The Creation of Scientific Psychology

David J. Murray with Contributions from Series Editor Stephen W. Link

Routledge
Taylor & Francis Group
NEW YORK AND LONDON

First published 2021
by Routledge
52 Vanderbilt Avenue, New York, NY 10017

and by Routledge
2 Park Square, Milton Park, Abingdon, Oxon, OX14 4RN

Routledge is an imprint of the Taylor & Francis Group, an informa business

Library of Congress Cataloging-in-Publication Data
A catalog record for this title has been requested

ISBN: 978-1-138-65815-8 (hbk)
ISBN: 978-1-315-62098-5 (ebk)

Typeset in Bembo
by SPi Technologies India Pvt Ltd (Straive)

The Creation of Scientific Psychology

With an emphasis on developments taking place in Germany during the nineteenth century, this book provides in-depth examinations of the key contributions made by the pioneers of scientific psychology. Their works brought measurement and mathematics into the study of the mind.

Through unique analysis of measurement theory by Whewell, mathematical developments by Gauss, and theories of mental processes developed by Herbart, Weber, Fechner, Helmholtz, Müller, Delboeuf and others, this volume maps the beliefs, discoveries, and interactions that constitute the very origins of psychophysics and its offspring Experimental Psychology. Murray and Link expertly combine nuanced understanding of linguistic and historic factors to identify theoretical approaches to relating physical intensities and psychological magnitudes. With an eye to interactions and influences on future work in the field, the volume illustrates the important legacy that mathematical developments in the nineteenth century have for twentieth and twenty-first century psychologists.

This detailed and engaging account fills a deep gap in the history of psychology. The Creation of Scientific Psychology will appeal to researchers, academics, and students in the fields of history of psychology, psychophysics, scientific, and mathematical psychology.

David J. Murray is Emeritus Professor of Psychology, Queen's University, Canada.

Stephen W. Link is Emeritus Professor of Psychology, McMaster University, Canada.

Scientific Psychology Series

Stephen W. Link
McMaster University, Hamilton, Canada

James T. Townsend
Indiana University Bloomington, USA

26 The Creation of Scientific Psychology
David J. Murray with Contributions from Series Editor Stephen W. Link

25 Invariances in Human Information Processing
Edited by Thomas Lachmann and Tina Weis

24 Mathematical Models of Perception and Cognition Volume II
A Festschrift for James T. Townsend
Edited by Joseph Houpt and Leslie Blaha

23 Mathematical Models of Perception and Cognition Volume I
A Festschrift for James T. Townsend
Edited by Joseph Houpt and Leslie Blaha

22 Mathematical Principles of Human Conceptual Behavior
The Structural Nature of Conceptual Representation and Processing
Ronaldo Vigo

21 Measurement With Persons
Theory, Methods, and Implementation Areas
Edited by Birgitta Berglund, Giovanni B. Rossi, James T. Townsend, and Leslie R. Pendrill

20 Information-Processing Channels in the Tactile Sensory System
A Psychophysical and Physiological Analysis
George A. Gescheider, John H. Wright, and Ronald T. Verrillo

19 Unified Social Cognition
Norman Anderson

18 Introduction to the Theories of Measurement and Meaningfulness and the Use of Symmetry in Science
Louis Narens

17 Measurement and Representation of Sensations
Edited by Hans Colonius and Ehtibar N. Dzhafarov

16 **Psychophysics Beyond Sensation**
Laws and Invariants of Human Cognition
Edited by Christian Kaernbach, Erich Schröger, Hermann Müller

15 **Theories of Meaningfulness**
Louis Narens

14 **Empirical Direction in Design and Analysis**
Norman H. Anderson

13 **Computational, Geometric, and Process Perspectives on Facial Cognition**
Contexts and Challenges
Edited by Michael J. Wenger and James T. Townsend

12 **Utility of Gains and Losses**
Measurement-Theoretical and Experimental Approaches
R. Duncan Luce

11 **The War Between Mentalism and Behaviorism**
On the Accessibility of Mental Processes
William R. Uttal

10 **Localist Connectionist Approaches To Human Cognition**
Edited by Jonathan Grainger and Arthur M. Jacobs

9 **Recent Progress in Mathematical Psychology**
Psychophysics, Knowledge Representation, Cognition, and Measurement
Edited by Cornelia E. Dowling, Fred S. Roberts, and Peter Theuns

8 **Toward A New Behaviorism**
The Case Against Perceptual Reductionism
William R. Uttal

7 **Adaptive Spatial Alignment**
Gordon M. Redding and Benjamin Wallace

6 **Sensation and Judgment**
Complementarity Theory of Psychophysics
John C. Baird

5 **Signal Detection Theory and ROC Analysis in Psychology and Diagnostics**
Collected Papers
John A. Swets

4 **Multidimensional Models of Perception and Cognition**
Edited by F. Gregory Ashby

3 **The Swimmer**
An Integrated Computational Model of A Perceptual-motor System
William R. Uttal, Gary Bradshaw, Sriram Dayanand, Robb Lovell, and Thomas Shepherd

2 **Cognition, Information Processing, and Psychophysics**
Basic Issues
Edited by Hans-Georg Geissler, Stephen W. Link, and James T. Townsend

1 **The Wave Theory of Difference and Similarity**
Stephen W. Link

This book is dedicated to
Ian Hacking
in recognition of his contributions
to the history of science.

Contents

Editor's Introduction

Five years ago I asked David J. Murray to think about writing a history of nineteenth-century Scientific Psychology. Over the course of my career, I read many histories of psychology that minimize or sometimes even lack a treatment of Psychology as a science, especially with respect to the contributions of mathematics in the early days. Therefore, I looked for an Experimental Psychologist and Historian to help to create a more accurate view. I knew of David's translation to English from German of Ernst Heinrich Weber's *Der Tastsinn* (1846) and many other historical articles. I co-authored with David and Helen Ross in 2009 a review of a delightful book on Gustav Fechner by Michael Heidelberger. I felt confident with David's knowledge of history.

A few years later, David provided me a very lengthy manuscript entitled *From Mind to Matter: A History of 19th-Century Psychology*. Impressed, I began my first reading. Due to the importance of mathematics in any science, I asked about the manuscript's presentations of mathematical ideas due to Herbart, Fechner, Helmholtz, and others. David informed me that mathematics was not really part of his history.

After my reading of the manuscript I suggested improvements to show how some missing mathematical ideas were important systems of deep thought about mental processes. David suddenly looked like a sailor standing at the edge of a very rough sea of mathematical equations. He looked sceptically into the distance at one equation then followed by a very large equation. But, his remarkable courage soon revealed itself when he said, "Where's our sailboat?"

We began sailing, first with Johann Friedrich Herbart, then with the other giants of early scientific psychology. We discovered the mathematical representations of mental processes created by Herbart (1824). David began the arduous climbing of mathematical ropes, learning a more accurate understanding of the equations as we sailed along, first a bit against the wind but later on, more smoothly, with the wind at our backs. At the end of our voyage emerged a historian with a remarkable new, deeper, knowledge of mathematical reasoning, enriched by his mastery of the German language, especially in its far from trivial forms of the nineteenth century. I thank David for his stellar presentation of the interactions between so many significant historical figures. The result is a new account of the creation of scientific psychology that fills a gap in the histories of Psychology—a new view that we hope will fascinate and excite both the lay and experienced readers alike.

Preface

The word "psychophysics", which is obviously a hybrid of "psychology" and "physics", first appeared in printed form over a century and a half ago, in the year 1860. It was coined by a famous German professor of physics named Gustav Theodor Fechner (1801–1887). Its first appearance was actually in the title of Fechner's two-volume *Elements of Psychophysics* [*Elemente der Psychophysik*]. Fechner had an agenda: he wanted to show that the world of mind (the subject of psychology) and the world of matter (the subject of physics) were not rigidly separated one from the other.

Fechner believed that mind could be shown to be intimately connected to matter because of the following phenomenon. If a strong feeling of sensation is mentally experienced when a strong physical stimulus exerts its impact on one's nervous system, then the fact that the magnitude of the sensation goes *up* as the intensity of the stimulus goes *up* suggests that the magnitude of the sensation-experience, and the intensity of the physical stimulation, increase together in some kind of lockstep. If a small canister holding lead shot is laid on the back of a person's hand and more lead shot is added to its contents, gradually increasing its weight, the person will almost certainly report that the *feeling* of heaviness increases with the amount of lead shot that is added to the canister. The person will be unlikely to say that, as the amount of lead shot being added to the canister goes *up*, the feeling of heaviness goes *down*.

Fechner believed that he made a major discovery that mind and matter could be unified scientifically by virtue of the fact that the two increased or decreased together in what is technically called a "monotonic" relationship. For example, as the physical stimulus intensity goes up, so does the corresponding feeling of heaviness. As the physical stimulus intensity goes down, so does the corresponding feeling of heaviness. Stimulus intensity and sensation-magnitude rise and fall one after the other. Indeed, Fechner devised a "psychophysical law" that "gave teeth" to these statements by asserting that sensation-magnitude was a particular kind of monotonic function of stimulus intensity, namely, a logarithmic function.

One notices immediately that a law such as Fechner's Law might not be taught in high school, college, or university courses on physics because it strays too far from whichever traditional sub-discipline of physics (e.g., mechanics, optics, or acoustics) is being taught. Likewise, Fechner's Law might prove a hindrance or stumbling block to instructors in many sub-disciplines of psychology because it involves mathematics. Understanding Fechner's Law involves knowing what is meant by a "logarithm".

I entered the University of Cambridge with a concentration in modern languages (French and German), but when I switched into psychology, the faculty member charged with teaching statistics to psychology students, E. G. Chambers, gave each one of his students, in their very first class, a booklet he wrote, explaining, from scratch, what a logarithm was.

Helen E. Ross, with whom I was a graduate student in experimental psychology at the University of Cambridge in the early 1960s, received a BA degree from the University of Oxford that included qualifications in the classical languages Greek and Latin. I still remember our discussions that took place in the lab space of her PhD supervisor, Richard Gregory (1923–2010), who was recognized as a foremost expert on visual sensation and perception (e.g., Gregory, 1966, 1981/1984). We made the decision to translate Weber's works on the touch-sense into English.

Helen's job was to translate, from Latin, Weber's *De Tactu*. My job was to translate, from German, Weber's *Der Tastsinn*. The procedure for doing so would be leisurely, because after obtaining our respective doctorates, Helen had to establish herself in a new teaching position at the University of Hull in England, and I at Queen's University in Canada.

The first edition of the translations of *De Tactu* and *Der Tastsinn* was published by Academic Press, under the auspices of the Experimental Psychology Society, United Kingdom, in 1978. The Hon. Secretary of the Society at that time, John D. Mollon, added a preface on the need for more English translations of early scientific research written in Latin or German. A second edition, with some updating of the historical introduction, appeared in 1996. The title of the first edition was *E. H. Weber: The Sense of Touch*. The title of the second edition was *E. H. Weber on the Tactile Senses*. In the present volume, the second edition will be referred to as Ross and Murray (1996). Helen's translation of Weber's *De Tactu* will be referred to as Weber (1834/1996a) and my translation of *Der Tastsinn* will be referred to as Weber (1846/1996b).

As just noted my first full-time faculty position was as Assistant Professor of Psychology at Queen's University in Canada. The university was founded in 1841 at Kingston, which is located where Lake Ontario empties into the St Lawrence River. My first teaching obligations included a focus on human short-term memory, because that was the topic of my doctoral dissertation. But, later in my career, I taught the history of psychology, and soon discovered that even graduate students in psychology showed signs of nervousness when I came to teach the derivation of Fechner's Law. But Fechner's work on psychophysics played an amazingly large role in the founding of the first university departments of psychology, starting with the establishment of Wundt's laboratory at the University of Leipzig in 1879.

Leipzig was where Fechner was based for almost the whole of his career; and it should be pointed out right away that, in 1860, when he wrote his *Elemente der Psychophysik*, Leipzig was the largest city in a country then called Saxony. Only when Saxony united with Prussia, Bavaria, and other now-extinct "countries", was modern Germany formed in about 1870. Leipzig's sheer importance in the Central European economy is illustrated by the fact that, in the early twentieth century, a railway station was built there, which was then, *and still is*, the largest railway station in the world.

I am now retired, but, having written a number of specialized articles on the history of psychophysics, I was very pleased to accept the invitation, made by the editors of this Scientific Psychology Series, that I write a history of the origins of psychophysics. Chapter 1 is about Johann Friedrich Herbart (1776–1841), whose mathematical model of what we typically call the flow of mental experiences included his discussion of "thresholds" of consciousness. Fechner adopted Herbart's concept of a "threshold" into his proof of Fechner's Law. Because Herbart referred to the distinction between "extensive" and "intensive" measurement-units that was introduced by Kant, an account of this distinction is included in Chapter 1. Chapter 2 is about the mathematical and measurement theory backgrounds to Fechner's psychophysics. It introduces William Whewell's (1794–1866) use of "extensive" and "intensive" measurement-units in the history and philosophy of early nineteenth-century physics. It then discusses de Moivre, Laplace, and Gauss on the Gaussian distribution.

Chapter 3 is about Weber's Law, which constituted a foundation stone of Fechner's Law. Chapter 4 is about the life and psychophysical contributions of Fechner himself. Chapter 5 is about the research on psychophysics conducted by G. E. Müller and his students at the University of Göttingen in the late nineteenth century. Chapter 6 extends the scope of the second topic of Chapter 2, namely, the Gaussian distribution. Now it is discussed exclusively in the context of Fechner's psychophysics. Chapter 7 is devoted entirely to the idea that sensation-magnitudes simply cannot be measured in the way stimulus intensities can. Chapter 8 describes the emergence of a rival to Fechner's logarithmic law, namely, the power law, with its huge implications for twentieth-century psychophysics as developed by S. S. Stevens (1906–1973). Chapter 9 focusses on the dismissal, by the American psychologist William James in 1890, of Fechnerian psychophysics. The chapter closes with a description of American research that showed how measures of the accuracy of performance in psychophysical tasks could be supplemented by measures of confidence ratings and of response times. "Passing the Torch" relates the psychophysics of the nineteenth century to the psychophysics of the twentieth century.

Because our understanding of Herbart's achievements to be described in Chapter 1 demands at least some understanding of the progress made in the sciences prior to 1800 (when Herbart would have been 24 years old), Chapter 1 is preceded by a short Prologue that summarizes, as succinctly as possible, those aspects of that progress that would most impress Herbart himself.

David J. Murray
Toronto, Canada

Acknowledgements

The Prologue and "Passing the Torch" were added after the first draft of the whole volume was completed. They were added at the suggestion of Stephen W. Link, who, with James T. Townsend, edit the Scientific Psychology series. At Steve's suggestion, the Prologue refers, not only to Western science and mathematics, but also to Chinese contributions to those topics. Science is truly international, so reference to the history of non-Western science is no longer a specialist luxury, it is a matter of common courtesy. But Steve also took time from his activities as an editor and as a practising psychophysicist to go, more than once, through my first draft sentence-by-sentence. His guidance allowed me to correct mistakes (often mathematical) in the first draft, to render more flowing many an overlong sentence, and to create several figures and tables in order to make them more user-friendly to present-day psychophysicists. Many of the figures were created by Steve. His help is so appreciated that his name appears on the title page as Editor of this volume.

I am deeply indebted to Steve and to Jim Townsend for their suggestion that I write this volume; to Marissa E. Barnes and Christina A. Bandomir, both PhD candidates, for research assistance with the preparation of this volume; to my daughter, Rachel G. Breau, MLIS, my grandson Colin Breau, and her family for their patience, cooperation, and support throughout the writing process; to Ian M. Hacking, Emeritus Professor of Philosophy at the University of Toronto, for his open encouragement of my endeavour and his very generous help in putting me onto relevant books from his extensive collection of literature on the history and philosophy of science; to Susan Ward, whose interest in the progress of the book at every stage was inspiring and who suggested the last chapter be titled "Passing the Torch"; to Michael Heidelberger, whose recent biography of Fechner is indispensable to any historian of psychophysics; to Matthew Friberg of Routledge (Taylor & Francis Group) for his help and advice at all stages of the submission process; and to Helen E. Ross, my co-translator of works by E. H. Weber into English, collaborator on several articles, and wonderful companion at many Annual Conferences of the International Society for Psychophysics.

I am also grateful to the Department of Psychology at Queen's University at Kingston. When I retired from full-time teaching at Queen's, my Emeritus status allowed me to continue borrowing books on term loan and accessing, on the internet, journals subscribed to by the Queen's University Library system. Other friends among psychophysicists with whom I interacted over the years and to whom I owe debts of gratitude for collaborative communication, include: Ekhtibar Dzhafarov, Mark Elliott, Simon Grondin, Åke Hellström, Peter Killeen, Donald Laming, Serge Nicolas, Kenneth Norwich, David Pantalony, Bertram Scharf, Bruce Schneider, Paul Whittle, and Willy Wong. Thank you, all of you.

Prologue

Physical Science Before 1800

Introduction

This book tells the story of how a few nineteenth-century scientists, including E. H. Weber and G. T Fechner, extended the application of scientific principles from the study of matter to the study of mind. Understanding the behaviour of matter revolutionized nineteenth-century theoretical physics. These new scientific principles depended on the use of mathematics. A brief account of how advances in physics went hand-in-hand with developments in mathematics is appropriate in order to understand the intellectual background known to the pioneer psychophysicists.

Peter Watson (2010) subdivided the history of Western science over the past millennium into five periods, namely, a First Renaissance (about 1200 to 1400), a Second Renaissance (about 1400 to 1600), a First Scientific Revolution (about 1600 to 1700), a Third Renaissance (about 1700 to 1800), and a Second Scientific Revolution (about 1800 to 1900). The first three of these periods involved many of the European countries, including Italy, France, Britain, and the Low Countries (Belgium and the Netherlands). The last two periods, according to Watson (2010), were contributed to mainly by Germany because of its large and efficient university system. This prologue also includes a brief account of Chinese mathematics during each of these five periods.

Chapter 1 is devoted to J. F. Herbart (1776–1841), a professor of philosophy for most of his career. Herbart (1822/1890b) contended that a psychological theory, based as firmly on mathematics as Newton's physical theory, was not only possible, but actually necessary. Readers may appreciate an introduction to Herbart's mathematical psychology. In order to facilitate the presentation of Herbart's pioneering work, this Prologue also serves to indicate the knowledge of philosophy, mathematics, and physics that Herbart acquired before he presented his most detailed exposition of his theory in his book titled *Psychology as Science* [*Psychologie als Wissenschaft*] (Herbart, 1824/1890a).

Gustav Theodor Fechner (1801–1887) created the name "Psychophysics" in 1860. He hoped that psychophysics would allow the study of mental processes to be integrated into the study of processes about physical objects. Psychophysics is important in the history of science for two main reasons. First, at an administrative level, psychophysics played a crucial role in persuading certain German universities to add a new discipline to their core teaching curricula, namely, experimental psychology. Second, psychophysics was a striking example of a would-be science, the validity of which was *not* agreed upon by many physicists, philosophers, mathematicians, and even some psychologists. Yet its controversial nature led to a game-changing new emphasis on the importance of measurement as a topic in its own right, and thereby contributed to the successful reception of Einstein's relativity theory.

Mathematics Before the First Renaissance

Europe, the Middle East, and India

Civilizations tend to come and go for reasons that many of the best scholars "nailed down" and explained. For example, Gibbon (1776–1789/2005) put forward his explanation of why the Roman Empire attained a pinnacle of political power before collapsing after invasion by several loot-hungry armies between about 400 and 500 CE. The Roman Empire was not completely destroyed because organized Christianity set up a clergy-run "Holy Roman Empire". A short account of the political history of Europe and North America, against which the history of psychology was enacted, was given by Murray (1988, pp. 1–7). Here something similar is offered, but it is restricted to those topics in intellectual history that presumably most influenced Herbart in his role as a theorist of mental science.

Kline (1972), in his magisterial history of Western, but not Chinese, mathematics, gave examples of the written symbols for individual whole numbers that were used by the Sumerian/Akkadian (p. 5), Babylonian (p. 7), Egyptian (p. 16), Greek (p. 132), and Hindu (p. 183) merchants, astronomers, and mathematicians. Multiplication and division are found in the Sumerian, Babylonian, and Egyptian civilizations, and the number 60 was used by the Babylonians as a "base" in their arithmetic in much the same way as we use the number 10.

Around 600 CE, the Hindu notation was adopted by the Arabs. It was easier to work with in arithmetic and geometry than was the case for the Greek letters that were used also as numerals. Roman numerals (e.g., I, II, III, IV, V...) were especially clumsy when used for fractions. But, in the Middle Ages (about 1000 to 1500), the Greek mathematics of Euclid and Archimedes, which used Hindu/Arab numerals, quickly came to dominate European mathematics.

Questions about the subdivision of land into plots or the values of bartered objects tended to be the earliest applications of mathematics. As a consequence of problems arising when land was divided, the Sumerian, Babylonian and Egyptian civilizations investigated square roots. A field with four sides, each of whose length, L, is one unit, will have an area of L^2 units.

To halve the area means finding $(L^2)/2$, and it was from situations like this that fractions came to exist. The length of the diagonal of a square is known to us from the relationship that later came to be called Pythagoras's theorem.

According to this theorem, the length of the diagonal is the same as the length of the hypotenuse, h, of a right-angle triangle. This length is given by $1^2 + 1^2 = h^2$, so h was the square root of 2. The use of the square root sign, $\sqrt{}$, was not introduced until the Second Renaissance (Kline, 1972, pp. 259–263).

The ancients did refer, however, to "square numbers", in which a number would be represented by a set of, say, four or nine dots organized in the form of a square (Ross & Knott, 2019). What we now call irrational numbers, such as $\sqrt{2}$, were present from the very beginning of mathematics, yet were not recognized as anything "special" separating them from ordinary fractions. The Babylonians never explored negative numbers, but did discover that the value of x in a quadratic equation such as $x^2 - bx + 1 = 0$ had two answers ("roots").

From papyri dating from about 1700 BCE, we know that the Egyptians also dealt with fractions, irrational numbers, and simple quadratic equations. They also investigated the properties of circles. If the diameter of a circle was 1 unit in length, they calculated the area of the circle to be 0.7023, whereas the correct answer, using π, would be 0.7854.

Neither the Babylonians nor the Egyptians came close to rivalling the Greeks when it came to mathematical progress. Eudoxus (ca. 408–ca. 355 BCE) developed the methods of proof that were employed by geometers ever since, and Euclid (born ca. 325 BCE) summarized an enormous number of geometrical proofs, including Pythagoras's theorem. Archimedes (287–212 BCE) calculated π to lie between 3.1408 and 3.1429, which is amazing considering that the value of π is 3.141592 … Euclid also compared lines of different lengths to explore the properties of proportions (ratios).[1] Euclid's 13 books appeared in English in one convenient volume (Euclid, 2013).

Later Greek mathematicians, who included Archimedes, investigated conic sections and solid geometry. They argued, I think rather persuasively, that if we divide the geometric world into "points" and "lines", as Euclid had, arithmetic concerns numerosity, that is, how numbers of individual points can be added, subtracted, multiplied or divided, whereas algebra concerns magnitudes (e.g., the variable-name x can stand for the length of one side of a triangle).

China

From about 1605 onwards, Jesuit missionaries introduced European mathematics into China (Martzloff, 1987/2006, pp. 20–31). The decisive role played by Euclid in Western mathematics was paralleled in Chinese mathematics by a book titled *Nine Chapters*. According to O'Connor and Robertson (2003), it was written some 200 years after Euclid's *Elements*. Euclid-type proofs of mathematical propositions were rarely given in early Chinese writings, but numerical demonstrations of the correctness of some of those mathematical propositions parallel many of those found in European mathematical texts written prior to about 1600.

1 The ratio to each other of the length of two stretched strings determines whether, if they were plucked simultaneously, the resulting chord sounds harmonious. This was known to the Greeks. Pesic (2014) pointed out that many famous physicists started their careers by studying harmony.

More precisely, the *Nine Chapters* discussed problems in land-surveying, including the measurement of the areas of circles. An approximate solution is given for π that is comparable with Archimedes' solution. As in Euclid, special attention is given to ratios and proportions; the problems include the extraction of square roots and cube roots, and included a numerical method for finding the values of a and b in linear equations of the form $ax + b = c$. The problems of solving simultaneous linear equations led to work on negative numbers and to a foretaste of the matrix algebra that would not be employed in European mathematics until about 1800. The solution of quadratic equations is approached from a geometrical point of view rather than from the algebraic view created by Newton in seventeenth-century Britain.

Prior to the First Renaissance in Europe, we find the earliest named mathematicians in China. According to Martzloff (1987/2006, pp. 13–40), two mathematicians who flourished in the third century CE were Zhao Shuang (p. 76) who did much of the early work on right-angle triangles. The content (though not the actual proof) of Pythagoras's theorem was known as well to the Chinese as to their Greek-influenced contemporaries in Europe. Another was Liu Hui (p. 14), whose commentary on the *Nine Chapters* was accompanied by original research on equations with several unknowns (p. 250) and on solid geometry (p. 285).

Prior to the First Renaissance, from about 600 to 900, mathematics in China was taught using textbooks. A compilation of 12 such textbooks (known under the misleading title *The Ten Computational Canons*) included the *Nine Chapters* (p. 15).

In Chinese mathematics, certain applied problems, too complicated to quickly describe here, had names based on the objects in the problems, such as the "round town" problem answered by Li Zhi and the "remainder" problem by Qin Jiushao (thirteenth century). The "hundred fowls" problem was introduced by Zhang Qiujian in the fifth century, and had its equivalents in European, Hindu, and Arabic mathematics (Martzloff, 1987/2006, p. 309). As early as about 1050, Jia Xian essentially extracted roots by using the binomial expansion $(a + b)^n$. He used his version of what later became known as Pascal's triangle (Martzloff, 1987/2006, p. 142).

The First Renaissance

The First Renaissance is most famous for the rediscovery of ancient Greek philosophy, including the works of Plato and Aristotle. In mathematics, a major name was Leonardo of Pisa (ca. 1170–1250), better known as Fibonacci. According to Kline (1972), Fibonacci's writings described Greek and Arab mathematics, but the language in which he wrote was Latin.[2] The notion of gravity as a downward-pulling force competing with a force associated with an

2 Latin remained the language of international scholarship long after literature in general was being written in local languages such as English, French, German and Russian. For example, E. H. Weber's first book on the touch-sense was written in Latin as late as 1834, as will be seen in Chapter 3.

object's being flung horizontally can be found in the writings of several medieval European scholars (Kline, 1972, pp. 211–212).

In contrast, Chinese mathematics saw one of its most productive periods in the 56 years between 1247 and 1303. Li Zhi (1192–1279) wrote on the solution of polynomial equations, including negative powers of the unknown variables, work that was followed up by Guo Shoujing (1231–1316) on the solution of a quartic equation whose first term was x^4 and who essentially started what became known as "Chinese spherical trigonometry". Finding formulae for *approximations* to the numerical values of algebraic variables or geometrical distances was better developed in China than in Europe.

Pascal's triangle appeared in China much earlier than it did in Europe, a point stressed by Needham (1959) in his volume on mathematics in his multi-volumed *Science and Civilization in China*. Pascal stressed that each row, n, of the triangle held the coefficients of $(a + b)^n$ and that each coefficient itself represented the number of ways (combinations) in which n things could be sampled k things at a time (for more on this please see the next section). Martzloff (1987/2006, pp. 304–305) claimed that, in a book written in 1303 by Zhu Zhijie, one can find evidence that the author not only understood the relevance of Pascal's triangle to the binomial expansion, but also to combinatorial theory. In this book, the triangle was named Yang Hui's triangle, after Yang Hui (1238–1298).

The Second Renaissance

According to Watson (2010), the Second Renaissance is bounded by the period 1400 to 1600. For exactly those same years, Kline (1972, p. 216) provided a special chapter devoted to European mathematics. In the Second Renaissance, the rediscovery of the Roman scientific writer Lucretius led to scepticism about religious interpretations of scientific findings (Greenblatt, 2011). The invention of printing by Gutenberg (1398–1468) and others helped spread those works, not only to the Church, but also to the aristocracy and to wealthy patrons of the merchant class. In the humanities, the rediscovery of Homer's *Iliad* and *Odyssey*, Greek dramas, and Roman lyric poetry and fiction, laid a foundation for much of modern European literature. The Second Renaissance became even more renowned for its achievements in painting, sculpture and architecture, which included the artworks of Leonardo da Vinci (1452–1519), Michelangelo (1475–1564), and Raphael (1483–1520).

During the Second Renaissance in Europe, China experienced many mathematical innovations. The earliest tools for assisting in Chinese computation were counting rods. The earliest Chinese mathematicians used rods made of bamboo, wood, and other materials, at first about 14 cm in length, then shortened later to about 8 cm. In 1337, a spelling book illustrated something that *might* be an abacus (please see Martzloff, 1987/2006, Figure 13.5, p. 213). One piece of evidence that the abacus did not come into popular use until late in the period corresponding to the Second Renaissance in Europe, was that no mention was made of it in the *Nine Chapters* or in the narratives brought back from China, prior to 1400, by European travellers, such as Marco Polo (1256–1325). In 1592, Cheng Dawei (1533–1606) wrote a general guide to computation methods that went into many printings, even into the twentieth century (Martzloff, 1987/2006, p. 20). This book included instructions on how to use the abacus (Martzloff, 1987/2006, p. 159).

The abacus consists of a set of vertical bars intersected horizontally by a crosspiece. Above the crosspiece are two balls that can be slid up and down a bar freely; below the crosspiece are five equally slidable balls. Usually each of the upper balls is worth 5 units, and each of the lower balls is worth 1 unit. The use of the abacus to carry out the four usual operations of arithmetic, as well as to calculate square and cube roots, involves memorizing a large set of rules.

The First Scientific Revolution

Progress in the sciences, including mathematics, lagged progress in the humanities, which reached its peak in the Second Renaissance. The "First Scientific Revolution" emerged in the seventeenth century, the era of Boyle, Descartes, Hooke, Leibniz, Newton, and Pascal. Wootton (2015) considered that the voyages of discovery by European navigators (including Columbus's explorations of America from 1492 onwards) and the discovery, by Mercator (1512–1594), of a way to represent the Earth's three-dimensional near-spherical surface in maps containing only two dimensions, were important antecedents to the First Scientific Revolution. Therefore, Wootton dated the First Scientific Revolution to the period "between 1572, when Tycho Brahe saw a nova, or new star, and 1704, when Newton published his *Opticks*, which demonstrated that white light is made up of all the colours of the rainbow" (p. 1).

Although the word "algebra" originated in Arabic, many of the modern symbols representing mathematical operations (including +, −, x, ÷ and =) were developed in the fifteenth and sixteenth centuries (Kline, 1972, pp. 259–263).[3] Francois Vieta (1540–1604) introduced the notion that variable-names, the values of which could range over an ordered sequence, and might not be known in advance, should be denoted by letters late in the alphabet (*x*, *y*, *z*), whereas constants were labelled by letters early in the alphabet (*a*, *b*, *c*). Two-dimensional graphs labelled the horizontal axis the x-axis (or, more generally, the "abscissa") and the vertical axis the y-axis (or, more generally, the "ordinate").

Major mathematical discoveries made during the First Scientific Revolution include the invention of logarithms by John Napier (1550–1617) in 1614, although both Kline (1972, p. 258) and Wootton (2015, p. 90) pointed out that Joost Bürgi (1552–1632) discovered them in 1588 but did not publish them until after Napier published them. We can add the invention of coordinate

3 "The symbols + and − were introduced by German craftsmen of the fifteenth century to denote excess and defective weights of chests and were taken over by mathematicians; they appear in manuscripts after 1481. The symbol x for 'times' is due to William Oughtred (1574–1660). … the sign = was introduced by Robert Recorde (1510–1558) of Cambridge" (Kline, 1972, p. 259). The symbol ÷ for division was introduced by G. H. Rahn in 1659 (Rouse Ball, 1908/1960, p. 211).

geometry by René Descartes (1596–1650) in 1637; the general solution of quadratic equations, along with the stipulation of whether the two roots are real and unequal, real and equal, or imaginary and unequal, by Sir Isaac Newton (1642–1727); and the "binomial theorem" and "binomial expansion", also by Newton.[4] Blaise Pascal (1623–1662) in 1653 observed that the coefficients of the binomial expansion of $(p + q)^n$, where $p + q = 1$, where p and q represent probabilities, could be represented by successive rows in Pascal's triangle.

If y is a function of x, one can determine, for any particular value of x, the instantaneous rate of change of y. Kline (1972, pp. 211–213) showed that several medieval mathematicians had discussed this topic. Using differing notations, Leibniz (1646–1716) and Newton independently developed differential calculus, though research on some recently discovered writings suggests that Archimedes came within a hair's-breadth of discovering it first (Netz & Noel, 2007). The much-debated question of whether Leibniz or Newton should be credited for the original discovery of calculus was reviewed by Bardi (2006).

Bardi (2006) stated that Newton "did discover calculus first, twenty years before Leibniz published anything" (p. 245). But Bardi also stated that, for other scientists,

> Leibniz was the one who deserved full credit, since his methods were the ones that progressed and survived. He invented calculus independently, was the first to publish his ideas, developed calculus more than had Newton, had far superior notation, and worked for years to move calculus forward into a mathematical framework that others could use as well.
>
> (p. 245)

The instantaneous rate of change of y with respect to x was notated by Leibniz as "dy/dx", the notation we still use today.

By 1800, the older geocentric systems of celestial mechanics due to Ptolemy (flourished about 140 CE) were replaced by the heliocentric system of Copernicus (1473–1543). A model of the solar system based on "vortices" put forward by Descartes was superseded by Newton's system based on gravitational forces. An axiomatic model of the mechanics of moving objects offered by Galileo (1564–1642) was supplemented by Newton's axiomatic model based on his three laws of motion. Prior to 1800, Newton's system was often resisted in France and Germany by believers in Descartes' cosmology. Newton's calculus was also resisted by supporters of Leibniz's calculus. But, by the end of the eighteenth century, Newton's system was adopted throughout Europe (Wootton, 2015, pp. 473–475).

The best-known achievement of the First Scientific Revolution was Newton's (1726/1999) theory that the objects of the solar system—the sun, the planets and their moons, the comets and asteroids—all behaved as a united system kept

4 The words "generalizable binomial theorem" apply particularly to Newton's extensions of the binomial theorem of the form $(x + y)^n$, where n is a positive whole number, to forms where n is fractional (e.g., 0.5) and/or negative (e.g., -2).

in place by a force of attraction known as the gravitational force. Gravity kept the moon from flying away from the earth and the earth from leaving its orbital trajectory around the sun. The moon's gravity also caused the earth to wobble slightly as it rotated, which in turn caused the oceans to rise and fall in a tidal pattern.

Newton was a founder member, in 1662, of the Royal Society, a gathering of like-minded scientists in London, England, whose membership included the physical chemist Robert Boyle (1627–1691) and the microscopist, town planner, and physicist Robert Hooke (1635–1703). In 1682, Hooke gave a set of lectures to the Royal Society on the topic of light. His mention of time, necessitated in part by the discovery, in 1604, of a kind of stone that was phosphorescent in the dark for a limited time that depended on how long the stone had been exposed to daylight beforehand, led him to write about how humans formulated their concept of Time partly via their inspections of their own thought-processes when retrieving spontaneously (or laboriously) memories of past events in their own lives (Singer, 1976).

Hooke and Newton continually disagreed on scientific matters. Jardine (2003) wrote a life of Hooke in which this matter is discussed in some detail. Only after Hooke's death did Newton agree to be the President of the Royal Society (Singer, 1976, p. 115) and then publish his *Opticks* in 1704. Newton actually carried out much of his research on light, reported in the *Opticks*, many years earlier, but delayed publication to avoid public controversy with Hooke.

In the seventeenth century, Jesuit missionaries, representing the Roman Catholic Church, came to China with the express purpose of introducing the Chinese people to Christianity. The arduous training of a Jesuit priest included instruction in mathematics and physics. A Jesuit missionary of Polish origin, Nikolaus Smogulecki (1610–1656), brought logarithms to China in 1653. The Jesuits brought with them, therefore, books of European mathematics, including the tables of logarithms to base 10 calculated by Henry Briggs (1561–1631).

The Emperor Kangxi, who reigned from 1661 to 1722, was taught as a young man by the Jesuit missionary Ferdinand Verbiest (1623–1688). Kangxi did all he could to introduce some of the European mathematics of the First Scientific Revolution to China. At the same time, the missionaries learned Manchu in order to instruct the Emperor. Much of Euclid's *Elements* was translated into Chinese in 1614. In 1671, Ignace-Gaston Pardies (1636–1673) wrote a manual of geometry in French titled *Élemens de géométrie* (Pardies, 1960–1967). This book was designed to make Euclid's arguments easier to follow. Pardies' book was translated into Manchu in 1690. In 1713, Kangxi founded a college for teaching mathematics and recruited over one hundred Chinese scholars to compile an encyclopaedic account incorporating both Chinese and European mathematics, particularly as applied to astronomy and to the theory of harmony. The contents of the Chinese-language *Collected Essential Principles of Mathematics* are summarized by Martzloff (1987/2006, pp. 163–166).

The best-known mathematician in late seventeenth-century China was named Mei Wending (1633–1721). He focused on astronomy using mainly geometrical methods. Newtonian mechanics as applied to the solar system had yet to be introduced to China.

Eighteenth-Century Science

A major mathematical development of the eighteenth century was the exploration of the properties associated with the irrational number $e = 2.718281\ldots$, which is the limit of $[1 + (1/n)]^n$ as n tends to infinity. In particular, e has the property that, if y equals e^x, then its derivative (dy/dx) also equals e^x. The constant e plays many roles in mathematics (Maor, 1990). Particularly important roles are played in equations that describe the "growth" or "decay" in the value of a variable when that value is a function of how far that variable has already increased or decreased. Equations involving e often involve values that "snowball" or "die away" over the course of time. Such equations can readily be adapted to describe the behaviour of a variable the value of which grows increasingly slowly as it approaches (but may never actually reach) an upper limiting value (an "asymptote").

The eighteenth century also yielded considerable progress in probability theory, some of which will be reviewed in Chapter 2. For an introduction to the history of probability theory in the seventeenth and eighteenth centuries, Hacking's (1975) book is particularly rewarding.

The founding of research institutes intended to emulate the Royal Society led to the expansion of science in the eighteenth century. The Royal Academy of Sciences (often referred to as the "*Académie des Sciences*") was founded in Paris in 1665. The Royal Prussian Society of Sciences was founded in Berlin in 1701. Its name was later expanded by Frederick the Great, in 1747, into the Royal Prussian Society of Sciences and Belles-Lettres. Peter the Great of Russia founded the St Petersburg Academy of Sciences in 1724. The adjective "Imperial" was added to its name by Catherine the Great in 1747. A difference between the institutes located in Berlin and St Petersburg and those located in London and Paris was that the institutes in Berlin and St Petersburg provided, to their elected members, accommodation and board, whereas the societies in London and Paris did not. A splendidly illustrated history of the founding of these state-supported academies on the European continent is provided by Heidelberger and Thiessen (1981).

The great Swiss mathematician Leonhard Euler (1707–1783) taught first at the University of Basel in Switzerland, then flourished at the St Petersburg Academy of Science. This was followed by a stay at the Berlin Society of Sciences. Then Euler finally moved back to St Petersburg. Calinger (2015) wrote a compendious life of Euler in which one can read at first-hand about life in those royal academies; about the struggles between supporters of Newton and Descartes, and those between supporters of Newton and Leibniz, on the European continent; and about Euler's championship of both the differential and the integral calculus in solving mathematical problems concerning, not only the celestial bodies, but also weaponry, the design of harbours, and countless other practical situations encountered by military and civil engineers.

Frederick II, known as the Great (1712–1786), wished to enhance the prestige of Prussia in European intellectual circles. He therefore invited the French savant Voltaire (1694–1778), the atheist doctor La Mettrie (1709–1757), and the geographer Maupertuis (1698–1759), as well as the great mathematician Lagrange (1736–1813), to stay with him in Berlin. Similarly, Catherine the Great (1729–1796) had in mind the prestige of Russia when she invited many of these famous theorists, and the French encyclopaedia-writer Denis Diderot (1713–1784), to visit St Petersburg.

The Third Renaissance

The Third Renaissance incorporated a revival of classical scholarship based mainly in universities in Germany. Why Germany? Some famous German universities were founded prior to 1600, notably those of Heidelberg (1386), Leipzig (1409), Königsberg (1544) and Jena (1558). Nevertheless, in the course of recovering from the Thirty Years' War (1618 to 1648) between Catholics and Protestants that almost destroyed the infrastructure associated with both urban and rural buildings, the opportunity arose for the founding of new universities in many of the states where German was a widely spoken language. These states included some large areas that were once kingdoms (including, ordered from north to south, Prussia, Hanover, Saxony, and Bavaria), dukedoms (including the city-state of Weimar in what is now central Germany), principalities, and margravates or electorships (a "Markgraf" was a count with voting privileges in the Holy Roman Empire). German was also spoken in Switzerland, Bohemia (part of what is now the Czech Republic), and the independent and wealthy Austria.

According to Watson (2010), the "Third Renaissance" was contributed to extensively by academics associated with the new universities. These scholars critically studied not only ancient literary works including the Bible, but also the ancient masterpieces of architecture. Examples include the ruins of the temple of Athena (known as the Parthenon, located on a hill called the Acropolis in Athens) and the temple of Diana (in the city of Ephesus, now located in Turkey). German, French, and British collectors of antiquities scoured many of the European countries bordering the Mediterranean (including Spain, Italy, Greece, and Turkey) for statues, vases, weapons, coins and other Greek or Roman artefacts. A recent reference-work describing this new mania for classical artefacts, as well as the beginning of extensive research on the origins of various languages, including Greek and Latin, is provided by James Turner's (2014) intellectual history titled *Philology: The Forgotten Origins of the Modern Humanities*.

With respect to the universities, Watson (2010) has noted:

> The eighteenth-century German universities differed from the British ones in a number of important ways. In the first place, early eighteenth-century Germany had far more universities—about fifty as compared with, for example, just Oxford and Cambridge in England. ... Although many were small... their

> number and local character meant it was much easier in Germany to obtain higher education.
>
> (pp. 49–50)

In 1670, a new form of evangelical Protestantism called Pietism took hold in North Germany. In 1694, a new university was established in Prussia in the small town of Halle. Theologians of a pietistic bent were appointed to teach on the theological faculty at Halle. Eleven years later, in 1708, King Friedrich Wilhelm I (1688–1740) of Prussia, father of Frederick the Great, adopted Pietism himself and ruled that all the Lutheran ministers in Prussia were to study for at least two years at Halle. Perhaps the most famous of the new eighteenth-century universities was the University of Göttingen, founded in 1737 in the state of Hanover.

The best-known German philosophers in this Third Renaissance were G. W. Leibniz (1646–1716), Christian Wolff (1679–1754), and Immanuel Kant (1724–1804). Leibniz is remembered for his belief that perceiving the world involved unconscious cognitive processing of raw sense data, a process he called "apperception", a word later adopted by Herbart (De Garmo, 1894). Christian Wolff (1734/1968, 1736/1972) made a distinction between "empirical" and "rational" psychology, which continued well into the nineteenth century (see e.g., Hickok, 1854; Richards, 1980). "Empirical" psychology involves the assemblage of facts about human behaviour and mental processing. "Rational" psychology offered explanations, including religious ones, purporting to account for the existence of that assemblage. The material in Herbart's (1834/1891) *A Text-Book in Psychology* [*Lehrbuch der Psychologie*] was also organized to discuss empirical and rational psychology separately. Wolff ran afoul of the pietist theologians of Halle for daring to deal, in his lectures and writings, with unorthodox beliefs, including Chinese Confucianism. To avoid hanging for his secular approach to psychology, he was forced to leave Halle.

Wolff also invented the word "psychometrics". Reviews of early research on "psychometrics" by Ramul (1960, 1963) brought to light many forgotten cases of attempted measurements of sensory and cognitive abilities. Rydberg (2017) wrote a thesis about how Wolff and many other psychology faculty, particularly at the University of Halle, believed that a study of psychology could play a part in the inculcation of mental health.[5]

Kant argued that there was an inborn component in the way humans perceived reality. The human "soul" was so constructed that there was an "intuitive" or "unlearned" knowledge of certain "categories" of experience, notably Space, Time, and Cause. Mathematics involves an *a priori* understanding of all three of these.[6] Because we can know Space and Time as experienced mentally, Kant

5 Kilpatrick (1996) has shown that psychotherapy may also have been practised in the schools founded by Aristotle and Plato in ancient Athens.

6 The distinction between *a priori* and *a posteriori* was stressed particularly by Wolff, as explained by Richards (1980).

maintained that, from these empirical observations, we can develop a rational physics. Because there is no innate "category" of experience that might be labelled Soul (or Mind or Spirit), it followed, for Kant, that a science of psychology based on mathematics would be unlikely to be achieved. Because we do not have an analogous knowledge of Mind, from the empirical observations, say, of one's own behaviour or thought processes, or of the behaviour of other humans, we cannot develop a rational psychology. According to Kant (1798/1974), all we can do is collect facts about human behaviour, which amounts to what he called a "pragmatic anthropology".

Events in China that took place contemporaneously with Europe's Third Renaissance included the following. The compiler-in-chief of Kangxi's encyclopaedia was Mei Juecheng (1681–1763), who was the grandson of Mei Wending, mentioned above as the most prominent Chinese mathematician flourishing at the end of the First Scientific Revolution in Europe. He himself worked on infinite series, now that some of his sources were European. Minggatu (? – 1764) specialized in the use of infinite series in the expansion of circular functions. Perhaps the most important event in eighteenth-century Chinese mathematics was yet another encyclopaedic compilation devoted to the presentation (in its first edition) of short accounts of the lives of 41 European and 275 Chinese mathematical astronomers. Its compiler, Ruan Yuan (1764–1849), started work on this biographical dictionary in 1795; its first edition appeared in 1799. It continued to be updated and reprinted throughout the nineteenth century (Martzloff, 1987/2006, pp. 166–173). The list of entries given by Martzloff included, of course, Euclid; but it also included Archimedes, Descartes, Galileo, and Newton; and, with respect to the Third Renaissance, we find the names of Leibniz, Euler, Laplace, and Gauss.

The Second Scientific Revolution

Watson (2010) named the extraordinary growth in all of the sciences in nineteenth-century Germany the "Second Scientific Revolution". Eighteenth-century mathematicians such as Euler and Daniel Bernoulli (1700–1782) provided a solid mathematical basis for late eighteenth-century science, especially physics. New universities were founded at Berlin (in 1810) and at Bonn (in 1818) by King Friedrich Wilhelm III of Prussia (1770–1840). A new teaching method, involving the oral presentation of an essay written by a student to a group of fellow students, was called the "seminar". New German-language scientific journals, notably in mathematics and chemistry, were founded. A new value was placed on research productivity as a criterion for evaluating the prestige of a university department. An "Abitur examination" had to be passed if a student were to be accepted into a university. After 1830, research on chemistry, biochemistry, physiology, and anatomy was often carried out in state-funded well-equipped laboratories that included radically improved microscopes (Ford, 1973) and apparatus for tone-generation (Pantalony, 2009).

The study of physics increasingly demanded sophisticated mathematical innovations. The history of nineteenth-century German physics was chronicled by Jungnickel and McCormmach (1986a, 1986b) in two volumes with the common title *The Intellectual Mastery of Nature: Theoretical Physics From Ohm to Einstein*. The first volume is titled *The Torch of Mathematics 1800–1870*; the second is titled *The Now Mighty Theoretical Physics 1870–1925*. Scientists discussed in these volumes whose names will be familiar to most psychologists included Karl Friedrich Gauss (1777–1855), Ernst Heinrich Weber (1795–1878), his brother Wilhelm Weber (1804-1891), Hermann von Helmholtz (1821–1894), Heinrich Rudolf Hertz (1857–1895), Ernst Mach (1838–1916), and Gustav Fechner himself. According to Martzloff (1987/2006, p. 172), no reference was made in Ruan Yuan's biographical dictionary to the names of E. H. Weber, W. E. Weber, Helmholtz, Hertz, Mach, or Fechner. The name of Gauss did appear, however, in later editions. The launch of the new discipline called "psychophysics" was therefore part-and-parcel of this Second Scientific Revolution.

The history of nineteenth-century mathematics in China has two major topics. First, the Roman Catholic Church, under Pope Clement XIV in 1773, decided to suppress the activities of the Jesuits. This proclamation led to the Jesuits' leaving China in 1775. They left a magnificent library of European books. The Jesuits were replaced by Protestant missionaries, who, in the nineteenth century, did sterling work in translating, into Chinese, books concerning mathematical topics that were not translated by the Jesuits. As a translator, pride of place should probably go to Alexander Wylie (1815–1905), who translated Elias Loomis's *Elements of Analytical Geometry and of the Differential and Integral Calculus* (1852 edition). This was the first introduction of calculus to the Chinese. The adaptation into Chinese appeared in 1859, and was written in collaboration with Li Shanlan (1811–1882), who is considered to be the foremost Chinese mathematician of the nineteenth century.

Martzloff (1987/2006, pp. 371–389) provided a list of books translated from European languages into Chinese, either by the Jesuit or the Protestant missionaries. The list contains each of the following topics: algebra, arithmetic, differential and integral calculus, conics, geometry, instruments, logarithms, mechanics, perspective, probability, and trigonometry. Not until 1896 was an article on probability (taken from the 8th edition of the *Encyclopaedia Britannica*) made available in Chinese. The first account of (Newtonian) mechanics to be translated into Chinese (as late as 1865) was a translation of William Whewell's (1819) *An Elementary Treatise on Mechanics*. Again, Li Shanlan collaborated with the Protestant missionary Joseph Edkins (1823–1905) in preparing the translation.

Second, Li Shanlan made major contributions to combinatorial theory, published in 1867, and described in detail by Martzloff (1987/2006, pp. 341–351). Li Shanlan generalized Pascal's triangle in such a way as to arrive at equations describing the sum of the first *n* terms of a series based on that generalized triangle. He also made use of Chinese mathematics, especially that of the 1303 book by Zhu Shijie that explored combinations using accumulated "heaps" of individual cube-shaped solids (pp. 342–345).

From a psychophysical point of view, the major lesson to be learned from the history of Chinese mathematics in the Second Scientific Revolution is that the European contributions called calculus, Newtonian mechanics, and probability theory were only translated into Chinese in 1859, 1865, and 1896 respectively. All three of these concepts were employed, in Europe, from 1860 onward, by the early psychophysicists.

The above also allows us to conclude what Herbart would have known prior to his writing *Psychology as Science* [*Psychologie als Wissenschaft*] (Herbart, 1824/1890a). He knew about Newton's gravitational explanation of how the physical objects in our solar system are held in a state of equilibrium. His text itself reveals his sophisticated understanding of differential and integral calculus. He also took into account Euler's work on exponential and logarithmic functions. His skill in these topics will be demonstrated many times in Chapter 1, which is devoted to showing the role played by Herbart's mathematical psychology in preparing the way for Fechner's development of psychophysics.

1 Johann Friedrich Herbart (1776–1841) and Psychophysics

Introduction

Two world-changing events happened in May 1776. On May 4, 1776 the Rhode Island General Assembly declared its independence from Great Britain, the first of the original 13 American colonies to do so. Earlier that same day, Johann Friedrich Herbart was born in Oldenburg, Germany. The event in Rhode Island signalled the American Revolution. Herbart signalled a revolution in psychology, when he considered psychology to be a science based on mathematics, rather than a topic in metaphysics.

Herbart's Career

Herbart's life was a success, insofar as he attained a stellar reputation as a university teacher and thinker. As noted, he was born on May 4, 1776, in Oldenburg, a town in northwest Germany not far from the cities of Bremen and Hamburg. His father was a judicial administrator in Oldenburg and his mother was the daughter of an Oldenburg doctor. He was precocious, a good amateur pianist, and in 1808 published his three-movement piano sonata just prior to the appearance of Beethoven's "Appassionata" (Rausch, 1975).

He entered the local Gymnasium (the German term for a school for teenaged students hoping to enter university) at the age of 12, and in 1794, at the age of 18, he entered the University of Jena. He showed an interest in philosophy at the Gymnasium (where he started his studies of Kant). At university, he was considerably influenced by one of his instructors, Johann Gottlieb Fichte (1762–1814). At that time, discussions about psychology in most of the German universities were dominated by Wolff's distinction between rational and empirical psychology.

Herbart's participation in the cultural milieu of his era was facilitated by Jena's being near the dukedom of Weimar. The aristocracy there financially supported the dramatists J. W. von Goethe (1749–1832) and J. C. F. von Schiller (1759–1805), and offered what was almost a perpetual festival of theatre. Herbart made the most of this unusual opportunity to play a part in the major German literary events of the late eighteenth century.

In 1799, at the age of 21, he was a private tutor to a wealthy family in Switzerland. He stayed there for two and a half years, until 1800. This year was a stormy one for most of Europe because Napoleon Bonaparte (1769–1821), having managed to stamp out some of the atrocious guillotinings of clergy and aristocracy that occurred at the end of the French Revolution, embarked on a mission to bring all of Europe under French control. Herbart left Switzerland because the family who employed him found themselves billeting some of the French army.[1]

He returned to Bremen, in North Germany, where he improved his teaching skills by tutoring and by lecturing at the local Gymnasium, and devoting considerable time to catching up on recent developments in mathematics. Herbart wanted a university position, which in 1802 he did obtain at the University of Göttingen. Henceforward, his academic career was stellar: at Göttingen from 1802 to 1809, at Königsberg from 1809 to 1833, and at Göttingen again from 1833 to his death in 1841.

His move from Göttingen to Königsberg in 1809 was motivated by his dislike of the French forces that occupied Göttingen in 1806. His new appointment as Chair of Philosophy at Königsberg in 1809 was highly prestigious. His predecessor but one was none other than Immanuel Kant. Herbart began a comfortable domestic lifestyle here: in 1811, he married Marie Drake, the daughter of an English merchant. Though childless themselves, they welcomed students and even children to gatherings at their home, where innovative educational methods were tested and discussed.[2]

The move from Königsberg back to Göttingen in 1833 also had a flair of drama. Kant spent his whole life in Königsberg. Kant was so impressed by a visit by the 22-year-old Fichte, who studied at Jena and Leipzig, that he recommended Fichte for a good teaching position at Jena despite his youth.

1 It is appropriate here to mention that Napoleon's exploits caused considerable distress throughout Germany. Soldiers were billeted on unwilling families, and large-scale battles took place on German soil with considerable loss of life on both sides. For example, Goethe and his family found themselves in physical danger following the battle of Jena (1806); and the impact of the Napoleonic wars on Goethe's private life has been documented by Damm (1998) in the course of her account of Goethe's relationship with Christiane Vulpius (1765–1816). Beethoven was so angry that his hero Napoleon, in 1804, had proclaimed himself an emperor, that he scratched out the dedication to Napoleon in the manuscript of his Third Symphony, the "Eroica." Later, in 1809, Beethoven feared that his patron in Vienna, the Archduke Rudolf, would not return from exile when French forces invaded and occupied Vienna. His piano sonata known as "Les Adieux" is a musical expression of Beethoven's hopes and fears concerning whether Rudolf would return safely to Vienna.

2 Herbart could not escape foreign soldiers even in Königsberg; they came there when, in 1812, Napoleon rashly invaded Moscow, which defended itself so well that Napoleon had to drag his weary army back to Germany. There, he was defeated by a coalition of British, Prussian, Austrian, Swedish, and Russian troops at the Battle of Leipzig (1813). Napoleon was captured by the British and exiled to an island off Italy named Elba; but he escaped and had to be defeated again at the Battle of Waterloo (1815). In 1821, he died on St. Helena, a tiny British-owned island in the middle of the South Atlantic. In 1840 his remains were moved to an impressive tomb located at the Hôtel des Invalides in Paris, where it is still frequently visited by tourists and Parisians alike. Napoleon's attack on, and retreat from, Moscow in 1812 was the subject of Tolstoy's (1869/1968) novel *War and Peace*, as well as of Tchaikovsky's "1812" overture, written in 1880.

Here, not only did Fichte teach Herbart, but Fichte also had Hegel as a departmental colleague.

Towards the end of their careers, both Fichte and Hegel moved from Jena to the newer, but more prestigious, University of Berlin. Hegel exerted so much dominance over what was taught at Berlin that Herbart's work was neglected. After Hegel died, Herbart reputedly hoped to be appointed to the chair of philosophy that Hegel occupied at Berlin. Instead, he accepted a call to return to Göttingen, where he spent the rest of his life. He died at the age of 65, on August 14, 1841. A short and informative life of Herbart was written by Flügel (1905), and a scholarly account of Herbart's life as an educationist by Asmus (1968/1970).

Herbart was one of a quartet of major German philosophers that straddled the turn of the nineteenth century. These four consisted of Kant, Herbart, Fichte, and J. W. F. Hegel (1770–1831). Prior to 1824, Herbart published a few papers on his mathematical theory about how ideas entered and left consciousness during a short period of time. As mentioned in the Prologue, his full theory (Herbart, 1824/1890a, 1825/1892) appeared in his *Psychology as Science* [*Psychologie als Wissenschaft*].

Herbart's Educational Psychology

Today, Herbart is best known for the creation of new principles of educational psychology. For example, both the late nineteenth-century book titled *Herbart and the Herbartians* (De Garmo, 1896) and the twentieth-century book titled *Herbart and Herbartianism: An Educational Ghost Story* (Dunkel, 1970) describe the rise of a pedagogical movement, largely centred on Germany and the United States. The movement recommended choosing reading material for the classroom that genuinely *interests* the students of a given grade. New material should always be introduced in such a way that the student can easily add it to the student's already acquired corpus of knowledge. The aim of education was to create well-rounded and civil-minded members of the community.[3]

Curtis and Boultwood (1963, pp. 352–368) show how Herbart's principles spread in Germany at educational institutes in the cities of Halle and Leipzig and at the University of Jena. As a consequence, many of the 9,000 American students attracted to Germany for university studies discovered Herbart's educational theory. Subsequently, "the cult of Herbartianism flourished in the United States for many years" (p. 367). Boudewijnse, Murray, and Bandomir (2001, pp. 122–124) surveyed several late nineteenth-century books on Herbartianism.

3 As told by Daniel Defoe (1660–1731), the novel *Robinson Crusoe* (Defoe, 1719/2003) was certainly of interest to adventurous-spirited teenagers in eighteenth-century English boys' schools. An admirer of Herbart named Johann Rudolf Wyss (1782–1830) wrote a family-oriented version of *Robinson Crusoe* designed to instil in its readers a sense of community obligation and selflessness. *The Swiss Family Robinson* (Wyss, 1812/2007) appeared in German in 1812 and in English in 1820. At least two Hollywood movies were made with that title, an earnest one in 1940, and a more light-hearted Disney version in 1960 (Maltin, 2008, p. 1356).

They concluded that "Herbart's mathematical theory was almost entirely absent from the writings of Herbartian educationists. One searches in vain through the English-language corpus of Herbartian books on education in the 1890s for any extended discussion of his mathematics" (p. 123). Herbart himself felt that the mathematics he used to describe conscious events that might be immediate responses to stimulus-combinations, or involved retrieval from short-term memory, could not predict how well a student would perform weeks or months later in his or her classroom performance (Herbart, 1812/1888a).

Herbart's philosophical approach, in which his mathematical psychology first appeared, received scholarly treatment in Stout (1888a, 1888b, 1889a, 1889b), Ward (1910–1911), Weiss (1928) and Kim (2015). For newcomers to Herbart's mathematical psychology, two papers by Boudewijnse, Murray, and Bandomir (1999, 2001) are recommended. This chapter can be read independently of those two sources.

A Short Introduction to Herbart's Theory

"Clear and Distinct" Ideas: Vorstellungen

This brings us immediately to a consideration of the word that Herbart used to refer to "ideas", namely, *Vorstellung* (plural, *Vorstellungen*). A *Vorstellung* (pronounced "fore-shtell'-ung") was translated as an "idea" in Boring's (1950, pp. 250–261) account of Herbart's theory. In Stout's (1888a, 1888b, 1889a, 1889b) articles expounding the psychology of Herbart for the benefit of English-speaking philosophers and psychologists at the end of the nineteenth century, the word *Vorstellung* was translated as a "presentation". In Smith's translation of the second edition of *The Text-Book of Psychology* written by Herbart (1834/1891), *Vorstellung* was translated as a "concept". And Ward (1910–1911, p. 337) translated *Vorstellungen* as "elementary ideas or presentations". Boudewijnse, Murray, and Bandomir (1999, 2001) preferred to leave *Vorstellung* untranslated because, in their opinion, no equivalent English translation exists.

Boring (1950, p. 255) had it right when he said that Herbartian *Vorstellungen* included not only Locke's mental ideas but also those conscious experiences, ostensibly caused by external physical stimuli, that Boring called "perceptions". These include "sights", "sounds", "tastes", "touches", "smells", and "pains". There are also somewhat amorphous experiences caused by internal stimuli such as feelings of dizziness, hunger, thirst, and drowsiness, as well as a gamut of vague feelings to do with movement, such as muscle-strain, stiffness, and other "kinaesthetic" experiences. None of these were called "ideas" by Locke, who called them "sensations". For Herbart, *Vorstellungen* were conscious experiences; and conscious experiences include sensations and perceptions as well as mental ideas. On occasion, Herbart used the term "perception-*Vorstellung*".

Herbart's *Psychologie als Wissenschaft* is usually translated as "Psychology as Science". This title can, somewhat pedantically perhaps, be interpreted as meaning "Psychology Presented as if it Were a Science". Herbart's awareness of his priority in applying mathematics to psychology—so long considered to be a sub-discipline within philosophy—led him to be ultra-careful in specifying how his theory related to previous theories about the mind/brain system put forward in a philosophical context.[4] So, for example, in the Introduction to the first volume of *Psychologie als Wissenschaft*, he attests that his contemporary view of how the "soul" or "mind" (here the German word was *Geist*) relates to the body owes an immeasurable debt to Descartes, followed by Locke, Leibniz, Wolff, Kant, and Fichte (Herbart, 1824/1890a, pp. 212–231).[5]

To make this clear, Table 1.1 shows the general layout, in terms of headings and subheadings, of *Psychologie als Wissenschaft*; the mathematical portions are found in the second and third sections of the First Part, while the applications of his theory to psychology in general are in the Second Part. The copy I used was

Table 1.1 The main section-headings in Herbart's *Psychology as Science* [*Psychologie als Wissenschaft*]

In Kehrbach & Flügel, Volume 5
Preface (*Vorrede*)
Introduction (*Einleitung*). Seven chapter-like headings, subsections §1–§23
First Synthetic Part[6]
First section. Investigations of the "I" and its closest relations
Four chapters, subsections §24–§40
Second section. Foundations of the statics of the mind
Seven chapters, subsections §41–§73[7]
Third section. Foundations of the mechanics of the mind
Seven chapters, subsections §74–§102
In Kehrbach & Flügel, Volume 6
Second Analytic Part
First section. On mental life in general
Five chapters, subsections §103–§128
Second section. On human development in particular
Four chapters, subsections §129–§152
Third section. On the external relationships of the mind
Two chapters, subsections §153–§168

4 According to Ramul (1960), a book by C. A. Körber (1746) was the most complete treatise on mathematical psychology before the appearance of the First Part of Herbart's (1824/1890a) *Psychologie als Wissenschaft*. I could not find it listed in the National Union Catalog of Pre-1954 Imprints.

5 *Collins Gem German-English Dictionary* (1953/1982, pp. 127–128) translates *der Geist* as meaning "spirit," "ghost," or "mind." A "mental illness" in German is *eine Geisteskrankheit*. "Soul-destroying" is *geistestödend*. And *geistlich* translates as "spiritual, religious." The "Holy Ghost" or "Holy Spirit" in Christian theology is *der heilige Geist* in German. *Geisteswissenschaften* is often translated as "human sciences" and *Naturwissenschaften* is often translated as "natural sciences."

6 The first "Synthetic Part" appears in Volume 5 (1890) of the edition, by Kehrbach and others, of Herbart's works arranged in chronological order and is referred to in the text as Herbart (1824/1890a). The second "Analytic Part" appears in Volume 6 (1892) and is referred to in the text as Herbart (1825/1892).

7 §41–§51 were translated into English in Shipley's (1961, pp. 22–48) edited volume. Shipley writes that he "wishes to acknowledge the assistance of Frank Gaynor in making the first, and very fine [draft] of the Herbart.... The final form of the translation is the full responsibility of the editor. Because of the difficulty of Herbart's writing, the translation of his work is quite free" (p. 19).

included in Volumes 5 and 6 of the 19 volumes of Herbart's works edited by Karl Kehrbach, Otto Flügel, and Theodor Fritsch between 1887 and 1912.

Herbart's mathematical model itself is not presented until subsection §41, which opens the section on statics. The Preface, followed by subsections §1–§40, explain how Herbart began his odyssey towards his mathematical model of psychology. A summary of these subsections now follows.

How Herbart Arrived at His Mathematical Psychology

The first sentence in the Introduction to *Psychologie als Wissenschaft* (Herbart, 1824/1890a) is: "The intention of this work is to present an investigation into the soul (*Seele*) that can be likened to investigations into natural phenomena.... The investigation, when possible, will consider magnitudes (*Grössen*) and calculations (*Rechnungen*)" (my translation, p. 185). The whole of the seven chapter-like divisions of the Introduction (*Einleitung*, subsections §1–§23) as well as the first four chapters of the first section of the First Synthetic Part (subsections §24–§40) are devoted to establishing that "magnitudes and calculations" *can be* applied to psychology.

Herbart's argument stated why he believed that metaphysics was *not* the best approach to founding a science of psychology. He specifically focused on the metaphysics underlying his mentor Fichte's theory of *das Ich* ("the I"). Near the end of this long argument (subsections §1–§23), Herbart carefully analysed Fichte's claim that the I was both object and subject. Fichte's rationale was that *Vorstellungen* are both (a) the *object* of the I's observations and (b) the *subject*, I, who makes those observations. Herbart showed that (a) and (b), when pursued to their logical conclusions, contained self-contradictions that trap the metaphysician in an unending series of wordy arguments, none of which comes to a clear conclusion.

Let more than one *Vorstellung* be present in consciousness at a given moment. These *Vorstellungen* will differ from each other in content. For example, two *Vorstellungen* may consist of two differing tones heard simultaneously or two differing colour-patches viewed simultaneously. If the listener hears tones that sound close together in pitch (e.g., on the piano, middle C and the adjacent D), then the *Vorstellungen* of the two tones are assumed to offer little contrast or "opposition" to each other. If the two tones sound further apart in pitch (e.g., middle C and the G above middle C), their *Vorstellungen* are assumed to be more strongly contrasted with, or "opposed", to each other than was the case for middle C and D.

Herbart asserted that, the greater the degree of opposition between two or more *Vorstellungen*, the greater the energy needed by each *Vorstellung* if it is to successfully strive (*streben*) for its own self-preservation. This striving has as its outcome a reduction, in the energy of each *Vorstellung*, from its initial energy-level to a lower level. The energy remaining after this reduction is spread across all the *Vorstellungen* that are not concurrently in consciousness. The fact that there is any change at all in the energy of a *Vorstellung* when another

Vorstellung is concurrently in consciousness led Herbart to claim that a "force" had been generated. This force affected the energy of each of the *Vorstellungen* involved.

Each of the forces generated by multiple *Vorstellungen* concurrently in consciousness represents a level of energy associated with the ability of each *Vorstellung* to resist the inhibition exerted by each of the other *Vorstellungen* concurrently in consciousness. In the present text, three cases, to be called Case I, Case II and Case III, are singled out for discussion. In Case I, the energy-level permitting *Vorstellung* V_a to resist inhibition from *Vorstellung* V_b is postulated to exceed the energy-level permitting *Vorstellung* V_b to resist inhibition from *Vorstellung* V_a. These energy-levels equal *a* and *b*.

The assumption that forces represented interactions between simultaneously experienced *Vorstellungen* led Herbart to draw an analogy between (a) the laws determining the magnitudes by which the initial energies of *Vorstellungen* were reduced in their striving for self-preservation and (b) the laws determining the magnitudes of distances moved by physical objects subjected to forces such as gravity. According to subsection §40 (p. 280), when a change in the energy of a *Vorstellung* occurs *suddenly*, the laws of statics describe the equilibrium-state arrived at almost instantaneously. When a change in the energy of a *Vorstellung* occurs *gradually*, as happens when a *Vorstellung* vanishes from consciousness and then later reappears in consciousness, the laws of mechanics must be applied.[8]

In subsection §35 (p. 272), Herbart used a metaphor to pinpoint the disadvantages of metaphysics, and the advantages of mathematics, in the development of a scientific model of psychology. Using the metaphysics associated with Fichte's concept of *das Ich* led to a continuous flow of reasoning with only momentary opportunities for stopping and resting. It is as if one were walking through a museum or art-gallery. The only valid way to arrive at a more permanent stopping-point, for Herbart, was to find a magnitude within the confines of psychological self-observation that would then permit mathematics to provide a conclusion to the reasoning process. That stopping-point occurred when the interactions between two or more simultaneously experienced and mutually opposed *Vorstellungen* altered the energy-level of each *Vorstellung*.

At the opening of *Psychologie als Wissenschaft*, Herbart (1825/1890a, p. 189) emphasized one kind of conscious experience in particular. Conscious experience provides evidence about our own feelings. We perceive this evidence in as direct a manner as we perceive the phenomena of Nature. This self-provided evidence was, therefore, Herbart's preferred starting-point for the development of a science of psychology. Evidence about our own feelings demands self-observation, which in turn is possible because of the existence of

8 There is a difference between Herbart's mathematical psychology and mathematical physics. *Vorstellungen* are assumed to have no spatial dimensions. Herbart's mathematical psychology does not refer, therefore, to many concepts used in mathematical physics, including acceleration, directional vectors, and trigonometrical definitions. *Vorstellungen*, however, do change in energy as time progresses, hence can be said to operate in a time-dimension.

self-consciousness. Only in the final pages of the Second Analytic Part of *Psychologie als Wissenschaft* does Herbart (1825/1892, subsection §132, pp. 168–171) use his model of psychology to explain how self-consciousness emerges slowly during an individual's childhood as a consequence of multiple experiences.

Herbart provided a rationale for preferring a model of psychology based on mathematics rather than on metaphysics. He also provided an account of what was meant, mathematically, when a numerical value was assigned to a *Vorstellung*. Let *Vorstellung* V_a be assigned a value 5 and *Vorstellung* V_b be assigned a value 4. The value 5 indicates that the energy exerted by V_a (to resist V_b's energy) exceeds the value 4, the energy exerted by V_b (to resist V_a's energy). As noted above, Herbart himself sometimes used "strength" (*Stärke*) as a synonym for "energy".[9]

Herbart's Statics

We need to understand the uniquely Herbartian concept of a "total inhibition" (*Hemmungssumme*).[10] That total inhibition is apportioned across the *Vorstellungen*

9 One can ask: Is there anything overlooked when one asserts that a *Vorstellung* has a specific "energy" or "strength"? Yes. The question itself assumes that a single *Vorstellung* might exist that can totally dominate one's conscious experience at a given moment. Herbart's theory made the "energy" or strength" of a *Vorstellung* contingent on there being an opposition between at least two *Vorstellungen*. Herbart (1824/1890a, p. 281) therefore argued that the assumption that any *Vorstellung* could exist as an isolated entity was a "fiction." He also implied that no *Vorstellung* could vanish completely from consciousness if a second *Vorstellung*, simultaneously present, exerted an inhibiting force on that first *Vorstellung*. To conceive of a single *Vorstellung* as having a strength whose value was independent of the strength of other *Vorstellungen* concurrently in consciousness would be an "idealization." Because this idealization, however, might greatly facilitate the discussion of the interplay of *Vorstellungen* in conscious experience, Herbart himself did assign "energies" or "strengths" to those *Vorstellungen* individually.

10 We are improving the translation of *Hemmungssumme* by rendering it as "total inhibition," rather than the literal translation of *Hemmungssumme* as "inhibition-sum" or Shipley's (1961, p. 24) "sum of the inhibitions." We add that a *Vorstellung* is clearly not a physical object we can see, and to which we can assign spatial coordinates. The word "*Vorstellung*" is an abstract word with strong connections to near-synonyms such as "idea," "concept," "presentation." If we assign human-like attributes to a *Vorstellung* we risk the error of anthropomorphizing something inanimate. Nevertheless, Herbart chose to teach his model by frequently assigning human-like attributes to his *Vorstellungen*. For example, a *Vorstellung* can "strive" (*streben*) to survive inhibitory forces exerted by other *Vorstellungen* and thereby preserve itself. One *Vorstellung*, A, can "help" (*helfen*) to lift back into consciousness a forgotten *Vorstellung*, B, because A can partially "fuse" (*verschmelzen*) with B. One *Vorstellung*, A, can "suffer" (*leiden*) when it "resists" (*widerstehen*) opposing forces that "compete" (*widerstreiten*) with A. There is no denying, however, that the kind of verbal laxity associated with anthropomorphism can appeal to teacher and learners alike. In particular, the term "*Vorstellung*-strength" is so widely used in both the primary and secondary literature concerning Herbart's model that the Editor and I decided to continue to use it here. A *Vorstellung* should perhaps be quantified as having a "magnitude" or an intensity, rather than a "strength." That is because the word "strength" does have anthropomorphic implications for some readers. More generally, these considerations have persuaded me to aim for verbal consistency throughout the present volume. I have therefore used "strength" as well as "energy" in the context of Herbartian *Vorstellungen*; "intensity" in the context of physical stimuli; and "magnitude" in the context of psychological experiences such as sensations. For example, in Chapter 4, Fechner's Law relates a "sensation-magnitude" to the "stimulus intensity" of its associated physical source.

concurrently in consciousness. The second section of the First Part is about "statics", wherein Herbart defines a threshold. Let Ψ denote this threshold. Herbart wanted to define a "threshold-*value*", that is, a number that uniquely defines a level of *Vorstellung*-strength that a *Vorstellung* must have to survive in consciousness.

Herbart's theory of the total inhibition is given in the first three chapters of the section on statics. The final three chapters of that statics section describe how *Vorstellungen* can combine in various ways. Herbart made two predictions that are so different from each other that it comes as a pleasant surprise to learn that one single model can justify both predictions. The first prediction is that, if there are two *Vorstellungen* in consciousness, then neither can cause the other to vanish from consciousness. The second prediction is that, if there are three *Vorstellungen* in consciousness, then one of them can (but not necessarily) vanish from consciousness due to inhibition exerted by the other two *Vorstellungen*.

Herbart's Model Applied to Two Vorstellungen

The intricate workings of the mind were a puzzle for Herbart's philosophical predecessors. Herbart resolved this puzzle by creating an ingenious theory of the opposition between *Vorstellungen* that led to their fusion, combination, or disappearance from consciousness.

The theory is remarkable for its simplicity and depth. Let each *Vorstellung*, V, have a strength in consciousness. For example, let the strength (i.e., energy) of *Vorstellung* V_a equal a. Another *Vorstellung*, V_b, has its own strength. Let V_b equal b. The total strength is $T = a + b$. Each *Vorstellung* also has an inhibitory strength equal to the reciprocal of its strength. This inhibitory strength plays a major role in the interaction between conscious *Vorstellungen*. The inhibitory strength of V_a is $1/a$ and for V_b it is $1/b$.

A necessary property of consciousness is that if both V_a and V_b are in consciousness they must interact. When they interact, they compete with each other through their mutual inhibitions $1/a$ and $1/b$. Let S equal the total inhibition for two *Vorstellungen* in consciousness.

$$S = \frac{1}{a} + \frac{1}{b} = \frac{b}{b}\frac{1}{a} + \frac{a}{a}\frac{1}{b} = \frac{a+b}{ab}$$

The two *Vorstellungen* strive to remain in consciousness. Their struggle results in a reduction in their strengths due to their mutual inhibition. Herbart's theory of how this decrease occurs due to the competition reveals the inventiveness of his ideas about the processing of *Vorstellungen* in consciousness. The amount of inhibition of one *Vorstellung* caused by the other depends on the proportion of total inhibition, S, caused by each *Vorstellung*. In this regard let p_a be the proportion of total inhibition due to V_a.

$$p_a = \frac{\frac{1}{a}}{S} = \left[\frac{\frac{1}{a}}{\frac{a+b}{ab}}\right] = \frac{b}{a+b}$$

The proportion of total inhibition due to V_b is p_b

$$p_b = \frac{\frac{1}{b}}{S} = \left[\frac{\frac{1}{b}}{\frac{a+b}{ab}}\right] = \frac{a}{a+b}$$

This result shows that the stronger *Vorstellung* V_a contributes a smaller proportion of the total inhibition caused by V_a and V_b. This very surprising outcome shows how the stronger *Vorstellung* with a smaller inhibition reciprocal influences the competition between two *Vorstellungen.*

The competition between V_a and V_b results in a loss of strength in both. How can each *Vorstellung* affect the other? Herbart proposes a startling observation. Suppose each *Vorstellung* consists of a string of components, call them quanta. The strength of V_a suggests a greater number of quanta, each contributing to the total strength of V_a. Since V_a has a greater strength than V_b, the number of quanta in V_b must be less than the number of quanta in V_a. Therefore, the greatest amount of interaction in strengths between the two quanta is limited by the smaller number of quanta in V_b that can influence the number of quanta in V_a.

The context within which the *Vorstellungen* oppose each other influences the strength of the opposition between the two *Vorstellungen.* The grade of opposition is characterized by a parameter m ($0 \leq m \leq 1$). The strength of this influence on V_b and V_a equals V_b's proportion of the total inhibition multiplied by mb. The inhibiting influence of V_b on V_a is

$$mb\frac{a}{a+b}$$

When $m = 1$, this equals

$$\frac{ab}{a+b}$$

Notice that this also equals the reciprocal of S, the total inhibition.

Similarly, the effect of V_a on V_b equals V_a's proportion of the total inhibition times b. That is

$$mb\left[\frac{b}{a+b}\right] = \frac{b^2}{a+b} \quad \text{when } m = 1.$$

The competition between V_a and V_b leads to the following reductions in their strengths to new values. Let R_a = V_a–loss caused by inhibition from V_b. Then when $m = 1$:

$$R_a = a - b\left[\frac{\frac{1}{a}}{\frac{1}{a}+\frac{1}{b}}\right] = a - b\left[\frac{b}{a+b}\right]$$

and for V_b, let R_b = V_b–loss due to inhibition from V_a. Then when $m = 1$:

$$R_b = b - b\left[\frac{\frac{1}{b}}{\frac{1}{a}+\frac{1}{b}}\right] = b - \frac{ab}{a+b}.$$

These examples show quite clearly how the inhibition affects the strength (the "remainder") of each *Vorstellung*. As an example, suppose $a = 5$ and $b = 4$ and $m = 1$. Then

$$R_a = 5 - 4\left(\frac{4}{9}\right) = \frac{45}{9} - \frac{16}{9} = \frac{29}{9}$$

and

$$R_b = 4 - 4\left[\frac{5}{9}\right] = \left(\frac{36}{9}\right) - \frac{20}{9} = \frac{16}{9}$$

Notice that

$$R_a + R_b = \frac{29}{9} + \frac{16}{9} = \frac{45}{9} = 5 = a,$$

the strength of V_a. This result will always occur given the proportional basis of the model.

In Herbart's day an important method of reducing errors in a calculation involving division was to keep the computation in integers until the final calculation, as shown here.

The remainders of two *Vorstellungen*, V_a and V_b can be illustrated in a broader context by setting $V_a = 5$, $V_b = 1, 2, 3, 4$ or 5, and letting $m = 1$. Figure 1.1 shows that the remainder of V_a falls from 5 when $V_b = 1$ to 2.5 when $V_b = 5$. The remainder of V_b rises from 1 when $V_b = 1$ to 2.5 when $V_b = 5$. The sum of the remainders of V_a and V_b always sum to 5 when $m = 1$. The sum equals the greatest-valued *Vorstellung*, which here is V_a. The *Vorstellungen* values are easily seen in Figure 1.1.

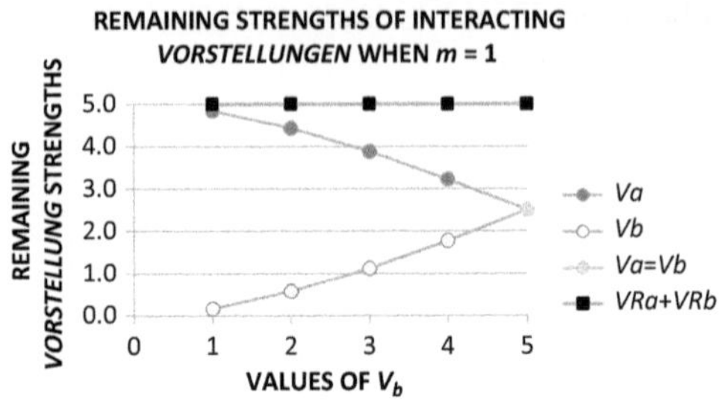

Figure 1.1 The strengths of the remaining two *Vorstellungen*, V_a and V_b, when $V_a = 5$, $V_b = 1, 2, 3, 4$ or 5, and $m = 1$.

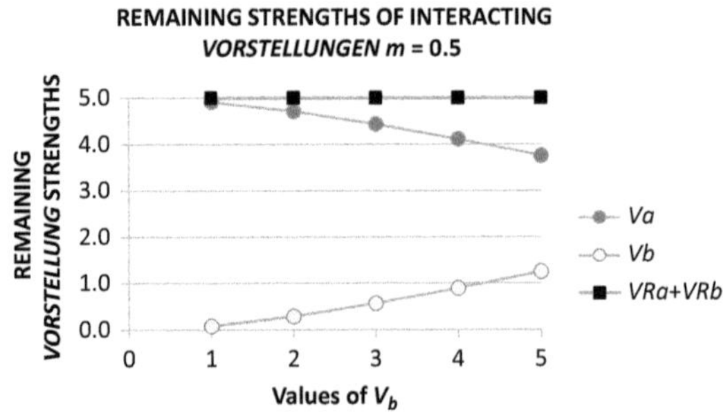

Figure 1.2 The strengths of the remaining two *Vorstellungen*, V_a and V_b, when $V_a = 5$, $V_b = 1, 2, 3, 4$ or 5, and $m = 0.5$.

Figure 1.2 shows that when $m = 0.5$ the decrease in R_a as V_b increases is less than was the case when $m = 1$. The increase in R_b as V_b increases is also less steep than was the case when $m = 1$.

Herbart's Model Applied to Three Vorstellungen

Given three *Vorstellungen*, V_a, V_b, and V_c, let $V_a > V_b > V_c$. The total energy, T, will equal $(a + b + c)$. The total inhibition, S, will be

$$S = \frac{1}{a} + \frac{1}{b} + \frac{1}{c} = \frac{abc}{abc}\left[\frac{1}{a} + \frac{1}{b} + \frac{1}{c}\right] = \frac{bc + ac + ab}{abc}$$

The proportions of the total inhibition caused by V_a, V_b, and V_c respectively will be

$$p_a = \frac{\frac{1}{a}}{S} = \frac{bc}{bc + ac + ab}$$

$$p_b = \frac{\frac{1}{b}}{S} = \frac{ac}{bc + ac + ab}$$

$$p_c = \frac{\frac{1}{c}}{S} = \frac{ab}{bc + ac + ab}$$

The influence of V_b and V_c on V_a equals the proportion of the total inhibition caused by V_b and V_c times $[m(b + c)]$, where m is the grade of inhibition ($0 \leq m \leq 1$). The remainders of V_a, V_b, and V_c respectively will then be

$$R_a = a - \left[m\left(b + c\right)\right]\frac{bc}{bc + ac + ab}$$

$$R_b = b - \left[m\left(b + c\right)\right]\frac{ac}{bc + ac + ab}$$

$$R_c = c - \left[m\left(b + c\right)\right]\frac{ab}{bc + ac + ab}$$

In Case II, let $V_a = 5$, $V_b = 4$, $V_c = 3$, and $m = 1$. Substituting these integer values into the above expressions for R_a, R_b, and R_c, then converting them to decimal notation leads to $R_a = 3.21$, $R_b = 1.77$, and $R_c = 0.02$. As shown in Figure 1.3 these values sum to 5, the value of the strongest *Vorstellung*, V_a.

In Case III, let $V_a = 5$, $V_b = 4$, $V_c = 2$, and $m = 1$. Substituting these integer values into the above expressions for R_a, R_b, and R_c, then converting them to decimal notation, leads to $R_a = 3.74$, $R_b = 2.42$, and $R_c = -1.16$. As shown in Figure 1.4, these values sum to 5, the value of the strongest *Vorstellung*, V_a.

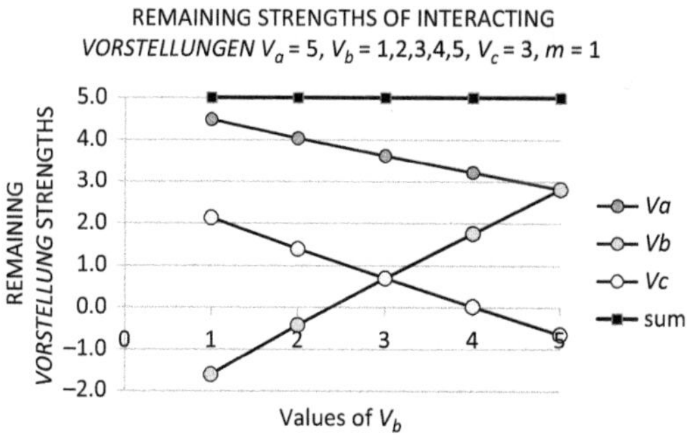

Figure 1.3 The strengths of the remaining three *Vorstellungen*, when $V_a = 5$, $V_b = 1, 2, 3, 4$ or 5, $V_c = 3$, and $m = 1$.

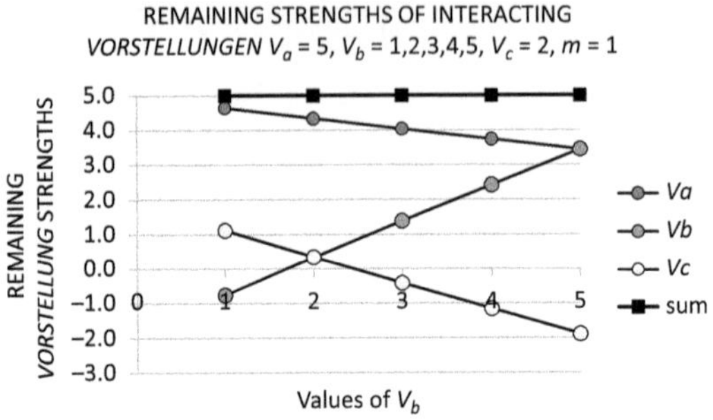

Figure 1.4 The strengths of the remaining three *Vorstellungen*, when $V_a = 5$, $V_b = 1, 2, 3, 4$ or 5, $V_c = 2$, and $m = 1$.

The Threshold Equation

Herbart (1824/1890a, p. 293) proved that, when we have two *Vorstellungen*, V_a and V_b, the value that Ψ, a common threshold (*gemeine Schwelle*), must have is:

$$\psi = b\sqrt{\left[a/(a+b)\right]} \tag{1.1}$$

Equation 1.1 represents what Herbart called the "threshold equation" for the particular situation where the number of *Vorstellungen* concurrently in consciousness equals two. When a third *Vorstellung* V_c is added, the inhibition by V_a and V_b, may force the remaining value of V_c to fall below Ψ, that is, $V_c < \Psi$.

Using Equation 1.1, we can look back over Figures 1.3 and 1.4 to find cases where the remainder of V_c is above or below Ψ. In Figure 1.3, $a = 5$, $b = 4$, and $c = 3$. Inserting these values of a and b into Equation 1.1 yields a value of $4\sqrt{[5/(5 + 4)]} = 2.9814$. The value, $c = 3$, exceeds the value Ψ by 0.02. Therefore, c remains in consciousness. In Figure 1.4, where $c = 2$, this same predicted value of Ψ, 2.9814, exceeds the actual value, $c = 2$, by 0.9814. Therefore, the value of c is less than Ψ and vanishes from consciousness.

If $V_c = \Psi = 2.9814$, the remainder $R_c = 0$. That is, V_c vanishes from consciousness, as predicted by the threshold equation.

Combinations of Vorstellungen

A combination of *Vorstellungen* V_a and V_b is one in which *Vorstellung* V_a shares a unity with *Vorstellung* V_b. If that combination vanished from consciousness, then a reappearance of *Vorstellung* V_a in consciousness can facilitate the reappearance of *Vorstellung* V_b along with V_a in consciousness.

Herbart postulated that there were two kinds of combination. One he called a "complication", where *Vorstellungen* V_a and V_b remain independent but travel in pairs, so to speak. The other kind of combination between *Vorstellungen* was called by Herbart a "fusion". Here, *Vorstellungen* V_a and V_b no longer remain independent, but are considered to have (partially or wholly) fused together, so that a particular portion of *Vorstellung* V_a is fused with a particular portion of *Vorstellung* V_b.

For Herbart, one of the major implications of fusing together *Vorstellungen* was that it explained serial (or "rote") learning by humans. A rote repetition of the number sequence 548706 could lead to fusions forming between the separate *Vorstellungen* representing 5, 4, 8, 7, 0, and 6. Herbart (1834/1891, pp. 22–23) argued that the strength of the fusion between the *Vorstellungen* "5" and "4" was greater than the strength of the fusion between *Vorstellungen* "5" and "7". The more "distant" the two *Vorstellungen*, the smaller the fused portions of both *Vorstellungen*. Ebbinghaus (1885/1964, pp. 90–123) confirmed experimentally the prediction that the strength of an association between two elements of a learned list decreased, the more distant those two elements were in that list.

Herbart's Mechanics

In Herbartian mechanics, the interest shifts from the statics-question "What equilibrium state is arrived at after the total inhibition has reduced a *Vorstellung* to a remainder?" to two questions: "How long will it take before a given *Vorstellung* vanishes from consciousness?" and "How long will it take for a given *Vorstellung* to reappear in consciousness?" Herbart (1822/1890b) himself distinguished between the statics and mechanics of a system in the following quotation. He recognized, as did Daniel Bernoulli and Euler in their studies of fluid dynamics, that a mathematical treatment can only be tractable if certain idealizations are incorporated into the theory:

> Statics denotes the study of equilibrium-states; mechanics denotes the study of changes [*Veränderungen*] which either proceed from the equilibrium-states before that state has actually been reached, or follow as a consequence when that equilibrium-state no longer holds … it will always be the case that statics will precede the much more difficult, though more widely generalizable, mechanics, even if a complete equilibrium-state should in fact represent an *ideal*, never fully realizable, situation.
>
> (my translation, p. 110)

Both in classical mechanics and in Herbartian mechanics, the emphasis shifts to discussions about how objects in a given equilibrium-state behave when subjected to forces that set them in motion. In classical mechanics, being set into motion means being relocated from one position to another, where each "position" can be identified by the values on the coordinates of a graphical representation of space (usually in two or three dimensions). In Herbartian mechanics, spatial coordinates do not exist. Changes are represented by changes in the strengths or energies of *Vorstellungen*, taken singly or in groups, that are represented as points located on a single coordinate called time.

These changes in individual *Vorstellung*-strengths develop into the total inhibition.

Let S = total inhibition. The amount of inhibition, $\sigma(t)$, increases over time t. Herbart assumed that the instantaneous rate of change equals

$$(S-\sigma)dt = d\sigma \tag{1.2}$$

The solution of the differential equation is stated by Herbart (1824/1890a, subsection §74, p. 339) to be

$$\sigma(t) = S(1-e^{-t}) \tag{1.3}$$

According to Equation 1.3 the value of $1-e^{-t}$ increases towards an asymptote equal to one. Therefore the upper limit of this equation is S, the total inhibition as shown in Figure 1.5.

The next few sections of Herbart's discussion of his mechanics are devoted to proving that, if the total inhibition, S, fades over time, then the N *Vorstellungen* concurrently in consciousness are subjected to amounts of inhibition that also fade over time. Only if a certain amount of inhibition is reached will one *Vorstellung* be driven out of consciousness. This means that the number of *Vorstellungen* remaining in consciousness will be reduced by one. A new total inhibition will be apportioned across those remaining (N–1). This happens spontaneously, and one of those (N–1) remaining *Vorstellungen* could then, in its turn, be driven below the static threshold.

Herbart drew some conclusions of considerable practical interest from this possibility that the loss of any one remaining-*Vorstellung* out of N *Vorstellungen* could take place so quickly as to appear to be a "sudden" mental event. It meant that one's mood could change "in the twinkling of an eye" given the right circumstances. It meant that what one was concentrating on mentally could vanish from consciousness if a sudden noise inserts new *Vorstellungen* into one's

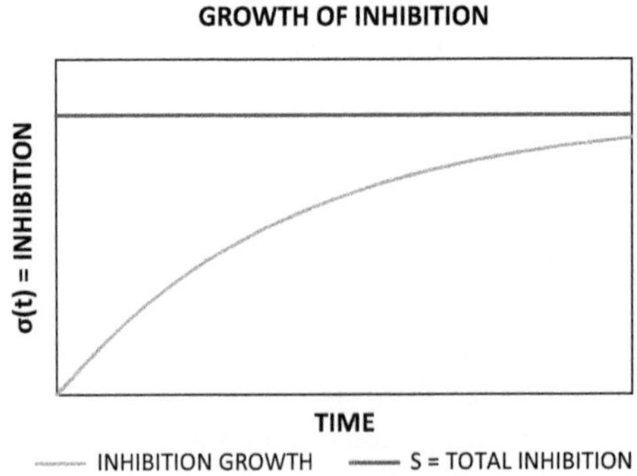

Figure 1.5 The inhibition grows as a function of time according to the Differential Equation 1.2.

train of thought. In his educational theory, Herbart devoted considerable attention to the teacher's difficulty in forcing certain pupils to concentrate on their schoolwork and not be distracted by minor events in the classroom. Distractions, particularly frustrating for the teacher, cause a switch of attention away from a pupil's current work and onto thoughts about events in the pupil's recent past. The pupil's consciousness now contains a host of new *Vorstellungen* that make it even harder for the pupil to resume the work that was interrupted (Herbart, 1812/1888a, pp. 149–151).

The above argument dealt only with independent *Vorstellungen*, none of which was fused to any other. Herbart (1824/1890a, subsections §67–§76, pp. 324–342) began his chapter on fusions by distinguishing between two kinds. For example, a perception-*Vorstellung* whose content was red could fuse with another perception-*Vorstellung* whose content was blue to yield a fused perception-*Vorstellung* whose content was purple. The second kind of fusion comes about when two *Vorstellungen* that stand in complete contrast to each other are both inhibited to such a degree that there is no longer any competition between them (i.e., their contrast was reduced to zero).

In the metaphysical background that determined what kind of mathematics should be applied to the mind, all *Vorstellungen* that are not competing with each other unite to form a grand whole. Any two *Vorstellungen* that were inhibited to such an extent that they no longer competed are fused with each other. The degree of fusion was specified by Herbart as being given by the proportion, r, of the first *Vorstellung*, V_a, that was fused with the proportion, q, of the second *Vorstellung*, V_b.

In his section on mechanics, which applied when dealing with two independent *Vorstellungen*, Herbart went on to derive an equation for two *Vorstellungen* that are fused.[11]

Let *Vorstellung* V_b reappear in consciousness because of the influence of *Vorstellung* V_a. This is because a proportion r of V_a is fused with a proportion q of V_b. It takes time for this influence to make V_b reappear fully in consciousness. Let the proportion of V_b that does reappear by time t be denoted by $\omega(t)$. The differential equation is:

$$d\omega = \left[(rq)/b\right]\left[(q-\omega)/q\right]dt \tag{1.4}$$

11 This equation was quoted in his largely non-mathematical book titled *Lehrbuch der Psychologie* (first edition, 1816; second edition, 1834). The second edition, Herbart (1834/1891), was translated into English by Margaret K. Smith (1846–1934) as *A Text-book in Psychology*. Margaret Keiver Smith was born in Amherst, Nova Scotia, Canada, and earned her teaching diploma in 1883 at the Oswego State Normal School, New York, where she was promoted to a teaching position until she decided to study psychology. It was during this period that she translated Herbart's *Text-book* into English. After making contact with a prominent American pioneer of experimental and educational psychology, G. Stanley Hall (1844–1924), she travelled to Switzerland and obtained her PhD in experimental psychology under Ernst Meumann (1862–1915), a close colleague of Ebbinghaus. After her return to the United States, she continued as a school teacher, although she had really hoped to be appointed to "a collegiate level position in psychology" (Young, 2013).

and its solution is:

$$\omega(t) = q\left\{1 - e^{\left[-(rt/b)\right]}\right\} \tag{1.5}$$

The derivations of these equations appear in Herbart (1824/1890a, subsection §86, pp. 369–371).

According to Smith's translation, Herbart (1834/1891) wrote about Equation 1.5 that

> it contained the germ of manifold investigations which penetrate the whole of psychology. [Equation 1.5] is indeed so simple that it can never really occur in the human soul, but all investigations began with such simple presuppositions as only exist in abstraction—e.g., the mathematical lever or the laws of bodies falling in a vacuum.
>
> (p. 19)

Herbart's Theory Compared to Alternatives

Herbart's Success Compared with Newton's

One of the reasons that Newton's physics was so successful was that his theories were quantitative and allowed for numerical predictions. His observations of natural phenomena and the results of experiments, both of which involve measurement, provided tests of his ideas. His gravitational theory included measurements of mass, time, and distance. He investigated light by an experiment in which he used a prism to separate white light into individual beams of light that differed in colour. He then reconstituted these beams back into white light by using another prism. Moreover, Newton's use of calculus to develop his theory of physics had a later application in Herbart's use of calculus in his mental mechanics.

Wootton (2015, Chapter 13) stressed that a major outcome of the Scientific Revolution in the seventeenth century was that Newton's mathematically difficult theory was widely accepted. As opposed to Britain, a delay of 50 years in its acceptance on the European continent was due to rivalry from supporters of Descartes and Leibniz. Wootton (2015, pp. 473–475) presents a formidable list of books appearing from 1687 to about 1750 that instructed lay readers in Newton's theory.

Herbart was extremely sceptical that he could devise an experiment designed to test the real-life validity of any equations in *Psychologie als Wissenschaft*. This was not because he believed an equation was "incorrect" because it rested on erroneous foundations or involved mistaken mathematics. Herbart did not create experiments to test the validity of his equations. Carrying out experiments on human individuals, who were so far from "ideal", would not allow for comparisons against predictions from "ideal" equations. Herbart was excessively sceptical about the trustworthiness of any experiment designed to test what we would today call the "reliability" and "validity" of any of the hypotheses suggested in *Psychologie als Wissenschaft*.

Herbart gave the following reasons for his scepticism. Humans varied from moment to moment in the degree of attention they paid to the cognitive task assigned to them. Another variable was their degree of wakefulness, which varied with the time of day and with the amount of time they spent working before the experiment. Another was their intake of coffee, alcohol, and so on, shortly before the experiment. Above all, there was the variety of *Vorstellungen*, fused or unfused, that are aroused by the stimuli being used in the experiment. If those stimuli were words, semantic factors would influence the results.

On the other hand, in Part Third of his *Text-book*, titled "Rational Psychology", Herbart (1834/1891) provided a conceptual framework in which specific interactions between *Vorstellungen* are characterized as being subject to measurement.

Herbart's discussion of rational psychology in the *Text-book* opened on familiar territory, namely, the mind/body problem. Herbart, more than many psychologists today, took seriously the notion that the "mind" can also be treated as if it were a "soul" that can potentially be immaterial and immortal. According to Herbart, the soul is postulated (a) to have no space relations and (b) a tendency towards self-preservation. In humans, the soul has the ability to think about, and conceptualize Space. Herbart suggested that the abstract concepts of Space and Time hinge upon the fact that our minds can conceive that, given two points, a third point lies between them. For example, in Time, an object memorized at time t_1 is separated by a series of temporal events from the recovery of the memory of that object at a later time t_2. This notion of "betweenness" of temporal events was, for Herbart, the foundation of the notion that there is a "magnitude" that can be called Time. Indeed, Herbart (1834/1891, pp. 130–132) went on to specify, in terms of interactions between *Vorstellungen*, the origin of the human representation of the concept of Time.

Herbart's Theory of the Origin of the Time-Concept Compared with Hooke's

Both Herbart's and Hooke's concept of Time depend on the concept of memory.[12] It is worth taking a moment to ask how similar Hooke's (1682/1971) theory that the time-concept originated in the ability of humans to remember "Ideas" is to Herbart's (1834/1891) theory of the origin of the time-concept. On one particular matter, Hooke and Herbart differed as to whether a mathematics-based theory of storage and retrieval *needed* to make use of the word "memory" at all. Hooke thought that it was necessary in order to communicate his own theory. Herbart thought it was not necessary.

The English language uses the word "memory" to represent two quite separate notions. One is of "memory" as being the ability (faculty, disposition) for a given species of animal to store and to retrieve information concerning past

12 A brief history of research on human memory was provided by Murray (2012).

experience. The second notion refers to the contents of memory.[13] Hooke called a memory representation a member of the class of "Ideas". Herbart called a memory representation a member of the class of *Vorstellungen*.

Hooke claimed that there was a "Repository" in which individual memories, "Ideas", were stored in the order in which they were experienced. Herbart claimed that his mechanics and statics explained how individual *Vorstellungen* were successively experienced. Any *Vorstellung* concurrently in consciousness could be a memory-*Vorstellung*, a perception-*Vorstellung* or an imagined *Vorstellung*. Its placement in time (in the person's past, present, or imagined future) was simply irrelevant insofar as the mechanics and statics were concerned. In order to expound Herbart's theory, it was not logically *necessary* to introduce a word like "memory-the-ability".

Both Hooke's and Herbart's theories were also profoundly influenced by the scientific merits of cosmological systems introduced in the First Scientific Revolution. Hooke was particularly impressed by the use of the inverse square law to describe the force of attraction of one celestial object, say, a moon, to another, say, a planet. Canonical examples were, of course, the forces of attraction between the sun and the planets. Hooke surmised that an Idea could be represented as being located at a distance *D* from the present moment, where *D* represented the number of other Ideas that were laid down between the moment the Idea entered the Repository and the present moment, called the "Centre". If the Centre was attending to an Idea, A_1, when A_1 was similar in some way to an earlier Idea, A_2, then, from the present moment, radiations could be initiated by A_1 that would irradiate A_2, leading to the event we call, in everyday parlance, "being reminded, by A_1, of A_2". Likewise, the sun, at the centre of the solar system, could radiate a beam of light that would illuminate the surface of a distant planet. Hooke did suggest that a mental equivalent of the inverse square law in planetary mathematics could be derived that predicts the ease with which Idea A_1 could irradiate Idea A_2, given that A_1 and A_2 were separated by *D* Ideas.

Herbart, on the other hand, was most impressed by the fact that gravitational forces could lead to the solar system's being in a state of "equilibrium". He therefore conceived of thought-events as involving a perpetually shifting state of equilibrium as new thoughts entered consciousness. New thoughts could come from outside ourselves (perception-*Vorstellungen*) or from inside ourselves (memory-*Vorstellungen* or imagined *Vorstellungen*).

Hooke's broadly based notion of the origin of the Time-concept in humans was that we essentially derive the notion of Time from a comparison of the ease with which recently deposited Ideas come to mind as contrasted with the greater difficulty associated with the retrieval of Ideas deposited much earlier.

13 These two meanings of "memory" are sharply distinguished in French and German. In French, memory-the-ability is called *la mémoire*, and an individual memory representation is called *un souvenir*. In German, memory-the-ability is called *das Gedächtnis* and an individual memory representation is called *eine Erinnerung*.

Hooke also tried to estimate how many Ideas were stored during the lifetime of a person celebrating his or her hundredth birthday. The initial calculation estimated that number to be 3,155,760,000; after corrections for time spent asleep, or in infancy, or in old age, or by inattention, the number was whittled down to one hundred million, a number that still seemed excessive. Mechanisms for forgetting were therefore introduced, including what we would now call forgetting-by-decay and forgetting-by-interference-from-other-Ideas.[14] Forgetting by interference from later memories was, for Hooke, analogous to the blocking of the sun's rays from reaching the earth during a lunar eclipse.

The Measurement of a **Vorstellung***'s Strength Presented a Dilemma for Herbart*

Herbart and Hooke each developed a theory of how the concept of Time originated. Herbart assigned the emergence of the Time-concept to interactions between *Vorstellungen* and Hooke assigned the emergence of the Time-concept to interactions between Ideas. In so doing, they brought numbers into their reasoning, but there was no discussion of how the strength of a *Vorstellung* or an Idea could be scientifically *measured*. In essence, this means that there was no suggestion as to how a *Vorstellung* experienced by person A could be measured by another person B.

Kant argued that we do *not* have intuitions about the Soul in the way we do have intuitions about Space and Time. For Kant, this entailed that psychologists could not assign measurement-units to mental events in the way physicists could assign measurement-units to physical events taking place in Space and Time. Also, the belief that the theological Soul was "immaterial" could be used as a religious objection to any attempt to assign measurement-units to Soul events, i.e., mental events. Herbart's quandary, therefore, was that his claim that Psychology was a "science" was highly debatable because no ways existed that would allow a scientist (Person B) to measure the strength of a *Vorstellung* (experienced by Person A).

The whole superstructure of Herbart's model rested on hypotheses about how *Vorstellungen* opposed each other. Any strengths assigned to individual *Vorstellungen* described the grade of opposition between two or more *Vorstellungen*. Herbart had ingeniously constructed a theoretical superstructure that embodied interactions between *Vorstellungen*. Unfortunately, any description of a "*Vorstellung*-strength" was only based on an arbitrary assignment of a number to that strength. That number could not be ascertained by a measurement from outside the person experiencing that *Vorstellung*. Herbart came face to face with the disturbing question: "Can a *Vorstellung* be measured?".

14 Hooke was not the first person to make this distinction; according to Murray and Ross (1982), it was also made, in 1538, by a Spanish educator named Juan Luis Vives (1492–1540).

CHAPTER 1A

Herbart's Fragment on the Measurement of *Vorstellungen*

A measure of the disturbance faced by Herbart was exposed by new evidence that Herbart was more preoccupied than is usually thought with the objection that his theory was not verifiable scientifically because *Vorsellungen* could not be measured. Among his belongings found after his death in 1841, was an unfinished hand-written fragment of an imagined dialogue in which two individuals confront each other over the question of whether *Vorstellungen can*, or can *not*, be measured. Individual A represents Herbart, who takes the position that *Vorstellungen can* be measured. Individual B is a critic who argues that *Vorstellungen* can *not* be measured. This document provides us with a unexpected theoretical link between Herbart and Fechner.

My translation of this fragment appears as a separate chapter for two reasons. First, despite the fragment's theoretical relevance to psychophysics, it was probably never actually read by early psychophysicists including E. H. Weber and G.T. Fechner. Neither refer to it in their writings on psychophysics. The fragment cannot be claimed, therefore, to represent an influence by Herbart directly on the scientific thought of Weber or Fechner. Second, the fragment itself is not always easy to read, in part because much of its content is concerned with philosophical issues rather than mathematical models. Following the translation in Chapter 1A, I have commented on some of these difficulties. Overall, therefore, the fragment is an example of the philosophical issues that surrounded the early history of psychophysics.

A Confrontation

The Discovery of the Confrontation

In the final pages of a lecture Herbart gave on the "possibility" and "necessity" of a mathematical approach to psychology (Herbart, 1822/1877), he claimed that attempts to use physical measurement-units in place of his postulated "energies" ("strengths") is potentially as erroneous as are attempts to carry out experiments designed to "prove" his theory right or wrong. For Herbart, the risk is that a reader might fail to be compelled by a supposed proof, based on laboratory measurements. In Herbart's eyes, the sheer number of variables, all of which can have numerical values that fluctuate from moment to moment, or that make the results obtained from one individual different from those obtained from others, made laboratory experimentation a dubious venture.

Nevertheless, Herbart did write an unfinished manuscript confronting the problem of what *would* be problematic if an experimental venture attempted to measure the sensation-magnitude of a perception-*Vorstellung*. The manuscript was first published by Gustav Hartenstein (1808–1890), a colleague and friend of Herbart, who undertook the enormous task of editing and publishing Herbart's collected works after Herbart's death in Göttingen in 1841.

Hartenstein's edition, which appeared between 1850 and 1852, contains 12 volumes.[15] The first time the present author saw the Hartenstein edition was in the historical building of the Research Library of the Eighteenth Century at the University of Göttingen in September 2004. He thanks Hermann Kalkofen and Jürgen Jahnke for their assistance in accessing the library and in providing a photocopy of Herbart's fragment as published by Hartenstein.

Hartenstein found this handwritten unfinished fragment (Herbart, 1837/1851) among Herbart's papers. Hartenstein reproduced it in volume 7 of his edition. Its apparent date, 1837, puts it firmly after the main exposition of Herbart's mathematical psychology in 1824, and firmly prior to 1860, the year of publication of Fechner's *Elements of Psychophysics* [*Elemente der Psychophysik*]. The fragment was not included in the 19-volume edition of Herbart's collected works edited by Kehrbach, Flügel, and Fritsch between 1887 and 1912. Because I used their edition during my early research on Herbart, I was unaware of this fragment until I spotted it.

The fragment takes the form of a conflict between two people, A and B. In the dialogue, A represents Herbart and B represents an opponent who offers resistance to whatever A asserts. Interlocutor B is set, from the start, to argue that the measurement scale used to measure mental magnitudes must satisfy a criterion characteristic of the scales used to measure spatial and temporal magnitudes. In the case of spatial extents, IF we choose, say, a metre as the measurement-unit, THEN *n* one-metre-long rods that are laid end-to-end between two points P and Q, will measure *n* metres. B insists that this "concatenation criterion" be satisfied with respect to mental, as well as to physical, magnitudes. Often, B "turns the tables" on A by ironically providing a counterexample to what is claimed by A. As a result, A is often obliged to highlight the irrelevance of B's counterexample to A's original claim.

Herbart's manuscript implies that there are three differences between physical objects and the corresponding mental experiences. First, *Vorstellungen* do not have spatial properties. Second, the magnitudes of mental sensation-*Vorstellungen* are not necessarily linear functions of the intensities of the corresponding sensation-arousing events. And third, measurements applicable in the physical world are not necessarily applicable in the world of corresponding mental experiences.

Herbart used two words that require explanation. The words are "intensive" and "extensive" as applied to measurement-units. They were introduced by Immanuel Kant (1781/1929, pp. 131–134). Kant distinguished between these two measurement-units in *physics*. As I read Heidelberger's (2004) Chapter 6 on Fechner's role in the history of psychophysics, I came across a sentence that took me by surprise. The sentence was "after a detailed report on Kant's distinction between intensive and extensive magnitudes … sensation cannot be represented in the form of numbers" (Heidelberger, 2004, p. 216).

15 Hartenstein's edition of *Psychologie als Wissenschaft* is available in facsimile as a stand-alone book (Herbart, 1824/1850/1968).

Kant used the word "extensive" to denote measurement-units such as length, in which a concatenation criterion holds. On the other hand, a knowledge of size and shape only are insufficient to characterize *all* the properties a physical object might possess. For example, depending on the porousness of the objects, one object might be "denser" than another, and might therefore be harder to set into motion than might be predicted on the basis of its size and shape alone. This "extra" magnitude is needed if Newtonian laws of physics are applied to physical objects. The extra magnitude was denoted by Kant as being an example of an "intensive magnitude".

In Herbart's lost fragment, we shall see that A is irritated by B's insistence that the magnitude of a sensation (a perception-*Vorstellung*) can only be established if that magnitude is conceived to be "extensive". Later, when Fechner (1860/1964) tried to measure sensation-magnitude in the laboratory, there is no doubt that his task was facilitated by the fact that Kant and Herbart laid the foundations for the psychophysical assumption that a sensation-magnitude was indeed an example of an intensive magnitude.[16]

My Rendering of Herbart's Confrontation

Herbart's (1837/1851) dialogue was preceded by the following paragraph, written by Hartenstein:

> While Herbart (1839/1906a, 1840/1906b) was engaged in writing the Introduction to the second volume of his *Psychological Investigations* [*Psychologischen Untersuchungen*], he [must have] felt it would be of benefit to some readers to write the following essay, which takes the form of a dialogue. Despite its fragmentary state, I have arranged for it to be transcribed from Herbart's handwriting and printed here as a supplement to the *Investigations*.
>
> (p. 49)

The conflict is as follows. [The fragment starts here]:

A1. Surely, sir, you will agree with me that something that can grow larger can also grow till it becomes two or three times its original magnitude?

B1. If that is the case, sir, is it then your opinion that the sine of 89 degrees, which can certainly grow larger, can, because of that fact, grow to two or three times its original value?[17]

A2. But surely you will concede that, at the very least, something that can become smaller can also be reduced to half, or even a third, of its original magnitude?

16 A critical examination of Kant's distinction between "extensive" and "intensive" magnitudes has been provided by Jankowiak (2013).

17 Translator's Note: the sine of 89 degrees is 0.99985; no sine value exceeds 1.0, which is the sine of 90 degrees.

B2. In that case, then, would you assert that one could take a dozen persons, remove half of them, then remove half of the remainder, and so on until one arrived at half-persons or even one-third-persons?

A3. You persist in finding examples of exceptions that limit the degree to which certain presuppositions can be generalized to all cases. Let me demonstrate how little value I place on those exceptions by offering an example of my own. Just as I deny that a number of persons can be infinitely subdivided, I also deny that matter [*die Materie*] itself can be infinitely subdivided.[18]

B3. Even better! Does that mean that you don't know that matter fills space and that space itself can be infinitely subdivided?

A4. Let me remind you that our conversation was originally inspired by the question of whether *Vorstellungen*, when they are considered to be entities that possess intensive magnitudes, are measurable. Because of this, I do not wish at this time to enter into a discussion of the validity of the presupposition that matter does indeed, when defined appropriately, fill the space it occupies. But let me ask a question about this concept of space, which does appear to provide a starting-point for all discussions of measurement in general. How long is one [Paris] foot?[19]

B4. One [Paris] foot consists of 10 inches, or, if you prefer, 12 Paris inches.

A5. And one Paris inch?

B5. Ten or twelve Paris lines.

A6. And one Paris line?

B6. You should be reminded that spatial magnitudes only become quantities after the outer limits of those magnitudes have been specified; spatial magnitudes do not become quantities merely by virtue of the fact that their individual parts can be concatenated.

A7. In that case, perhaps I need to remind you that *Vorstellungen* likewise can only be assigned a specific magnitude [*Grad*] when it is known that the *Vorstellungen* are neither stronger nor weaker than that particular magnitude. If I am to establish that you can hear sounds whose intensities can be increased or decreased, must I do so by speaking more loudly or more softly at different moments?

B7. Nobody would doubt you on this. But how do I measure sounds in such a way that I can conclude that one sound is twice as loud as another? What

18 Translator's Note: According to Heidelberger (2004, pp. 137–164), Herbart was an early believer in physical atomism.

19 Translator's Note: Although the metric system had been devised and adopted in France between 1790 and 1799, pre-metric units of length remained standard in other countries until those countries elected to adopt the metric system. In Germany, in 1837, units called 'Paris lines, inches, and feet' were in use. In this system, 12 Paris lines equalled 1 Paris inch; and 12 Paris inches equalled 1 Paris foot. In modern terms, 1 Paris inch equalled 1.066 Imperial inches, or 2.71 cm (Ross and Murray, 1996, p. 20). So, 1 Paris foot equalled 12 Paris inches, or 12.79 Imperial inches, or 32.49 cm. B's next remark suggests that he is jestingly referring to the tussle for acceptance between the new metric measures (based on 10s) and the old pre-metric measures (based on 12s).

measuring device can you put into my hand that can be laid 'alongside' a sound successively in a manner analogous to that in which I customarily lay a measuring-rod alongside an object successively in order to measure its length?

A8. If you are prepared (even though it be only in your imagination) to step a little aside from the way in which you normally think, then make the effort to accompany me, in your imagination, to a school, where, following Pestalozzi's teaching precepts, the children have practiced coordinated rhythmic speech that is so clear that one can distinctly hear each syllable even though it has been intensified by fifty to eighty throats.[20]

B8. I would much rather listen to a chorus sung by twelve well-practiced singers; but I would be afraid that they would provide you with a reason for drawing the following conclusion: Because vibrations transmitted through the air are what cause hearing, and because the air is here transmitting vibrations from twelve throats simultaneously, the heard *Vorstellung* associated with each tone is twelve times as strong as it would have been had the vibrations been created by a single voice.

A9. You are thinking ahead of me; so I would ask you not to lose sight of the original question while I am raising an issue similar to the one you have just raised. If you hear the clock strike twelve, how often is the *Vorstellung* (of the tone associated with each stroke of the bell) created, once or twelve times?

B9. What are you driving at? It's always the same tone and always the same *Vorstellung*!

A10. And now we're back to the old prejudice [*Vorurtheil*]! I urge you to ask yourself exactly what you mean when, one minute after the chimes have finished, you say to somebody that you heard the clock strike twelve.

B10. I would mean that I was referring to one and the same *Vorstellung*; I would mean that it was equally strong each time I heard it; and I would say that I had experienced one and the same *Vorstellung* twelve times.

A11. So you would not have forgotten any of the twelve strokes?

B11. No.

A12. On the contrary, each of the twelve strokes would have been retained by you?

B12. Yes.

A13. Moreover, you are sure that all of these strokes were equally strong. But how do you know that? Were you up there in the tower? Did you investigate the clock's mechanism in order to convince yourself that the hammer struck the bell always with the same force, the same velocity, and at the same angle, on each occasion?

B13. No, but I could hear it directly.

20 Translator's Note: More on Pestalozzi's educational theory is provided by Curtis and Boultwood (1963, pp. 316–351).

A14. It almost appears that your ear had measured the strength of the sounds and, by way of these measurements, had convinced itself that the intensive magnitude associated with each sound was always identical. The result would have been somewhat different had you been rapidly approaching, or retreating from, the tower at the same time as the clock was striking.

B14. Then I would have heard stronger or weaker tones, but would never have measured one with respect to another.

A15. That's strange! Your ear measures equal tones and says that they are equal! Yet you are unwilling to measure unequal tones and are unwilling to believe for a moment that two identical and equally strong sounds (such as would be evoked by striking a single key on the fortepiano, thereby causing two strings of equal length to vibrate) would result in your experiencing a heard *Vorstellung* that had twice the strength of a representative *Vorstellung* of the sound evoked if each string were sounding simultaneously and independently of the other. Even less are you willing to believe that the repetition of one of those representative *Vorstellungen*, will strengthen that representative *Vorstellung*; you would prefer to believe that, in the case of repetitions (for example, when the clock strikes twelve), you retain all twelve strokes in your memory, but not in the form of a single *Vorstellung* [German: *ohne Multiplication*]. You would believe that each *Vorstellung* is isolated from each of the others. But just what *is* memory? It resembles a storage room in the brain in which, however, each *Vorstellung*, once it has been established, is also retained; but, despite being crammed together, each is individually retained in isolation and never fuses with one of the other *Vorstellungen*.

B15. What memory is, I do not know.

A16. And you do not even want to know what it is! Otherwise you would long ago have searched mathematical psychology for an answer, instead of dismissing memory as something foreign to you.

B16. I would rather be ignorant than deceived.

A17. But one has to swim if one is to learn to swim.

B17. I repeat: I am not interested in hearing about measurements when I do not have a single reliable measure that I can hold on to.

A18. So it is by repeating yourself that you hope to buttress your objection? I suspect that it is less likely that you would win your argument that way than it would be for the bell to multiply its associated *Vorstellung*-magnitude by twelve simply by striking twelve.

B18. So at last you seem to be conceding that in this case, at least, there does not exist a measurement of the kind that would have been provided had a repeated *Vorstellung* yielded a multiple version of itself in a manner analogous to that obtained had a measuring-rod been laid down alongside it repeatedly. It is as if one could count one, two, three and so on without worrying about the question of where in one's brain the measured

***Vorstellungen* would be retained. Or do you mean to say that my *Vorstellung* of twelve feet is twelve times as large and as intense as my *Vorstellung* of one foot? And that the *Vorstellung* of twenty million miles is twenty million times larger than that of one mile?**

A19. If you are correct, you are implying that the magnitude of the *Vorstellung* of twenty million miles is really no larger than the magnitude of a *Vorstellung* of one mile. How are you able, then, to distinguish *between* twenty million miles and one mile? How are you even able to conceptualize the difference between 'more' and 'less'?

B19. Those are pointless questions that have never troubled my head before.

A20. But you cannot have remained ignorant of the fact that certain measurement craftsmen less well practiced than you, namely, those primitive scientists who first tried to establish the distances of the heavenly bodies, were astounded by their findings and were almost overwhelmed by the degree to which their imaginations had to be stretched. You must also be aware of the complementary finding that practice at a level more advanced than yours can lead to estimations of magnitude in which the measuring-rod is not held in the hand but in the mind. Examples of such mental measurements are the judgments by eye accomplished by architects and the beating of strict time accomplished by music directors.

B20. You are blatantly diverting the discussion away from matters you do not wish to hear about. Our question concerned what happens when a clock strikes twelve—in particular what happens if one or other perception be repeated. Should we give *any* credence to the idea that the number of repetitions of a perceived stimulus has the effect of multiplying the *Vorstellung* of that stimulus by the same number? I agree that it cannot be denied that each single perception is retained within us, because one can remember not only each single one of them but also remember specifically that there was a sixth and a seventh, as well as a first and a second. Otherwise one would never know how many times the clock had struck. But, apart from that, I am unwilling to assert that the *Vorstellungen* are somehow separated in our brains, and I will even admit that repeated *Vorstellungen* that are identical in content can combine (*verbinden*) with each other and may even be strengthened thereby, because it is from this perspective that one can begin to examine, by referring to one's own experience, the processes involved in memorizing, practising, and habituating oneself to repeated events. But now, in contrast, think about how much would be missing if the initial perception were to serve as a measuring-rod for the intensity of the total *Vorstellung* yielded after having heard [the first *Vorstellung*] repeated twelve times. If this first *Vorstellung* did indeed serve as a standard, then the number of repetitions would indeed indicate the magnitude of the *Vorstellung*. And just as certainly as twelve times twelve makes one hundred and forty-four, just as certain would it be that, after twelve days on each of which you heard the clock strike twelve, your *Vorstellung* of this sound would be strengthened to a magnitude indicated by the number 144. But you don't have to wait that long to arrive at this conclusion. The same result would be obtained if, within a duration of a few minutes, you listened to one hundred and forty-four identical sounds. In fact one can state, even more briefly, that, during a sustained period of continuous perception, time itself can provide the multiple by which the magnitude of the resulting *Vorstellung* must be increased. It would then follow that the strength of the resulting *Vorstellung* is proportional to the time required to establish it. If events are indeed allowed to unfold appropriately, then there will be a total *Vorstellung* [*Gesammtvorstellung*] available at the end of an uninterrupted period of perceiving. This total *Vorstellung* may be considered to have a magnitude given by the sum of each of the individual *Vorstellungen* occurring within each very small unit of time (—as you can see, I am getting used to employing your vocabulary according to which there are as many *Vorstellungen* as there are time units each of which contributes to the number of memories to be retained in memory—). If the strength [of that total *Vorstellung*] is to be commensurate [with the strength of the individual *Vorstellungen* of which it is composed], then the total *Vorstellung* must be measurable in terms of units that reflect the strength that was associated with some chosen unit of time, for example, one second. But is this compatible with one's experience? You had recourse earlier to refer to architects and to music directors; there is no doubt that both possess extended experience that renders them responsible, following a preferred period of study involving the prolonged contemplation of a single object or the prolonged listening to a set of sounds, for creating a set of *Vorstellungen* that concern those objects that had been seen and those sounds that had been heard. But this set of *Vorstellungen* is one in which each of the various *Vorstellungen* possesses a desired degree of strength. So what answer were you expecting?

A21. I had hoped for an answer that has already been given in the treatise entitled *de attentionis mensura*.[21]

B21. What treatise is that?

A22. It is a treatise in which, fifteen years ago, the foundations and consequences of the theory that you have just outlined as if it were new, were first evaluated.

B22. So in that treatise is it claimed that the *Vorstellung* that can be attained in a [pre-determined] unit of time during a period of uniformly continuous perceiving can serve as a measuring-unit concerning the total *Vorstellung* in existence when the end of the preferred period of sustained perceiving has been reached?

21 Translator's Note: See Herbart (1822/1890c).

A23. Assuredly. But the claim is [also] made that this method of measurement is analogous to the method whereby you use your measurement-unit of a foot, not only to determine distances measured in multiples of feet, but also to determine fractions and irrational magnitudes [*Irrationalgrössen*] within the unit of measurement.[22]

B23. For measurement-units consisting of feet, that sounds acceptable, but fractions of *Vorstellungen*,—what are they? I don't even have my own *Vorstellung* of what you are trying to say.

A24. But you must allow at least that a musician, an architect, or, even more indubitably, a sculptor or a painter, do in fact work with fractions of *Vorstellungen*. The sculptor in particular is most immediately concerned with light and shade; but what is shade, other than a fractional unit of light?

B24. A fractional unit of *light*, but not a fractional unit of a *Vorstellung*.

A25. And why does the sculptor need light?

B25. Do you seriously think he could work in the dark?

A26. Work? Even if the work on a column has already been completed, the column still needs light if it is to be seen. And the onlooker, what does he see? There is no doubt that he will see what a skilled painter, who wished to depict the column and set it down on paper, would also see, namely, light and shade. Now imagine yourself in the place of the onlooker, and try to resist being too influenced by [your knowledge of] investigations by physicists of light and shade; these do not belong here. In the mind of this onlooker, try to find his *Vorstellungen* of the illuminated object and try to find the *Vorstellungen* of those parts that lie more or less in shade. You will then see fractions of *Vorstellungen*; the darker the shade, the smaller those fractions.

B26. I agree with what you say about the sculptor. But what would you find in the mind of a painter who does not use light and shade only, but also uses colours? Is blue some kind of fraction lying between red and green?

A27. Well, violet is a fraction equidistant from blue and red; and violet is also equidistant from green and orange.[23]

B27. That's a short theory of colour.

A28. Moreover, violet is not a fraction, and cannot be a fraction, in the sense of that word as used by a physicist; for here I am referring to *Vorstellungen*, not to rays of light.

B28. And presumably you would say the same about tone-*Vorstellungen* in the mind of a musician, but it cannot be said of sound waves in the air. If only

22 Translator's Note: The words "fractional" and "irrational" also appear in the title of Leibniz's first article on calculus (Leibniz, 1684/1987).

23 Translator's Note: IF a horizontal line represents the seven colours of the rainbow—red, orange, yellow, green, blue, indigo, and violet (ROYGBIV)—and is bent upwards to form a loop so that R is separated from V by a small space, THEN V is separated from B by I, and from R by the small space. Likewise, V is separated from G by I and B, and from O by the small space and R.

the hearing-nerve [*der Gehörnerv*] were not there! If it is to know what we refer to as consonance and dissonance, then surely the hearing-nerve, at some earlier time, must have experienced the pleasing and predictable relationships among the sound waves associated with consonance, and the displeasing and irrational relationships between sound waves associated with dissonance and wrong notes.

A29. The hearing-nerve itself knows nothing of that kind. It is the musician who knows it when he is composing at the same time as his hearing-nerve is quiescent.

B29. But even with all this we have still not arrived at a point where we are measuring *Vorstellungen*.

A30. What? If that's what you think, then you must be ignorant of the fact that the musician uses the octave as a measuring-rod for all the intervals that lie between the [upper and lower] tones of the octave.

B30. Well, a monochord is a magnificent instrument because, with its aid, one can control the length of the [vibrating] string; one can thereby convince oneself of various facts, including the fact that the octave would be a very bad measuring-rod. Or is it your opinion that all octaves are equal in magnitude?

A31. I don't merely hold that as an opinion; I know it for certain!

B31. But haven't you ever heard that one arrives at octaves that are higher or lower if one doubles or halves the lengths of the vibrating strings? When one does so, geometric proportions remain equal, but arithmetic proportions do not; as a consequence, the higher the octave, the narrower the distance between its [upper and lower] tones.

A32. And yet each of these higher octaves contains just as many musically distinguishable intervals as do the lower octaves. As a consequence of *that*, all octaves possess equal magnitudes; for these octaves represent dividing lines [*Unterschiede*] between *Vorstellungen*, and the smaller musical intervals are fractions within these dividing lines.

B32. It's impossible to make any progress with you, because you are always talking about *Vorstellungen* instead of about measures and measuring-rods. You even refute the evidence provided by the monochord, even though it is the only instrument which, from your point of view, permits comparison with our barometers and thermometers.

A33. Well now, since you've mentioned barometers and thermometers, can you tell me whether or not you consider that these instruments allow you to transform intensive magnitudes into extensive magnitudes? If warmth and heaviness are indeed intensive magnitudes, we must ask: do the differences between these intensive magnitudes actually behave identically to the differences between thermometer- or barometer-readings, or do they not?

Interpreting the Fragment

In the section on Herbart's success as compared with Newton's, I asserted that Herbart considered that "betweenness" is necessary for a measurement-unit to be rigorously defined. There are no fewer than five excerpts in the translation that attest to the importance of betweenness for Herbart. Here are the five excerpts, in the order in which they appear in the fragment. By "B6" is meant the sixth of B's comments and by "A7" is meant the seventh of A's comments. In the translation of the fragment given above, these excerpts are printed in **bold** for the reader's convenience.

Excerpt 1 (B6, A7):

B6. You should be reminded that spatial magnitudes only become quantities after the outer limits of those magnitudes have been specified; spatial magnitudes do not become quantities merely by virtue of the fact that their individual parts can be concatenated.

A7. In that case, perhaps I need to remind you that *Vorstellungen* likewise can only be assigned a specific magnitude [*Grad*] when it is known that the *Vorstellungen* are neither stronger nor weaker than that particular magnitude. If I am to establish that you can hear sounds whose intensities can be increased or decreased, must I do so by speaking more loudly or more softly at different moments?

Note:
The *Grad* (the degree or intensity in consciousness) of a *Vorstellung* is discussed by A in terms of such a *Grad's* being neither "stronger nor weaker" than it actually is. This is consistent with Herbart's stress on betweenness as an important characteristic of the strength of any scalable magnitude. In contrast, B uses the necessity of extremes to define a magnitude.

Excerpt 2 (B18, A19):

B18. So at last you seem to be conceding that in this case, at least, there does not exist a measurement of the kind that would have been provided had a repeated *Vorstellung* yielded a multiple version of itself in a manner analogous to that obtained had a measuring-rod been laid down alongside it repeatedly. It is as if one could count one, two, three and so on without worrying about the question of where in one's brain the measured *Vorstellungen* would be retained. Or do you mean to say that my *Vorstellung* of twelve feet is twelve times as large and as intense as my *Vorstellung* of one foot? And that the *Vorstellung* of twenty million miles is twenty million times larger than that of one mile?

A19. If you are correct, you are implying that the magnitude of the *Vorstellung* of twenty million miles is really no larger than the magnitude of a *Vorstellung* of one mile. How are you able, then, to distinguish *between* twenty million miles and one mile? How are you even able to conceptualize the difference between 'more' and 'less'?

Note:

B suggests that A must be wrong because, if A had used a concatenation criterion to determine whether a *Vorstellung* of a 12-foot distance is 12 times as "large" as a *Vorstellung* of a 1-foot distance, the implication is that the *Vorstellung* of a 20-million-miles-distance would occupy 20 million times as much space in the brain as would a *Vorstellung* of a 1-mile-distance. A says that, if B is silly enough to credit A with thinking along those lines, then B would probably believe the opposite, namely, that there's no difference between the strength of a *Vorstellung* of a 20-million-miles-distance and that of a *Vorstellung* of a 1-mile-distance. But if *Vorstellungen* did *not* differ between each other in terms of individual contents concerning intensities, B would never have learned to tell the difference between "more" and "less" in the first place.

This excerpt borders on the unpleasant, because A and B are actually insulting each other's intelligence-level, but, for me, the "bottom line" is that A makes a knowledge of the difference between "more" and "less" not only an essential part of any attempt to understand the nature of measurement; it also implies that there is a "value" of a variable that lies between another value above it (is "more" than it) and another value below it (is "less" than it).

Excerpt 3 (B22, A23):

B22. So in that treatise is it claimed that the *Vorstellung* that can be attained in a [pre-determined] unit of time during a period of uniformly continuous perceiving can serve as a measuring unit concerning the total *Vorstellung* in existence when the end of the preferred period of sustained perceiving has been reached?

A23. Assuredly. But the claim is [also] made that this method of measurement is analogous to the method whereby you use your measurement-unit of a foot, not only to determine distances measured in multiples of feet, but also to determine fractions and irrational magnitudes within the unit of measurement.

Note:

Gregson (1993) observed that Herbart (1812/1888b) actually did argue that, under certain ideal circumstances, the strength of a *Vorstellung* of a heard tone increased *linearly* with the duration of that tone. So Herbart has A declaring that this is a case where a mental entity (a *Vorstellung*) has a strength that can be measured in concatenated units of time (e.g., seconds). But Herbart also has A emphasize that any *Vorstellung* whose strength can increase linearly can thereby also use the number system to talk about "in-between states" in the form of fractions (e.g., 1.5 is in between 1.0 and 2.0) or irrational incommensurables (e.g., the irrational $\sqrt{2} = 1.4142 \ldots$, which is in between the commensurables $\sqrt{1} = 1$ and $\sqrt{4} = 2$).

Excerpt 4 (B31, A32):

B31. But haven't you ever heard that one arrives at octaves that are higher or lower if one doubles or halves the lengths of the vibrating strings? When one does so, geometric proportions remain equal, but arithmetic proportions do not; as a consequence, the higher the octave, the narrower the distance between its [upper and lower] tones.

A32. And yet each of these higher octaves contains just as many musically distinguishable intervals as do the lower octaves. As a consequence of *that*, all octaves possess equal magnitudes; for these octaves represent dividing lines [*Unterschiede*] between *Vorstellungen*, and the smaller musical intervals are fractions within these dividing lines.

Note:

This excerpt illustrates wonderfully how measurement-units appertaining to physical entities can have corresponding mental entities which can also be assigned measurement-units, but of a kind that are valid *psychologically* rather than in terms of physics. The *tone* of a sound, when the sound is measured by physicists in units of frequency of sound-waves, has its psychological equivalent in the perceived *pitch* of that sound. One measurement-unit that can be used in describing *what* pitch a human hears is its "note" with respect to the octave. Each of the 88 keys on a modern piano has a "name" that stands for the tone that is sounded when that key is struck; the middle note of the piano is called middle C and it is the first note on a white-note scale that runs as follows: C, D, E, F, G, A, B, C', where C' is the note that is psychologically one octave above middle C and is physically the tone that is sounded when the key representing C' is struck. Its associated physical frequency is 512 vibrations/sec, which is twice the vibration rate of middle C, namely, 256 vibrations/sec.

So Herbart takes B's attempt to disconcert A (by saying that physical vibration frequencies are not matched linearly in psychological octave measurements) as an excuse to let A say that octaves represent dividing lines between equal steps of psychologically perceived pitch. Again, Herbart shows that the musical tones produced by striking white keys A or B or … C' can be individually subdivided into smaller musical intervals (such as semitones). That is, tones can be produced that lie in between whole tones. And, once again, it is B who talks about extensive magnitudes (*lengths* of strings) and A who talks about intensive magnitudes (perception-*Vorstellungen* of tones with a *perceived* pitch).

Excerpt 5 (A33):

A33. Well now, since you've mentioned barometers and thermometers, can you tell me whether or not you consider that these instruments allow you to transform intensive magnitudes into extensive magnitudes? If warmth and heaviness are indeed intensive magnitudes, we must ask: do the differences between these intensive magnitudes actually behave identically to the differences between thermometer- or barometer-readings, or do they not?

Note:

Here, Herbart tantalizes us by phrasing, in his own astute way, a question that lies at the very heart of psychophysics. Feeling warm and feeling cold are *subjective* feelings. Measurements of degrees Fahrenheit, Celsius, or Kelvin are *objective* readings of a thermometer. Heaviness is a subjective feeling. Measurements of one's *personal* weight are normally obtained by scales. Measurements of the weights of objects are obtained by using balances, whether these be in a grocery store, jewellery shop or laboratory. But in all these examples, the weight is an *objective* reading.

Herbart chose, no doubt for reasons to do with his desire to integrate the study of mental events into the studies by physicists of physical events, to use measures of the weight exerted by the pressure of air acting downwards on the Earth's surface. That weight varies with whether one is in a valley or on top of a mountain, or whether one is at the North Pole or at the Equator. The appropriate recording device is a barometer. Just look at the clever phrasing with which confronter A attempts to integrate psychology with physics: "If warmth and heaviness are indeed intensive magnitudes, we must ask: do the differences between these intensive magnitudes actually behave identically to the differences between thermometer- or barometer-readings, or do they not?" Surely the answer is, they do not. Confronter B insists on arguing, not that they do, but that they *ought* to if the unity of Newtonian science is to be preserved.

For Herbart, one thing that intensive and extensive magnitudes had in common was their propensity to include values that lie in between other values. An important consequence is that incommensurables like e and π are included, and so are the infinitesimals, especially in the case of values of a variable that come closer and closer to equalling zero, but can never actually be identified with zero.

Summary

Noting that Herbart's educational psychology makes little use of his mathematical theory about the interactions between *Vorstellungen*, each of which has an "energy" denoted by a specific number, a brief explanation is offered as to why Herbart predicted that, if consciousness is occupied by two *Vorstellungen* only V_a and V_b, then V_a could not cause V_b to vanish from consciousness. But if there are three *Vorstellungen*, V_a, V_b, and V_c, it can happen, depending on the energies of those *Vorstellungen*, that at least one *Vorstellung* does vanish from consciousness. If V_c has the lowest strength of V_a, V_b, and V_c, a "threshold equation" (Equation 1.1) says that, in order *not* to vanish from consciousness, V_c must have a value above the threshold.

Herbart did not believe that his theory could ever be incontrovertibly proved or disproved by experiments. This was in part because he had not provided a proof that the strength of a given *Vorstellung* could be formally "measured" (as opposed to being assigned a numerical value of one's choosing). But he did leave, in his unpublished papers, a fragment of an unfinished article on whether one could measure the strength of a perception-*Vorstellung* (i.e., a sensation). He asserted that what was a valid measure on a scale used by physicists to measure the strength of a stimulus would not necessarily be identical to the measure on a corresponding scale used by psychologists. He also insisted that mental magnitudes should share, with physical measurements, the inclusion of fractional and irrational numbers.

2 The Measurement and Variability of Physical Intensities

Introduction

This chapter describes how Fechner's knowledge of ideas about measurement and about variability was initially grounded on measurements of *physical* intensity. This knowledge was then ingeniously applied by Fechner (1860/1964) to measuring the variability of *Vorstellungen*.

One of the strongest objections to Fechner's psychophysics was the claim that a "sensation-magnitude" was simply not a kind of magnitude that *could* be "measured" in the way a distance could be measured in terms of metres or a time-duration measured in terms of seconds. An increasing level of sophistication was lent by Kant to the discussion of measurement when he highlighted the differences between so-called "extensive" and "intensive" measurement-units. The historian and philosopher of science Wilhelm Whewell (1794–1866) also stressed these differences. The first part of this chapter describes Whewell's contributions to the study of *measurement*.

At the turn of the nineteenth century, prior to Fechner, major progress was made with respect to our understanding of the role played by the Gaussian (often called "normal") distribution in quantifying variability. Three pioneers with respect to the Gaussian distribution were de Moivre, Laplace and Gauss himself. The second part of this chapter describes their contributions, which introduced probabilistic reasoning into the description of the Gaussian distribution. As a result, this research enhanced mid-nineteenth-century scientists' understanding of *variability*.

William Whewell on "Extensive" and "Intensive" Measurements

Measurement From a Present-Day Perspective

Of all the writers concerned with measurement just prior to Fechner's invention of "psychophysics", the Rev. William Whewell, Master of Trinity College, Cambridge—Newton's College—from 1841 to 1866, must take precedence for his contributions both to the history of science and to the philosophy of science. To simply narrate his importance to our understanding of measurement theory without putting it into a proper historical context, would be to do his memory an injustice. Whewell's achievement is most appropriately viewed in the light of present-day measurement theory, a growing subdiscipline in the philosophy of science. Suppes' (2002) volume titled *Representation and invariance of scientific structures* and the three-volume *Foundations of Measurement* (Krantz et al., 2007) represent a pinnacle within that branch of the philosophy of science. We turn to Hand's (2016) *Measurement: A Very Short Introduction* as a convenient vantage point from which to obtain a perspective on Whewell's work.

Physicists made incredible progress in our understanding of how material objects, from planets to protons, respond to the forces exerted on them and by them. It is therefore with surprised gratification that I report that Hand's (2016) fact-rich treatise on twenty-first-century measurement theory gives full credit, not only to physicists, but also to psychologists, economists, and other social scientists for their deep concern with measurement as an issue in its own right in the advancement of science. Not only is credit given to Fechner as a pioneer of mental measurement (Hand, 2016, pp. 76–77), credit is also given to S. S. Stevens (1951, pp. 1–49) for his classification of types of measurement scale. Also discussed by Hand (2016, pp. 79–89) are various models of psychological tests and psychiatric questionnaires that make them both reliable (read "replicable") and valid (read "trustworthy").

Throughout the present volume, a distinction is made between the "physical" and the "mental". Any *two* scientists can agree or disagree on the truth of an assertion such as "this table is three feet long". But only *one* scientist can testify that "this table *looks* three feet long", namely, the scientist actually doing the looking. The second scientist might or might not agree that the table *looks* three feet long to him or her as well. There is no way, using a physical object such as a ruler, to test the accuracy of the assertion "this table *looks* three feet long". So, we continue to distinguish between the "physical" and the "mental", noting how central this distinction was to Herbart. Herbart argued that, despite the strictures of Kant, a system of "mental mechanics" *could* be developed that could parallel the already-in-place system of "physical mechanics" attributable mainly to Galileo and Newton.

Let's adopt Kant's distinction between "extensive" and "intensive" types of measurement-unit. "Extensive" measurements applied to physical entities are most easily exemplified by units of length. The fact that different *units* of length (cubits, inches, centimetres) were adopted in different geographical localities at different historical times should not blind us to the fact that all units of length, no matter what they are called, are subject to the concatenation axiom. That is, units of length can be "chained" end-to-end in such a way that a length of one unit chained end-to-end to a second length of one unit gives rise to a total length of two units. "Intensive" measurements applied to physical entities are most easily exemplified by units of temperature. If a beaker of water at one degree Celsius is added to a beaker of water already at one degree Celsius, the temperature of the two-beakers'-worth of water remains at one degree. Adding the second beaker does *not* give rise to a new total temperature of two degrees Celsius. This matter will be amplified below, when we discuss Whewell's own account of measurement-units of temperature.

When we try to apply the distinction between "extensive" and "intensive" measurement-units to mental, as opposed to physical, entities, controversies erupt. Because no mental entity can be measured with a ruler in order to pronounce that it is "so-and-so feet long", the concatenation axiom that characterizes measurements of length clearly does not apply to mental entities. Therefore, so the argument goes, any measurement-unit applicable to mental entities cannot possibly be extensive, and therefore must be intensive. This sounds so obvious as to seem to be incontrovertible and it is consistent with what Kant said about sensation-magnitudes.

Yet, Herbart insisted that extensive measurements were concerned with time as well as with space, and that time-measurements *could* be applied in his "mental mechanics". He was precise, not vague, in predicting the duration of time, in seconds, it could take for a third *Vorstellung* to be pushed below the static threshold *and then resurface*. Then, of course, knowledge would be required of the new strengths of the two *Vorstellungen* that remained in consciousness after they had pushed the third *Vorstellung* below consciousness. Herbart argued that the strength of a perception-*Vorstellung* of a tone could sometimes be a *linear* function of the duration of that tone (Herbart, 1812/1888b). An objection to the view that a measurement-unit of the strength of a mental entity (here, a Herbartian *Vorstellung*) must necessarily be intensive, arises from Herbart's insistence that units of time that can be concatenated can also be *Vorstellung*-strengths in his "mental mechanics".

A similar claim can be made that certain applications of Fechner's Law (later discussed in Chapter 4), those based on the measurement-unit he called the "just noticeable difference" (JND), involved extensive rather than intensive measurements. If Sensation 2 differs from Sensation 1 by being one JND stronger than Sensation 1; and if Sensation 3 differs from Sensation 2 by also being one JND stronger than Sensation 2; then, for Fechner, Sensation 3 differs from Sensation 1 by being two JNDs stronger than Sensation 1. This claim would appear to be consistent with the concatenation axiom. Of course, it can be objected that Fechner's invention of the JND as a unit was just a pipe-dream of his, resulting from his trying to find a parallel, using mental entities, to Newton's application of extensive measurement-units to physical entities. Nevertheless, I maintain, using these historical examples, that not *all* measurement-units applied to mental entities need be intensive.

Whewell's Beliefs

Whewell's treatment of the difference between intensive and extensive measurement-units seems exemplary for its time. This is, in part, because he was probably the most knowledgeable historian of science of his generation. His three-volume *History of the Inductive Sciences, From the Greeks to the Present Times* (Whewell, 1832, reprinted 1966) and his two-volume *Philosophy of the Inductive Sciences, Founded Upon the History* (Whewell, 1st edition 1840, 2nd edition 1847, reprinted 1967) represented a magisterial contribution to the history and philosophy of science.[1] Whewell said practically nothing in his *Philosophy* about the measurement of mental entities, although he did give reasons for believing that psychology had a necessary place in the biological sciences (Whewell, 1847/1967, pp. 611–618).

Whewell was born, in 1794, in Lancaster, a town in north-west England. He found himself, as a teenager, brought up at the same time as the budding Romantic movement, represented by the poets William Wordsworth (1770–1850) and Samuel Taylor Coleridge (1772–1834), emerged in the small town of Grasmere, a few miles to the north-west of Lancaster. The Industrial Revolution, at the peak of its ugliness and cruelty, was dominated by Manchester, some forty miles to the south-east of Lancaster.

Whewell was born into this ferment. Whewell took Holy Orders (a requirement for many instructors at the University of Cambridge). His strong mathematical gifts and valuable discoveries in the science of mineralogy (especially on crystals) eventually qualified him for the coveted intellectual prize of being elected Master of Trinity College, Cambridge. His scholarship concerning the German Gothic style as exemplified in German cathedrals provided a basis for applying new scientific information to the history of architecture. All of these facts steered him towards a conservatism both in academic practice and in academic writing.

He fought hard against atheism, ascribing, with little hesitation, the creation of the world to a First Cause, which is clearly asserted by Whewell to be the God of the "Scriptures", by which he meant the authorized version of the Holy Bible used by the Church of England (Whewell, 1847/1966, Vol. 1, pp. 680–708). He died wealthy enough to build "Whewell's Court", a Gothic-inspired set of rooms just across a busy street from Newton's rooms in Great Court. He also set up a Professorship of International Law, still in existence, whose mandate was essentially to try to replace wars between nations by negotiated peace settlements. In the Ante-Chapel to the main body of the Chapel at Trinity College will be found, not only Roubiliac's magnificent eighteenth-century statue of a standing Newton, but also Thomas Woolner's nineteenth-century statue of a seated Whewell.

Whewell's work is best understood, I think, as being that of a dedicated scientist who wanted to preserve the intellectual collegiality conducive of friction-free scientific research at the same time as he wanted to resist the blandishments of commercial enterprise motivated by greed. He also relished the peace and quiet associated with the acceptance of the existence of a benevolent Creator. He was brought up in a world where extreme beauty (the Lake District) and extreme squalor (Manchester) lay within what nowadays would be called "commuting distance" of his home-town of Lancaster. These contrasting world-views

1 It is worth noting that Whewell's *History* was translated into German in 1840 to 1841 and may have been known to Fechner; but the *Philosophy*, which includes a chapter on extensive and intensive measurements, was not available in German.

would surely predispose him to adopt a religious conservatism that, only seven years before his death from a fall from his horse in 1866, would receive its greatest challenge of all time from Darwin's natural selection theory of evolution as expressed in *The Origin of Species* (Darwin, 1859/2004).

In approaching psychophysics, the magnitudes of particular interest to us are clearly specifiable stimulus intensities and, more controversially, sensation-magnitudes. In the *Philosophy of the Inductive Sciences*, Whewell (1847/1966) devoted Book IV, Chapters I to IV, to the "Philosophy of the Secondary Mechanical Sciences". The word "secondary" is here taken from Galileo's distinction between "primary" and "secondary" qualities, which was also promulgated by John Locke (1700/1947). In Whewell's (1847/1966) Book IV, Chapter I (pp. 277–285), he starts with the discussion of the "medium" by which a person receives the sensation caused by a given stimulus. For example, air is the medium by which undulations in air pressure are conducted to the ear. So we first consider the medium through which stimulus characteristics are transmitted prior to arousing their associated sensation characteristics.

Of the Idea of a Medium as Commonly Employed

This is actually the title of Chapter I of Book IV as given by Whewell (1847/1967, p. 277). He now argued that "the sciences which have as their subject Sound, Light and Heat, depend for *their* principles upon the Fundamental Idea of Media by means of which we perceive those qualities" (p. 277). Although Galileo invented the distinction between primary and secondary qualities, Whewell, without mentioning Galileo, briefly reviewed and criticized what Locke, Thomas Reid (1710–1796), and Thomas Brown (1778–1820) had to say about that distinction.[2] Locke listed as primary qualities solidity, extension (which includes length), motion or rest, and number. Brown added to this list the quality of resistance. Secondary qualities include sound, colour, heat, and fragrance. Whewell acknowledged that the primary qualities of an object were those that determined the effects exerted by mechanical forces on that object. He added that secondary qualities, while negligible with respect to the effects of mechanical forces, were also transmitted to the human observer via a medium. He wrote:

> Certain of the qualities of bodies, as their bulk, figure, and motion, are perceived immediately in the bodies themselves. Certain other qualities as sound, colour, heat, are perceived by means of some medium. Our conviction that this is the case is spontaneous and irresistible; and this difference of qualities immediately and mediately perceived is the distinction of primary and secondary qualities.
>
> (Whewell, 1847/1967, p. 280)

2 Reid and Brown were members of the "Scottish School" (Murray, 1988, Figure 5-2, p. 144).

He discussed a number of problems familiar to all students of perception. In vision, one problem is why we see objects as upright despite the fact that their image on the retina is inverted. Another problem is why we see only one object most of the time despite the fact that the object subtends two different images, one on each retina. Whewell hones in on the roles played by the intervening medium in sound, light and heat. He attributes to Newton our first understanding of undulations. Although Newton's detailed theory of the propagation of undulations through the air was questioned by several of his contemporaries, Whewell claimed that Euler's and Lagrange's research on the calculations of motions in fluids led to the following view:

> a medium, in conveying secondary qualities, operates by means of its primary qualities, the bulk, figure, motion, and other mechanical properties of its parts…, the elasticity of the air, called into play by its expansion and contraction, lead, by mechanical necessity, to such a motion as we have described.
>
> (Whewell, 1847/1967, Vol. 1, p. 313)

Whewell pointed out that Thomas Young (1773–1829) and Augustin-Jean Fresnel (1788–1827) introduced the notion that light might differ from sound insofar as vibrations associated with light might run transversely to the direction of a ray, and not exclusively, as was the case with sound, in the same direction as the ray. Whewell considered that, because the hypothesis that light was essentially undulatory, with undulations being capable of being transverse as well as codirectional with respect to a ray of light, the transmission of light through a medium shared with sound a "conformity to the fundamental principle of the Secondary Mechanical Sciences, that the medium must be supposed to transmit its peculiar impulses according to the laws of mechanics" (p. 317).

Yet, when it came to demonstrating that heat was analogous to light and sound because it was conveyed by undulations through a medium, Whewell was brought up short by there not being, in his time, conclusive evidence that "the heat of a body consists in the undulations of its particles propagated by means of the undulations of a medium" (p. 317). While evidence in support of this view was introduced, a problem remained: what *was* the medium in which vibrations of heat were conveyed? Whewell, correctly for his time, pronounced it "unsafe" to proceed upon any principle to the effect that heat necessarily shared the same medium as light, despite evidence of the many similarities between heat and light.

On the Measurement of Secondary Qualities

Given that the "special impressions" of sound, light, and heat are conveyed through a medium, it was, for Whewell, "interesting and important to measure the effects which we observe", even if we are unsure of the mechanisms underlying light and heat (Whewell, 1847/1967, Vol. 1, p. 318). Whewell introduces the difference between extensive and intensive measurements as follows:

> The idea of a medium affects our proceeding in this research also. We cannot measure secondary qualities in the same manner in which we measure primary qualities, by a mere addition of parts. There is this leading and remarkable difference, that while both classes of qualities are susceptible of changes of magnitude, primary qualities increase by addition of *extension*, secondary, by augmentation of *intensity*. A space is doubled when another equal space is placed by its side; one weight joined to another makes up the sum of the two. But when one degree of warmth is combined with another, or shade of red colour with another, we cannot in like manner talk of the *sum*.
>
> (p. 319)

Perhaps even more clarity is brought to the issue, not by considering how parts may or may not be added to each other (concatenated), but by considering how parts may be divided. Whewell wrote:

> Extended magnitudes can at will be resolved into the parts of which they were originally composed, or any other which the nature of such extension permits; their proportion is apparent; they are directly and at once subject to the relations of number. Intensive magnitudes cannot be resolved into smaller magnitudes; we can see that they differ, but we cannot tell in what proportion; we have no direct measure of their quantity. How many times hotter than blood is boiling water? The answer cannot be given by the aid of our feeling of heat alone.
>
> (p. 320)

According to Whewell, it is *because* our sensations of sound, light, and heat arise from vibrations transmitted through a medium that the means used to measure extensive primary qualities (rulers, clocks, weighing-devices) cannot be used to measure the *sensations* of sound, light, and heat. Possibly worse, they cannot be used to measure intensive magnitudes, such as loudness, brightness, and warmth either. All we can do is measure them by "artificial means and conventional scales ... for light and heat we must have Photometers and Thermometers, which measure something which is assumed to be an indication of the quality in question" (Whewell, 1847/1967, Vol. 1, pp. 320–321). According to Whewell, in extensive measurements, we talk about measurement-*units*; and in intensive measurements, we talk about the *degrees* by which the intensity ascends.

Whewell then worked his way through measurements of sound, light, heat, and one or two other modalities, as follows. In the case of sound, Whewell (1847/1967) first noted that we do not really have a word describing the "faculty by which the relations of sound are apprehended", so simply call it a "musical ear" (Vol. 1, p. 323). Acknowledging the differences, and recognizing the similarities, between individuals with respect to a "musical ear", Whewell assumed that concords (agreeable harmonies) are the groundwork of our musical standard. Such a standard requires a "musical scale". The origination of the familiar eight-note scale C, D, E, F, G, A, B, C' lay probably in the singing of these notes, rather than in their employment in musical instruments.

With respect to colour, Whewell pointed out that, prior to the discovery of Fraunhofer lines (see below), we had no parallel, in precision, to the division of musical intervals into agreeable ones like octaves and fifths as contrasted with disagreeable ones like seconds and sevenths. According to Newton (1730/1970), the range of perceptible colours was represented by the seven colours of the rainbow. Scientific discoveries led to a dissatisfaction with Newton's view (Pesic, 2014). In particular, the variation in the colours caused by variations in the glass of which a prism is made, and differences between individuals in colour perception—what one person calls *bluish green*, another calls *greenish blue*—justified the dissatisfaction. This dissatisfaction was ameliorated by the discovery that passing sunlight through prisms produced certain fine black lines. These lines were first observed by William Hyde Wollaston (1766–1828) in 1802.

Joseph von Fraunhofer (1787–1826), a maker of optical devices such as lenses and prisms out of specialty types of glass, rediscovered Wollaston's lines. Fraunhofer tested the refractive indices of different types of glass that could be combined in such a way as to avoid "chromatic aberration" (unwanted coloured edges seen around objects, due to the lenses used in the microscopes of the eighteenth century). According to Asimov (1972), Fraunhofer found in 1814 that

> the solar spectrum was crossed by numerous dark lines. Even slight imperfections in the prism would have reduced the sharpness of the image sufficiently to fuzz out the lines and that may explain the puzzling fact that Newton had not observed them in his pioneering studies a century and a half before.
>
> (p. 379)

Much later, G. R. Kirchhoff (1824–1887) established that each of the (very many) Fraunhofer lines was determined by a particular chemical element through which the light passed (e.g., sunlight passed through sodium vapour gave rise to line D, suggesting that sodium existed around the sun).

For Whewell (1847/1967, Vol. 1), the importance of Fraunhofer's discovery was that we have greater clarity as to what coloured light we are speaking of,

> when we describe it as that part of the spectrum in which Fraunhofer's line C or D occurs. And thus, by this discovery, that prismatic spectrum of sunlight became, for practical purposes, an exact chronometer.
>
> (p. 328)

Moving to the measurement of the intensity of light, Whewell considered as "inadmissible" all so-called photometers that appeared to measure light intensity in terms of the amount of heat that produced that light. The measurement of light intensity is an unusually complicated matter. I particularly like the introduction by Riggs (1965) to the topic of photometry. Riggs first gets to grips with the difference between the radiant power, flux, and intensity of a point source of light before discussing the problem of measuring the intensity of light after it is reflected from a surface. Whewell wrote in 1847; Fechner wrote in 1860: their discussions of the measurement of the intensity of light did not come close to possessing the sophistication that mid-twentieth-century visual scientists, such as Riggs, applied to photometry.

With respect to scales of heat, Whewell gave a wonderful history of progress in the invention of thermometers. These include thermometers invented by Francis Bacon and Newton. Whewell emphasized that the problem was as much a matter of building a scale of degrees of temperature that included *fixed points* about which scientists could universally agree, as it was about inventing a measuring-device. These are the words in which Whewell (1847/1967, Vol. 1) described the discovery of fixed points:

> Newton had taken freezing water, or rather thawing snow, as the zero of his scale which was really his fixed point; Halley and Amontons discovered (in 1693 and 1702) that the heat of boiling water is another fixed point; and Daniel Gabriel Fahrenheit [1686–1736] of Dantzig, by carefully applying these two standard points, produced, about 1714, thermometers which were constantly consistent with each other. This result was much admired at the time, and was, in fact, the solution of the problem just stated, the fixation of the scale of heat.
>
> (p. 337)

Fahrenheit also noted that degrees of heat could suitably be measured in terms of a mapping of the degrees of heat onto the number of units of expansion of a column of mercury when heat was applied to the mercury. Later, a Swedish astronomer named Anders Celsius (1701–1744) devised the "centigrade scale", in which the difference between the boiling point and the freezing point of water was evenly divided into 100 degrees.

Fahrenheit's contemporary, René Antoine Ferchault de Réaumur (1683–1757), independently developed a scale of temperature that, like the Fahrenheit scale, is based on the expansion of a column of liquid. But whereas Fahrenheit had used mercury, Réaumur used a mixture of alcohol and water. This led to the Réaumur scale of temperature in which the freezing point is represented by zero degrees and the boiling point by eighty degrees. Although the Réaumur scale is rarely used today, it was the scale used by Weber and by Fechner in their discussions of temperature sensations.

The introduction of the metric system in 1799 adopted the centigrade (Celsius) scale for the obvious reason that it was based, analogously to the scale of length in which 100 centimetres equals a metre, on a decimal scale rather than on Fahrenheit's hard-to-think-in scale where freezing is given by 32 degrees and boiling by 212 degrees.

Whewell asked whether there was some scale of temperature that could be derived "naturally" from observations of terrestrial phenomena (compare the "natural" scale implied by the Fraunhofer lines, which are not necessarily confined to terrestrial origins). His discussion is fascinating to a scholar knowledgeable in the history of physics. For example, he asks whether a temperature scale might be derived from a study of the laws of the cooling of liquids, or of the laws determining the expansion of a gas when it is heated. Then Whewell concluded that any attempts to measure heat by extrapolating from "the general assumption of a caloriferous and luminiferous medium" would be "entirely foreign to the course of inductive science and cannot lead to any stable and substantial truth" (Whewell, 1847/1967, Vol. 1, p. 342).

Whewell's mid-nineteenth-century achievements were far-sighted anticipations of twentieth-century theories of measurement of sound, light, and heat. Hand (2016) surveyed more recent contributions to the problems of measurement. In 1960, the 11th General Conference for Weights and Measures introduced seven basic units. These are known as SI units—"Système International d'Units". For length, mass, and time, the units were the metre (m), the kilogram (kg) and the second (s) respectively. And there were also measures of electric current (ampère, A), temperature (kelvin, K), quantity of substance (the mole, mol) and luminance intensity (the candela, cd). Units of energy such as the joule and units of frequency such as the hertz (the number of undulations or "cycles" a second), can all be derived from these seven basic units (Hand, 2016, p. 7). Whewell's search for a "natural" way of measuring temperature seems to have been fulfilled by the discovery that

> the pressure of a fixed volume of gas decreases as the temperature is lowered. Extrapolation down to zero pressure suggested that there might be a minimum possible pressure—*an absolute zero*. … Using this notion, we can redefine standard scales like the Fahrenheit and Celsius scales, so that they start at the absolute zero. … When this is done with the Celsius scale, we obtain the kelvin scale, with units denoted K (note, not "degrees K"). The freezing point of pure water under normal atmospheric pressure is 273.15 K.
>
> (p. 54)

Hand (2016) noted that the second fixed point on the Kelvin scale, apart from absolute zero, is the *triple point* of water, where the triple point is "the temperature and pressure at which water exists in equilibrium in its gaseous, liquid and solid form, and it occurs at 273.16 K, so that the kelvin is defined as 1/273.16 of the temperature of the triple point of water" (p. 55). Whewell discussed only the measurement of intensive magnitudes applied to physical entities. Despite his acquaintance with contemporary German science, he appears not to mention the work of Herbart or of Daniel Bernoulli, Fechner's predecessors.

The Gaussian Distribution

The Problem it Poses for Non-Mathematicians

Many holders of a BA or BSc degree in psychology, as well as many graduate students in that discipline, know that a Gaussian distribution is a symmetric bell-shaped curve. An example is given by the fact that, if the heights are measured of a sample of 8,585 adult males born in the United Kingdom and Ireland (Kendall, 1947, p. 8), and one plots how many men possess a certain height, most of the men will have heights clustering around a midpoint (the peak of the bell curve; in Kendall's survey, that height was 5 feet 7 inches). Only a few men are extremely short or extremely tall in height (the two "tails" of the bell curve).

There are other features that might not be known about the Gaussian distribution. Among these facts are the following. The normal probability density function describes the bell shape of the Gaussian distribution. The equation of the function is

$$f(x) = \frac{1}{\sigma\sqrt{2\pi}} e^{-\frac{1}{2}\left[\frac{x-\mu}{\sigma}\right]^2} \tag{2.1}$$

expressed in terms of μ (the mean) and σ (the standard deviation). In the standard form of the equation, $\mu = 0$, $\sigma = 1$ and the height of the normal density curve at $x = 0$ is 0.3989. The area within the bell-shaped curve is a measure of probability equal to 1. See Figure 2.1.

Areas beneath the bell shape between limits on the abscissa define the probability that the measurement will lie between these limits. For example in Fechner's time, a measure of the "spread" or "dispersion" associated with a bell curve was the "probable error". This area is defined by values +P and –P on either side of the mean μ of a Gaussian distribution. The area of the bell-shaped curve between the limits from –P to +P equals 0.50. Thus, a single measurement

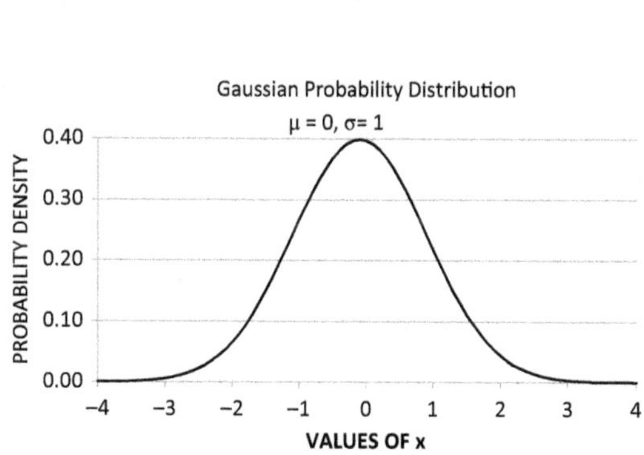

Figure 2.1 Illustration of a Standard Gaussian Probability Density Function.

has probability 0.50 of being either inside or outside the region defining the probable error. A single measurement will, like a coin flip, be either inside or outside the limits –P to +P with probability 0.50.

After Fechner's time, the probable error, as a measure of dispersion, was eclipsed by the standard deviation. The distance from the mean μ to the value of $+1\sigma$ is called one standard deviation. The area under the curve bounded by the limits μ and $+1\sigma$ contains an area equal to 0.3413. The symmetry of the bell shape ensures that the area from -1σ to the mean μ also equals 0.3413. Thus the area bounded by -1σ and $+1\sigma$ will then include 68.26% of the area under the Gaussian curve. Thus an observation, a measurement, will have a probability of 0.6826 of lying within these limits. This is a slightly broader range of possible measures than that of the probable error.

There are *two* versions of what we refer to as a "Gaussian distribution". The first is the familiar bell curve, which is known by the technical term "the normal probability density function". The second is a curve that climbs like a plane taking off from zero at the left end of the abscissa and reaching its cruising altitude at 1.00 at the right end. This is known as the "cumulative normal distribution". In the early twentieth century, the psychometric function was described as a cumulative Gaussian distribution by Urban (1910).

On the History of the Gaussian Distribution

Abraham de Moivre (1667–1754)

One of Newton's most admired colleagues was Abraham de Moivre, who was aged 20 when Newton's *Principia* was first published. His parents were French Protestants, members of a group usually known as Huguenots. According to the Edict of Nantes, agreed upon in 1598 after some 36 years of warfare between Catholics and Protestants in France, the Huguenots were allowed to reside outside the boundaries of Paris, build their own places of worship, and attend four universities in particular, those of Montauban, Montpellier, Sedan and Saumur. De Moivre entered the University of Sedan at the age of 11, where he discovered his talent for mathematics. Following the revoking of the Edict of Nantes in 1685, when De Moivre was 18, the University of Sedan was closed down, so he moved on to study philosophy at Saumur and physics in Paris. He may himself have been imprisoned in 1685. We do not know about the fate of his parents. We do know he moved to London in 1687 or 1688 to escape religious persecution. After his immigration as a refugee to Britain, nearly everything he wrote was in English.[3]

De Moivre's first publication was about Newton's differential calculus. He was elected to the Royal Society in 1697, to the Berlin Academy in 1735, and to the Académie des Sciences, in Paris, in 1754. He befriended the Swiss

3 In D.W. Griffith's classic silent movie in 1916 titled *Intolerance*, one of the four examples given of intolerance down the ages was the persecution of the Huguenots in late seventeenth-century France (Maltin, 2008, p. 683).

mathematicians Johann and Jakob Bernoulli, and Newton's friend Nicolas Fatio de Duillier, as well as Newton himself. He was also embroiled in a number of disputes with eminent mathematicians of his time (Walker, 1967, pp. 358–362). Moreover, he never obtained a university position in Britain, apparently because he was a foreigner. He survived by tutoring. It is gratifying to report that, when elected as a Foreign Associate to the Paris Académie des Sciences in 1754, it was none other than Christian Wolff whom he replaced.

His best-known work was *The Doctrine of Chances: A Method of Calculating the Probabilities of Events in Play* (De Moivre, 1756/1967), which went through four editions widely spaced in time (1711 in Latin, 1718, 1738, and 1756 in English). Although the selling point of the book was that it might be of aid to gamblers, the 1738 edition is now considered to be *the* stepping stone between Newton's proof of the binomial expansion and Gauss's equation for the normal probability density function. The name "Law of Errors" given to the Gaussian distribution emerged when De Moivre apparently got the idea of measuring the degree to which an error of measurement exceeded or was less than a measure of central tendency such as a mean. He did so by adopting measurement-units based on how widely dispersed those errors were around a measure of central tendency.

It was a short step from there to estimating the *probability* that an error of a particular magnitude would be found, given a symmetric bell-shaped distribution of errors. In a facsimile of the third edition (final) of the *Doctrine of Chances* (De Moivre, 1756/1967), the first part of the book is about games involving coin-tossing or dice-throwing, or card-games such as piquet, or one's chances of winning a lottery. Pages 243 to 259 represent the link between the binomial expansion and the Gaussian distribution that interests us. Fortunately, Michael Cowles (1989, pp. 67–72) rewrote De Moivre's argument for a psychological readership. Essentially, De Moivre's great insight was that, IF the abscissa of a binomial distribution of the form $(1 + 1)^n$ was changed from a labelling that ran from say, $X = 0$ to $X = 12$, to a labelling where the middle value (here, 6) is taken to be zero, THEN, as the n-values increase, the ratio of the middle value to the sum of all the terms in the expansion of $(1 + 1)^n$ will tend to a precise limiting value.

In De Moivre's formulation of that ratio, he introduced the proof, made known to him by its discoverer James Stirling (1692–1770), that if c is a circumference of a circle and n is the very large power to which $(1 + 1)$ is raised, then that ratio is given by a number. In Cowles's reformulation of the ratio for twentieth-century readers, this value is $[2/\sqrt{(nc)}]$. Let Y_0 denote the middle term of the expansion of $(1 + 1)^n$. If the sum of all the terms in the expansion of $(1 + 1)^n$ is given by 2^n, then that ratio, in de Moivre's own argument, is given by:

$$Y_0 / 2^n = 2 / \sqrt{(2\pi n)} = 0.3989. \tag{2.2}$$

De Moivre then went on to ask what the area would be between the middle term and the point below the inflection of the Gaussian curve. Using logarithms, De Moivre calculated that area to be 0.3413. De Moivre calculated that the area between the two points of inflection would therefore be 0.6826. De Moivre therefore anticipated the general idea that, if we expand $(p + q)^n$ to very large values of n, we will obtain the normal probability density function, the area under the curve of which is 1.0, the abscissa of which is measured in terms of standard deviations centred around the midpoint, and for which the area between the perpendiculars representing −1 and +1 standard deviations will be 0.6826.

Pierre-Simon Laplace (1749–1827): After 1817, the Marquis de Laplace

Although his father wanted him to become a Roman Catholic priest, Laplace gained such a good reputation as a mathematician at the University of Caen (located in Normandy, northwest of Paris) that he was sent to Paris with a letter of introduction to the mathematician Jean le Rond D'Alembert (1717–1783). Shortly thereafter, D'Alembert helped secure a teaching position for him at the École Militaire (Military School) in Paris. This position was started in 1769, when Laplace was 20, and he was elected as a member of the Académie des Sciences a week after his 24th birthday.

In 1779, Laplace introduced the terminology that is still used in reference works on statistics and probability; a probability is defined as the ratio of "favourable" cases to all the possible cases combined of "favourable" and "unfavourable" cases. For example, let an urn hold 100 counters on each one of which is written a different number from 1 to 100, some counters having a number from 1 to 25 and the others having a number from 26 to 100. Then the "Laplacian probability" that a draw of a single counter will yield a counter with a number between 26 and 100 will be [75/(25 + 75)] = 75/100 = 0.75.

In the 1780s, Laplace's publications were mainly on astronomy (in which he clarified some problems unanswered by Newton) and on gravitational theory (to which he applied Euler's work on fluid dynamics). In 1788 he married a girl some 21 years younger than himself; they had two children. He wrote a short book titled the *System of the World* (Laplace, 1796/1809) as a forerunner to his massive five-volume work titled *Celestial Mechanics* (Laplace, 1799–1825/1966–1969), in which he presented his revisions of Newton's cosmology, with all the mathematics presented in calculus and incorporating the nebular hypothesis of Kant and others (see Laplace, 1966–1969).

The French Revolution (1789–1793), from which Laplace took refuge outside Paris, was followed by the foundation of the French Republic by Napoleon. Napoleon briefly employed Laplace as the Minister of the Interior for six weeks in 1799. When it looked as if Napoleon's empire was going down to defeat, Laplace contacted the Bourbon royal family and was ennobled with the status of marquis in 1817 when the Bourbons returned to power. Napoleon at that time was in captivity on St. Helena, where he died in 1821. Laplace himself spent his final years at Arcueil, just outside Paris, where he died six years after Napoleon, in 1827.

From our point of view, Laplace's major contributions to probability theory included his huge *Théorie Analytique des Probabilités*, which appeared in 1812. His *A Philosophical Essay on Probabilities* appeared in 1814. According to Laplace, the *Essay* originated in some lectures given in 1796. It was clearly intended to be read by people unfamiliar with mathematics. This Laplace (1840/1951) achieved without using a single equation in the entire text of 196 pages in the English translation of the sixth edition of the *Essay*! The first quarter of the *Essay* is devoted to expounding the basic principles of probability theory. But it is Principles 8, 9, and 10 that are of most interest here, because Laplace took Daniel Bernoulli's (1738/1954) work on *fortune physique* and *fortune morale* (please see Appendix 1 to Chapter 4) as an important application of probability theory.

The bulk of the *Essay* is concerned with stressing the usefulness of probabilistic thinking in 12 everyday problem-situations. Here I focus only on Applications 3 and 12, where Laplace gets to grips with the Gaussian distribution. We begin with Application 3, which is about choosing the best estimate of a measured magnitude.

Imagine we are carrying out an exercise in "geodesy" (the science of measuring distances, mountain heights, etc. on the surface of planet Earth). Let us make a hundred measurements of the distance from one signpost A on a straight road to another signpost B on the same road. Let the true distance between A and B be one kilometre (i.e., 1,000 metres), but we do not know that in advance. Furthermore, we do not have modern laser equipment that can measure distances very accurately indeed (including distances inside one's house should one be planning renovations). Instead, we have one metre-long wooden ruler. This ruler must be laid end to end in a straight chain going from A to B. Perhaps the first measurement of the distance from A to B was 1,012 metres, the second 983 metres, and so on and on for a total of N measurements. Let N be 100. Then if one takes the sum of all hundred measurements and divides the sum by 100, one will obtain a measure of central tendency called the arithmetic mean. The question is whether the arithmetic mean is also the "best" estimate of the distance AB. And what is meant here by "best"?

Let X denote an obtained value of distance. It turned out that the "best" estimate of a central tendency was given by the arithmetic mean, [$\Sigma X/N$], because, as Gauss proved, this value minimizes the sum of the squared deviations from the mean. From Gauss's time, it became known as the "method of least squares" for estimating the "true" value of a distance-measurement (Stahl, 2006, pp. 102–107).

In his widely circulated *Essay*, Laplace also helped to propagate a general knowledge of what was signified by the Gaussian distribution. The Gaussian distribution describes large samples. In Chapter VIII of the *Essay*, Laplace praised Jacques Bernoulli (1655–1705) for proving the following theorem, known, in its varying forms, as the "central limit theorem" (Cowles, 1989, p. 119).

Consider the binomial distribution, derived from a sequence of tosses of a fair coin. As the number of coin-tosses grows, say, from 12, to 18, to 40, the most likely number of heads changes from 6 out of 12, to 9 out of 18, to 20 out of 40. When we go to 20 heads out of 40 coin tosses, we see how the appearance of a jagged triangle, with a peak at 6 heads when there are 12 coin tosses, is transformed to a relatively smooth bell curve with a peak at 20 heads when there are 40 coin tosses.

Laplace made the following observation with respect to the notion that the Gaussian distribution represents the distribution of errors made up of different deviations from a "true" measure of central tendency. Let the influence of errors be such as to lead to a hypothesized measure of central tendency that does indeed deviate from the true measure of central tendency. Call this deviation a "disadvantage" imparted to the calculation of the true measure of central tendency. Then Laplace showed that, for that disadvantage to be at a minimum, the midline on the abscissa should divide the total distribution into two equal parts.

Johann Karl Friedrich Gauss (1777–1855)

Born into a working-class family in the city of Brunswick (German, *Braunschweig*), which is located in North Germany about half-way between Hanover and Berlin, Gauss has a reputation for being precocious at doing mental arithmetic. At the age of six, he is said to have figured out for himself that the sum of the first N whole numbers is $\{[N(N + 1)]/2\}$(Wertheimer, 1945, pp. 89–97).[4] A work he wrote on number theory at the age of 21 is still considered a breakthrough publication (Gauss, 1801/1986). He proved, for the first time, how to make a 17-sided polygon using a ruler and compass. His statue in the city of Göttingen has a 17-sided polygon as its base.

Gauss did not actually publish on the method of least squares until 1809, when he applied it to the problem of how far the motions of comets and asteroids might be thrown off course by the gravitational forces associated with the planets (Gauss, 1809/1963). The method of least squares was equally useful in geodesy, and much later, in the 1820s, Gauss published three essays on the role of the Gaussian distribution in the formulation of probability theory in general. It was Gauss's (1809/1963) book on planetoid motions that Laplace read shortly before the publication of his *Théorie Analytique des Probabilités* (1812). Later in his life, Gauss gave two other proofs that he thought avoided the objection that his first proof had taken too much for granted that the arithmetic mean was indeed an appropriate measure of central tendency.

So, armed with roughly the same amount of knowledge of the theory of the Gaussian distribution and of the theory of measurement that Fechner himself

4 This formula was first explicitly described, in Western science, in the third century by the Greek mathematicians Diophantus and Iamblichus. It was then introduced into European mathematics by an Irish monk named Dicuil, who worked at the French court in the ninth century, and may have read Greek. According to Ross and Knott (2019), however, "possibly Dicuil invented [the formula] independently of other sources" (p. 8).

might have possessed, we are ready to embark on an examination of the new branch of science Fechner himself named "psychophysics". Psychophysics depends heavily on the notion of "absolute" and "differential" thresholds. As shown in detail in Chapter 1, it was Herbart (1824/1890a) who introduced the word "threshold" into psychology. The first measurements of sensory thresholds were made by Ernst Heinrich Weber (1795–1878), who is the topic of our next chapter.

Summary

The problem of measuring "intensive" magnitudes (i.e., magnitudes that cannot easily be conceived of as following the concatenation axiom) was as difficult for physicists as was measuring subjective magnitudes for psychologists. Whewell's historical account of the difficulties associated with the measurement of physical sound intensities, physical light intensities, and physical heat intensities, was summarized. His assertion that extensive magnitudes can be measured in terms of "units", whereas intensive magnitudes have to be measured in terms of "degrees" echoed what Kant (1781/1929) argued. Whewell, however, added little to our understanding of how mental entities, as opposed to physical entities, are measured either extensively or intensively.

Nowadays, the most widely used measure of dispersion (variability) associated with the Gaussian distribution is called the standard deviation. The distance along the horizontal axis of the normal probability density function from the midline to the point delineating one standard deviation, is the distance from the midline to a line dropped perpendicularly from the point of inflection on the downward right-hand curve. The same goes for the point of inflection on the downward left-hand curve, where the standard deviation equals −1.

Historically, de Moivre predicted that the area under the normal probability density function between the two lines demarcating one standard deviation on either side of the midline would be 0.6826 of the total area under the curve. Laplace emphasized that the larger the sample, the more accurately the midline could be predicted. Gauss emphasized that the "true" midline of a distribution was the arithmetic mean, because the method of least squares showed this value to minimize the sum of the squared deviations from that mean.

3 An Introduction to Weber's Law

Introduction

Preliminary Remarks

Asimov's Biographical Encyclopedia of Science and Technology (Asimov, 1972) contains short entries on the lives and achievements of 1,195 major scientists. I was also given a copy of a more recent book entitled *The Britannica Guide to the 100 Most Influential Scientists* (Gribbin, 2008). The name of Herbart is missing from the entries of both books. In Chapter 1, I introduced Herbart's work in the context of his education theory, simply because that is what Herbart is best remembered for nowadays. I now introduce Ernst Heinrich Weber's (1795–1878) work as a predecessor to the work of Gustav Fechner. This is partly because, in most texts of introductory psychology, the names of Weber and Fechner are closely linked. It is now customary among professional psychophysicists to distinguish Weber's Law quite sharply from Fechner's Law. For many years, Fechner's Law was not clearly distinguished from Weber's Law, and various sources called Fechner's Law the "Weber–Fechner Law". Fechner (1860/1966, p. 54) himself recognized that Weber's discovery that, in order for a sensation-magnitude to feel just noticeably different, the associated stimulus intensity had to be increased by a constant proportion of itself, deserved to be named "Weber's Law".

The Connection between Gauss and the Scientist Members of Weber's Family

Ernst Heinrich Weber was one of three brothers who all obtained high status as scientists. Wilhelm Weber (1804–1891) was an exceptional mathematician and therefore gravitated naturally towards a specialization in physics. Wilhelm's older brother, Ernst, held two chairs at the University of Leipzig, one in Anatomy from 1821 to 1866 and the other in Physiology from 1840 to 1871. That is, on paper at least, Ernst Heinrich Weber was a physiologist. The youngest of the three scientist brothers was Eduard Friedrich Weber (1806–1871), a medical specialist who collaborated with Wilhelm on a study of the biomechanics of human walking.

Wilhelm, before moving in 1831 to collaborate with Gauss at Göttingen on the theory of magnetism and electricity, resided at Halle and at Leipzig. With E. H. Weber, he collaborated at Halle on the study of the behaviour of waves of several kinds, particularly water waves for which they constructed a 190-foot-long indoor trough. In addition, they studied sound waves (E. H. Weber & W. Weber, 1825). After Wilhelm worked with Gauss at Göttingen for some six years, he was dismissed because he was one of a group of academics known as "the Göttingen Seven", who rebelled in favour of academic freedom.

From its founding in 1737, the University of Göttingen was a source of patriotic pride for the state of Hanover. Hanover was then ruled by an Elector (of the Holy Roman Empire) until 1820, when the King of England, George IV, was installed as King of Hanover. George IV died in 1830. His successor as King of England and of Hanover was William IV, whose reign lasted from 1830 to 1837. In 1833, the state of Hanover, as well as the University of Göttingen, adopted a liberal constitution. William IV was succeeded by Queen Victoria, who could not be permitted to be Queen of Hanover because Hanoverian law did not allow the state to be ruled by a woman. The next in line for the Hanoverian throne was therefore German, namely, King Ernest Augustus (1771–1851).

Both constitutions of 1833 were abolished in 1837 by Ernest Augustus. Some professors refused to sign an oath of loyalty to the king. These included the physicist Wilhelm Weber, the experts on German literature, language and folklore Jacob Grimm (1785–1863) and his brother Ludwig Grimm (1786–1859), the jurist Wilhelm Eduard Albrecht (1800–1876), the political historian F. C. Dahlmann (1785–1860), the biblical historian H. A. Ewald (1803–1875), and the literary historian G. G. Gervinus (1805–1871). All were forced to resign from the university in December 1837. Their memory lived on because they protested in favour of academic freedom. The Göttingen Seven are commemorated by a group of bronze statues located in the city of Hanover.

Wilhelm Weber refused to swear an oath of loyalty because "he had already sworn an oath of office on the state's constitution and would not dishonor it" (Jungnickel & McCormmach, 1986a, Vol. 1, p. 131).[1] Later, in 1843, Wilhelm was offered the chair of physics at Leipzig, previously occupied by Gustav Fechner. He accepted the offer, and found himself back with his brothers in the same university. Here, he set up a new laboratory for measuring terrestrial magnetism, and also concentrated on the theoretical problem of ascertaining what were the optimal

1 The careers at Göttingen of neither Gauss nor Herbart were seriously affected by this controversy. Gauss, however, had to deal with a loss of staff. Herbart was criticized by Wolman (1968, p. 44) for not joining his colleagues in their protest for academic freedom.

measurement-units applicable to electrical currents in particular. His ability at advanced mathematics was honed by his early studies, carried out with Ernst Heinrich, of wave motions. He derived an equation describing the forces exerted on each other by two electrically charged masses in relative motion. The equation, important in the history of research on electricity, became known as Weber's Law (Jungnickel & McCormmach, 1986a, Vol. 1, pp. 138–146, esp. p. 143).[2]

Given that our primary interest is E. H. Weber, I believe it is crucial to establish that the two brothers shared an interest in physics (as judged by their collaboration on the book about waves in 1825), and also in physiology. Wilhelm Weber, during his period at Halle, before going for the first time to Göttingen in 1831, wrote about the influence of acoustic waves upon human hearing. His work related to the design of concert halls. Moreover, Wilhelm and the third brother, Eduard, co-authored a book about the physics involved in human walking (W. Weber & E. F. Weber, 1836). Meanwhile, Ernst Heinrich applied the knowledge of fluid dynamics he acquired in the study of waves to problems of blood flow. His contributions to our understanding of the physics underlying the operations of the human vascular system included observations on the elasticity of the walls of the veins and arteries, and the study of the rate of propagation of the pulse-beat.[3] All three Weber brothers were experts in integrating physics with physiology.

Wilhelm was able to return to Göttingen in 1849. Late in his career, he proposed theories according to which all physical laws pertaining to mechanics, light, heat, electricity, and so on, were themselves based on simple—and speculative—theories about how electrically charged particles interacted.[4] This work is summarized by Jungnickel and McCormmach (1986b, Vol. 2, pp. 72–79).

2 Wilhelm Weber's Law extended Coulomb's Law by including the effects of time. Coulomb's Law, applied to two spheres, was that the force of electrical attraction or repulsion between the spheres increased as the product of the electrical charges on the spheres increased, but fell as the square of the distance between the centres of the spheres increased.

3 Much later, Wilhelm Weber (1867) developed a differential equation showing how the density and the pressure of blood flow in a blood vessel with a radius, *r*, accelerated the rate of flow.

4 Newton himself had devised such a theory, but was afraid it would be greeted as over-speculative. In theories about the unification of such forces as gravitation and light, pride of place as a pioneer must go to Michael Faraday (1792–1867). Born in humble circumstances, his research on electricity and magnetism was largely supported by the Royal Society in London. He discovered that if magnets were rotated around a stationary wire, an electric current could be generated in the wire. He also discovered that if electrically charged wires were wound around a magnet, a magnetic force could be generated. Not only were magnetic and electrical forces interconnected, but Faraday's work paved the way for the postulate by the Scottish physicist James Clerk Maxwell (1831–1879) that there was an "electromagnetic spectrum" of waves varying enormously in wavelength. To understand how such waves were generated, imagine a bar magnet shrunk to a tiny spot which is set into oscillation; this produces electromagnetic activity that Maxwell deduced would have been like a wave (Einstein & Infeld, 1938, pp. 129–156). Maxwell conjectured that one portion of the spectrum consisted of very long waves, a conjecture confirmed in 1888 by H. R. Hertz (1857–1894); the term "radio waves" was conferred on them by M. G. Marconi (1874–1937), who invented a "radio telegraph" that was the precursor of our present-day system of radio communications. Another portion of the spectrum affects human sensation, because the eye is the transmitter of medium wavelength information to the brain that creates colour.

E. H. Weber's Experimental Work on the Touch-Sense

Weber's Writings on the Touch-Sense

Weber's family provided the basis for his development as a scientist. Neither of E. H. Weber's parents were aristocratic. They did own land. His father, after serving as a Protestant minister in Leipzig, moved to the University of Wittenberg, where he married the daughter of another Protestant minister. They had 13 children, of whom seven survived. The three children who became university professors were the physiologist Ernst Heinrich, the physicist Wilhelm Eduard, and the doctor Eduard Friedrich. Ernst Heinrich was a precocious student and entered the University of Wittenberg at age 16. Following some political turmoil, the University of Wittenberg was merged with the University of Halle, so the whole family moved to Halle. For his *Habilitationsschrift* (a thesis required if one were to be hired to *teach* at a university), Ernst Heinrich wrote about the sympathetic nerves in various species (E. H. Weber, 1817), which earned him an invitation to teach at Leipzig.[5]

Intrigued by the patterns induced by motion in a set of particles lying on the surface of a vial of mercury, he invited his brother Wilhelm, who at that time was teaching at Halle, to collaborate with him on the experiments that ultimately led to E. H. Weber and W. Weber's (1825) book on wave motion.

The indoor trough they constructed revealed that, when waves were propagated along a surface of water (or other medium), particles near the surface moved in circular paths while those deeper down described elliptical trajectories with the axes being longer in the horizontal direction than in the vertical. In a separate series of studies, they showed that waves can move with equal rapidity along the surfaces of water and mercury, but were faster, the deeper the water or mercury.

Later, in E. H. Weber's (1850/1851) research on the pulse-beat, he showed that the rapidity of a wave in small elastic tubes (likes veins and arteries) was not affected by the increase of pressure on the walls of these blood vessels. Typically, a pulse-beat has a rapidity of about thirty-five feet per second, and so is felt in the chin before it is felt in the foot (Royal Society Obituary of E. H. Weber, 1879).

E. H. Weber obtained the Professorship of Anatomy at the University of Leipzig. He settled into a productive lifetime of teaching and research on a variety of problems in physiology, both human and animal. In the period in which he discovered the perceptual regularity later known to psychologists as Weber's Law, Weber was aged between 35 and 55. Details about these problems were written about by Ross and Murray (1996, pp. 1–4).

Two publications stand out in particular. First was a monograph written in Latin that appeared in 1834. Its full title was *On the Pulse, Breathing, Audition, and Touch Senses* [*De Pulsu, Resorptione, Auditu et Tactu*]. The section on the touch-senses formed pages 44–174 of that work and was given the subtitle *On the Sensitivity of the Touch Sense* [*De Subtilitate Tactu*]. The subtitle is often shortened to *De Tactu.*

5 In 1821, at the age of 26, he married Friedericke Schmidt, with whom he had eight children. A family photo taken about 1850 is reproduced by Schreier (1993, p. 2). It shows, from left to right, the two daughters Sophie and Laura, mother Friedericke, son Theodor, daughter Anna, father Ernst Heinrich, daughter Amélie, and sons Georg, Julius, and Heinrich.

Second was Weber's major monograph on the touch-sense, which was a contribution to a handbook of physiology edited by R. Wagner. Weber's title was *The Touch Sense and Common Sensibility* [*Tastsinn und Gemeingefühl*], often referred to briefly as *Der Tastsinn.*[6] It first appeared in 1846, in the third volume of the handbook (pp. 481–588). It was also reissued as an independent monograph in 1849 and 1851. It was published again, with an introduction by the prominent physiologist Ewald Hering (1834–1918), in 1905.

The Contents and Importance of Weber's De Tactu *(1834)*

A quick flip through *De Tactu* shows an amazing number of pages containing tables of experimentally obtained data. The work is also curious insofar as a four-page "index" is presented prior to the main text and a 23-page "summary" is presented after the main text. The main text consists of 77 pages of which one (p. 31) is devoted to a modern drawing showing Weber's adjustable compass for measuring the two-point threshold. Of the remaining 76 pages, 39 (i.e., 51.32%) have no tables and 37 (i.e., 48.68%) have one or more tables. These tables can be divided into five classes, whose order here is not the same as in *De Tactu*.

Class TPT (standing for "two-point threshold") comprises tables naming a large number of different regions of the human body (Weber, 1834/1996a, pp. 34–45). I represent this class, in Table 3.1, as a shortened list showing how the body-regions can be ranked, from most sensitive to least sensitive.

The distance between the two compass legs represents the shortest distance on the skin separating the places where the participant judges when he or she first felt two sensations of touch, rather than one. The distances shown are in Paris lines. Ross and Murray (1996, p. 20) indicate that

$$1 \text{ Paris line} = 0.226 \text{ cm} = 0.089 \text{ inches}$$

These were measurements used in France prior to the introduction of the metric system in 1799. They continued to be used in Germany and elsewhere until they were replaced by millimetres, centimetres, etc.

The two-point threshold in the middle of the back over the spine is 60 times that of the two-point threshold on the tip of the tongue. Subsequent research by Weinstein (1968) has substantially confirmed Weber's mapping of tactile acuity over the surface of the human skin. Weber also discovered that the two-point threshold was lower if the two compass legs touched the skin successively with a brief interval between the two touches, than if the two compass legs touched the skin simultaneously. Much of Weber's discussion of the data shown in Table 3.1 concerned differences in tactile acuity on closely contiguous body-regions.

6 "Common sensibility" is also called "coenaesthesis"; it deals with all sensations that do not neatly fit into the categories of seeing, hearing, smell, taste, and touch. It includes feelings related to internal organs, such as nausea or dizziness, but also sensations arising from physical movements, sensations that emanate from the muscles themselves or from associated tissues such as tendons and ligaments. "Common sensibility" has fallen into almost complete disuse now, having been replaced by more specialist terms such as "kinaesthesis", "visceral sensations", and others.

Table 3.1 A reproduction of Weber's table, showing the two-point threshold (measured in Paris lines) as measured for the body parts shown. From Ross and Murray (1996, pp. 43–45)

Place	*Separation in Paris* lines
Tip of tongue	1/2
Palmar surface, 3rd segment of fingers [fingertips]	1
Red skin on lips	2
Palmar surface, 2nd segment of fingers	2
Dorsal surface, 3rd segment	3
Tip of nose	3
Palmar surface of metacarpal joints	3
Mid-back of tongue, 1 *thumb* from tip	4
Non-red part of lips	4
Edge of tongue, 1 *thumb* from tip	4
Tip of tongue	4
Tip of big toe	5
Skin covering cheek muscle	5
Dorsal surface, 2nd segment of fingers	5
Palm of hand	5
External skin of eyelid	5
Mucous membranes, mid-hard palate	6
Skin in front of cheekbone	7
Under surface, metatarsus of big toe	7
Dorsal surface, 1st segment of fingers	7
Dorsal surface, metacarpal joints	8
Mucous membrane of lips near gums	9
Skin behind cheekbone	10
Lower part of forehead	10
Back of heel	10
Lower part of scalp	12
Back of hand	14
Neck under lower jaw	15
Top of head	15
Kneecap, and thigh near knee cap	16
Sacrum (lower back)	18
Top of shoulder blade, and upper arm near same	18
Buttock muscle, and thigh near same	18
Upper and lower part of forearm	18
Skin near knee and near foot	18
Dorsal surface of foot near toes	18
Breast-bone	20
Spine, towards upper 5 vertebrae	24
Spine, on upper neck	24
Spine, lumbar and lowest pectoral region	24
Spine, mid neck	30
Spine, mid-back	30
Mid-upper arm, except where girth of muscles is widest	30
Mid-thigh, except where girth of muscles is widest	30

Weber's own title: Of the degree of tactile acuity in the main parts of my body. I measured this as the minimum separation of the compass legs at which I could feel whether the orientation was perpendicular or horizontal, and detect the gap between the legs.

Table 3.2 A reproduction of Weber's data on the time elapsing before a finger was withdrawn from hot water of temperatures between 50 and 57 degrees R. From Ross and Murray (1996, p. 94)

Temperature of water in which 1st joint of index finger immersed (in degrees R)	*Time elapsed between immersion and retraction of finger (in seconds)*
57 degrees	3½
53 degrees	4½
52 degrees	4
51 degrees	5
51 degrees	4
50 degrees	4
49 degrees	8
48 degrees	5½
56 degrees	2½
55 degrees	3½
54 degrees	3½
53 degrees	4
52 degrees	4
51 degrees	5
50 degrees	5

Class TEMP (standing for "temperature") includes tables showing variations in the sensitivity to heat, cold, and warmth in various body-regions (Weber, 1834/1996a, pp. 88–89 and 93–94). An example is shown in Table 3.2. In this experiment, a colleague immersed the top joint of alternative index fingers in hot water until the discomfort could not be borne and he retracted his finger. The table shows the time elapsing, in seconds, between the moment of immersion and the moment of retraction, for water whose temperatures step down from 71.25 to 60 degrees Celsius (57–48 degrees Réaumur) and then the cycle is repeated from 70 to 62.5 degrees Celsius (56–50 degrees Réaumur).[7] It becomes clear, when these immersion times are plotted as a function of temperature, that the hotter the water, the shorter the time Weber's colleague could endure its heat. For temperatures in the hottest range, 67.5–71.25 degrees Celsius (54–57 degrees Réaumur), the mean immersion time was 3.25 seconds; for temperatures in the middle range, 63.75–66.25 degrees Celsius (51–53 degrees Réaumur), the mean immersion time was 4.36 seconds; and for the coolest temperature, 60–62.5 degrees Celsius (48–50 degrees Réaumur), the mean immersion time was 5.63 seconds.

Again, much of Weber's discussion about the measurement of temperature sensitivity concerned experimental issues and problems related to bodily surface area, and the exposure time of an area to a given temperature. These observations

7 The Réaumur scale has only 80 degrees between the freezing-point of zero and the boiling-point. The equation converting to degrees Celsius from degrees Réaumur is $T_C = T_R(5/4)$. The distance from 48 to 57 degrees Réaumur would cover a wider range of temperature sensations than would a distance from 48 to 57 Celsius.

reveal that the measurement of temperature sensitivity was probably as least as hard to quantify as the temperature scales themselves.

Class PRESSURE used two methods to determine the pressures *experienced* when two different weights were placed on the body (Weber, 1834/1996a, pp. 71–82). The weights consisted of coins called *Joachimtalers*, illustrations of early versions of which are given by Ross and Murray (1996, p. 70). These early coins originally weighed about one ounce each, but the coins Weber used weighed about two ounces each. One pile of coins served as a constant standard weight and weighed about 12 ounces. The other pile of coins varied in weight.

In Method 1, Weber *successively*

> placed two different weights on the two palms of the hands, the backs of the hands, the two forearms ... We see whether the subject discriminates the same difference in all these places, or whether a greater difference is needed for tactile weight discrimination on the back of the hand than on the palm, and on the forearm than the back of the hand, and so on.
>
> (Weber, 1834/1996a, p. 69)

His results showed that weights evoked the greatest feelings of pressure when placed on the palm side of the fingers (i.e., the volar), the sole of the foot and the forehead.

In Method 2, the two weights were placed *simultaneously* on two body parts. Weber's rationale was that

> Equal weights do not seem to exert the same pressure on organs that differ in sensitivity; the pressure feels greater when the sensibility is greater. If you place one of the weights on a less sensitive organ, and reduce its weight until the two feel equally heavy, the difference in weight will then tell you the difference in sensitivity of the two organs.
>
> (Weber, 1834/1996a, p. 69)

In these experiments a colleague placed weights on Weber himself, who then made a verbal judgement about how much pressure was felt to be exerted on one body part or the other. For example, when two equal weights (2 ounces each) were placed simultaneously, one on the immobile lips, the other on the forehead, the sense of pressure was judged to be greater on the lips. The two sensations of pressure were judged "equal" both when 2 ounces and 4 ounces were placed on the lips and the forehead simultaneously and when 1 ounce and 4 ounces were placed likewise. When half an ounce was placed on the lips and 4 ounces on the forehead, the sense of pressure was judged to be greater on the forehead. Weber (1834/1996a) therefore concluded that "tactile sensitivity for weight estimation is about *three times greater* in the *lips* than the *forehead*" (p. 73).

Because of the impracticality of comparing all body parts to all other body parts, Weber decided to take one single body part (the palm-side or "volar" surface of the second and third segments of the third and fourth finger of the right hand) and compare it to 14 other body parts. After making an interesting analogy between "our weight-sensitive organs" with the "arms of weighing scales of unequal length", Weber (1834/1996a) concluded that

> in no type of experiment were the observations sufficiently certain and constant for it to be possible to determine the sluggishness of the touch sense of any individual organs. We must therefore accept the fact that our conclusions on the subject are of a general nature.
>
> (p. 83)[8]

Nowadays, we might refer to the 15 comparisons the results of which were reported by Weber in the PRESSURE tables as "pilot studies".

The final two classes of tables, which I can't resist calling SUCCESS and LIFTOFF, used the same test for touch sensitivity, namely, that two weights, W_A and W_B, are placed on the skin surface, usually on the ends of certain fingers with the hand lying immobile, palm side up, on a table. The experimenter tries to establish the smallest difference between the two weights that can make them just discriminably different to the participant. The participant must judge which one of the weights is heavier than the other. The group of tables called SUCCESS was devoted primarily to demonstrating that, under a variety of conditions, the difference between the two weights that made them perceptibly different in heaviness was smaller when the two weights were placed successively, as opposed to simultaneously (Weber, 1834/1996a, pp. 96–100).

Five conditions, denoted by Weber as (a), (b), (c), (d), and (e) were examined, as follows. By *N* is meant the number of trials devoted to each of the five conditions. As Table 3.3 shows, each trial involved its own set of W_A-values and W_B-values. Table 3.3 therefore represents a summary of Weber's findings.

Table 3.3 The five conditions under which Weber examined judgments of which of two weights, W_A or W_B, was the heavier. From Weber (1834/1996a, pp. 64–67, "Experimental Series 1") as given by Ross and Murray (1996, p. 67)

Name of condition	*Number of trials*	*Weight on fingers 2 & 3*	*Weight on fingers 4 & 5*	*Order of placement*	*Position of hand*	*% of "true" judgments*
(a)	4*	W_A	W_B	Simultaneous	Immobile	75%
(b)	11	W_A	W_B	Successive	Immobile	54.54%
(c)	4	W_A	W_B	Simultaneous	Raised	75%
(d)	2	W_A	W_B	Successive	Raised	50%
(e)	1	W_A = 15 ounces W_B = 14.5 ounces	–	"Repeatedly in succession"	Raised	100%

* Each of the four trials on condition (a) involved weight values as follows. On Trial 1, W_A = 15 ounces and W_B = 9 ounces; on Trial 2, W_A = 15, W_B = 10; on Trial 3, W_A = 11.5, W_B = 15; on Trial 4, W_A = 11.5, W_B = 15.

8 In a footnote to this passage, Helen Ross, the translator of Weber (1834/1996a, p. 133), explained why she chose to translate the Latin word *torpor* as "sluggishness". Weber compared the *torpor* of the touch-organs with the inertia of weighing-scales (p. 83).

Now we can, for the first time in our discussion of these five classes of table, reasonably bring Weber's Law into the discussion. We start with the Law in its simplest form, namely,

$$k = \Delta I / I \tag{3.1}$$

Let the lighter weight of the two weights used in one measurement in the SUCCESS class of tables be thought of as I. Let ΔI be thought of as the increment that is added to I in order to make the new weight just noticeably heavier than I. This new weight will be equal to $I + \Delta I$.

In the one measurement made by Weber (1834/1996a, p. 96), using condition (e), the lighter weight was 14.5 ounces and the heavier weight was 15 ounces.[9] So, in this case, $I = 14.5$ ounces, $\Delta I = 0.5$ ounces and $I + \Delta I$ was $14.5 + 0.5 = 15$ ounces.[10] In terms of Weber's Law, these findings imply that $\Delta I / I$ would have the numerical magnitude 0.5/14.5. Weber preferred to represent his results as integers, so, 0.5/14.5 equalled 1/29. That is, condition (e) showed that a weight difference of 1/29 sufficed to yield a judgment that one weight was heavier than the other.

This is what led Weber to write in *De Tactu* (Weber, 1834/1996a) that:

> weight discrimination is most sensitive and accurate if the objects are placed *successively on the same finger* and are *held with the hand in a raised position*: for under this condition a weight ratio of 29:30 is correctly discriminated.
>
> (p. 97)

Later, in *Der Tastsinn*, Weber (1846/1996b) wrote, concerning the smallest difference between two weights that we can distinguish, that, "if we go by the feeling of pressure exerted by the two weights on the skin, we can actually distinguish a weight-difference of 1/30, i.e., when the weights are in the relation 29–30" (p. 210). Weber arrived at that conclusion from the measurements reported from the SUCCESS tables.

In the LIFTOFF series of tables (Weber, 1834/1996a, pp. 64–67), Weber's aim was to establish experimentally that weights perceived by "touch" only, as when placed on the fingertips, were less easy to discriminate between in terms of judged heaviness than were weights perceived by a combination of "touch" and "kinaesthesis". By the latter, Weber meant the feelings aroused in the muscles and related tissues of the hand when the hand was raised along with the weight(s) still resting on the fingers.

9 The Latin for the first two column-headings is *semunciis expressa*, which can be translated as "listed in half-ounces" or as "listed with half-ounces", which is consistent with Weber's other tables.

10 In Weber's measurements, W_A could be either the heavier or the lighter weight of the two. This clouds the issue somewhat, but it can be avoided by replacing "W_A" and "W_B" by the "lighter" or the "heavier" weight as necessary. In this case, W_A was the heavier of the two.

Table 3.4 A reproduction of Weber's table, showing estimates of the smallest perceptible difference in heaviness perception when weights are placed on, as opposed to lifted by, the hands. From Ross and Murray (1996, p. 67)

Subject's number in the experiments		*Smallest perceptible difference when ounces or drachms were placed on the hands*		
1.	Touch	32 oz: 17 oz	difference	15 oz
	Touch & kinaesthesis	32 oz: 30½ oz	difference	1½ oz
	Touch	32 dr: 24 dr	difference	8 dr
	Touch & kinaesthesis	32 dr: 30 dr	difference	2 dr
2.	Touch	32 oz: 22 oz	difference	10 oz
	Touch & kinaesthesis	32 oz: 30½ oz	difference	1½ oz
	Touch	32 dr: 22 dr	difference	10 dr
	Touch & kinaesthesis	32 dr: 30 dr	difference	2 dr
3.	Touch	32 oz: 20 oz	difference	12 oz
	Touch & kinaesthesis	32 oz: 26 oz	difference	6 oz
	Touch & kinaesthesis	32 dr.: 26 dr	difference	6 dr
4.	Touch	32 oz: 26 oz	difference	6 oz
	Touch & kinaesthesis	32 oz: 30 oz	difference	2 oz
	Touch & kinaesthesis	32 dr: 29 dr	difference	3 dr

Of all the tables dealing with weight perception in *De Tactu*, one stands out for its coming close to what we now call a factorially designed experiment. It provided a large enough number of measurements to forestall criticisms of the small number of observations. Indeed, it was the only table that Fechner apparently deemed worthwhile to repeat verbatim in his *Elements of Psychophysics* (Fechner, 1860a/1966, p. 116). It is found in *De Tactu* (Weber, 1834/1996a, p. 67), and is reproduced here as Table 3.4.

In a previous experiment, Weber had taken ten participants from various walks of life. In order to measure weight discrimination using touch only, Weber (1834/1996a) wrote that he:

> placed two-pound weights on many subjects' hands, which were motionless on a table, and inserted a [vertical] cardboard sheet between [the two hands]. Then I reduced the magnitude of one of the weights without the subject's knowledge, and then changed the hands supporting the weights by switching the lighter weight alternatively to the right and left, of course. In addition, I often lifted the weights and replaced them on the same hands, so that the subject could not guess, but could feel the heavier side only by touch. I recorded it only if the subject discriminated the heavier from the lighter weight correctly on repeated attempts and with frequent changes of hand.
>
> The same experiments were next repeated on the same people, but in such a way that they lifted both their hands and the weights together, and weighed the weights by hand. Then, if I discovered the size of the just

noticeable difference, I again made a note of it, and compared the numbers representing the difference between the weights.

(pp. 63–64)[11]

The first three tables in the LIFTOFF series (reported on pp. 64, 65, and 66 respectively) clearly show that the "difference threshold", as Weber himself called the measure denoted by ΔI in Weber's Law, was much larger when the weights were discriminated by touch only (i.e., were not lifted) than when the weights were discriminated by touch and kinaesthesis (i.e., were lifted). However, the fourth table, shown here as Table 3.4, differed from the preceding three tables by using *two* starting weights instead of one.

The single starting weight used in the preceding three tables had been 32 ounces. In Table 3.4, Weber used two starting weights, a heavier one of 32 ounces (as before) and a lighter one of 32 drachms equalling approximately equals 4 ounces. I think Weber deliberately contrasted 32 ounces with 32 drachms in order to make a point that multiplying the weights by a constant maintained what later came to be known as Weber's constant. In other words, Weber's starting weight of 32 ounces weighed eight times as much as his other starting weight of 32 drachms. Yet each would be as discriminable as the other.

Results are reported in Table 3.4 for four of the subjects out of the original ten used in all the experiments that employed a starting weight of 32 ounces. For Subject 1, the table shows that the weights needed to yield the smallest perceptible difference when the hands rested motionless on the table bore the ratio 32:17 ounces. The difference between these is 15 ounces, a value of ΔI. The standard weight is 32 ounces. It follows that $\Delta I/I$, will equal $(15/32) = 0.47$. For Subject 1, *lifting* the hands, however, yielded the smallest perceptible difference when the weights were in the ratio 32:30.5. Letting $I = 32$ and $\Delta I = 1.5$, yielded a value of $\Delta I/I$ equal to $(1.5/32) = 0.047$. Obviously, for this subject, lifting a starting weight of 32 ounces yielded a Weber fraction (0.047) that was some 10 times smaller than that obtained (0.47) when the hand remained motionless on the table.

We now do the same calculation, for the same subject, when the starting weight is only 4 ounces (32 drachms) as compared with 32 ounces. When the

11 According to Helen Ross (personal communication by email, received October 26, 2019), Weber used some unusually cumbersome Latin to refer to the smallest difference in the perceived heaviness of two weights that could be detected by a participant. She translated the Latin into normal English, which is "the just noticeable difference". In her words, "it is clear to me that Weber had the concept of the Just Noticeable Difference in 1834, but could not express it neatly in Latin. It goes better in German and English". There is no entry for the Just Noticeable Difference in the Index to Ross and Murray (1996). Adler's English translation of Fechner's (1860/1966) *Elements of Psychophysics* states, in its Index, however, that the term first appears on page 60 of that translation, where Fechner's "Method of Just Noticeable Differences" is introduced.

hands were motionless, Table 3.4 shows that, when I = 32 drachms, ΔI = 8 drachms, then $\Delta I/I$ becomes a dimensionless fraction because the units of measurement cancel each other out. Then $\Delta I/I$ = (8/32) = 0.25. When the hands were lifted, I = 32 drachms and ΔI = 2 drachms, so that $\Delta I/I$ = (2/32) = 0.06. For this subject, lifting a starting weight as small as 4 ounces yielded a Weber fraction (0.06) that was some four times as small as that obtained (0.25) when the hand remained motionless on the table.

Taken by themselves, these calculated values of the Weber fraction seem somewhat chaotic except for the fact that the fraction is clearly smaller when the weights were lifted than when they were not. I, nevertheless, wondered what would happen if the values of $\Delta I/I$ that were calculated for the four conditions investigated with Subject 1 were calculated for Subjects 2, 3, and 4. Table 3.5 shows the Weber fraction for all the subjects mentioned in Table 3.4.

Each calculated value of $\Delta I/I$ was computed in a manner identical to those described above for Subject 1, whose four Weber fractions appear in the first row of data in Table 3.5.

Table 3.5 shows that, for Subject 2, when the weights were placed on his motionless hands, the Weber fraction for the large starting weight (32 ounces) *equalled* that for the small starting weight (4 ounces). In both cases, ($\Delta I/I$) was 0.31. Moreover, for Subject 3, when the weights were lifted by the hands, the Weber fraction for the large starting weight (32 ounces) *equalled* that for the small starting weight (4 ounces). In both cases, ($\Delta I/I$) was 0.19.

For each of the eight possible conditions, both a low and high magnitude of the standard weight were investigated. The results show we have found an *exact* fit of Weber's Law to two out of the six comparisons (two comparisons were not tested by Weber) for which the "smallest perceptible differences" between weights placed on the hands were ascertained experimentally. In the remaining four comparisons the following were found: for Subject 1, large and small lifted weights, the fractions were 0.05 and 0.06 respectively; for Subject 2, the corresponding fractions were 0.05 and 0.06; and for Subject 4, the corresponding

Table 3.5 A demonstration that the discrimination data for subjects 2 and 3 obeyed Weber's Law

Subject	*Touch (non-lifting)*		*Touch and Kinaesthesis (lifting)*	
	Large starting weight (32 oz)	*Small starting weight (32 dr or 4 oz)*	*Large starting weight (32 oz)*	*Small starting weight (32 dr or 4 oz)*
1	0.47	0.25	0.047	0.06
2	**0.31**	**0.31**	0.05	0.06
3	0.38	–	**0.19**	**0.19**
4	0.19	–	0.06	0.09

All ($\Delta I/I$)-values are expressed as decimal fractions.

fractions were 0.06 and 0.09. These values exemplify what we now call "near-misses" to Weber's Law.

The Contents and Importance of Weber's Der Tastsinn *(1846)*

The purpose of Weber's (1846/1996b) *Der Tastsinn* was to provide an encyclopaedic reference that could be consulted by researchers concerned with the anatomy and physiology of the skin senses. *De Tactu* (Weber, 1834/1996a) was more concerned with the sensitivity (*subtilitate*) of the skin senses to changes in pressure, localization, temperature, and weight as they affected various regions of the body. In the years elapsing between 1834 and 1846, considerable progress was made in the identification of specific sensory receptors lying under the skin. This was largely because of improvements in the microscopes of the time.

In fact, Murray and Farahmand (1995) claimed that there were three main reasons for Weber's initial lack of knowledge of the physiology of the skin senses when he started the work on measuring the acuity of those senses eventually published in *De Tactu*. First, Christianity dominated eighteenth-century medical schools, and it was felt to be sacrilegious to study the "mind" because the mind was part of one's immortal soul (Jacyna, 1994). Second, the study *in vivo* of muscles and nerves was hampered by a lack of anaesthetics. Third, microscopes prior to about 1800 were subject to spherical and chromatic aberrations that made most histological observations unreliable (Ford, 1973). But matters quickly improved, and the first photographs of microscopic images were made in 1836, that is, two years after the publication of *De Tactu*, but ten years before the publication of *Der Tastsinn*.

In *Der Tastsinn*, Weber (1846/1996b) wrote for a second time about many of the phenomena first reported in *De Tactu*. Now the emphasis was as much on the underlying neurophysiology as it was on the sensitivity of the individual skin-surface being discussed. In this translation, *Der Tastsinn* was divided into three main sections, the first being devoted to perception in general (pp. 141–168), the second devoted to the touch-sense (pp. 168–213), and the third devoted to coenaesthesis, which refers to what we now call kinaesthesis, visceral sensations, proprioception, and other internal sensations (pp. 213–236).

At the end of the section on the touch-sense a short passage is devoted to comparing the "smallest differences in weight perceptible to the touch-sense, the smallest differences in length of lines perceptible to the visible sense, and the smallest differences in pitch perceptible to the auditory sense" (pp. 210–212). Little is added to what had been said on these matters in *De Tactu*. In fact, the most useful précis of Weber's own evidence concerning the Weber fraction comes, not from *Der Tastsinn*, but from a passage towards the end of Weber's *summary* of the evidence presented in *De Tactu* (Weber, 1834/1996a). It is here that we find the following:

Now to describe my pronouncements in a few words:

> we do not find weight discrimination by *touch* unless the difference between the weights is at least a fifteenth or thirtieth part;
>
> we do not find discrimination between lines by *vision* unless the difference between them is a hundredth part;

> we do not find discrimination between sounds by *hearing* unless there is a pitch difference of a three hundred and twenty second part of the vibrations.
> (p. 125)

The equivalent passage in *Der Tastsinn* (Weber, 1846/1996b) consists of two opening paragraphs, which read as follows:

> It appears from my experiments that the smallest difference between two weights which we can distinguish by way of feeling changes in muscle-tension is that difference shown by two weights roughly bearing the relation of 39–40, i.e., when one is about 1/40 heavier than the other. If we go by the feeling of pressure exerted by the weights on the skin, we can actually distinguish a weight-difference of 1/30, i.e., when the weights are in the relation 29–30.
>
> If two lines are perceived one after the other, a person excellent at visual discrimination can, according to my experiments, detect a difference between two lines bearing a ratio of 50:51 or even 100:101 to each other. Persons with a lesser ability in this regard can distinguish lines differing in length by about 1/25. The smallest difference between the pitches of two tones almost in unison which can still be detected by an artist who hears them in sequence is, according to Delezenne, 1/4 comma $(81/80)^{1/4}$. A music-lover, according to this author, can distinguish only 1/2 comma $(81/80)^{1/2}$. If the tones are heard simultaneously, such small differences in tone cannot be detected, according to Delezenne's experiments.[12] 1/4 comma represents a ratio of approximately 321:322. 1/2 comma represents approximately 160:161.
> (p. 210)

Weber's conclusion in *De Tactu* about the Weber fractions for perceived heaviness, perceived line length, and perceived pitch is replaced by a longer passage in *Der Tastsinn*. Again, the difference between Weber fractions is highlighted by Weber's reference to "persons with a lesser ability", who have a Weber fraction of 1/25 for line lengths, instead of the 1/100 associated with persons of greater ability.

On the other hand, the first part of *Der Tastsinn* is devoted to what is essentially a lengthy discussion of the relationship between what a person *feels* on receiving a particular sensation (of vision, say, or touch) and how a person *interprets* that sensation. For example, Fechner, who was only six years younger than Weber, approached Weber to ask for an explanation of the following phenomenon. If we hold in our hand a rod and touch a table top with the end of the rod, we

12 According to Ross and Murray (1996, p. 20), "the comma of Didymus = 0.22 of an equal-tempered semitone". The value of $(81/80)^{1/4}$ is 1.003, and the value of $(81/80)^{1/2}$ is 1.006.

> have the impression of feeling the pressure in two places, one where the rod touches our finger-tip, and the other where the lower end of the rod touches the table. It is as if we simultaneously received two sensations, separated by the length of the rod … Only when a tooth is noticeably loosened and moves in its socket, and a rigid object is pressed against the tooth, do we—as I myself have experienced—feel two sensations, one on the surface of the root, the other on the surface of the crown.
>
> (Weber, 1846/1996b, p. 143)

Weber himself confirmed the acceptability of this analogy by showing that two sensations were felt if the rod were held loosely by the fingertip against the table top at the other end of the rod, but only one sensation was felt in the fingertip *either* if the rod were fixed rigidly to the table *or* if the fingertip were fixed rigidly to the rod.

This example of how we use touch to navigate our ways around objects, large and small, in our immediate environment, was explored in depth by Brodie (1995). Brodie drew a historical analogy comparing Weber's distinction between our bodily sensations and our interpretations of them and Thomas Reid's (1785/1853) distinction between "sensation" and "perception". Moreover, Brodie also carried out experiments showing how a participant can concentrate directly on *either* the environment *or* the bodily sensations. Brodie inferred that, in the case of weight perception, a *direct* perception of an object's weight can arise if we lift that weight. Weber intimated that weight perception could only be attained indirectly by adding muscle-sensations to pressure-sensations.

Der Tastsinn raised theoretical issues about how the brain interpreted sensations arising in the peripheral nervous system. Weber and his contemporaries knew about the Pacinian corpuscle, which mediates sensations of pressure that are propagated deeply below the surface of the skin. Weber considered that "pain" was a kind of "common sensibility" rather than a cutaneous modality of sensation, because pain can arise not only if the skin is cut, but also when muscles are overstrained and when we experience pains in the viscera, not to mention headaches. Pain is also aroused when the skin surface is extremely hot or cold (as was indicated by Table 3.2). Weber speculated that some kinds of temperature-induced pain resulted from peripheral messages activating an unusually large number of nerve-fibres in the brain. But the notion that some cutaneous pain might be mediated by "free nerve endings" was not investigated by Weber.

Weber as a Pioneer of Experimental Psychology

This chapter concludes by noting that Weber is ranked by some present-day historians of science as the first person in modern times to provide experimental support for assertions concerning *mental* events. The section of the Prologue devoted to the Third Renaissance, showed that a number of academics initiated quantitative research on sensation and perception in German-speaking countries in the eighteenth century (Ramul, 1960, 1963). Weber's research on differential thresholds, though comprising only a small proportion of his total published research on physiology, was greeted enthusiastically by his colleagues. His research on differential thresholds was destined to furnish a large number of experiments on the discriminatory powers of the human mind when Wundt established his Institute of Experimental Psychology at the University of Leipzig in 1879. This act probably inspired the University of Göttingen to found its own Psychological Institute, with a splendidly well-equipped laboratory, in 1881 (Krohn, 1893). Its first director, Georg Elias Müller (1850–1934) was perhaps the third, in chronological order, of the founders of psychophysics (after Weber and Fechner).

Asimov (1972) rated the importance of Weber's achievements in the following words:

> [Weber's] law is not exact but it served as the groundwork for all kinds of experimentation into the manner in which the human being senses the environment about him and how he interprets his sense impressions. Weber by his observations may be said to have founded experimental psychology and introduced the working of the mind into the realm of the natural sciences.
>
> (p. 412)

We close this chapter by indicating that, in the nineteenth century, at least one psychologist of considerable note was rather optimistic that the calculation of Weber fractions represented an important stepping stone in the quantification of sensory science. Théodule Ribot (1839–1916) holds an important place in the history of psychology. One reason is because he postulated "Ribot's Law" (which was to the effect that, in cases of progressive global amnesia, the first memory representations to be lost were of recent origin, and were therefore "unstable"). A second reason is because he became the first professor of psychology, as opposed to philosophy, in France, at the Collège de France in 1888 (Nicolas & Murray, 1999).

Ribot also rendered stalwart service to his countrymen by writing articles, later compiled into two books, introducing the new advances in evolutionary and experimental psychology. One was about English psychology (Ribot, 1875) and one was about German psychology (Ribot, 1879). The second edition of the book about German psychology was translated into English (Ribot, 1886). Anxious to prove that Weber's approach would be of benefit, not just to psychologists, but also to physiologists, Ribot deliberately searched for estimates of the numerical value of the Weber fraction that extended to the senses beyond those concerned with judgments of perceived heaviness. In his book on contemporary German psychology, Ribot (1886, pp. 134–187), presented an insightful introduction to Fechnerian psychophysics, and, on page 152, he provided the following table of Weber fractions:

For touch	1/3	(weight placed on participant's hand)
For muscular effort	1/17	(lifting a weight)
For temperature	1/3	(hands dipped in water)
For sound	1/3	(loudness)
For light	1/100	(luminous intensity)

Most of the evidence supporting these Weber fractions was extracted by Ribot from Weber's (1834/1996a) *De Tactu* and Fechner's (1860/1964) *Elemente der Psychophysik*.

To complement Ribot's assertions, it is salutary to jump a century ahead of *De Tactu* (Weber, 1834/1996a) to Woodworth and Schlosberg's (1954) section on Weber's Law. Woodworth and Schlosberg (1954, p. 223) reproduced a table of eight Weber fractions that were compiled by Boring, Langfeld, and Weld (1948, p. 268). The *lowest* of these Weber fractions was 0.003 for a perceptible difference in perceived pitch, given a tone of 2,000 cycles per second. The *highest* of these Weber fractions was 0.200 for the increase in perceived saltiness of saline, given that 8 moles of salt (NaCl) were dissolved in one litre of water. In between these extreme values was a Weber fraction of 0.019 for lifted weights, a fraction based on combining the results from four experiments, all conducted after the data of Table 3.4 were presented by Weber. Weber's own estimate of the *minimal* Weber fraction for lifted weights, it will be recalled, was 0.0345 (1/29). These experiments were conducted by Fechner (1860a/1966), Brown (1910), Woodrow (1933), and Oberlin (1936).

Gregory (1981/1984) wrote that "it should be added that Weber's Law … is not precise, and breaks down markedly at extreme- and especially-low stimulus intensity, when greater incremental intensities are needed for discrimination than his formula indicates" (p. 502). Laming (1989) later made a plea that Weber's Law might be found to be accurate for a wide variety of sensory discriminations, provided we knew exactly *how* to present the standard and comparison stimuli in such a way as to avoid artefacts peculiar to each sensory dimension. There is a large literature on a "near-miss" to Weber's Law that was associated with differences in perceived loudness between two tones presented at a frequency of 1,000 Hz. Viemeister (1972) offered an explanation of the near-miss in terms of harmonics generated by the ear itself. If correct, this would be an excellent example of an artefact affecting results that would normally be expected to follow Weber's Law fairly exactly. Green (1995), summarizing the evidence obtained subsequent to 1976 on the topic, was obliged to conclude that "our current theorizing is inadequate to explain many aspects of the data" (p. 1).

One of the major contributions made by Fechner's psychophysics was to replace Weber's somewhat arbitrary choice of weight comparisons with choices made on the basis of more principled and more explicitly described methodology and implemented in experiments using many more trials for each condition than Weber used.

Summary

The first part of the chapter was devoted to placing Ernst Heinrich Weber in the context of the multiple scientific activities concurrently taking place, particularly at the Universities of Halle, Göttingen, and Leipzig, in the first half of the nineteenth century. The three brothers, Ernst Heinrich, Wilhelm Eduard, and Eduard Friedrich, all became experts on the applications of physics to the workings of the human body.

Ernst Heinrich Weber's first investigations of the touch-sense were designed to measure its "sensitivity" or "acuity" in a large number of skin surface areas. The acuity with which two touches could be distinguished from one touch was mapped for most of the body by "two-point threshold" tests. Sensitivity to variations in pressure was measured by whether a participant could say which of two weights placed simultaneously on two different parts of the body seemed to exert the most pressure. Weber also started a program of research on the sensitivity of warm body parts to changes in temperature. The ability to discriminate small differences in the perceived heaviness of two weights placed simultaneously or successively on the same or a closely contiguous part of the body (mainly using the fingertips) was evaluated by determining, over a series of trials, which of the two weights seemed heavier. In general, the fineness of discrimination was greatest if the hands on which the two weights were placed were raised into the air rather than rested motionless. The greatest sensitivity (or "smallest difference-threshold") was found when a weight of 29 ounces was successively alternated with a weight of 30 ounces placed on the *same* two fingers of one hand, and the hand was then raised. The ratio of the two weights was described as being 29:30.

A table of Weber's obtained difference-thresholds under four conditions (a starting weight of 32 ounces or a starting weight of 4 ounces, the hand motionless or lifted) was re-analysed. When the standard weight was assigned the intensity I, the comparison weight that was just noticeably heavier was assigned the intensity, $I + \Delta I$. Weber's Law was discovered to be $k = (\Delta I/I)$. For one participant, the results were exactly as predicted. The same Weber fraction ($\Delta I/I$) held for the starting weight of 32 ounces as for the starting weight of 4 ounces, when the weights were placed on the stationary fingers of one hand. For another participant, the same was true if the weights located on the fingers were also raised by the hand (Table 3.5).

Weber's discussion, in *De Tactu*, of the smallest perceptible differences for weights were complemented by short discussions of the comparable differences for line lengths (viewed successively), and for pitch differences (heard in very close succession). Later, his remarks in *De Tactu* on these topics were discussed in *Der Tastsinn*. *Der Tastsinn* went into much more detail on how we interpret our sensations in such a way as to provide a coherent representation of how objects create those sensations.

4 An Introduction to Fechner's Law

The Historical Background to Fechner's Law

Fechner's Early Research on Electricity

Chapter 3 made clear that the Weber brothers, either as joint or as sole authors of books and articles on various scientific topics, laid the foundations for some of the most important advances in scientific knowledge in the nineteenth century. Their *Wellenlehre* [wave theory] of 1825 was a precursor of important studies of fluid mechanics, blood flow, acoustical theory, and the waves found in the electromagnetic spectrum (including light waves, radio waves, and waves emitted as by-products of subatomic interactions, such as X-rays). A more detailed treatment of these contributions was made by Schreier (1993) in the context of a conference celebrating the life and work of Wilhelm Weber.

Table 4.1 shows how the three Weber brothers interacted with Gustav Theodor Fechner (1801–1889), mainly at Leipzig, but also at Halle. Wilhelm Weber also interacted with Gauss at Göttingen at a time when Herbart was also teaching at Göttingen. From 1831, Weber and Gauss improved the technology of telegraphy (Kline, 1972, p. 871). In Germany, the first telegraph system was installed, in 1834, between Dresden and Leipzig.[1] I dated the last entry in Table 4.1 at 1867 because it was then that Wilhelm Weber (1867) described how a study of the flow of fluids through elastic tubes could be applied to blood flow. A book on the same topic was written by his brother Ernst in 1834. Their collaboration on the *Wellenlehre* (1825) inspired them to study blood flow.

Of the various lessons that can be learnt from Table 4.1, two stand out. First, Fechner's early career was that of a highly respected physicist (specializing in electricity). Second, when Ernst Heinrich wrote *Der Tastsinn* in 1846, both his brothers and Fechner were resident in Leipzig (although Wilhelm was only temporarily so).

Fechner was born in 1801 in a small town, Gross-Sährchen, that in his time was in the German Electorate of Saxony, later in Prussia, and is now in Poland

1 The initial theory and implementation of telegraphy was due mainly to Joseph Henry (1797–1878). It was put into practical use only when Henry collaborated with Samuel F. B. Morse (1791–1872). In the United States, telegraphy was first installed, in 1844, between Baltimore and Washington DC (Asimov, 1972, pp. 298–299).

Table 4.1 The interacting career-paths of E. H. Weber, Wilhelm Weber, and Fechner

Date	*Leipzig*	*Wittenberg*	*Göttingen*
1795		Ernst H. Weber born	
1801		G. T. Fechner born (in Gross-Sährchen)	
1804		Wilhelm E. Weber born	
1806		Eduard F. Weber born	
1824			Herbart's *Psychology as Science*
1825		E. H. and W. E. Weber's book about wave motions (written at Halle)	
1831	Fechner on Ohm's Law		W. E. Weber hired by Gauss
1834	E. H. Weber's *De Tactu*		
1836			W. E. and E. F. Weber's book about human walking
1837			The "Göttingen Seven": W. E. Weber loses his position
1843	W. E. Weber hired at Leipzig		
1846	E. H. Weber's *Der Tastsinn*		
1849			W. E. Weber reinstated at Göttingen
1860	Fechner's *Elemente der Psychophysik*		
1867			W. E. Weber (1867) on blood flow

(Heidelberger, 2004, pp. 19, 321). His grandfather and father were both Protestant clergymen and Fechner was at first inclined to follow in their footsteps. But he entered the University of Leipzig in 1817 to study medicine and obtained an undergraduate degree in that topic. His adolescence was one of extreme intellectual inquiry. It found him swinging from studies of Herbart and of Romanticism to a uniquely German approach to life called *Naturphilosophie* (nature-philosophy) that was propagated by Lorenz Oken (1779–1851). Like almost all turn-of-the-nineteenth-century academics, Oken was influenced by Kant. I would point out specifically that Kant argued that humans were so "adapted" to the world around them—knowing, for example, how to navigate in space and time quite spontaneously—that I consider Kant to have been a proto-evolutionist. Kant's notion that humans were born "attuned" to their external environment was seized upon by the nature-philosophers, who were among the first to say that the development of a child into an adult in some ways recapitulated the development of the human species from primitive ancestors.[2]

At the same time, Oken and his colleagues made frequent sweeping analogies between natural phenomena that brought the movement into disrepute among more conscientious scientists. For example, an idea, first formulated by Goethe (see Lewes, 1855/1908, pp. 369–373), that the human skull had somehow evolved from a vertebra, was extended by Oken. Later, Thomas Huxley (1825–1899) disproved Goethe's theory (Lewes, 1855/1908, pp. 372–373).

Fechner soon tired of the over-generality of the nature-philosophers and indeed, in some writings of late adolescence written under the pen name Dr Mises, satirized them. In one rigmarole of logic, he argued that, since a sphere is a perfect geometrical solid, and an angel was a perfect being, angels must be spherical (Fechner, 1825; English translation by Corbet & Marshall, 1969). Fechner, as Dr Mises, also wrote a parody in which he claimed that the moon was made of iodine (Fechner, 1821/1832). This youthful phase—partly spurred on by his dissatisfaction with the lack of rigour in medical practices of his day—was summarized by Marilyn Marshall (1969).

During these student years, Fechner earned some income by translating, from French into German, major textbooks in physics and chemistry. In later editions, some of the final chapters in those translations were written by Fechner himself.

Fechner's curiosity concerning the laws of electricity that were formulated by Georg Simon Ohm (1787–1854) were a consequence of his translations of more than one edition of a textbook by Biot (1824).[3]

Fechner found the fact fascinating that, using highly sophisticated mathematics, Ohm was able to generate the law that thousands of students who nowadays study high-school physics probably learn by heart as something like: amps = (volts divided by ohms). Fechner was convinced that the law needed to be confirmed experimentally. Eventually, after hours of carefully planned experiments, he published a monograph that succeeded in doing just that (Fechner, 1830). Because of the quality of this research and because many academic physicists had a high regard for his translations and annotations concerning the textbooks of Biot and others, Fechner was elected as extraordinary professor of physics at Leipzig in 1831. He was promoted to ordinary professor of physics at Leipzig in 1834.[4]

2 This idea was promoted, later in the nineteenth century, in a book by G. J. Romanes (1848–1894) titled *Mental Evolution in Man* (1888). Romanes was a close colleague of Darwin.

3 For a full account of the somewhat complicated events that led Ohm, who was working as a Gymnasium teacher without a permanent university position in the 1820s, to derive, from a partial differential equation, the extraordinarily simple relationship we now call Ohm's Law, consult Jungnickel and McCormmach (1986a, Vol. 1, pp. 51–58).

4 "Extraordinary" is a somewhat unfortunate translation of *ausserordentlich*, meaning that one is "outside" the elite group of professors who are *ordentlich*. The former were allowed to teach at the university but did not necessarily receive a salary; the "ordinary" professors had permanent fulltime positions with pay and, usually, research funding.

Fechner the Invalid

Reports about particular events in a person's life can either be autobiographical or biographical, written by somebody else. There is a large (and underknown) literature of autobiographical accounts by persons who have undergone illnesses of a psychological nature and then written about it themselves; such accounts have come to be called "self-reports" in the psychiatric literature.[5]

Psychophysicists know that Fechner suffered a severe illness in his early 40s. Reports about that illness in the English-language literature on Fechner are fragmentary. Many attendees at the annual meeting of the International Society for Psychophysics know that Fechner's "insight" obtained on October 22, 1850, led to October 22 being referred to as "Fechner Day". According to Fechner's own diary, it was on that date that Fechner intuited how the mental (psychological) could interact with the material (physical) world. The new discipline based on this insight was therefore called "psychophysics". Table 4.2 provides key background details, but also illustrates that Fechner himself provided four separate self-reports about his illness.

The first self-report was written in 1845, after his recovery was well underway, but not published during his lifetime. Five years after his death, a nephew on his sister Emilie's side, named Johannes Emil Kuntze (1824–1894), wrote the first biography of Fechner (Kuntze, 1892). Heidelberger (2004, p. 9) noted that Kuntze provided information about Fechner's life that is now unavailable because a lot of archival information concerning Fechner was lost in bombing-raids of Leipzig during the Second World War. According to Heidelberger (2004, p. 49), this self-report was described by Fechner himself as "a history of my illness". The first self-report was never fully translated but long extracts from it are in English (Lowrie, 1946, pp. 36–42) and in German (Lasswitz, 1896/1902, pp. 39–47).[6]

The second self-report was very short, only two pages. After four years of illness, Fechner entered his garden not wearing the mask that covered his eyes for many years. He was overwhelmed by how beautiful everything looked, especially the flowers. This event appeared in Fechner's *Nanna* (1848). We here quote from Lowrie's (1946) translation into English:

5 Alvarez (1961) collected autobiographies by "people who have been mentally upset, highly eccentric, alcoholic, or otherwise ill or handicapped" (p. 5), and published abstracts of some of those autobiographies in his valuable book, *Minds That Came Back*. These autobiographers included the Swedish dramatist August Strindberg (1849–1912), the Russian ballet dancer Vaslav Nijinsky (1892–1950), and the English poet William Cowper (1731–1800). Daniel Paul Schreber (1842–1911) was a lawyer who practised in Leipzig contemporaneously with Fechner, G. E. Müller, and Wundt. Schreber described his own psychotic episodes (Schreber, 1903/1988). Reading his autobiography led Freud (1911/1958) to invent the word "narcissism." In our own time, the recently deceased American feminist Kate Millett (1934–2017) wrote an informative account of her experience with a bipolar disorder requiring hospitalization (Millett, 1990). Self-reports about psychotic episodes are often published in the journal *Schizophrenia Bulletin*.

6 Kurt Lasswitz (1848–1910) was the second, after Kuntze, to write a biography of Fechner. It was evaluated favourably by Heidelberger (2004, pp. 12–13). Lasswitz also wrote science fiction.

Table 4.2 Fechner's self-reports about his illness

1801	Born in Gross-Sährchen, between Dresden and Breslau.
1834	Promoted to ordinary professor of physics at Leipzig.
1839	First eye strain and headaches; beginning of his mental isolation.
1841	Serious loss of appetite.
1842	Worries about his own mental health.
1843	Beginning of recovery; the experience in the garden.
1845	**First self-report** (Fechner, 1845/1892). An account of his illness, including his first description of his experience in the garden. First *published* posthumously by Kuntze (1892, pp. 105–126).
1848	**Second self-report** (Fechner, 1848/1946). A second account of his experience in the garden; First *published* in *Nanna*; English translation by Lowrie (1946, pp. 211–212).
1850	**Third self-report** (Fechner, 1850/2001). Fechner describes his "insight" into the relation between stimulus intensity and sensation-magnitude. First *written* in his diary on October 22, 1850 ("Fechner Day"); First *mentioned* by Fechner (1860/1964, Vol. II, p. 554); First English translation circulated at the 2001 ISP Conference in Leipzig; a brochure titled *From Fechner's Diary: Oct. 22nd, 1850.*
1885	**Fourth self-report** (Fechner, 1885/2004). A short autobiography requested by academic authorities in Prussia. First *published* by Heidelberger (German: 1993, pp. 387–389; English: 2004, pp. 321–322).

> I still remember well what an impression it made upon me when, after suffering for some years from an ailment which affected my sight, I stepped out for the first time from my darkened chamber and into the garden with no bandage upon my eyes. It seemed to me like a glimpse beyond the boundary of human experience. Every flower beamed upon me with a peculiar clarity, as though into the outer light it was casting a light of its own. To me the whole garden seemed transfigured, as though it were not I but nature that had just arisen.
>
> (p. 211)

Fechner's third self-report was a diary entry about how he created his insight that a mathematical relationship could be found between the intensity of a physical stimulus and the magnitude of the sensation aroused by that stimulus. Strangely, this self-report was not readily available in English because Fechner himself had only referred to it in a single short sentence in Volume II of his *Elements* (Fechner, 1860/1964, p. 554). In a single short sentence, Boring (1950, p. 280) referred to this self-report.

The 31st annual meeting of the International Society for Psychophysics took place in Leipzig in 2001. The meeting had many participants and our hosts arranged for us to have a tour around the section of the Library that houses the Fechner archives and to display to us a (very rare) first edition of Fechner's

(1860/1964) *Elemente der Psychophysik*. They gave each of us a brochure with photographs of the pages in Fechner's diary for October 22, 1850, and prepared a translation of the key passage in which Fechner claimed to have had a sudden insight into how physical stimulus intensities and sensation-magnitudes could be mathematically related (Fechner, 1850/2001). October 22 is still called "Fechner Day" by psychophysicists.[7]

Finally, at the age of about 84, after German unification, when Fechner was still writing as prolifically as he had early in his career, he was asked by the authorities of the University of Berlin to prepare a short autobiography of his career. This fourth self-report makes no attempt to hide his illness. This document was handwritten and is currently conserved in the Library of the University of Berlin. Heidelberger (1993, pp. 387–389) reproduced it in full in German, and, later, Heidelberger (2004, pp. 321–323) arranged for it to be translated into English by Cynthia Klohr.

The following extract from this fourth self-report shows how Fechner viewed his own illness in the light of his career. Fechner (1885/2004) wrote the following:

> In 1831 and 1832 I was a university lecturer, and after Prof. Brandes died I was given a professorship in physics in 1834. But then I ruined my eyesight by doing experiments in subjective color perception, looking often at the sun through colored glass, and by frequently observing minute divisions well into the evenings, so that by Christmas 1839 I could no longer use my eyes and had to interrupt my lectures. When I finally could no longer bear daylight, at all, I gave up my position. I also had headaches from previous intellectual strain. Then, in the autumn of 1843, peculiar circumstances led to a fairly quick, almost sudden considerable improvement.
>
> (p. 322)

According to Fechner (1845/1892) what caused an improvement or "break" was a visit by a lady friend of the family to give Fechner a dish (raw ham without fat and soaked in wine and lemon juice). His enjoyment of this renewed his appetite and helped him recover his strength (Lowrie, 1946, p. 38). In his own account of his own illness, he himself acknowledged that "my state was close to that of mental disorder; nevertheless, gradually everything settled into symmetry" (as cited in Heidelberger, 2004, p. 49).

Between 1839 and 1843 Fechner's oversensitivity to light was so distressing he blindfolded himself. He often experienced pain when he tried to move around. His hearing, sleeping, and eating were severely impaired. Heidelberger

7 An annual conference is held by the International Society for Psychophysics (founded in 1985). Early conferences were held so as to coincide with October 22, but because October 22 falls within the academic teaching year in the northern hemisphere, some would-be participants could not attend the conference. In recent years, the conference was held occasionally in August.

(2004, pp. 49–50) lists several attempts to give a diagnosis of Fechner's affliction; several of the diagnoses offered include words such as "depression" or "neurotic", implying that his symptoms were essentially psychogenic rather than somatic in origin. Fechner reported, two years later, that he felt God had chosen him to do extraordinary things, and that "the riddles of the world seemed to reveal themselves" (as cited in Heidelberger, 2004, p. 49).

Fechner's scientific bent was so strong that, after his illness, he described how some of his own visual experiences differed from those of others viewing the same visual stimulus. For example, Fechner (1860b) published a long article on contrast in which he noted two examples of such differences. The first concerned a heightened sense of contrast when the sunlight fell on small objects through the window of his darkened room:

> Such a strong impression was made on my hypersensitive eyes when individual isolated patches appeared in my room that I could hardly endure it; yet I could go out into the street in full sunlight, or look up into a bright sky without feeling it as burdensome. This was despite the fact that the whole retina would have been stimulated to an identical or greater extent than it would have been in the former case, where the stimulation would have been confined to a small area.
>
> (p. 75)

The second phenomenon concerned the appearance of the moon in the early evening. Because of his failing eyesight, Fechner would stop reading and writing when the sun started to set, and go for a walk. If the evening were clear at the start of his walk, then, if the moon should also happen to be visible, its contrast with the blue sky was striking. At the end of his walk, he claimed he would always see a golden shine (a "halo"?) around the moon even though the sky remained equally clear, but the moon had climbed higher. This shine, Fechner affirmed, was probably visible when he had started his walk, but he had not seen it at that time. When accompanied on his walk by another person, he was persuaded that she could see no sign of the halo. If the evening should be foggy, both of them could see a shine surrounding the moon (Fechner, 1860b, p. 117).[8]

Fechner developed his own philosophy between his years as a graduate student and the end of his years as an invalid. Marshall (1974) proposed that Fechner's first serious contribution to philosophy was his attempt to place the "organism" within its appropriate domain in the subject matter of the sciences. It appeared in his master's dissertation at the University of Leipzig (Fechner, 1823).

Marshall's account of Fechner's 24-page dissertation was mainly concerned with establishing how far Fechner's views were consistent with those of three of the most prominent post-Kantian philosophers of the 1820s, namely, Fichte,

8 Fechner argued that the shine he saw surrounding the moon was caused by an usually high degree of light-diffusion within his eyes.

Schelling, and Hegel. We know that Fechner's interest in *Naturphilosophie* led naturally to Schelling's work, with its idealization of Nature and its emphasis on the beautiful as an intrinsic part of any philosophical worldview. Marshall firmly brings out the fact that these post-Kantian thinkers took strong umbrage against Kant's insistence that a difference existed between *phenomena* and *noumena*. *Phenomena* represent our conscious experiences of physical objects outside ourselves (Marshall used the word "extramental" to refer to physical objects). *Noumena* are aspects of those extramental objects we would never know directly. These post-Kantians disliked the idea that any sort of barrier or dividing-line could separate phenomena from noumena because they wanted "everything" to be a "unity" held together by scientific law. This view is consistent with the view that mind was omnipresent, known as "panpsychism", associated with Fechner's later thought. It also coincides in many ways with the thinking of Baruch Spinoza (1632–1677).

Fechner introduced into his purely verbal arguments a distinction that mathematicians made from antiquity, namely, the distinction between multiplication and addition. This peculiarity of Fechner's viewpoint led Marshall (1974) to write that

> Fechner's forms of combination and ideas, multiplication and addition, could have had as their models Herbart's "fusion" and "complication" … and Fechner's thesis that forms of natural objects must be expressed [in terms of] mathematical equations is probably made under Herbart's influence as much as Schelling's.
>
> (p. 46)

According to Heidelberger (2004, p. 51), this worldview seemed to be a reconciliation between the romantic nature-philosopher Fechner had once been tempted to adopt as his persona, and the mechanistic scientist he became thanks to his work on Ohm's Law.

After his illness had largely subsided, between 1845 and 1851, he wrote some of his most controversial books, writings whose apparent mysticism may have had the effect of alienating him from many of his fellow academics: *Uber das höchste Gut* [On the Highest Good; Fechner, 1846]; *Nanna oder über das Seelenleben der Pflanzen* [Nanna, or on the Soul-Life of Plants; Fechner, 1848]; and *Zend-Avesta oder über die Dinge des Himmels und der Jenseits* [Zend-Avesta or on Matters of Heaven and Beyond; Fechner, 1851].[9]

9 "Nanna," according to Boring (1950, p. 278), was the Norse goddess of flowers. Boring noted that "Zend-Avesta" means "practically 'a revelation of the world.' Consciousness, Fechner argued, is in all and through all" (p. 279). The soul does not die; and, before his illness, Fechner had written *Das Büchlein vom Leben nach den Tode* [A Little Book About Life After Death; Fechner, 1836]. *Zend-Avesta* was also the title of the prayer-book of Zoroastrianism, a religion dating back to ancient Persia. The language of the Persian *Zend-Avesta* was similar, but not identical, to Sanskrit, the language of ancient Hinduism.

In 1850 he worked on the *Zend-Avesta* and, in his diary entry for October 22, 1850, Fechner (1850/2001) wrote the following. This passage is clearly a follow-up to his thesis topic of 1823, some 27 years earlier, in which his scientific view of reality incorporated the difference between multiplication and addition (Marshall, 1974).

> For a long time now I have been thinking—along the lines of my views on a connection between body and soul—that mental intensity could be demonstrated to be a function of the corporal, i.e., the kinetic energy [*lebendige Kraft* (life-force)] of the body.[10] But nothing came of it, first, because I only took into consideration the absolute increase, and not the relative increase, and second, I considered only the momentary increase, and not the sum or the integral of the increase. … In expanding further on this scheme, I had the idea of using geometric expressions instead of arithmetic ones. … Combining that with my earlier idea of using the differential of the kinetic energy as a measurement-unit of mental intensity, I therefore took into consideration not the absolute but the relative increase. … I also remembered that kinetic energy increases by summing its absolute increases from a definite beginning-point. Concomitantly, therefore, the soul would sum the respective relative increases. … It was on October 22, while lying in bed, that I had these ideas.
>
> (Fechner, 1850/2001, pp. 1–2)[11]

We now explain this passage more thoroughly. Assume that Fechner's task is to relate the magnitude of a psychological sensation to the intensity of a stimulus. We know from Weber's Law, that when the intensity of the stimulus increases by a certain fixed proportion of itself, the magnitude of the resulting sensation is just noticeably increased.

A geometric expression provides an increase in psychological magnitude that is given by adding to I a fixed proportion, k, of I. Fechner thereby asserted that his great insight of October 22, 1850, was "the idea of using geometric expressions instead of arithmetic ones".

Please note that the terms I, k, and kI refer to physical *stimulus* intensities. In Fechner's thinking, as stimulus intensities themselves increase, stimulus intensity differences also increase. The corresponding sensation-magnitudes, Fechner predicted, would increase with *equal* steps between individual sensation-magnitudes. That is, sensation-magnitude increases arithmetically. Each step in sensation-magnitude would, according to Fechner, represent a unit on a

10 A stationary object, prior to being dropped from a height, has "potential energy"; when the object actually is dropped, it gathers "kinetic energy" as it falls.

11 An "arithmetical progression" consists of a series of numbers, each one of which is the previous number *plus* a constant term. For example, in the series "2 4 6 8 …," each number is the previous number *plus* two. A "geometrical progression" consists of a series of numbers, each one of which is the previous number *multiplied* by a constant term. For example, in the series "2 4 8 16…," each number is the previous number *multiplied* by two.

hypothetical scale of sensation-magnitude. He identified each one of those units with one "just noticeable difference".

Fechner's aim was to find a mathematical function that related the magnitude of a sensation-experienced-by-the-person to the actual intensity of the physical stimulus that activated that person's sensory receptors. We learned in Chapter 3 that Weber's Law says that, in order to increase a sensation-magnitude, the increment to be added to a weight of W ounces is a constant fraction of W. It was Fechner's genius that created the insight that Weber's Law would be an appropriate starting point for the derivation of a law relating sensation-magnitude to stimulus intensity. This insight formed the groundwork for Fechner's (1860/1964) monumental *Elements of Psychophysics* [*Elemente der Psychophysik*]

From Weber's Law to Fechner's Law: Fechner's Own Argument

In Fechner's notation, β refers to I. He asserted that the differential $d\beta$ was equivalent to ΔI as used in Weber's Law.[12] A crucial piece of information about how Fechner thought of ΔI is conveyed by Fechner (1860/1964, Vol. 2), who wrote:

> We shall assume, as is generally the case in experiments purporting to confirm the validity of Weber's Law, that the difference between two stimuli, or, putting it another way, the increase required of a stimulus, is very small in proportion to that stimulus. Let the stimulus to which the increase is applied be denoted by β, and the small increase be denoted by $d\beta$, where d should not be interpreted as standing for a particular magnitude, but only as a sign that $d\beta$ represents a small increase in β; this allows one to consider from the very outset that $d\beta$ can be taken as a sign denoting a differential. So the increase considered in relation to the stimulus intensity is given by $d\beta/\beta$. Let, on the other hand, the magnitude of the sensation evoked by the stimulus β be denoted by γ, and let the small increase in sensation-magnitude that arises when the increase in the stimulus reaches $d\beta$, be denoted by $d\gamma$, where once again d is to be understood as referring to a small increase.
>
> (*Elemente der Psychophysik*, Vol. 2, pp. 9–10 as translated by the author)

Next, I now offer my translation of Fechner's complete derivation of Fechner's Law as expressed in his notation. Here is how Chapter XVII of the *Elemente der Psychophysik* (Fechner, 1860a/1964, Vol. 2) opens:

> In the course of the previous chapter [on page 24 of the *Elemente*, Vol. 2, Chapter XVI], a fundamental formula was described, namely,

12 The use of β to refer to stimulus intensity and γ to refer to sensation-magnitude was first introduced in Appendix 2 of Fechner's *Zend-Avesta*, not in the *Elements of Psychophysics* (Fechner, 1860/1966). This Appendix was translated into English by Eckart Scheerer and is referred to here as Fechner (1987a). A key passage states that his theory can explain "in particular why the increase in *sensation* is less than the increase in the *stimulus*" (p. 207).

$$d\gamma = Kd\beta/\beta. \tag{4.1}$$

This formula was supported by experimental evidence on differences that were on the borderline of being noticeable.[13] From here on, $d\gamma$ and $d\beta$ will be considered as, and manipulated as, differentials. We can start by noting that, when it is assumed that natural logarithms are being discussed, the integration [i.e., the solution] of the above equation yields

$$\gamma = K\log\beta + C, \tag{4.2}$$

where C is the constant of integration.[14] The value of C can be determined by the condition that the sensation γ disappears when the threshold value of the stimulus intensity β is attained. Let this threshold value of β be denoted by b. It follows that

$$0 = K\log b + C, \tag{4.3a}$$

$$C = -K\log b \tag{4.3b}$$

$$\gamma = K(\log\beta - \log b). \tag{4.3c}$$

Inasmuch as a common logarithm is equal to a natural logarithm multiplied by a modulus $M = 0.4342945$, the above formula can be transformed into common logarithms.[15] If we also denote (K/M) by k, then the final formula above can be written as

$$\gamma = k(\log\beta - \log b) = k\log(\beta/b)(pp.33-34). \tag{4.4}$$

We can express Equation 4.4 in a more contemporary fashion by substituting S (sensation-magnitude) for Fechner's γ. For Fechner's β, substitute I (stimulus intensity); and for Fechner's b, substitute I_0 (absolute threshold value, as named by Fechner). We preserve Fechner's K, which is in units of sensation-magnitude. This leads to:

$$S = K\log_e(I/I_0). \tag{4.5}$$

13 Equation 4.1 is still called Fechner's "fundamental formula."

14 This is the first derivation of Fechner's Law.

15 In mathematics a modulus is a particular number that, when used in order to multiply one expression, thereby transforms that expression into another. Fechner here was concerned with transforming a log in one base to a log in another base. The rule for transforming logs in one base to logs in another is usually given by $\log_a x = \log_b x/\log_b a$. For example, $\log_e x = \log_{10} x / \log_{10} e$. Fechner, however, preferred to write this as $\log_{10} x = (\log_{10} e)(\log_e x) = (0.4342945)(\log_e x)$. The number 0.4342945 is the "modulus" that allows the natural logarithm $\log_e x$ to be transformed into the common logarithm $\log_{10} x$. Please note that, from Equations 4.2 to 4.4, Fechner wrote just "log b" instead of "$\log_e b$" or "$\log_{10} b$." I have kept Fechner's notation out of a sense of historical accuracy. Once we are past Equation 4.4, however, the notation will revert to "$\log_e b$" for the remainder of this volume.

For the remainder of this book, Fechner's Law will be given by Equation 4.5.

A criticism of Fechner's Law is that, if I_0 is greater than I, then Fechner's Law predicts that a sensation will have a negative value. The criticism of the negative values predicted by Fechner's Law led to his being plagued for the rest of his life by accusations that he believed in negative sensations. Murray (1990) provided a short review of the relevant literature. Here, I would emphasize that a negative sensation intensity can only arise if I_0 is *greater* than I, which is impossible IF I_0 is defined to be an absolute threshold intensity that the value of I must necessarily exceed.

Although Fechner does not belabour this issue in the *Elemente* (Fechner, 1860/1964, Vols. 1 and 2), Wundt (1887) misinterpreted its importance. In the third edition of his *Principles of Physiological Psychology* [*Grundzüge der physiologischen Psychologie*], which contained 1,106 pages, he wrote that:

> The noticeability of a [change in] sensation grows proportionally with the logarithm of the stimulus. But it should be noted here, for simplicity's sake, that the size of the absolute threshold stimulus intensity has been assumed to be itself a unit of stimulus intensity; that is, the sensation has its absolute threshold value somewhere between being noticeable and not being noticeable. If I is a fraction smaller than 1.0, S becomes negative because the logarithm of a fraction is always negative.
>
> (Wundt, 1887, Vol. 1, p. 383; author's translation)

By definition, this negative value cannot occur because I is greater than I_0. At this point Wundt introduced a graph illustrating Fechner's Law. In this graph, Wundt confuses axes by plotting sensation-magnitude on the abscissa and the logarithm of the stimulus intensity on the ordinate. This diagram was reproduced by Boring (1950, p. 290). Fechner (1860/1964) himself presented no graphs in which Cartesian coordinates were divided into measurement-units. Boring also preferred to use the German notation that had been used by Wundt (1887), namely, R (for *Reiz*, stimulus) and E (for *Empfindung*, sensation).

To summarize: starting from Weber's Law and asserting that ΔI can be written as a differential, dI, Fechner's Law can be described as saying that the sensation-magnitude, S, associated with a stimulus intensity, I, is given by the logarithm to base e of I. But I has often been expressed as I/I_0 where $I_0 = 1$ and is taken to be an "absolute threshold value" of I.

The Absolute Threshold

"Sense-Distances"

Titchener (1905a, pp. xix–xli) meticulously discussed what was meant by the "magnitude" (or the "strength" or the "intensity") of a stimulus. Let us imagine a Weber-type weight-lifting study in which a "standard" weight, that stays the same from trial to trial, is judged against a "comparison" weight, that varies from trial to trial. On one particular set of trials, the "intensity" of the comparison weight might be 312 g and that of the standard weight 300 g. The difference of 12 g that makes the comparison weight objectively heavier than the standard weight could be represented on a horizontal line that has a series of equally spaced marks. The standard weight of 300 g could be represented by the 300th mark and the comparison weight of 312 g could be represented by the 312th mark. So, the "difference" of 12 g could be represented geometrically by a "distance", on the horizontal axis, of 12 marks.

We shall see that Titchener eventually adopted the general view that it was the distance between stimuli that was the operative variable determining the subjective distance between sensations, which he called "sense-distances". Dzhafarov and Colonius (2011) argued that "sensation magnitude need not, however, be taken as a primitive of Fechner's theory. The logic of the latter is more consistent with the view that the notion of sensation magnitude is *constructed* by means of a more basic concept of *difference sensation*" (p. 3). The author italicized the word "constructed".

Two just noticeably different sensations aroused by two stimuli might also be influenced by a context. A "spatial context" could be the placement of the two weights on the left or the right side of the table at which a participant is seated. A "temporal context" could be the order in which the two weights were lifted. In other words, a judgment that the comparison was "different" from the standard can be influenced by variables other than stimulus intensity.

The meaning of "contextual background" can vary between sensory modalities. In psychophysical studies of "levels-of-greyness" discrimination, of the kind to be discussed in more detail in Chapter 8, the stimulus I might be a particular grey displayed against the background of a different grey. In weight discrimination, a weight of a given heaviness might be presented against the background of "no weight" (e.g., when the weight resting on a participant's palm is mentally contrasted with no weight). In loudness discrimination, a tone might be presented against a background of white noise, or silence. In each case no stimulus is an island unto itself. A stimulus is always viewed within a background. The notion took hold that "sensation-magnitude" was more appropriately described as a feeling of contrast between the corresponding stimulus and its background.

I think that there is a real problem with treating the absolute threshold stimulus intensity, I_0, as the appropriate "background" for any stimulus of intensity I. Let a stimulus be presented but also let a participant, when presented with that stimulus, report "no sensation". The probability that there actually *is* no stimulus will not necessarily be 1.0. A report of "no sensation" can arise *either* when there was no detectable second stimulus at all (i.e., call this background I_{NULL}) *or* when the stimulus did activate the nervous system but was so low in intensity that the stimulus could not be discriminated from its background. These are quite separate cases, and, I suggest, clarity will be brought into the discussion of what "I_0" means if we distinguish between two kinds of threshold, I_{NULL} and I_0. I_0, according to Fechner, is the minimal intensity of a stimulus that is just discriminable from I_{NULL}, its background. Stimuli lying between I_{NULL} and I_0 can excite the nervous system, but be too low in intensity to be consciously detectable. It will be necessary to represent the separate values I_{NULL} and I_0 *as* separate values on the abscissa of a two-dimensional Cartesian graph, where stimulus intensity such as I_{NULL} and I_0 are represented on the abscissa, and sensation-magnitude is represented on the ordinate.

A Numerical Demonstration of Fechner's Law

Let us consider weight discrimination experiments. Temporarily replace "I" by "W" to make it clear that we are dealing with weights measured, for example, in grams.

Let the names of the weights represented on the abscissa be written (from left to right) as W_{NULL}, W_0, W_1, W_2, ... W_{N-1}, W_N. Let W_{NULL} yield no noticeable sensation. Unlike Fechner, let W_0 be the heaviest weight that is not yet, however, heavy enough to elicit a just noticeable sensation. Let W_1 be the weight that can be felt to be just noticeably different from W_0. Weber's Law, based on $\Delta W/W$ as a constant k, provides that $W_1 = W_0 + kW_0 = W_0(1 + k)^1$. Let W_2 be the weight that is just noticeably different from W_1. $W_2 = W_1 + k[W_0(1 + k)^1]$, which equals $W_0(1 + k)^1 + k[W_0(1 + k)^1] = W_0(1 + k)^2$. In general,

$$W_i = W_0\left(1+k\right)^i. \tag{4.6}$$

The value of W_0 is not known in advance, but we often know the value of W_1 in advance. W_1 is the *stimulus* weight that is just noticeably different from its background. Then, given a knowledge of $(1 + k)$, we can derive from W_1 a value of W_0.

We now estimate the sensation-magnitude, S_i, associated with a given weight, W_i. Fechner's Law was given by Equation 4.5 as:

$$S = K\log_e\left(I/I_0\right). \tag{4.5}$$

Replace I_0 by W_0 and I by W_i. And replace S by S_i. Then:

$$S_i = K\log_e\left(W_i / W_0\right). \tag{4.7}$$

We can replace W_i in Equation 4.7 by $W_0(1 + k)^i$ to obtain

$$S_i = K\log_e\left\{\left[W_0\left(1+k\right)^i\right] / W_0\right\}. \tag{4.8}$$

Cancelling W_0 from the right side gives:

$$S_i = K\log_e\left[\left(1+k\right)^i\right]. \tag{4.9}$$

This is a second version of Fechner's Law.

To give a numerical example of how the above argument is consistent with Fechner's Law, it will be helpful if we assign numerical values to K, k, and W_1.

Table 4.3 How a weight intensity, W_i, that increases geometrically is predicted by Fechner's Law to yield a sensation-magnitude, S_i, that increases arithmetically

Name of Weight	*i*	W_i	$W_i - W_{i-1}$	S_i	$S_i - S_{i-1}$
W_{NULL}	n.a.	unknown	unknown	n.a.	n.a.
W_0	0	9.3120	unknown	0.0000	n.a.
W_1	1	9.6333	0.3213	0.0339	0.0339
W_2	2	9.9655	0.3322	0.0678	0.0339
W_3	3	10.3096	0.3441	0.1017	0.0339
W_4	4	10.6651	0.3555	0.1356	0.0339

Let *K*, the coefficient in Equation 4.9, be set at 1.0 for simplicity. Weber used a standard and a comparison weight placed successively on the same finger and held with the hand in a raised position to discover the Weber fraction equal to (1/29) (Weber 1834/1996a, p. 97).

The value of W_1 will be given by the lightest weight in a container that is judged by the lifter to be just noticeably heavier than that same container when it holds nothing. A rough estimate of W_1 for lifted weights was reported by Sanford (1898), and cited by both Titchener (1905b, pp. 82–85) and Woodworth and Schlosberg (1954, pp. 246–247).[16]

Three participants were each given 118 envelopes containing strips of lead varying in weight from 5 to 100 g. They were to sort the envelopes into five piles ordered in such a way that the average weight of the second pile was at a "sense-distance" from the first pile that was equal to the sense-distance between pile 3 and pile 2, pile 4 and pile 3, and pile 5 and pile 4. The first pile would necessarily include the lightest envelope (containing 5 g), but also a number of others. On the first trial, the average weights of pile 1 for participants 1, 2, and 3, were 11.6, 11.3, and 6 g, yielding an average weight of 9.6333 g.

In Table 4.3, Column 1 shows the names given to the six weight intensities used in the Table, namely, W_{NULL}, W_0, W_1, W_2, W_3 and W_4. Column 2 shows the *i*-values associated with the W_i-values in Column 1.

W_{NULL} is the weight intensity that can activate the observer's nervous system but is too small for the observer to detect W_{NULL}. The notation *i* here refers to felt heaviness-levels when $i = 1, 2, 3$ … It is surely semantically unacceptable to assign a value of *i* (which concerns sensations) to W_{NULL} (which concerns no sensations). Hence, the label "n.a.", standing for "not applicable" is assigned to W_{NULL} in Column 2. The weight W_0 is the heaviest weight that nevertheless yields no sensation. The weight W_1 is the weight intensity that is just noticeably different from its background.

Column 3 shows the values of W_i predicted by Equation 4.6:

$$W_i = W_0\left(1+k\right)^i. \tag{4.6}$$

16 Sanford's (1898) course on experimental psychology was the first such course in English to be published. Titchener (1901b, p. xxxii) expressed his indebtedness to Sanford for doing a lot of hard preliminary work that greatly facilitated Titchener's task.

There is no reason why recording-equipment should not be used to estimate the value in grams of W_{NULL}. In practice, this is so rare that the value of W_{NULL} is "unknown" in most psychophysical experiments. So W_{NULL} is listed as having an "unknown" value. Surprisingly, W_0 may be estimated by noting that, from Equation 4.6, $W_0 = W_1/(1 + k)^1$. Sanford (1898) estimated W_1 to be 9.6333 g. Thus, $W_0 = 9.6333/(1 + 1/29) = 9.3120$ g (Column W_i of Table 4.3). The value of W_2 was given, to nine decimal places, by Equation 4.6 as

$$W_2 = (9.3120)\left[1+(1/29)\right]^2 = 9.965482762.$$

The reason for using nine decimal places in the calculation was that it ensured that, in Column 6, the values of sensation-magnitude associated with W_0, W_1, W_2, W_3 and W_4 would differ by an identical amount when taken to four decimal places.[17] So the value of W_2 in Column 3 was 9.9655. Identical derivations were obtained for W_3 and W_4.

Column 4 shows the value of $(W_i - W_{i-1})$ for each value of W_i. For weights $(W_{NULL} - W_{NULL-1})$ and $(W_0 - W_{NULL})$, both values remain "unknown". For the weight W_1, the value $(W_1 - W_0) = (9.6333 - 9.3120) = 0.3213$. For W_2, the value $(W_2 - W_1) = 0.3322$. Identical derivations were obtained for $(W_3 - W_2)$ and $(W_4 - W_3)$. Column 4 shows that the values of $(W_i - W_{i-1})$ are not identical for $(i - 1) = 0, 1, 2$ and 3. In fact each value of W_i, is given, to four decimal places, by

$$W_i = 1.0345 W_{i-1}$$

This means that, as W_i increases, the value of W_i is given by W_{i-1} *multiplied* by 1.0345. This is already implicit in Equation 4.6 because $1.0345 = (1 + 0.0345) = (1 + k)$. So W_i increases *geometrically* as i increases.

Column 5 shows the sensation-magnitudes, S_i, predicted by Equation 4.9:

$$S_i = K \log_e\left[(1+k)^i\right] \tag{4.9}$$

W_{NULL} again received a label of "not applicable". For W_0, Equation 4.9 predicts $S_0 = 0$, no sensation is felt, consistent with the definition of W_0. For W_1, Equation 4.9 predicts that

$$S_1 = K \log_e\left[(1+k)^1\right] = (1.0)\log_e(1.0345) = 0.0339$$

to four decimal places. Identical derivations were obtained for W_2, W_3 and W_4.

Column 6 shows the value of $(S_i - S_{i-1})$ for each value of S_i. S_{NULL} received a label of "not applicable", and so did $(S_0 - S_{NULL})$. Column 6 shows that the

17 These values were obtained using a hand-calculator, the Casio *fx*-991MS, that displayed a maximum of eleven characters.

values of $(S_i - S_{i-1})$ *are* identical for $i = 1, 2, 3$ and 4. In fact each value of S_i is given, to four decimal places, by

$$S_i = 0.0339 + S_{i-1}.$$

This is already implicit in Equation 4.9 because $0.0339 = \log_e(1.0345) = \log_e(1 + k)$. This means that, as W_i increases, the value of S_i is given by S_{i-1} *plus* 0.0339. So, sensation-magnitude S_i increases *arithmetically*. In contrast, stimulus intensity W_i increases *geometrically*.

Fechner's Own Research Findings

General Overview

In his *Elements of Psychophysics*, Volume I, Fechner (1860/1966) discussed past research on the discrimination of small differences in sensation and how they related to his plans for the methodologies he presumed would be needed in future psychophysical research. It was in the context of his discussion of his Method of Right and Wrong Cases that he reported the findings of one experiment, using lifted weights, that he had designed in order to test the validity of Weber's Law. This experiment will here be called Fechner's "large experiment".

In Volume II of his *Elemente der Psychophysik*, Fechner largely discussed how his own law, Fechner's Law, could be derived from Weber's Law, and how both laws were mainly concerned with outer psychophysics. He also asserted, at the end of Volume II, that the theoretical explanation for *why* the two laws were operative in human psychology rested on "inner psychophysics", to be discussed later in this chapter.

Weights were not the only kind of material employed by Fechner himself that were discussed in Volume I. He also reported that it was very difficult in practice to estimate the Weber fraction for temperature differences (tested by dipping two fingers of the same hand alternately into two vessels filled with water differing in temperature). Nevertheless, it seemed that Weber's Law was upheld for the middle range of temperature, but not for very cold or very hot water (pp. 168–175). He also reported a series of attempts to confirm that Weber's Law held for the extensive variable of line-length, whether the lines be perceived visually or tactually (pp. 176–197); these experiments were done in collaboration with his brother-in-law A. W. Volkmann (1801–1877). Their findings suggested that Weber's Law was indeed valid for visual estimates of just noticeable differences in the lengths of two lines viewed *successively*. The two lines, which could be horizontal or vertical, were not drawn on paper but were displayed as distances between compass points viewed from distances of one foot down to eight centimetres. When the compass points were applied to the skin (as if one were measuring a two-point threshold), there was no evidence that Weber's Law was upheld (pp. 196–197); on the other hand, before Fechner's *Elemente* was published, Volkmann (1858) had reported experiments in which he showed that the two-point threshold could be reduced, though not to a large extent, by practice.

His large experiment was something of a disappointment insofar as, in an extensive series of experimental trials in which lifted weights were used as physical stimuli, Fechner failed to demonstrate that Weber's Law was *always* confirmed. Volume I of the *Elements* is in three parts: an Introduction (pp. 1–18); a part on Outer Psychophysics, which includes a long chapter introducing his three psychophysical methods (pp. 19–111); and a final part on Fundamental Laws and Facts (pp. 112–278), the centrepiece of which is a chapter on Weber's Law (pp. 112–199). This chapter is so long that it accounts for about 31% of the whole of Volume I. It is in this chapter that the results of his large experiment using lifted weights will be found (pp. 152–167).

Using Lifted Weights to Examine the Validity of Weber's Law: Fechner's Large Experiment

Fechner (1860/1966) introduced his three methods of studying differential and/or absolute thresholds in the chapter immediately preceding the chapter on Weber's Law. He named them as follows: the Method of Just Noticeable Differences, the Method of Right and Wrong Cases, and the Method of Average Error (p. 60).[18] A quick description of the first of these methods was given by Fechner himself:

> In the applications of the method of just noticeable differences, a person compares the weight of two containers, A and B, by lifting them, after they have first been given slightly different loads. The difference in weights will be felt if it is large enough; otherwise it will be [notated].
>
> (p. 60)

The Method of Average Error, applied to line length, asks participants to judge whether a standard distance is equal to a variable distance. The difference between the variable distance and the standard distance associated with an incorrect judgment is called the raw error; this was the method used by Fechner and Volkmann in the experiments on line length, as judged visually and tactually, that appeared at the end of Volume I of the *Elements*.

The Method of Right and Wrong Cases, Fechner claimed, had probably originated at the University of Tübingen, under the auspices of Karl von Vierordt (1818–1884), who eventually became the Director of the Institute of Physiology there from 1855 onwards. Fechner was referring to a study by the young Christoph Friedrich Hegelmaier (1833–1906), who published an article on the

18 This is the first written appearance of "just noticeable difference" (*ebenmerkliches Unterschied*).

discrimination of line-length using that method, and who may well have been responsible for inventing it (Vierordt acted more as a supervisor to Hegelmaier than as a research collaborator).

Hegelmaier's (1852) article was translated into English by Laming and Laming (1992); it holds interest for memory theorists as well as for psychophysicists, because Hegelmaier showed that the ability to correctly discriminate that a standard line is different in length from a comparison line diminishes as the time elapsing between the perception of the standard line and the comparison line increases. For Fechner, however, the importance of the method of right and wrong cases is that he himself chose it as the most appropriate method for carrying out "very extensive experimentation in the judgments of weight" (Fechner, 1860/1966, p. 62).

The Method of Right and Wrong Cases was sometimes called the "Method of Constant Stimuli" in Fechner's time; this nomenclature was later criticized by Titchener (1905b). The method holds two particular sources of interest for historians of psychophysics. First, as just noted, it was the method employed by Fechner when he presented what was perhaps the first counterbalanced experimental design in the history of psychology. Second, as noted earlier in this chapter, it was Fechner's preferred method to test his theory that the stimulus-difference determined the probability of a correct judgment of difference. Here, the emphasis will be on what Fechner's data on heaviness judgments taught him about the difficulties of carrying out experiments in psychophysics in general.

Fechner designed his own weights, all equal-looking in size, by putting lead or zinc shot into metal containers. In sharp contrast to what Weber had done, Fechner built handles onto his weight-containers. Participants were asked to lift the two weights successively by grasping the handles either with the same hand or using both hands (this was one of the variables in the experimental design of the large experiment). They first lifted one of the weights to a height of about two modern inches (as indicated by a board located just above the table top at which the participant sat), taking about one second to do that lifting; holding it there for a second; then taking a second to put the weight down onto the table again. The other weight likewise took a second to lift, a second to hold there, and a second to put down.

Fechner said therefore that the time to execute a pair of weight lifts was held constant at five seconds, after which a verbal judgment was made as to which felt heavier, the first or second weight. The timing was controlled by having a metronome ticking away in the background. Fechner (1860/1966, pp. 93–96), noting that the two containers were located side-by-side on the table prior to being lifted, went to extraordinary lengths to allow for two biases that might have been affecting the data. One bias had to do with time: would the discrimination data vary with whether a weight was picked up first or second? The other had to do with space: would the discrimination data vary with whether a weight was located on the left or the right when the weights stood side-by-side?

Fechner suggested that there were four combinations of conditions to be considered in attempts to eliminate biases. That is, there were four sources of bias. The heavier weight could be placed:

1. On the left in the container lifted first
2. On the left in the container lifted second
3. On the right in the container lifted first
4. On the right in the container lifted second

(1860/1966, p. 93)[19]

The measure of accuracy used in the Method of Right and Wrong Cases demanded first, the establishment of the number of trials to be included in an uninterrupted sequence of trials. Fechner (1860/1966) preferred to use 64 trials (rather than, say, 100 trials) because "64, as a power of 2, could be broken into a greater number of subdivisions than 100, and I had wanted at first to keep the way open for any kind of partitioning" (p. 92).

In order to derive a score which could include not only correct (or "right") judgments of "heavier" but also "doubtful" judgments, Fechner assigned "each right judgment as two right, each wrong judgment as two wrong, and each doubtful judgment as one right and one wrong" (p. 78). He argued that this was fair because his *modus operandi* was always to measure accuracy in terms of the *proportion* of correct "heavier" judgments out of 64 (if 64 were the number of trials used in a sequence of trials devoted to the same condition).

So he denoted the number of right (*richtig*) "heavier" judgments as r, the number of wrong (*falsch*) "heavier" judgments as f, and then found the proportion $r/(r + f)$ of correct "heavier" responses for the $(r + f)$ trials on the same condition. If $(r + f) = n$, then the proportion $[r/(r + f)]$ can be written as (r/n) and this was a stepping-stone to the terminology Fechner would eventually use to denote both the accuracy *and* the variability of weight discrimination responses.

So, at last, we come to the counterbalanced design. The variable named P is the weight of a standard weight, and there were six values of P, namely 300 g (which equals about 0.6667 lb), 500 g (about 1.1 lb), 1,000 g (about 2.2 lb), 1,500 g (about 3.3 lb), 2,000 g (about 4.4 lb), and 3,000 g (about 6.6 lb). It should be noted that a weight of 7 lb is sometimes the heaviest weight in a butcher's shop for measuring retail purchases, for example, of ground beef. I remember as a child thinking how heavy a butcher's weight of 7 lb felt when I lifted it by grasping it around the middle with my right hand. Serving as his own participant, Fechner found himself subjected to a variety of discomforts and fatigue-states from lifting weights as heavy as 6.6 lb for extended periods; he actually reported the results of some experiments in which he measured his own

19 In some of his analyses of obtained data, Fechner devoted separate discussions to each of these four biases. The numbers of correct "heavier" responses obtained in each of the bias-conditions 1, 2, 3, and 4, were denoted by r_1, r_2, r_3, and r_4 respectively.

pulse-rate after lifting a long sequence of 6.6-lb weights in order to learn, not so much about weight perception, as about fatigue (Fechner, 1860/1966, pp. 252–268).

The counterbalanced design that Fechner (1860/1966) used was described in words on page 153, from which I have drawn a tree-diagram resembling the diagram that a present-day student might draw up as the design for a five-way analysis of variance. The five variables were:

1. The standard weight, denoted by *P*, had six values as shown above, namely, from 300 to 3,000 g;
2. The variable addition to the standard weight, denoted by *D*, had two values, either 0.04*P* or 0.08*P*; so the comparison weight had two values, namely, *P* (1 + 0.04) or *P* (1 + 0.08);
3. The order in which the two weights were lifted had two values; either the standard weight *P* was lifted first, while the comparison weight (*P* + *D*) was lifted second (ascending order); or vice versa (descending order);
4. The way the hands were used to lift the weights had two alternatives, namely, one-handed or two-handed;
5. The hand that was used in single-handed lifting had two alternatives, left or right.

The tree-diagram is shown in Figure 4.1. With (16 × 6) = 96 possible conditions being potential candidates for listing at the bottom of the tree, it was impractical to present all six values of *P* at the top row of the tree. So only one value, *P* = 300 g, is shown. The rest of the diagram, I hope, is self-explanatory; and the number of conditions listed at the bottom of the tree shown in Figure 4.1 is 16. On each of these 16 conditions, 64 liftings were undertaken.

Four remarks will be made about Figure 4.1. First, as just said, there is only room to illustrate one of six values of *P*, the weight of the standard. The design

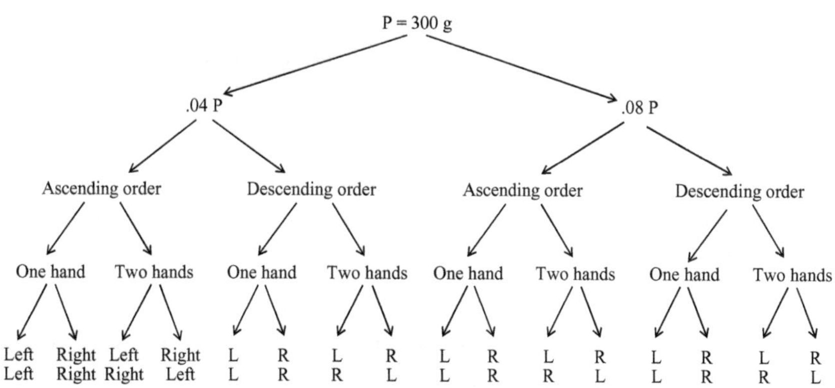

Figure 4.1 Fechner's factorial design for his experiment to test Weber's Law.

resembles what we would now call a $6 \times 2 \times 2 \times 2 \times 2$ factorial design with the factors being *P*, *D*, ascending or descending, ONE or TWO hands, and, for the case of ONE HAND only, whether that one hand was the participant's left or right hand; it was only that one hand that did the lifting of both weights (successively). In the case of TWO HANDS, either the left hand picked up the first weight and the right hand picked up the second, or vice versa. The upshot was that, for each *P*-value, a total of 16 conditions occupied the final row of the tree.

Second, in his discussion of how to eliminate biases, Fechner (1860/1966, pp. 93–96) had shown (in an argument too lengthy to give here) that the best way to minimize, if not eliminate, biases based on which of two side-by-side weights was picked up first, as opposed to second, was to design trials in such a way that each of the four sources of bias was tested equally often. This was the rationale underlying the design shown in Figure 4.1.

Third, the number of liftings included in a "trial" was somewhat ambiguous in Fechner's (1860/1966, p. 153) verbal description of his method. When I wrote about "64" trials, I did not mention that Fechner counted each *lift* in a trial as a "lifting". So in a one-handed sequence of lifting actions, a lift by the left hand of the first weight (one lift) would be followed by a lift, again by the left hand, of the second weight (a second lift). Fechner therefore referred to "two liftings" on that trial.

So the number of "liftings" on a session was given by $2 \times 64 = 128$. On the one-handed condition, therefore, there were 128 liftings using the left hand, and 128 liftings using the right hand, making a total of 256 liftings. Combining these with the two-handed condition led to $256 \times 2 = 512$ liftings. Combining these with whether the heavier weight was presented first or second led to $512 \times 2 = 1{,}024$ liftings. Combining these with whether *D* was $0.04P$ or $0.08P$ led to $1{,}024 \times 2 = 2{,}048$ liftings. Combining these with one of the six values of the standard *P* (in Figure 4.1, it was $P = 300$ g), led to $2{,}048 \times 2 = 4{,}096$ liftings for one *P*-value. Because there were six *P*-values, the total number of liftings in the experiment was $4{,}096 \times 6 = 24{,}576$ liftings.

Fourth, Fechner found that the best way to avoid fatigue was to test himself with only 12 sessions a day (with 64 liftings on each), which equals 768 liftings a day. It took him 32 days to finish the experiment this way; so the total number of liftings in the experiment was $32 \times 768 = 24{,}576$ liftings, confirming the conclusion of the previous paragraph.

Fechner (1860/1966) reported his accuracy findings from his large experiment in his Tables I (p. 154), II (p. 155) and III (p. 157). In that experiment, there was six standard weights with *P*-values of 300, 500, 1,000, 1,500, 2,000 and 3,000 g. Each standard weight was judged to be heavier or lighter than a comparison weight of $[P(1 + 0.04)]$ g or $[P(1 + 0.08)]$ g. If Weber's Law was operative, then the proportion of "right" (i.e., correct) responses, (r/n), should be identical for each of the six standard weights compared with the comparison weight $[P(1 + 0.04)]$ g. The same prediction would hold for the comparison weight $[P(1 + 0.08)]$ g.

Link (1992, pp. 13–17) analysed the mean (r/n)-values obtained by Fechner for all six standard weights compared with each of the two comparison weights. He did so in two stages. In the first stage, Fechner's (1860/1966, p. 155) Table II was reproduced in full in Link's (1992, p. 14) Table 1.1. This table was titled by Fechner (1860/1966, p. 154) as "Number of Right Cases r of the One-Handed Series".

The value of n was given by Fechner as 512. For each of the six P-values, r was given for each of the eight conditions yielded by two comparison stimuli $[P(1 + 0.04)]$ and $[P(1 + 0.08)]$ g, two hands (left and right) and two orders of lifting (ascending and descending). Link calculated the value of (r/n) for each of these $6 \times 2 \times 2 \times 2 = 48$ conditions.

In his Figure 1.3, Link (1992, p. 15) plotted the six P-values on the abscissa, and the six corresponding proportions of right responses on the ordinate of a two-dimensional graph. According to Weber's Law, a flat horizontal line intersecting the ordinate at the value of 0.75 should be the function relating (r/n) to P for each P-value.[20] For comparison weight $[P(1 + 0.04)]$, however, the obtained (r/n)-value for $(P = 300)$ fell below the predicted horizontal line and climbed in a negatively accelerated manner, as P increased. For comparison weight $[P(1 + 0.08)]$, the obtained (r/n)-value for $(P = 300)$ was above that predicted for $[P(1 + 0.04)]$, as well as above the horizontal line. The function climbed, in both cases, in a negatively accelerated manner, as P increased.

In the second stage of Link's (1992) analysis, he showed that these two functions deviated significantly from the horizontal function predicted by Weber's Law. He concluded this from chi-squared tests performed on the frequencies of "right" responses obtained for each P-value for each of the two comparison weights. For $[P(1 + 0.04)]$ g, Link found that chi-squared (23 df) = 44.9, $p < 0.01$. For $[P(1 + 0.08)]$ g, chi-squared (23 df) = 80.9, $p < 0.001$. These findings are consistent with the claim that the (r/n)-values obtained in Fechner's large experiment deviated significantly from those predicted by Weber's Law.

Fechner (1860/1966, pp. 155–157), however, argued that the tendency of the (r/n)-values to rise as P increased was an artefact, which, if corrected, would cause the (r/n)-values to remain constant as P rose. He argued that the artefact came about because of a failure to add the weight of the observer's arm to each P-value. Denote this arm-weight as P_{ARM}. Fechner (1860/1966) made the following claim.

> If we consider the same absolute addition, $[P_{ARM}]$, due to the weight of the arm, added to the standard weights P as they increase (whereas D increases only proportionately to P), then naturally $D/(P + P_{ARM})$, on which the number right depends, will increase as P_{ARM} tends to vanish compared to P in the divisor, that is, as P itself becomes larger. It will stay practically constant from

20 The value 0.75 equals the probability of a correct response obtained in the entire experiment.

> the point where P has become so large that P_{ARM} does not have to be considered as compared to it. This is just as the experiment demonstrates.
>
> (p. 156)

Fechner's (1860/1966) argument can be illustrated by a numerical demonstration. He used standard weights, P, of 300, 500, 1,000, 1,500, 2,000 and 3,000 g. Let P_{ARM} be 2,273 g.[21] Let $D = 0.04P$. Let the value of r (the number of right cases) depend on $[D/(P + P_{ARM})]$, as was stipulated by Fechner in the quotation just given. Then the values of $[D/(P + P_{ARM})]$ as P increases are 0.0047, 0.0072, 0.0122, 0.0159, 0.0187 and 0.0228 with respect to the six P-values given above. These values rise as P rises, and that rise is negatively accelerated. They are therefore consistent with the findings shown in Link's (1992, p. 15) Figure 1.3, where (r/n) was a negatively accelerated rising function of P when the comparison weight was $[P(1 + 0.04)]$.

Fechner's "artefact" can therefore be pinpointed as arising from the assumption that, in the expression $[D/(P + P_{ARM})]$, D in the numerator is assumed to be a proportion of P alone, whereas the denominator, instead of being P alone, was $(P + P_{ARM})$.[22]

Another criticism that can be levelled at Fechner's large experiment was that the proportion (r/n) itself might not be a suitable measure of accuracy in some psychophysical tasks. This is because it is not known beforehand how (r/n) is predicted to behave when, in an experiment, P is manipulated as an independent variable. Klemm (1911/1914) stressed that speculation had to play a somewhat unwelcome role in making inferences from proportions correct to the magnitude of a just noticeable difference:

> The method of right and wrong cases calls for numerous judgments upon one and the same stimulus [here, P] lying near to the difference threshold [here, $P + \Delta P$]. Rather hypothetical discussions in the theory of error are required in order to come to any definite conclusions as to the nature of the difference-threshold from the relation (r/n) between the number of right cases (r) and the total number of cases (n), which results from employing this method.
>
> (p. 223)

This speculation belongs to Klemm because Fechner's theory does not require or use hypothetical discussions based on the theory of error. Fechner's theory, now generally viewed as ideal observer theory, was a marked deviation from the theory of errors. This new recognition of Fechner's theory was put forward by Link (1992, 1994, 2015) and is summarized in Appendix 2 to the present chapter.

21 In the context of a criticism raised by Hering (1875), Fechner (1877, pp. 179–186) later estimated that Hering's arm weighed 2,273 g (5.01 lb).

22 As will be shown in Chapter 8, however, there is an alternative explanation of why (r/n) should rise with P. It is that sensation-magnitude is not a logarithmic function, but a power function, of stimulus intensity.

It should also be noted that Fechner (1886) himself realized that there were occasions on which experimentally obtained data, such as (r/n) proportions, are collected in an effort to confirm the validity of Weber's Law, and yet do not suffice to provide incontrovertible statements about sensation-magnitudes. This 1886 paper was designated to be a reply to two of his most recent critics, Adolph Elsas (1886) of Marburg and Alfred Köhler (1886) of Leipzig.[23]

Fechner's "Parallel Law" to Weber's Law

At the end of Volume 1 of the *Elements of Psychophysics* (Fechner, 1860/1966, pp. 249–273), Fechner ventured into the speculative realm. From the beginning of the book, Fechner insisted (a) that Weber's Law was probably true for differential thresholds, and that apparent deviations from the law meant that the experimenter had not been able to eradicate various sources of error (such as biases based on the order in which two weights were picked up) or had neglected to take into account, in estimating the value of the Weber fraction k, such variables as arm-weight or, in vision, the existence of a perceptible "eye-darkness" (*Augenschwarz*) visible when one closes one's eyes. Fechner also insisted (b) that Fechner's Law could be derived from a knowledge of the value of the Weber fraction k, which was the value of the fraction of I that had to be added to I if $(I + kI)$ were to be just noticeably different from I.

Fechner also insisted (c) that the value of the absolute threshold, served, so to speak, as a pedestal from which to derive the value of k. I_0 (as defined by Fechner) represented the minimal intensity of a stimulus that could make it just noticeably different from its background. It was inevitable that sooner or later Fechner would raise the question of how the Weber fraction, k, was related to I_0, the absolute threshold.

In this theoretical context, Fechner (1860/1964, pp. 249–250) offered his "Parallel Law" to Weber's Law. He expressed his views in three different formats, of which the shortest was: "When the sensitivity to two stimuli changes in the same ratio, the perception of their difference will nevertheless remain the same" (p. 250). Fechner saw this hypothesized "Parallel Law" both as a "transposition of Weber's Law from the external to the internal realm" (p. 250), and as a "bridge between inner and outer psychophysics" (p. 250).

His own attempts to confirm the validity of the Parallel Law involved comparing weight-lifting discrimination data, with and without fatigue induced by carrying other weights. For example, when P was 1,500 g, the non-fatigue condition yielded a higher value of r (the number of correct "heavier" judgments) than did the fatigue condition. But when P was 3,000 g, the opposite finding was obtained, that is, r was greater for the fatigue condition than for the

23 According to Tinker's (1932) list of the names of students whose dissertations were supervised by Wundt, A. Köhler's thesis had the title "On the Most Important Experiments Concerning the Mathematical Formulation of Weber's Psychophysical Law."

non-fatigue condition. One of the spin-offs from these experiments was the series of studies in which Fechner measured his own pulse rate as he became increasingly fatigued over the course of a session devoted to heaviness judgments using fairly heavy weights (e.g., $P = 3{,}000$ g).

More recent attempts to investigate the validity of the Parallel Law involved the manipulation of degrees of adaptation by participants to the sensory objects that are to be compared. Their findings were summarized by Murray and Ross (1988). Fechner was more enthusiastic, about the validity of the Parallel Law, than the data warranted, concluding that weight discrimination is not impaired by fatigue. Holway, Goldring, and Zigler (1938) and Gregory and Ross (1967) found the opposite. With respect to the perception of brightness/lightness, a review article by Cohn and Lasky (1986) on visual sensitivity led Murray and Ross (1988) to conclude that "the Parallel Law cannot be sustained as a useful hypothesis and must be replaced by modern theories of noise and adaptive mechanisms" (p. 82).

Nevertheless, Fechner's (1860/1966, Chapter XII) on the Parallel Law does try to relate the breakdown of Fechner's Law at low intensities of, say, weight or luminance, to a breakdown of the Parallel Law. The chapter provides a "bridge" to Fechner's important distinction between inner and outer psychophysics, the discussion of which occupies just under 30% of Volume 2 of the *Elemente* (pp. 377–547). To this topic we turn.

Fechner on Outer versus Inner Psychophysics

Fechner's Outer Psychophysics

Volume 1 of the *Elemente* has 336 pages of text and Volume 2 has 569 pages. Volume 1 contributes 36.8% to the total work and Volume 2 63.2%. Volume 2 is divided neatly into three sections. The first section of Volume 2, covering pages 1 to 237, is the mathematical derivation of Fechner's Law:

$$S = K \log_e \left(I / I_0 \right) \tag{4.5}$$

There is also a surprisingly wide variety of elaborations of Equation 4.5 to cover cases, for example, of stimuli subjected to the influence of simultaneous brightness contrast. As one elaboration of Fechner's formula 4.5, von Helmholtz (1860/1962) introduced the effect of "neural noise".

At the end of Volume 2, Fechner reported that he was only made aware of Helmholtz's addition of neural noise to Fechner's formula when Fechner was well into writing Volume 2. Fechner obtained permission to delay its publication until after Fechner had a chance to add a postscript (*Zusatz*) giving his opinions of Helmholtz's contribution (Fechner, 1860/1964, pp. 565–569).

The second section of Volume 2 covers pages 238 to 376 and concerns new findings relative to issues dealt with only briefly in Volume 1. These included, first, the establishment of absolute threshold intensity values for stimuli consisting of coloured lights, and a comparison of those thresholds with those for pure tones.[24] Second, there was an unusually detailed discussion of how far Weber's Law was applicable to the extensive stimuli consisting of line-lengths. Third, he corrected some equations used in Volume 1 in the context of his Method of Average Error.

Fechner's Inner Psychophysics

The third section of Volume 2, covering pages 377 to 547, discusses Fechner's inner psychophysics. During the last quarter of the nineteenth century, Fechner's Law, his arguments in favour of Weber's Law, his detailed discussions of his three psychophysical methods, and, above all, his assumptions about the feasibility of psychological measurement, had all played a major role in determining what was taught in psychology departments and what was published in psychology journals. Titchener's (1905a, 1905b) *Experimental Psychology: Quantitative* was a strikingly successful summary of progress in psychophysics over those years. But it was often forgotten that, apart from a short introduction, Fechner's (1860/1966) Volume 1 was entirely devoted to his "outer psychophysics". Indeed, it can be claimed that nowhere in Volume 1 does Fechner present *experimental* evidence that compellingly supports Fechner's Law!

In the history of measurement theory, Volume 1 represents an excellent example of how measurement-units were divided into extensive (distance, line-lengths, two-point thresholds) and intensive (brightness, colours, loudness, pitch, heaviness, heat, warmth, cold). The discussion of how Fechner's Law and Weber's Law might be related to the nervous system was deliberately left as the last issue that Fechner chose to discuss. The fact is that, at the turn of the twentieth century, his "inner psychophysics" was more or less ignored during the heyday of psychophysics.

For example, Klemm (1911/1914) noted that Fechner himself saw his Parallel Law as being a bridge—not the only one—between inner and outer psychophysics. Klemm felt constrained to remark that: "this inner psychophysics of Fechner has remained a world of shadows" (p. 244). A full century after Fechner's death, Scheerer (1987a) wrote: "even in Fechner's lifetime, his inner psychophysics was not taken seriously, and today is all but forgotten" (p. 200).

Because Eckart Scheerer (1943–1997) put forward a strong case that some of Fechner's (1987b) ideas about inner psychophysics foreshadowed some ideas prevalent in modern memory theory, notably hologram/resonance theories of the kind expressed by Pribram (1986), I decided to read Scheerer's (1987b) article devoted to Fechner's inner psychophysics *before* I read Fechner himself on the matter. My experience was as follows.[25] First, I find it expedient to cite

24 These descriptions mesh well with those of Whewell (1847/1967) because, like Whewell, Fechner viewed lights of a given colour and tones of a given frequency as the sensory outcomes of the transmission of vibrations *through a medium*. Fechner also used Fraunhofer's lines as indicative of the wavelengths associated with different hues, just as Whewell had recommended.

25 Scheerer's (1987b) article was published in German in an edited volume resulting from a 1987 conference held at the Karl Marx University in Leipzig to mark the centennial of Fechner's passing. But Dr Scheerer kindly gave me an English translation of that article, which I use here.

directly Scheerer's abstract concerning the four main points that he thought characterized Fechner's inner psychophysics. These were:

> (1) The transformation between neural and mental events is non-linear. (2) There is a cascade of "inner thresholds" intervening between neural and mental events. (3) Neural processes operate according to the oscillation principle... (4) The "psychophysical representation" of mental processes is highly parallel and distributed.
>
> (Scheerer, 1987b, p. 1)

Fechner's contemporaries criticized him for using such a scientifically precise word as "oscillation" in what they considered to be a carefree fashion. Fechner's (1860/1964) first use of the word in his section on "inner psychophysics" concerned the "oscillation" of day and night caused by the daily rotation of Earth in the course of its trajectory around the sun. He quickly moved on to talk about other natural "oscillations", such as the ebb and flow of the tides along the seashore, as well as his observation of the diurnal "oscillation" all of us experience in the daily cycle of "sleeping" and "waking".

In the second section (pp. 238–376) of Volume 2 of the *Elemente*, Fechner (1860/1964) also wrote about "oscillations" in the context of sound waves and light waves. From there it was a short step to elaborating on vibrations in the nervous system. In this context he quoted, with approval, three of Newton's (1730/1970) "Queries" from the *Opticks* (as cited in Fechner, 1860/1964, Vol 2, p. 284).[26] They were Nos 12, 13, and 14, in each of which Newton wondered if "vibrations" in the nerves (as opposed to "animal spirits") transmitted messages from the sense organs to the brain to give rise to sensations (Query 12) and from the brain to the muscles to give rise to movements (Query 13).[27]

Fechner's interest in "oscillations" was actually in keeping with the best science of his time. Newton's Third Law of Motion said that, to every action, there corresponded a reaction. In the middle of the nineteenth century, such notions as the Principle of the Conservation of Mass (an eighteenth-century idea) and the Principle of the Conservation of Energy (a definitely nineteenth-century idea that arose indirectly from engineering problems to do with steam-engines

26 For an illustration comparing modern views with ancient views about how "animal spirits" flowed through tube-like nerves, Murray (1988, Fig. 1–4, p. 41) may be consulted.

27 The first edition of Newton's *Opticks* appeared in English in 1704, but was followed, at Newton's earnest instigation, by a translation into Latin so that scholars in non-English-speaking countries could read it. Fechner's quotations of Queries 12, 13, and 14 were from the Latin, rather than the English version of the *Opticks*. Latin was still alive as the international language of science when Fechner was writing in 1860, but was clearly dying out. In the case of psychology, the importance of psychophysics as a University discipline is demonstrated by the fact that graduate students supervised by Titchener at Cornell University had examination questions that included a translation of a passage from German into English (Titchener, 1905b, pp. 415–416). The five examples given by Titchener were all taken from German writings on psychophysics. The Latin tradition was nevertheless continued in a few places well into the twentieth century. For example, in order to be accepted into the University of Cambridge as an undergraduate in 1955, I had to pass an examination in (elementary) Latin.

and from theories about the physics of heat transfer) were very much in the air. It is not too much a stretch of imagination to see an ebbing-and-flowing of the tides or the rising-and-falling of a sinusoidal wave as evidence that "oscillating" or "vibrating" can have the effect of preserving energy and conferring stability on an otherwise chaotic universe.

As Heidelberger's (2004) Chapter 7 shows in detail, Fechner anticipated many modern ideas about how a physiological system can be prevented from "run-away" behaviour by incorporating organic mechanisms that ensure that erratic behaviour is self-corrected (Wiener, 1948).[28] If such an organic system should prove itself capable of learning, and thereby *acquiring* the ability to correct itself in the event of behaviour that threatens the well-being of the organism, this system can be called "self-organizing". A good example from cognitive psychology is the "self-organizing consciousness" postulated by Perruchet and Vinter (2002). Murray and Bandomir (2001) also emphasized that Fechner's theory of oscillations was consistent with nineteenth-century work on the conservation of energy. The concept of "waves" came to generalize the ideas of "vibrations" or "oscillations". Waves were at the heart of Clerk Maxwell's (1864/1965) discovery of an "electromagnetic spectrum" that included radio waves. But Fechner's leap of *Naturphilosophie*-like imagination, from the sleep-waking continuum to the excitation-relaxation activities of the nervous system, probably irritated some of his scientific colleagues.[29]

Fechner established *mathematically* that a sensation-magnitude was a non-linear function of actual stimulus intensity. He established, to his own satisfaction, that the non-linear relationship was likely to be a logarithmic function. He therefore found himself obliged to surmise at what *location* in the mind/brain system this logarithmic translation from stimulus intensity to sensation-magnitude took place (see also Link, 1992).

In his inner psychophysics, he added a "psychophysical threshold" to his account of outer psychophysics. This threshold could actually be divided into two separate thresholds. Let a weight of intensity W activate the sensory receptors of the hand lifting the weight. Let the weight exceed W_{NULL} as well as the first discriminable weight whose value is W_1. Let the "oscillation" aroused in the nerves leading from the hand to the spinal cord and then to the brain, be sufficient to cross the first kind of threshold (W_{NULL}) in the brain, which suffices to sustain the oscillation for long enough to enable the

28 A system whose level of activity "snowballs" if it becomes overactive is often said to display "positive feedback"; if the system is brought back to normal by some corrective device, the system displays "negative feedback." A biological system that has built-in physiological devices that return the organism to a normal state if the organism is wounded (e.g., white blood cells) or suffering from over-indulgence in certain foodstuffs (one of the jobs of the liver is to correct for chemical imbalances in the body) was credited with having "homeostasis" (Cannon, 1915/1963). In such cases, negative feedback devices and homeostasis ensure a return to a normal level of "equilibrium" in the system.

29 Scheerer (1987b) noted that Fechner's academic position after his illness would have involved no student supervision, lecturing, or participation in examinations.

oscillation to cross the second kind of threshold (W_0) as well. This serves to arouse the *conscious* feeling in that person that he or she is lifting that weight. In other words, the first kind of threshold is purely neural, whereas the second kind is a threshold that an oscillation must exceed if the participant is to be aware of, and feel, a sensation that there is an actual weight, of a given magnitude. In a word, "inner psychophysics" brings *consciousness* into play in a manner that was, to say the least, underplayed in Fechner's exposition of his "outer psychophysics".

Not only does the new importance accorded to conscious experience in inner psychophysics bring Fechner's ideas closer to those of Herbart's, but we know it also influenced Freud (Link, 2001; Scheerer & Hildebrandt, 1988; Tögel, 1988). I was particularly impressed by the fact that Freud (1895/1966) thought to include, in his *Project for a Scientific Psychology*, three classes of neurons. First, a class involving neurons that are temporarily activated by stimuli from the external ("outer") world. Second, a class in which neurons are not only activated by the first class of neurons, but also by neurons sub-serving activations transmitted from locations in one's own body—this second class is capable of retaining memories of those activations. And third, a class in which the neurons received stimulations from the first class and from the second class, but also transformed them into the conscious experiences we call "perceptions". The above account is a shortened version of Ellenberger's (1970, pp. 477–480) description of how Fechner and others influenced Freud's views on how consciousness might be related to the nervous system.

The question that Fechner needed to answer was: Did the transition from a sensory input to a feeling of sensation occur in the sensory receptors of the hand and/or arm? Or was it at the first kind of threshold (W_{NULL}) where peripheral oscillations were transformed into brain oscillations? Or was it at the second kind of threshold (W_0) where brain oscillations were transformed into conscious perceptions? Fechner placed his nonlinear transformation, not at the consciousness level, nor at the level of the peripheral nervous system, but at one or the other of the two "psychophysical thresholds" (W_{NULL} or W_0). This theory suffers from the great Popperian ailment: It is hard to see how it can be *disconfirmed*, even nowadays when we know so much more about brain-processes than did Fechner.

Most of what I have just written about inner psychophysics was derived from Scheerer [1987a, 1987b (English Translation)]. When I actually turned to page 377 of Volume 2 of the *Elemente*, I was struck by the appropriateness of an analogy with the workings of a clock put forward by Fechner in the context of mind/brain matters. There then followed a sequence of 45 pages (pp. 381–426) concerning what could possibly be meant by the words "seat of the soul" (*Seelensitz*) and what was known in Fechner's time about where in the brain that "seat" might be located. Then came surprisingly few pages (pp. 428–439) in which Fechner affirmed that the logarithmic transformation *must* take place at the "psychophysical level"; probably his most striking expression on this matter is given by the following quotation:

> Does a sensation [a conscious perception] depend on activity (*Thätigkeit*) at the psychophysical level, or does a stimulus, following the rules determined by the fundamental formula and the measurement-formula, individually arouse activity at the psychophysical level, from which it will follow, first, that there will be an absolute increase in the psychophysical activity that must necessarily be proportional to that of the stimulus, and, second, that a sensation must be experienced whose intensity must necessarily be proportional to that of the psychophysical activity [?]
>
> (p. 429)

On page 439 comes the chapter on sleep and wakefulness that introduced the notion of "long-duration" oscillations exemplified by diurnal events like sleep and wakefulness, and day and night (pp. 439–449). Nearly all of the remainder of Volume 2 of the *Elemente* concerns cognitive activity, which is prevalent in waking rather than in sleeping states. His passage on how attentional processes determine the primary contents of conscious experience is interesting. For example, Fechner (1860/1964, p. 432) reported how his bedroom contained a large black stove-pipe (used then, as now, in many German houses for heating-purposes). Upon waking, a faint outline of this stove is one of the first things he sees, somewhat murkily. Then, as he slowly wakes up, it comes to dominate his attention. But in the everyday course of events, he is so busy thinking about other matters that he does not even notice the stove-pipe despite its stark visual contrast against the white wall. His conscious experience was determined by attentional processes.

From attention, Fechner (1860/1964) turned to memory. Here Scheerer (1987b) finds parallels with resonance theories of memory, as contrasted with the connectionist approaches to memory that dominated memory research in the 1980s. In fact, in Fechner's (1882) final book on psychophysics, *Review of the Main Points of Psychophysics* [*Revision der Hauptpunkte der Psychophysik*], he elaborated his ideas about memory and stated explicitly that memories were not stored in individual nerve cells, but as networks permeating the cerebral hemispheres. The section on inner psychophysics finishes with a speculative account concerning oscillations whose crests lie above the second kind of psychophysical threshold (the consciousness threshold, W_0). Conscious representations fuse into coherent *Vorstellungen*, while the troughs of those oscillations lie below threshold W_0. Yet they still lie above the first threshold (W_{NULL}) and persist but have no representations in consciousness.

Now we return to the clock analogy. Here is my translation of a passage from Fechner (1860/1964, Vol. 2):

> Although one cannot look into a clock from the outside, the movements of the clock-hands, assuming the clock to be working properly, can be taken as corresponding with the movements of the wheel that controls the clock-hands. For us, these exterior clock-hands represent the stimulus, while the psychophysical movements represent the movements of the wheel. In

> psychophysics we have a reversal of what happened in the clock, because it is as if the clock-hands [the stimulus] were turning the wheel [the psychophysical movements].
>
> (pp. 377–378)

The sheer invisibility of those hypothetical psychophysical movements viewed from outside more or less ensured that the word "psychophysics" would become synonymous with "outer psychophysics" for many years to come.

Fechner's Passing

It is appropriate to close this chapter with a short account of Fechner's final days, as reported by Lasswitz (1896/1902). My translation of his account of Fechner's passing is:

> Fechner took great inner pleasure at the unexpected number of people who helped him celebrate his eightieth birthday in 1881, his golden wedding in 1883, and his fiftieth year as *ordentliche* Professor. He was particularly pleased to be made an honorary citizen of Leipzig; and to be congratulated by the church community in his birthplace, Gross-Sährchen. In his honour the pastor then in charge of that community, whom Fechner had never met, arranged for the church-bells to be rung at the very hour at which Fechner had been born. Fechner wrote to him to say that, because he had been baptized in the church there, he would assume that the sound of the bells could worthily serve as an advance notice of the final day of his life.
>
> That last day came in the year 1887. Even on November 6, Fechner worked as normal. At nine in the evening he had a stroke and regained consciousness, but his strength gradually faded. He went into his final sleep at midday on November 18.
>
> (pp. 109–110)

During his long marriage, he had been close to his wife, née Clara Volkmann (1809–1900). She was sister to A. W. Volkmann, an early colleague of Fechner. In his first self-report about his illness, Fechner (1845/1892) wrote:

> I was almost estranged from my wife, partly because she could not stay in the same dark room that I occupied, and partly because she felt obliged (*musste*) to avoid any sustained conversation with me. So we sat together at table, where I took my place wearing a mask (to keep out the light, because I found a bandage irritating), with almost nothing being said. When I wanted something, I conveyed that want more through gestures than through words.
>
> (as cited by Lasswitz, 1896/1902, pp. 44–45)

In his fourth self-report, Fechner (1884/2004) wrote: "our otherwise happy marriage remained childless" (as cited by Heidelberger, 2004, p. 323). It comes as no surprise to learn that it was Clara who approached her nephew, Johannes Kuntze, with the request that he write Fechner's biography, which he did (Kuntze, 1892).

Summary

Following a survey of how Fechner, as a professor of physics at the University of Leipzig, interacted with the Weber brothers, an account of his famous illness is given that is based on the four self-reports he left us describing his experiences. His "insight" that the monotonic relationship between stimulus intensity and sensation-magnitude was of a logarithmic nature was expounded using his own arguments as given in the second volume of *Elemente der Psychophysik* (Fechner, 1860/1964). His own experiments, as given in the first volume of that work (Fechner, 1860/1966), are summarized with an emphasis on two issues in particular. The first is the importance of his "large experiment" on weight-discrimination in the history of the design of psychological experiments. The second is the importance of distinguishing between two "absolute thresholds". One represents a value, W_{NULL}, where the existence of a weight difference cannot be consciously experienced. W_{NULL} can be associated with an excitation of neural activity. The other threshold, W_0, is where the neural activity does not suffice to elicit a conscious experience of a sensation that *is* discriminable from the sensation of the background. The chapter ends with a discussion of Fechner's controversial "Parallel Law" that, nevertheless, ushered in his distinction between "outer psychophysics" and "inner psychophysics". The latter was rather neglected historically, but Scheerer (1987a) championed the view that inner psychophysics deserved reconsideration as an original contribution by Fechner to modern cognitive psychology.

APPENDIX 1

Fechner's Theory and D. Bernoulli's (1738) Conjecture

Fechner (1860/1964) noted that:

> One can pursue Weber's Law into a still more general field. Our physical possessions (*fortune physique*) have no value or meaning to us as inert material, but constitute only a means for arousing within us a sum of psychic values (*fortune morale*). In this respect, they take the place of stimuli.
>
> (p. 197)

Fechner here acknowledges that Weber's Law (which applies to perceived differences in sensation-magnitude) had a parallel in what is here called Bernoulli's

Conjecture (which applies to perceived differences in the value of one's wealth). Fechner's claim merits discussion.

Daniel Bernoulli (1700–1782) is justly famous for Bernoulli's Principle, which is the foundation on which present-day aviation science is built.[30] Less well known is his article that appeared in a journal published by the St Petersburg Institute entitled, in Latin, "Specimen Theoriae Novae de Mensura Sortis", translated into English by Louise Sommer as "Exposition of a New Theory on the Measurement of Risk" (Bernoulli, 1738/1954). As did many early investigators of probability, Bernoulli wished to advance the understanding of probability theory as applied to gambling, usually with dice or cards. But it was an issue concerning coin-tossing that piqued his particular interest.

The so-called St Petersburg Paradox was very much in the air at that time.[31] It asserted that a certain kind of coin-tossing game could predict that a player could, in theory, win an infinite amount of money. According to Jorland (1987), the rules of the game were as follows:

> A tosses a coin until it falls heads up and gives B one coin if it does so at the first toss, two if at the second, four if at the third, and, in general, 2^{n-1} if at the nth. The value of the game, or B's expectation, is the sum of the products of each expected gain by its probability. Since B has one chance out of two to win one coin, one out of four to win two coins and, in general, one out of 2^n to win 2^{n-1} coins, his expectation is the sum of an infinite geometric series of first term 1/2 but of common ratio 1, hence divergent. The series is not summable; there is no expectation.
>
> (pp. 157–158)

Jorland's (1987) article was devoted to the role played in the history of probability theory, up to 1987, by the following so-called paradox. If the number of trials, n, tends to infinity then so will 2^{n-1}. Let the probability that a coin falls heads on Trial 1 be $(1/2) = (1/2)^1$. The probability it will also fall heads on Trial 2 will be

30 Bernoulli's Principle concerns the flow of fluids, including air. Essentially it exemplifies the Principle of Conservation of Energy, because that principle underlies many phenomena Bernoulli's Principle tries to explain. Here are two examples. First, if air is forced to travel between the walls of two high buildings, it will travel faster between them than it would if the two walls had not been there. Second, if an aircraft wing is designed so that the underside is flat, but the topside is rounded convexly to the extent that the surface distance across the wing is longer on the topside of the wing than it is on the underside, then the air will travel faster over the topside of the wing than it does on the underside. The effect is to give the wings a "lift" when the aircraft accelerates during take-off, so that the plane ascends into the air. The lift comes about because, as the airflow increases in velocity, its density decreases, with the result that the air going over the topside of the wing exerts less pressure on the wing than does the air going under the wing. Bernoulli's Principle was enunciated in his 1738 book on hydrodynamics; it says that, as the velocity of a fluid increases, the density of that fluid, and hence the pressure it exerts, decreases.

31 The paradox had been studied, before Daniel Bernoulli published his 1738 paper, by his brother Nikolaus II Bernoulli (1695–1726), Pierre Rémond de Montmort (1678–1719), and Gabriel Cramer (1704–1752). Details of these early contributions, and of how the paradox has sustained an influence on mathematics up to modern times, were provided by Jorland (1987).

$(1/2)^1 (1/2)^1 = (1/2)^2$. The probability it will also fall heads on Trial 3 will be $(1/2)^1 (1/2)^1 (1/2)^1 = (1/2)^3$. So, by induction, the probability the coin will also fall heads on Trial $(n - 1)$ will be $(1/2)^{n-1}$.

The expectation of how many coins Player *B* will have gained before Trial *n* will be given by the probability that one coin is gained on Trial 1, or two on Trial 2, or four on Trial 3... summed over $(n - 1)$ trials. This expectation can be written in full:

$1(1/2) + 2(1/4) + 4(1/8) + \ldots + (2^{n-2}) (1/2^{n-1})$. It can be written more succinctly as $(1/2) + (1/2) + (1/2) + \ldots + (1/2)$.

It was argued by proponents of the St Petersburg Paradox, therefore, that *B*'s expected gain could approach infinity as $(n - 1)$ approached infinity. Criticisms of the logic behind this argument were discussed in detail by Jorland (1987). But Daniel Bernoulli also added a criticism.

It seemed to Bernoulli that the *subjective* value of the expected amount to be won in a game was a value that was not constant from player to player. The subjective value, or "moral value" (*fortune morale*) as it was often called in the eighteenth century, of a monetary gain would in part depend on how much money a player had to start with. For example, in the four-trial coin-tossing game above, if the first head had not appeared before trial 5, the expectation was $(1/2) + (1/2) + (1/2) + (1/2)$ ducats, that is, two ducats.[32] For a person living on starvation wages, an expected win of two ducats would be far more emotionally satisfying than it would be for a millionaire. Bernoulli, therefore, argued that the level of satisfaction provided by a *gain* of, say, two ducats, would decrease, the larger the player's "fortune" (or "wealth" or "capital"). He therefore distinguished between a "gain" and the "utility" (Latin, *emolentum*) of that gain. That is, he stipulated that there was a mathematical function relating the utility of a gain to the amount of the gain (as measured, in this example, by the number of ducats won). To be even more precise, Daniel Bernoulli conjectured that the utility of a gain on a particular trial was a function of the logarithm, to base *e*, of the number of ducats won on that trial.

This conjecture was proved by Bernoulli in an argument that was initially expressed in terms of a geometrical diagram. Bernoulli proved, using the diagram, that the utility of a gain was a natural logarithmic function of that gain. Figure 4A1.1 is a greatly simplified and a relabelled adaptation of that diagram: The diagram of Figure 4A1.1 has two coordinates. The horizontal abscissa represents the amount of money (or "wealth") a player has at a given moment. The vertical ordinate represents the *utility*, to that player, of that amount. The abscissa is intersected by Bernoulli's curve at the point w_P, which represents the wealth of the poor person before the game begins. To the right of w_P is a point, w_R, which represents the wealth of a rich person before the game begins. After the games begins, both persons make a gain of exactly the same amount, namely, *g* ducats. As shown in Figure 4A1.1, the increase in the utility of *g* ducats for the poor person exceeds the increase in the utility of *g* ducats for the rich person.

32 Ducats were coins made of gold, and therefore especially valuable.

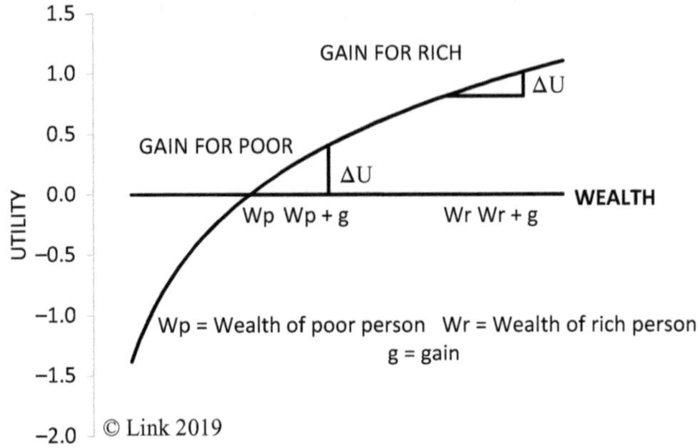

Figure 4A1.1 Bernoulli's illustration relabelled so as to demonstrate that the utility of a gain, *g*, is greater for a poor person than for a rich person.

Turning to algebra, let us denote the utility by U, a constant of proportionality by b_1, the gain by g, and the initial wealth by W. Bernoulli (1738/1954, p. 29) proved that:

$$U = b_1 \log_e W. \tag{4A1.1}$$

Bernoulli's Conjecture was used immediately, by Bernoulli himself, to show that the expectation of player B in the game used in the St. Petersburg Paradox need not be infinite, but take the form of a predicted number of ducats; this is because the logarithmic curve in Bernoulli's Conjecture does not diverge, but converges to a limit as n, the number of trials, tends to infinity.

In his article Bernoulli (1738/1954) went on to apply his theory to risk-taking in insurance, and to the reduction of the risk of loss when sending a cargo of goods by sea (using sail-power) by splitting the cargo between several ships. In modern times, evidence is accumulating that, apart from the rich being less affected by a given gain than the poor would be, the rich also behave differently from the poor both when making gambling decisions and when making investment decisions. Whereas the poor focus largely on the monetary gain they hope to win, the rich are more risk-averse, being very concerned not to lose any of the money they already have. Michael Lewis (2017, Chapter 10, pp. 268–290) shows how Kahneman, Slovic, and Tversky (1982) tried to incorporate individual differences in the personal utility of a gain or a loss into their Nobel-Prize-winning research on how biases and heuristics often influence so-called "rational" decision-making in a detrimental manner. "Heuristics" have been defined as "mental short cuts that often work well but can effectively be gamed by framing questions in a particular way" (Leith, 2017, p. 32).

It must be stressed that Fechner himself clearly acknowledged his indebtedness to Bernoulli (Fechner, 1860/1966, pp. 54, 197–198). Fechner did not present Bernoulli's Conjecture in full; he noted instead that Daniel Bernoulli had shown that the same mathematical function that Fechner used to relate sensation-magnitude to stimulus intensity could also describe "the dependence of *fortune morale* on *fortune physique*" (p. 54). According to Fechner (1860/1966, p. 197), these terms had been introduced first by Laplace and then given further credibility by Simon-Denis Poisson (1781–1840). Fechner (1860/1966) himself wrote that

> a dollar has … much less value to a rich man than to a poor man. It can make a beggar happy for a whole day, but it is not even noticed when added to the fortune of a millionaire.
>
> (p. 197)

Daniel Bernoulli (1738/1954) himself had written that "there is no doubt that a gain of one thousand ducats is more significant to a pauper than to a rich man though both gain the same amount" (p. 24).[33]

APPENDIX 2

Fechner's Theory and Ideal Observer Theory

Fechner's task was to find a measure of random activity in the nervous system that could be used to estimate the probability that a comparison stimulus would correctly be judged to be "heavier" than a standard stimulus. The Gaussian probability density function had, as its scale on the abscissa, values expressed in standard deviation units, namely, -4σ, -3σ, -2σ, $-\sigma$, 0, $+\sigma$, $+2\sigma$, $+3\sigma$, and $+4\sigma$. The ordinate shows the probability of a correct "heavier" response, given the value of σ on the abscissa; these probabilities must sum to one. The Gaussian probability density function had originally been derived for measurements of physical entities such as distances. Fechner wished to ascertain that the function also applied to psychological entities such as a feeling that one weight was heavier than another.

Link (2015) argued that Fechner found a new way of incorporating neural variability into his quantitative account of how a comparison stimulus was judged to feel "heavier" than a standard stimulus. Temporarily denote by E_N the Gaussian probability density function exemplified by Equation 2.1. Let us postulate that E_N can be developed in such a way as to include a variable whose value reflects a fact about neural functioning. Denote this variable by *t*

33 At the end of his article, Bernoulli (1738/1954, pp. 33–39) records how another distinguished Swiss mathematician, Gabriel Cramer, had written to Daniel's brother Nicolas expounding the notion that "*in their theory*, mathematicians evaluate money in proportion to its quantity, while, *in practice*, people with common sense evaluate money in proportion to the utility they can obtain from it" (p. 33). Cramer's work was brought out of oblivion by Stevens (1975, pp. 3–6), who claimed that it anticipated the "power law" of modern psychophysics.

(as Fechner did). As a result of his success at estimating the value of *t*, Fechner was able to replace E_N by a function of his own that involved *t*. Equation 6.4 in Chapter 6 describes this function.

He was also able to estimate the unknown value of σ, that characterized the variability of random events in the nervous system. Recall that the probability of a correct "heavier" response in Fechner's large experiment was 0.75. Imagine we have two Gaussian probability density functions, in each of which the abscissa represents subjective feelings of heaviness associated with one particular weight. The most common heaviness-feeling, represented by the midpoint of the function for weight a, would be the mean feeling, μ_a. Let the bell-shaped function associated with weight a be located on this abscissa. Let there also be placed, to the right of that function, another bell-shaped function with mean weight μ_b. This function for weight b is located there because weight b is objectively heavier than weight a.

Subjectively, however, let the two weights be "just noticeably different" in heaviness. The relative frequency of erroneous responses can be indirectly predicted by mentally "sliding" the two functions together, along their common abscissa, until they overlap. Let the point of intersection at the overlap be deliberately chosen so that the area associated with that point of intersection is 0.75. Let a straight line be dropped perpendicularly from that point of intersection to the abscissa. The point at which that line meets the abscissa is denoted by *t*. That is, *t* reflects a fact about neural functioning, namely, that the overall proportion of correct "heavier" responses in Fechner's large experiment was 0.75.

According to Link (1992, 1994, 2015), Fechner claimed the value of *t* to be:

$$t = \mu_a + (\mu_a - \mu_b) / 2. \tag{4A2.1}$$

Link (2015) wrote that *t* can be considered to be what we now call a decision-threshold:

> Fechner postulated that a (decision) threshold, *t*, for deciding which weight was the larger existed exactly midway between μ_a and μ_b. … A lifted weight sensed to be greater than this threshold was thought to be the heavier weight.
>
> (p. 470)

Fechner's incorporation of *t* into his version of the Gaussian probability density function was influenced by the fact that Gauss actually used two different measures of dispersion, σ and *h*. The standard deviation, σ, *increased*, the wider the spread of the density function. The measure of precision, *h*, *decreased*, the wider that spread. The inverse relationship between σ and *h* follows from:

$$h = 1 / (\sqrt{2})\sigma. \tag{4A2.2}$$

Let D be the objective difference between a comparison weight and a standard weight. In the present example, D is small enough to be only just noticeable by a participant. Fechner demonstrated that

$$t = hD/2. \tag{4A2.3}$$

Fechner incorporated Equation 4A2.3 into his version of the Gaussian probability density function as described in Chapter 6 by Equation 6.4.

"Ideal observer theory" is a special case of signal detection theory (SDT), the historical origins of which were outlined by Link (2015, pp. 472–473). According to SDT, a sensory discrimination can be described as the feeling that the sensation of a "signal-presented-in-noise" differs from the sensation of "noise" itself. Nearly all late twentieth-century versions of SDT have in common the notion that "noise" (N), and "signal-presented-in-noise" (S + N), can be represented by two overlapping Gaussian probability density functions with the same abscissa. This abscissa represents the subjective strength of the sensation associated with N as well as that associated with S + N. A "criterion value" is assigned to the abscissa in such a way that, IF a sensation is judged to exceed the criterion value, THEN the sensation was judged to have the signal as its source.

The criterion value is moveable, because its location can be influenced by such variables as the ratio of the number of (S + N) trials to the number of (N) trials; the strength of a participant's desire to avoid errors such as false alarms or missed signals; and the amount by which a participant's vigilance has been lowered by fatigue.

An "ideal observer" would be a participant unaffected by biases like these. Because Fechner's setting of t was based on an *obtained* probability of a correct "heavier" judgment, it is analogous to a criterion setting whose value is uninfluenced by these biases. Fechner's theory, therefore, can be viewed as an example of ideal observer theory.

5 Psychophysics at Göttingen

G. E. Müller (1850–1934)

G. E. Müller's Reputation among Historians of Psychology

At the end of Haupt's (1998) article on G. E. Müller's influence on American experimental psychology, Edward Haupt (1936–2001) specified that mid-twentieth-century writers on the history of memory theory, notably E. S. Robinson (1893–1937) and J. A. McGeoch (1897–1942), focussed on interference theory as the central building block of neobehaviorist theories of memory. Intrinsic to such theories was the distinction between "proactive inhibition" and "retroactive inhibition" as sources of interference when trying to recall material that was learned by heart, in a laboratory experiment, hours or days earlier. What puzzled Haupt was the almost complete neglect of G. E. Müller's nineteenth-century research on proactive and retroactive inhibition.

Müller's role in the early history of memory research was summarized by Murray (1995) as follows:

> Ebbinghaus (1885/1964) had invented nonsense syllables, shown that the amount retrievable of lists of nonsense syllables or of poetry was high immediately following learning, but fell rapidly to an asymptote as time progressed, and demonstrated that practice at memorizing carried out in a number of short bursts led to faster memorization than did a single extended period of practice receiving the same amount of time. G. E. Müller and Friedrich Schumann (1893) had shown how rhythmizing and grouping facilitate memorizing and Müller and Pilzecker (1900) had introduced the term "retroactive inhibition" to refer to interference with retrieval of some target item X, interference that seems to be caused by events (which may or may not involve memorizing) intervening between the time of learning X and the time of its retrieval ... This early research is reviewed by Murray (1976).
>
> (p. 53)

It may be added that Müller and Pilzecker (1900) also introduced the words "proactive inhibition," "perseveration", and "consolidation".[1]

The experiments that demonstrated proactive and retroactive inhibition involved "paired-associates learning". A pair of stimuli are to be associated in memory (for example, a letter-number pair such as K-9; a word-pair such as pencil-gasoline; or a nonsense syllable-pair such as mif-tas). A varied number of pairs constitute a "paired-associates list". Two paired-associate lists may be learned in sequence. When the lists contain common elements, an interaction between the learned lists influences recall of the elements. When the second list is tested (again) after the second list has been learned, the performance may exhibit interference from memories of the first list. This is said to demonstrate "proactive inhibition". When the first list is tested after the second list has been learned, the performance may exhibit interference from memories of the second list. This is said to demonstrate "retroactive inhibition".

Haupt asked why American researchers on human memory said so little about the paper by Müller and Schumann (1893), who designed an early version of a paired-associate task (called the *Treffermethode*, or method of hits).[2] As noted, Müller and Pilzecker (1900) clearly distinguished between *rückwirkende Hemmung* ("backward-working inhibition", i.e., retroactive inhibition) and *vorwärtswirkende Hemmung* ("forward-working inhibition", i.e., proactive inhibition).

In the course of his research on the history of memory experimentation, Haupt came across Müller's research on psychophysics.[3] As noted in Chapter 4, Woodworth and Schlosberg's (1954) textbook had lengthy sections on psychophysics and Woodworth's (1938) original first edition of that textbook had even more. Haupt learned that Woodworth's textbook on psychophysics was influenced by Guilford's (1936) text on psychometrical methods, which itself was influenced by the course on psychophysics that Guilford took from Karl M. Dallenbach (1887–1971). Dallenbach was taught by Titchener and used Volume 2 of Titchener's (1905b) *Experimental Psychology* as a textbook. And—this is the point I wish to get to—Titchener explicitly acknowledged that the psychophysical views espoused in his manuals for the guidance of students and instructors in psychophysics were based on those of Müller's psychophysics rather than those of Fechner.

Haupt (1998, pp. 33–34) conveniently lists exactly what those sources were: they were Müller's (1878) book titled *Zur Grundlegung der Psychophysik* [Towards

1 Interference can also be exhibited when participants cannot recall whether an element came from the first or second list. A review of the late twentieth-century literature on this matter was provided by Murray (1995, pp. 118–123).

2 This task had actually first been explored by Calkins (1894a, 1894b). Mary Whiton Calkins (1863–1930) taught for most of her career at Wellesley College near Boston. She thought at one time of studying with Müller, but decided instead to study with William James at Harvard. She became the first female president of the APA in 1905.

3 G. E. Müller's (1873) PhD thesis, submitted to the University of Göttingen, was about sensory attention.

a Fundamental Basis for Psychophysics], Müller's (1879) article on the use of the method of right and wrong cases to establish two-point thresholds on the skin, and Müller's (1904) book titled *Die Gesichtspunkte und die Tatsachen der psychophysischen Methodik* [The Points of View and the Facts of the Psychophysical Methods]. In a word, classical psychophysics, that had indubitably originated with Fechner, were probably propagated internationally as much through G. E. Müller's writings on psychophysics as through Fechner's. A discussion of the contents of Müller's 1878 and 1904 books will be presented in Chapter 6.

A particular question runs through this nearly century-long sequence of book-length accounts of psychophysics. The question was raised by Fechner (1860/1966) himself, in his discussion of the method of right and wrong cases in Volume 1 of the *Elements* (pp. 73–108), and continued to Woodworth and Schlosberg's (1954, pp. 192–266) discussion of the same issue. It is the question of whether the distribution of errors in psychophysical judgments can be Gaussian.

In the present chapter, however, we focus on two collaborative studies carried out by Müller, one with his research assistant, Friedrich Schumann (Müller & Schumann, 1889), and one with an American graduate student, Lillien J. Martin (Martin & Müller, 1899). Both studies clearly show that results in psychophysical experiments with lifted weights are not entirely determined by the order in which two weights are lifted successively, or by such "physical" factors as their objective weights in grams. The judgments made in psychophysical tasks can also be determined by "psychological" factors such as expectation, or by individual differences in mental processing that occur during the decision-period in which a judgment of "heavier", "equal", or "lighter", is formulated. That is, these are just as relevant to an evaluation of Fechner's inner psychophysics as they are to his outer psychophysics. Indeed, for Titchener (1905b), Müller and Schumann's (1889) experiments demanded that

> we must have recourse to subcortical preadjustments and to dispositions of the motor apparatus. The result of this change of attitude is the opening up of a new set of problems, and the writing of a new chapter in psychophysics.
> (p. 345)

Müller and Schumann (1889) on Expectation ("Set") in Psychophysical Tasks

Friedrich Schumann (1863–1940) worked in Müller's laboratory until obtaining his *Habilitionsschrift* there in 1892. He was then hired as a research assistant to Carl Stumpf (1848–1936) at Berlin, where he stayed from 1894 to 1905. His later career was more important in the development of Gestalt psychology than is often realized. Not only did the Gestalt psychologists Kurt Koffka (1886–1947) and Wolfgang Köhler (1887–1967) work alongside Schumann while obtaining their doctoral degrees with Stumpf, but Max Wertheimer (1880–1943), often recognized as the founder of Gestalt psychology, also worked with Stumpf from 1902 to 1904.

The weights that Müller and Schumann used were actually those used by Fechner himself. The purpose of their article was laid out in their first sentence. My translation of Müller and Schumann (1889) is as follows:

> Following Fechnerian procedures, if one has completed a lengthy series of trials lifting weights that are relatively heavy, and then turns to lighter weights, the latter, as Fechner … has observed, seem strikingly light. If, during the experimental trials, the weights are lifted briskly, then, after a series of lifting heavy weights, a lighter weight might be lifted so high that the participant is taken totally by surprise at first and finds it hard to decide anything about the relationship that had existed between the two weights that had been lifted quickly one after the other. This phenomenon clearly showed itself even when the trials with the light weights were undertaken a full 24 hours later than the trials with the heavy weights. Plainly, therefore, the force [*Impulse*] needed to lift the heavy weights had been so well practiced that it even showed itself in the lifting of the light weights. Moreover, this *Einstellung* [defined immediately below] of the force needed to lift a weight can also be demonstrated if one snatches up a light weight A in rapid alternation with a heavy weight B. If one suddenly replaces A with a weight C that, instead of being heavier than A as B had been, actually equals A in weight, then C will be lifted with the same force as had hitherto been used to lift B, so that C, as a result, appears markedly lighter than A [despite having the same weight as A].
>
> (p. 37)[4]

The word *Einstellung* (pronounced "ine-shtell-ung") has a variety of meanings in German. For example, it can mean the recruitment of a soldier, or a work-stoppage. My personal copy of *Cassell's German and English Dictionary* (Breul, 1940) also offers the English translations "attitude taken up" and "adjustment". The sentence involving *Einstellung* in the above translation could be translated as "moreover, the attitude taken up by the participant concerning the force needed to lift a weight". An alternative translation could be "moreover, the adjustment the participant is required to make to the force needed to lift a weight".

It has, however, become customary to translate *Einstellung*, when used in the context of scientific psychology, into the word "set". For example, in Duijker and van Rijswijk's (1975, Vol. 3, p. 64) trilingual psychological dictionary, *Einstellung* is translated as "mental set".[5] So perhaps the best translation of the

4 Translator's note: "Snatch at" is the translation offered by Breul (1940) of "*ruckweise*," the word used by Müller and Schumann when instructing their participants how to lift the weights. Here, I have used "lifted briskly." Please note that "*ruckweise*" has little to do with the German word for the back of the body, which is *das Rücken*, or with "backward-working" as in *rückwirkende Hemmung*.

5 Interestingly, in modern psychometrics, an "attitude-scale" is translated as an "*Einstellungsskala*" and an "attitude-questionnaire" as an "*Einstellungsfragebogen*." An employment interview is an "*Einstellungsgespräch*."

sentence would be "moreover, the participant sets himself or herself to adjust the force needed to lift a weight".

Two pages later, Müller and Schumann (1889) wrote explicitly that the purpose of their paper was

> not to offer a thorough investigation of Weber's Law but rather to improve our understanding of the influence, and effectiveness, of the *Einstellung* of the lifting-force, and especially to establish what the variables are that determine how well measurements can be made concerning comparisons between [lifted] weights.
>
> (p. 39)

Accordingly, they made some changes to Fechner's methodology, as follows, but continued to use the method of right and wrong cases.

Although the weights used by Fechner were now in the possession of the Göttingen laboratory, the experimenters were obliged to manufacture six more containers filled with metal and provided with handles on top. The weights were lifted at a table covered with a thick textile that served to reduce noise-cues and vibrations. The weights were not lifted as high as Fechner did, but only to a minimum height. The participant sat at one side of the table and was instructed to position his arm so as to keep as regular and as unvaried as possible the actions of lifting the weights. For investigating the effects of *Einstellung*, Fechner's timing of his lifting was deemed too slow, so they changed the ticking of a metronome to be more rapid. Furthermore, it was deliberately arranged that the participant "briskly lift and lower" each weight.

Seated behind a screen at the table, opposite the participant, was the investigator [*Protocollant*], whose main job was to reposition the weights between trials, as well as to redo any trials that were not properly conducted. For example, the participant would often grip the weight by one side of the handle, rather than in the middle. It should be recalled that, on almost all trials using the method of right and wrong cases, two weights were lifted, a "standard" and "comparison". A final important difference between Fechner's (1860/1966) method and that of Müller and Schumann (1889) was that Fechner permitted judgments of "heavier", "lighter", or "doubtful", whereas Müller and Schumann (1889, pp. 41–42) permitted "heavier", "heavier or equal", "equal", "lighter or equal", and "lighter". Which categories were used depended on the experiment; but in what follows, all of the categories "heavier", "equal", and "lighter" will be needed.

A record was always kept of which weight was lifted first, when only one hand was used ("one-handed trials"—the *same* hand was used to pick up both the first and second weights). But in several of their experiments, participants were instructed to lift the two weights simultaneously, one with each hand ("two-handed trials"). Müller and Schumann (1889, pp. 42–44), in order to investigate *Einstellung* effects, chose a general design that involved three sub-experiments, labelled here as SE_1 (two-handed), SE_2 (two-handed), and SE_3 (two-handed).

Using this design, the first *Einstellung* sub-experiment, SE_1 (two-handed), was carried out with the help of a participant named Wh., who knew nothing about the theoretical aims of the experiment and had not taken part in any previous weight-lifting experiments.

In SE_1 (two-handed), a standard weight of 676 g—which the authors were at pains to point out included the weight of the container as well as its contents—was paired irregularly (*unregelmässig*, presumably meaning roughly "randomly") with one of six comparison-weights, namely, 626, 676, 726, 776, 826, and 876 g, with five trials devoted to each comparison. Please note that this design includes the rare case where a comparison weight of 676 g *equals* the standard weight of 676 g. The standard was always to the right of the participant and was always the first weight to be lifted. The results were reported as follows

> the comparison weight 876 gm was judged as "greater" than the standard weight 676 gm on each of the five trials; the comparison weight of 826 gm seemed "greater" than the standard weight of 676 gm on four of the five trials, and "equal" on one of the trials.
>
> (Müller & Schumann, 1889, p. 43)

In fact, all of Müller and Schumann's data are reported like this, with the experimental results embedded in the text. There is not a single table in that section of the article where the *Einstellung* effect is demonstrated. So I present two tables compiled from Müller and Schumann's text.

Table 5.1 Part A shows the typical layout used in SE_2 (two-handed), which was their demonstration that the *Einstellung* effect can be obtained in a two-handed experiment. For 30 trials, the comparison weight, a heavy 2,476 g, is lifted with the left hand *at the same time as* the standard weight, 676 g, is lifted with the right hand. Then, on the 31st trial, the *Protocollant*, without the participant's knowledge, changes the comparison weight of 2,746 g to one weighing 926 g. Although this 31st trial still involves a comparison weight, 926 g, that is physically heavier than the standard weight of 676 g, it was, nevertheless, mistakenly judged to be "lighter" than the standard weight; on the 32nd trial, the comparison weight 876 g was judged "lighter" than the standard weight of 676 g; and on the 33rd trial, the comparison weight of 826 g was judged "lighter" than the standard weight of 676 g.

All the judgments of "lighter" obtained in SE_2 (two-handed) represented the effects of a "mental set" that predisposed the participant to believe, or expect, that the weight on the 31st trial would demand the same effort, in the physical lifting of the two weights, as was required for the first 30 trials of the demonstration.

SE_3 (two-handed) replicated the *Einstellung* effect using blocks of only five *Einstellung* trials followed by three comparison trials. The 2,746-g weight served as a comparison and the 676-g weight served as the standard for five trials without judgement. These five trials were followed by three trials using one comparison weight per trial of 926, 876, and 826 g. The findings are shown in Table 5.1 Part B. After only five *Einstellung* trials, the results are less tidy than

Table 5.1 Demonstrating an *Einstellung* effect: Sub-experiments SE_2 and SE_3 (two-handed lifting) with Participant Wh

Part A: First Einstellung-*experiment. Second sub-experiment,* SE_2 *(two-handed) with Participant Wh.*

	Lifted simultaneously			
	Number of trials	Comparison weight (left hand)	Standard weight (right hand)	Judgment of comparison weights
Einstellung trials	30	2,476	676	(no judgments)
Comparison trials	1	926	676	"lighter"
Comparison trials	1	876	676	"lighter"
Comparison trials	1	826	676	"lighter"

Part B: Three replications using 5 instead of 30 Einstellung *trials. Third sub-experiment,* SE_3 *(two-handed), with Participant Wh.*

Number of trials	Comparison weight (right hand, lifted second)	Standard weight (right hand, lifted first)	Judgments of comparison weights		
			"Lighter"	"Equal"	"Heavier"
5	2,476	676	(no judgements)	(no judgements)	(no judgements)
1	926	676	1	0	0
1	876	676	0	1	0
1	826	676	0	1	0
5	2,476	676	(no judgements)	(no judgements)	(no judgements)
1	926	676	0	1	0
1	876	676	0	1	0
1	826	676	1	0	0
5	2,476	676	(no judgements)	(no judgements)	(no judgements)
1	926	676	0	1	0
1	876	676	1	0	0
1	826	676	1	0	0

Table 5.2 Demonstrating an *Einstellung* effect: Third sub-experiment SE_3 (one-handed lifting) with Participant P

Number of trials in each block	*Comparison weight (right hand, lifted second)*	*Standard weight (right hand, lifted first)*	*Judgments of comparison weights*		
			"Lighter"	*"Equal"*	*"Heavier"*
10	2,476	676	(no judgments)	(no judgments)	(no judgments)
1	926	676	1	9	0
1	876	676	3	7	0
1	826	676	4	6	0

after 30 *Einstellung* trials, but the main finding leaps out, nevertheless. Not once was a comparison weight that objectively weighed more than the standard weight judged to be subjectively "heavier" than the standard weight.

Table 5.2 represents analogous *Einstellung* effects when the weights are lifted with one hand only. Like Participant Wh. in the two-handed study, a new participant, P, was naïve with respect to the goals of the investigator and was unpractised at the task. The 676-g standard weight was always located on a participant's right; it was always the first weight to be lifted; and it was always the right hand that did the lifting. Then the same hand, the right hand, briskly picked up the comparison weight which was always located on the participant's left side. As in Table 5.1, the standard weight was always 676 g, the comparison weights were 926, 876, and 826 g, and the *Einstellung*-inducing heavy weight was 2,476 g.

In SE_1 (one-handed), the comparison stimulus was always heavier than the standard. The 876-g weight was always judged "heavier" than the 676-g standard on ten trials. The 826-g weight was judged "heavier" than the 676-g standard on seven out of the ten trials, "equal" to it on two of the ten trials, and "lighter" than it on one of the ten trials.

In SE_2 (one-handed), the initial *Einstellung* trials consisted of 30 trials with the 2,476-g weight as the comparison, and a standard weight of 676 g. The comparison weights on each of the single trials were 926, 876, and 826 g, with the standard weight continuing to be 676 g. The results of SE_2 (one-handed) were not reported but I assume that the comparison was always judged "lighter" than the standard, as had been the case with two-handed judgments.

In SE_3 (one-handed), each block of trials consisted of 10 *Einstellung* trials followed by the three comparison trials, each devoted to one of the 926 g, 876 g, and 826 g comparison weights. The judgments obtained in ten such blocks of trials are shown in Table 5.2.

In Table 5.2, I follow Müller and Schumann's (1889, p. 45) strategy of reporting the number of "heavier", "equal", or "lighter" judgments associated with each comparison weight individually. One particular finding will be stressed. In the text, SE_1 (one-handed) was described as showing that comparison stimuli of

926, 876, and 826 g were, in the main, judged "heavier" than the 676-g weight. But, in Table 5.2, SE_3 (one-handed) was described as showing that the comparison stimulus was *never* judged "heavier" than the standard.

More convincing, however, than any references to the scholarly literature is Müller and Schumann's (1889) account of how we estimate weights in real life, say, when buying a large bag of sugar or flour:

> One can reconstruct the process that takes place when one wishes to estimate the absolute weight of objects. As can easily be observed, the object is taken by the hands and the purchaser lifts it several times for a small distance. The object may have already provided the purchaser with a visual impression, for example, that the object can be estimated to weigh 2 kg. The purchaser now applies this *Vorstellung* to lift the object with a force appropriate to lifting, just for a short distance, a 2-kg weight.[6] If this force suffices to achieve this lift, the purchaser will deem that his estimate was correct; but if the force does not suffice to lift the object, and/or the object is too large in dimensions to be conveniently lifted, then the person will try again but now use a force that has been increased to 3 kg (adding a kg), and so on.
>
> (my translation, p. 57)

I add here that we often estimate the weight of small objects by lifting them on the palm of one hand, moving the hand up and down, thereby obtaining our self-provided estimate of the speed required to raise and lower the weight. In English, we use the verb "to heft" to refer to this practise. In French, the word "*soupeser*" is used. In German, the task of repetitive lifting [*mit der Hand wägen*] was investigated neither by Fechner (1860/1966) nor by Müller and Schumann (1889).

Müller and Schumann's (1889) article was also recognized by Boring (1942, pp. 524–535, esp. pp. 532–533) as a contribution to our understanding of the physiological apparatus underlying kinaesthetic sensations. More than a third of their article (pp. 64–91) was devoted to a discussion of their belief that heaviness-judgments depended on the speed of lift and were related to the general topic of "internal" sensations arising from muscles, tendons and joints that activate sensory receptors.

Martin and Müller (1899) on Individual Differences in Psychophysical Tasks

Lillien Jane Martin (1851–1943) was born in Oleana, New York State, and obtained her undergraduate degree at Vassar College, situated at Poughkeepsie on the Hudson River upstream from New York City. The college was founded

6 Translator's note: Müller here uses the Herbartian term, *Vorstellung*. Haupt (1998) asserted that "Müller is virtually the last Herbartian" (p. 50). Here, Haupt referred to Herbart the mathematical psychologist, rather than to Herbart the educationist.

in 1861 by the philanthropist Matthew Vassar (1792–1868) and Martin obtained her BA degree there before starting a brief career as a high-school teacher of science. She went to study psychology with G. E. Müller at Göttingen from 1894 to 1898, and her research was written up the following year. Apparently, this was the only study Müller ever published in which he listed himself as the second author.[7]

Martin and Müller's (1899) monograph was titled *Toward the Analysis of Sensitivity to Differences. Experimental Contributions* [*Zur Analyse der Unterschiedsempfindlichkeit. Experimentelle Beiträge*]. Its 233 pages were summarized at some length both by Angell (1899) and by Titchener (1905b, pp. 300–309). Titchener wrote that "there can be no doubt that the work of Martin and Müller will stand as a landmark in the history of experimental psychology" (p. 309).

I prefer to start with a passage that Martin and Müller (1899, pp. 128ff) wrote towards the end of their monograph even though, in order to understand that passage properly, one needs to have studied some of the conclusions they arrived at earlier in their monograph. Here is the passage as paraphrased by Angell (1899):

> Excluding errors of space order … there are no less than five possible influences at work in determining judgments on "hefted" weights when all outer and inner conditions were made as constant as possible.
>
> 1. The general tendency of judgment, resulting in more correct judgments when the variable weight [i.e., the comparison] follows the standard.
> 2. Influence of the type—positive and negative.
> 3. Influence of the Fechnerian time error—positive and negative.
> 4. Influence of the size of the variable weight in the preceding judgment.
> 5. Influence of change of criterion for delivering judgments. Of all these, the only one that is theoretically eliminable is the Fechnerian time error.
>
> (p. 270)

The meanings of Influences 1 through 5 are as follows.

Influences 1 and 2: The "General Tendency of Judgment" and "Type—Positive and Negative"

In all that was written above about weight comparisons, little was said about the cognitive processes that enter into a judgment that a comparison stimulus is heavier than, equal to, or lighter than a standard weight. Let us assume that any

7 One of Wundt's American doctoral students, Frank Angell (1857–1939), had opened the Department of Psychology in 1892 at Stanford University in California. Angell was glad to hire Martin as an assistant professor because of her knowledge of the laboratory at Göttingen, and to put her in charge of designing, and obtaining apparatus for, the new laboratory. Martin's (1906) floorplan of that laboratory was reproduced by Hilgard (1987, p. 35). Martin left academia in 1916 to become a clinical psychologist in San Francisco. A full-length biography of Martin, stressing her dedication to good causes, was written by De Ford (1948).

errors in judging that the comparison weight (Co) was heavier than, equal to, or lighter than the standard weight (St) had *only* four possibilities, namely, the four combinations of Fechner's two time errors and two space errors.

Let *D* denote (Co–St). Fechner (1860/1966) wrote.

> I shall ... take *p*, the influence of temporal order of lifting, as positive when the weight that is lifted first appears heavier. I shall call it negative when the second container, independent of *D*, appears as the heavier. I shall call the effects of the spatial factors, [*q*] positive, when the left-hand container appears as heavier and negative when the right-hand container appears heavier. If I say, for example, that the influence of *p* was +10 gm, this means that, apart from [the question of which was] the truly heavier weight, the first container appeared 10 gm heavier than the second one.
>
> (p. 96)

Fechner's definitions of "positive" and "negative" concerned the *order* in which the two weights were lifted in the method of right or wrong cases. A quite separate matter is whether the *first* weight lifted was the standard or the comparison weight. Angell (1899) used the word "variable" instead of "comparison". He conjectured that:

> If there [were] practical equality of "lighter" and "heavier" in the order Standard—Variable, there should be [practical equality] in the order Variable—Standard; or, if there are more "lighter" judgments in the order Standard—Variable than in Variable—Standard, there ought to be correspondingly more "heavier" judgments in the order Variable—Standard: but the "heavier" in Standard—Variable about balance those in Variable—Standard.
>
> (p. 267)

A third influence on performance is whether St > Co or Co > St. Titchener (1905b, pp. 302–303) preceded his discussion of Martin and Müller's (1899) findings by making the following prediction. Let the number of trials, *n*, be the same for conditions when St > Co as for conditions when Co > St. Titchener proved that, IF Fechnerian time errors and space errors *alone* constituted all the errors in a weight-lifting task, using the method of right or wrong cases, THEN the obtained (r/n)-value when St > Co would equal the obtained (r/n)-value when Co > St. The proof relied on Fechner's distinction between *p* and *q*, "positive" and "negative" time errors and space errors.

Martin and Müller's (1899) data were not consistent with Angell's (1899) conjecture or with Titchener's (1905b) later prediction. Instead, their data led them to emphasize two novel findings. First, the number of correct judgments when the comparison weight was lifted second exceeded the number of correct judgments when the comparison weight was lifted first. Second, there were two types of participant, a "positive" type who gave more correct responses when the standard weight was objectively the heavier of the two weights, and a "negative" type who gave more correct responses when the standard weight was objectively the lighter of the two weights.

The expression "general tendency of judgment" referred to the first of these findings, namely, that if the comparison weight was lifted second, *most* participants gave more accurate judgments than they did if the comparison weight was lifted first. To quote Angell (1899), who used the word "reagent" as a synonym for a "participant":

> The influence producing this effect is termed the general tendency of judgment; it is present in all reagents, and comes from the prevalence of *absolute* impressions of heaviness or lightness,—i.e., impressions in which no comparison with another definite weight takes place ... The evidence for the existence of such absolute impressions comes, of course, from the reagents ... One reagent remarked "if I decide that a weight is clearly greater or smaller than another, the judgment does not rest on a difference in the weights but chiefly on the fact that weight appears to me in a general way very large or very small" [p. 45 in Martin and Müller].
>
> (p. 267)

Titchener (1905b) described the introduction by Martin and Müller of this new concept of "absolute impressions" as being "simple and convincing" (p. 304). He presented, in German only, a key paragraph from Martin and Müller (1899, p. 45), a paragraph that announces both the existence of absolute impressions *and* the subdivision into two types of individual participants.[8] Here is my English translation of that paragraph:

> The anomalous individual differences, their particular modes of behaviour, and their dependence on the type [of the reagent] can be accounted for in a completely satisfactory manner if one starts with the fact, confirmed by self-observation, that on many occasions judgments about the [two] weights are determined by *absolute impressions*; and, considering the matter further, it is obvious that the absolute impression of the lightness or heaviness of the comparison weight is more frequently determined by the magnitude $\pm D$ by which the comparison weight differs from the standard weight, than by the magnitude of the standard weight. Moreover, it is obvious that, when the absolute impression is that the comparison weight is judged to be the lighter of the two weights, it is because the comparison weight is lifted second rather than first [because, says Titchener (1905b), "the impression can influence the judgment only by way of memory" (p. 304)]. Finally, it is

8 Titchener demanded that his graduate students acquire a reading knowledge of German. The Instructor's Manual for the Quantitative volumes of his *Experimental Psychology* (Titchener, 1905b) is crammed with extracts from primary sources that are left untranslated. This means that present-day readers who have no German cannot read the Instructor's Manual without some feelings of irritation.

> also obvious that "strong lifters", given that they take into consideration the known extreme values of the weights they are lifting, will more easily attain an impression of lightness than an impression of heaviness, whereas "less strong lifters" will arrive more easily at the converse impression.
>
> (p. 304)

Titchener's conclusion was that "the validity of these two influences—the influence of the absolute judgment and, as a last resort, the influence of the type of participant in terms of differences in muscular strength—would itself form a sufficient justification of the method of qualitative analysis" (p. 304).[9]

Influence 3: "Fechnerian Time Error—Positive and Negative"

Angell (1899) pointed out that the Fechnerian time error could be reduced (e.g., by adopting a counterbalanced design), whereas neither the general tendency of judgment, nor the vagaries introduced by the type of participant, were eliminable. Angell's article actually had, as its central thread, the results of an experiment in which Fechnerian time errors were positive for the order Standard–Comparison, but were also positive for the order Comparison–Standard.[10] Angell explained how Martin and Müller accounted for this paradoxical result by invoking Influences 1 and 2, namely, the "general tendency of judgment" and the "type" of participant (pp. 266–269).

Influence 4: The Size of the Comparison Weight in the Preceding Judgment

A curious fact was reported in mid-twentieth-century experiments on immediate serial recall for verbal materials. Let the to-be-recalled material be a list of eight consonants, such as LVMKTNCS. Note that "N" is in the sixth position of these letters. An error, such as the mis-recall of "N" as "M", can be repeated on the next list, when the sixth letter (which need not necessarily be "N") of the next list is *also* recalled, erroneously, as "M". These "serial order intrusions" (named by Conrad, 1959) are likely to occur if something surprises the participant, leading him or her to repeat a previous response (Murray, 1966).

According to Angell (1899, pp. 269–270) and Titchener (1905b, pp. 307–308), Martin and Müller deliberately arranged for some trials, chosen at random, to involve a standard and a comparison that were *equal* in weight, although participants in that particular experiment had been asked only to

9 Titchener's incredible knowledge of the psychophysical literature is exemplified by a footnote here that describes no fewer than 16 references to other research articles that offer some support for Martin and Müller's analysis of the cognitive processes underlying a heaviness-judgment (Titchener, 1905b, p. 304, fn5). Martin and Müller's participants were six women and six men; the "strong lifters" who found it easiest to make "lighter" judgments were five men and one woman. The "less strong lifters" consisted of five women and one man.

10 A summary of these findings is given as a small table on page 266 of Angell (1899) and again on page 268.

provide "heavier" or "lighter" responses. Such a trial was called a hoax trial (*Vexierversuch*). Martin and Müller wrote that: "On the [hoax trials], the second weight to be lifted was compared with the comparison weight of the *preceding* trial and was judged, about equally often, as 'heavier' or 'lighter' than the first weight to be lifted" (as cited by Titchener, 1905b, pp. 307–308). If the participant detected the two weights to be equal, then a feeling of surprise or disillusionment could result.

Influence 5: The Change of Criterion for Delivering Judgments

Readers probably were taken aback when they read about a "criterion" in Influence 5 a few pages ago. But I was also taken aback to read Titchener's (1905b) version of this same Influence 5. He wrote that practice "may alter the scale of judgments, shift the subjective standard for the application of a determinate judgment-category" (p. 307). In a footnote Titchener stated that this passage is based on his reading of pages 128ff of Martin and Müller's book. He also noted that this subject is discussed, in Müller's (1904) second book on psychophysics, on pages 27ff. The keyword in Titchener's sentence is surely "subjective standard". It implies that the psychophysicists at Göttingen, under Müller's leadership, were amplifying their readiness to expand the discussion from constant errors to conscious psychological processes.

One of the unusual characteristics of Müller's (1878) first book on psychophysics was his concern, not merely with trying to disentangle the physiological determinants underlying comparison-judgments from those associated with psychology and conscious awareness, but of reconsidering Weber's Law from both perspectives. His mathematical efforts in this direction were summarized by Klemm (1911/1914, pp. 258–260) and need not be pursued here. The pioneering research of several of the doctoral students working with Müller, however, focussed on the study of psychological processes in themselves. For example, the approach to psychology *and* philosophy represented by the word "phenomenology" was expounded in the *Logical Investigations* [*Logische Untersuchungen*], published in 1900–1901, by Edmund Husserl (1859–1936). Its importance in the history of psychology was evaluated (positively) by Boring (1950, pp. 603–611). The enormous effect it had on mid-twentieth-century existentialist philosophy was described (entertainingly) by Bakewell (2016).[11]

David Katz (1884–1953) wrote his *The Appearances of Colours* [*Erscheinungsweise der Farben*] in 1911 under the influence of phenomenology; a revised version appeared in English as *The World of Colors* (Katz, 1935). It was also in G. E. Müller's laboratory in 1912 that Edgar Rubin (1886–1951) began his research on figure-ground effects that later had such a strong influence on Gestalt theory (Rubin, 1915/1921). Nor should we overlook the fact that it was Friedrich Schumann

11 Boring (1950) defined phenomenology as being "the description of immediate experience with as little scientific bias as possible" (p. 18).

who invented the tachistoscope that was used by Wertheimer (1912/1961) in his investigation of apparent movement, a study that is often considered to be the first major experimental contribution of the Gestalt movement.

Summary

In his compendious *Experimental Psychology*, Volume 2, Part 2, Titchener (1905b) stressed that he relied, for his information about psychophysical experimentation, quite as much on G. E. Müller's writings on psychophysics as on Fechner's.

The paper by Martin and Müller (1899) offered the first attempt to characterize the approach taken by participants in making a decision as to whether one weight was heavier than, equal to, or lighter than another. Participants in Martin and Müller's research sometimes claimed that they did not consciously compare the memory representations of the two weights, but instead formed an "absolute impression" of a feeling of heaviness associated with one of the two weights, usually the second. Physically stronger people tended to focus on the comparison weight and were inclined in general to make "lighter" judgments, while less muscled people tended to focus on the standard weight and were inclined in general to make "heavier" judgments. When, unexpectedly, the two weights used in a trial were objectively equal, there was a tendency to base the response, "heavier" or "lighter", on the response given on the previous trial (where the weights had been unequal). There was an early hint that a "subjective standard" could be set up mentally by participants themselves, a standard that could be shifted under different experimental circumstances.

In fact, subjective standards set up by participants had already been demonstrated in *Einstellung*-experiments described by Müller and Schumann (1889) a decade earlier. One experiment showed that, following exposure to a series of trials where a very heavy comparison weight (2,476 g) was lifted simultaneously with a much lighter weight (676 g), comparison weights of 926, 876 and 826 g were judged to be "lighter" than the 626-g weight. Presumably this was because these three weights were compared to a mental standard of "heaviness" determined by repeated exposure to the 2,476-g weight.

6 Measuring Psychological Magnitudes

I. Variability Measures

Measuring Variability

Titchener's Achievements

In Chapter 4, I briefly indicated that Fechner wrote extensively about three psychophysical methods, the method of limits, the method of average error, and Hegelmaier's method of right and wrong cases. When Titchener (1905a, 1905b) came to write his scholarly manual of how to do psychophysical experiments, his enormous knowledge of the literature in German and French led him to discuss a total of eight methods. In addition to the three just listed, there was also Weber's method of equivalences, Plateau's method of equal sense-distances, G. E. Müller's method of least differences, what Titchener called a method of constant stimuli, and a method of constant stimulus differences. I thought, before preparing this chapter, that the method of constant stimuli was just a synonym for the method of right and wrong cases, but, as will be explained later, this is not exactly correct.

Following the publication of Titchener's (1905b) book, new methods were added to the psychophysicist's toolbox, notably a short-lived "method of simple stimuli" that paved the way for the method of magnitude estimation in Stevens's (1975) theory of psychophysics.

In addition, confidence ratings were added to the data collected from participants usually engaged in some variant of the method of right and wrong cases (Link, 2003; Peirce, 1877). In the present volume, Chapter 9 discusses the late nineteenth-century research on the use of confidence ratings and response times in psychophysical contexts. After about 1955, confidence ratings were often obtained from experiments conducted in the context of signal detection theory.

In the late eighteenth century, it was discovered that astronomers differed among themselves in their recording of the time at which a star crossed the wires of a telescope (on this, see Boring, 1950, Chapter 8; Burke-Gaffney, 1963; Murray, 1988, pp. 195–197). This was the starting point in psychological research on response times. Response times can be divided into "simple" and "choice." F. C. Donders (1818–1889), a Dutch ophthalmologist, invented a mechanical device (a "chronometer") for measuring response times. Donders (1868/1969) did not restrict his interests to individual differences in response times. He also collected simple response times, such as when a person repeated aloud, as soon as possible, what an experimenter said (e.g., respond "ko" when the experimenter says "ko"). He also measured choice response times, such as when a person repeated aloud, as soon as possible, only one of several possible sounds spoken by the experimenter (e.g., respond "ko" only to "ko" and not respond at all to "ki" or "ku").

Turning to psychophysics, Cattell (1886a, 1886b) reported simple response times in experiments in which the participant responded, as soon as possible, to the onset of a visual stimulus varying in intensity. Fullerton and Cattell (1892) reported choice response times in studies of how quickly and accurately participants could decide which of two stimuli was the more intense. In the 1950s, there was an upsurge in research on response times viewed as indirect measures of the efficiency of human information-processing. Reviews of early twentieth-century research on simple and choice response times were provided by Laming (1973).

All this seems daunting. Upper-year students and graduate students in psychology in the first half of the twentieth century probably *were* daunted by the emphasis placed on the psychophysical methods in the syllabi of laboratory classes in experimental psychology. This explains, for example, the careful attention paid to psychophysics in two chapters of Woodworth's (1938) widely used textbook. In its second edition, Woodworth and Schlosberg (1954) toned down the emphasis on psychophysics, but only slightly. That left more space for the selection of alternative topics that were just as suitable for psychology laboratory classes, notably experiments to do with human memory or with choice reaction times. The fact remains that, in the eyes of Fechner, G. E. Müller, and Titchener, carrying out laboratory classes in psychophysics represented a copy of what students of physics, chemistry, and engineering were doing in *their* laboratory classes. Following this tradition, we discover an almost excessive fastidiousness and care given by Titchener to psychophysics in his magnum opus, the four volumes of his *Experimental Psychology* (Titchener, 1901a, 1901b, 1905a, 1905b).

Volume I dealt with experiments in "qualitative" psychology, with the first part being written for students and the second for instructors (Titchener, 1901a, 1901b). Volume II, whose appearance was delayed so that Titchener could read Müller's (1904) second full-length book on psychophysics, deals with experiments in "quantitative" psychology. It is divided into the same two parts, one for students and the other for instructors (Titchener, 1905a, 1905b). Both in the "qualitative" and "quantitative" volumes, the chapter headings in the instructor's manual are identical to those in the student's manual. In the qualitative and quantitative volumes, the instructor's manual is about twice as long as the student's manual. Each manual consists of a general Introduction (whose pages are numbered in Roman numerals) followed by several chapters.

Table 6.1 The Contents of Titchener's *Experimental Psychology*

Volume I	*Volume II*
Qualitative	Quantitative
Part I: Student's Manual (xviii + 214)	Part I: Student's Manual (xli + 208)
Part II: Instructor's Manual (xxxiii + 456)	Part II: Instructor's Manual (clxxi + 453)
Introduction (5 sections)	Introduction (7 sections)
Chapters:	Chapters:
I. Visual sensation (4)	I. Preliminary experiments (12)
II. Auditory sensation (5)	II. The metric methods:
III. Cutaneous sensation (4)	The law of error (2)
IV. Gustatory sensation (3)	The method of limits (0)
V. Olfactory sensation (3)	Fechner's method of average error (1)
VI. Organic sensation (1)	The method of equivalents (2)
VII. The affective qualities (4)	The method of equal sense-distances (2)
VIII. Attention and action (2)	The method of constant stimuli (1)
IX. Visual space perception (3)	The determination of equivalent stimuli (1)
X. Auditory perception (3)	The method of right and wrong cases (2)
XI. Tactual space perception (3)	III. The reaction experiment (3)
XII. Ideational types and association of ideas (2)	IV. The psychology of time (1)
	V. The range of quantitative psychology

In each chapter, several experiments are described in detail, indicating the procedure, the apparatus, and the calculations to be carried out when the data were collected. In Table 6.1, the number of experiments introduced in each chapter is shown in parentheses after the chapter's title. The chapter headings are identical for Parts I and II of each volume.

Titchener (1901a, 1901b) on Qualitative Experimentation

We look very briefly at Volume I of Titchener's manual, concerned with "qualitative" experiments, in which numerical data are collected. Data usually do not demand any major statistical manipulations. In Table 6.1, we can see that 9 of the 12 chapters in Volume I are concerned with sensation and/or perception. Chapter VII concerns the measurement of a participant's *preferences* for particular stimuli. For example, in Chapter VII, the first experiment has the participant (whom he called "*O*", meaning "observer") seated at a table with closed eyes. Opposite him sits the experimenter who sets two squares of coloured paper in a neutral grey cardboard frame in front of *O*. Each pair of squares has a "standard", made up of one of nine colours, and a "comparison" of the same colour but lighter or darker than the standard. Titchener (1901a) wrote "at the word of command, *O* opens his eyes, views the two coloured squares in the neutral frame, and gives an immediate decision as to which of them is the *more pleasant*" (p. 94).

Titchener (1905a, 1905b) on Quantitative Experimentation

Our interest in Volume II of Titchener's *Experimental Psychology* is focussed on what he says about the measurement of the variability found in the data collected in psychophysical experiments. Chapter 2 of the present volume narrates the history of the formulation of the Gaussian distribution. The rationale for discussing this distribution was to introduce the basis for Fechner's adoption of the Gaussian distribution as a representation of sensory variability. Accordingly, I prepared Table 6.2, which summarizes the psychophysical methods discussed in the student's manual (Titchener, 1905a) and the instructor's manual (Titchener, 1905b). I kept a special eye open for (a) passages in the general narrative where the Gaussian distribution is used and (b) passages specific to individual psychophysical methods that involve its use.

Before coming to grips with the Gaussian distribution, I learned, from Titchener's (1905b) manual for instructors, that Titchener discovered that too few psychologists could properly understand the equation defining the normal probability density function. In fact, he divided "psychologists" into two extreme

Table 6.2 Titchener's Discussions of the Gaussian Distribution in Volume II of his *Experimental Psychology*

Methods introduced by Fechner	*Student's manual (Part I)*	*Instructor's manual (Part II)*
	pp. i–xli: the meaning of "measurement"	pp. i–clxxi: Fechner and his critics
	pp. 38–55: the law of error	**pp. 93–99: the law of error**
Method of limits (also called Method of minimal error) (also called Method of just noticeable differences)	pp. 55–69	pp. 99–143
Method of average error	pp. 70–77	**pp. 143–187**
Method of constant stimuli	**pp. 92–106**	**pp. 248–263**
Method of constant stimulus differences	**pp. 106–119**	**pp. 263–275**
Methods introduced by others	**Student's manual (Part I)**	**Instructor's manual (Part II)**
G. E. Müller's Method of least differences		pp. 4–99
E. H. Weber's Method of equivalences	pp.77–81	pp. 187–194
Plateau's Method of equal sense-distances	pp. 81–92	pp. 194–248
Hegelmaier's Method of right and wrong cases		**pp. 275–318**

The passages shown in **bold** font include his discussions of the Gaussian distribution.

kinds. There were those who, because they had a limited grasp of mathematics, worked largely "by rule of thumb". There were those who did have a good command of mathematics. Titchener, somewhat slyly, accused the latter of often being more concerned with applying their mathematics to psychology than they were with developing psychology with the aid of mathematics. Referring to himself, Titchener wrote that

> the author has attempted in the text to strike a middle course between these extremes: not because the *via media* [the middle road] is here the safest,—it is, on the contrary, the most perilous of the three,—but because it promises to lead most directly to psychological results.
>
> (p. 93)

Fechner's Own Equation Expressing How Variability Can Be Determined for Response Proportions

Fechner's own concept of his task was to determine the proportion of "correct" heavier responses, (r/n), as a function of h. Fechner's (1860/1966, p. 86) equation was:

$$\Theta = \left(2/\sqrt{\pi}\right)\int_{0}^{hD/2} \exp\left(-t^2\right)dt \qquad (6.1)$$

Fechner proved that:

$$\left(r/n\right) = \left(1+\Theta\right)/2 \qquad (6.2)$$

Fechner showed his proof, involving Equations 6.1 and 6.2, to a professor of mathematics at Leipzig, A. F. Möbius (1790–1868), who approved it, but offered an alternative derivation, which he believed to be more applicable than Fechner's when investigating stimuli other than weights.[1]

Equation 6.1 says that the function Θ equals a constant, namely, $(2/\sqrt{\pi})$, multiplied by the area under a Gaussian curve. Link (1994) showed that t represented the difference in perceived heaviness, D, between the comparison stimulus (Co) and the absolute-threshold stimulus, (St), when (Co – St) was measured in units of h. Fechner maintained that a normal probability density function was a description of variability in the magnitude of sensation.

Using numerical data taken from Fechner's large experiment, Link (1994) spelled out how Fechner's Law predicts, from a knowledge that (Co – St) equals, say, 10 g, that the associated standard deviation equals 7.4 g. Link wrote that:

1 Möbius is nowadays considered the father of topology. He introduced the "Möbius strip" by "taking a strip of paper, giving it a twist so that one side is reversed and sticking the two ends together to form a loop" (Glendinning, 2013, p. 346). The Möbius strip of paper has only one side and one edge.

> In this way, the previously unknown measure of σ, the spread [variability] of errors generated by the sensory system, became measurable in units of the physical stimulus. A previously invisible property of the mind became observable. Psychology became a science.
>
> (p. 337)

The Cumulative Gaussian Distribution

The Psychometric Function

According to Link (1992/2020, p. 40), the psychometric function was introduced into psychophysics, at a rather late date, by Urban (1910).[2] Urban gave the name "psychometric function" to "a mathematical expression which gives the probability of a judgment as a function of the comparison stimulus" (p. 230). In the same year, Brown (1910) reported psychometric functions obtained in a weight-discrimination experiment. Psychometric functions were discussed in considerable detail by Guilford (1936, pp. 171–176), by Woodworth (1938, pp. 400–427) and, in its second edition, by Woodworth and Schlosberg (1954, pp. 192–217), who give a particularly useful drawing of the psychometric function (see Woodworth & Schlosberg, 1954, p. 203). Of course, neither Fechner (1860/1964) nor Titchener (1901a, 1901b, 1905a, 1905b) used the term "psychometric function". From a historical point of view, the shift from discussing the bell curve of the normal probability density function to the "flight path" of the cumulative Gaussian distribution had two important consequences.[3]

2 According to Ertle et al. (1977), Friedrich Johann Victor Urban (1878–1964) was born in what is now the Czech Republic and wrote articles on psychophysics both in German and in English. He obtained his PhD from the University of Pennsylvania, but was trapped in Europe when World War I broke out; he never returned to America even after the war ended in 1918.

3 The relationship between the normal probability density function, the cumulative normal probability function, and the psychometric function is less straightforward than it might seem. The values of the abscissa for a normal probability density function are the differences between a fixed absolute-threshold stimulus (St) and each value of Co. Let (Co – St) be plotted as zero when Co = St. When (Co – St) exceeds zero, it is positive and is plotted on the right of the zero setting. When (Co – St) is negative, it is plotted on the left of the zero setting. The values along the abscissa range from $-\infty$ to $+\infty$.

The ordinate shows y, the probability density associated with each (Co – St)-value. For a normal probability density function, the y-value has a maximum of 0.39894228 for the case where (Co – St) = 0 and the variance = 1.

The cumulative Gaussian distribution is also called the "normal distribution function." The distribution functions of some well-known probability density functions that are not Gaussian, is covered in detail by Parzen (1960, pp. 180–251). The abscissa of the normal distribution function ranges from $-\infty$ to $+\infty$. The normal distribution function is derived by integrating the normal probability density function over the range of (Co – St) that runs from $-\infty$ to (Co – St). This value shows the probability of a response such as "heavier" or "lighter." When (Co – St) = 0, the value of this cumulative probability is 0.50.

The abscissa of the psychometric function has values restricted to the range used by an experimenter. The ordinate shows the probability of a response, such as "heavier" or "lighter" associated with each value of (Co – St), with values ranging from 0 to 1.

The normal probability density function looks like a bell-shaped curve and the cumulative Gaussian function has the shape of a flight path (often called "ogival" or "S-shaped").

First, the measure of precision, Gauss's h, was a parameter in Fechner's normal probability density function. The value of h can be represented visually by drawing a tangent to the mid-point of a psychometric function. The slope of that tangent gives the value of h. The steeper the psychometric function, the more tightly clustered about its midpoint would be the responses. Larger values of h are taken to indicate a better precision of measurement.

The Müller-Urban Weights

Second, G. E. Müller (1879) identified a potential source of error in the calculation of h. It is best understood by stepping back and re-examining the expression (Co – St).

Restrict the standard to the case where St represents an "absolute-threshold stimulus", W_1 in Chapter 4, that is just noticeably different from its background. Let an abscissa denote the perceived heaviness associated with a given stimulus intensity along a particular sensory dimension. As explained in detail by Link (1994, p. 336), the "perceived heaviness" comprises two parts, its "true" heaviness (mediated by the nervous system) and Gaussian variability. Let a given value of Co "feel" heavier than St. Then, as explained by Link (1994, pp. 335–337), a threshold value of [(Co – St)/2] will represent that value of perceived heaviness such that Co is correctly judged to be "heavier" than St on 75% of trials, and St is correctly judged to be "lighter" than Co on 75% of trials.

Now use D as shorthand to denote the difference between the stimulus intensity of Co and the absolute-threshold intensity, W_1. Then the "threshold value" of perceived heaviness, $(D/2)$, can substitute for [(Co – St)/2]. Fechner then assumed that the stimulus heaviness that would be the most "precise" predictor of the absolute threshold would be given by $(D/2)h$. For any participant in an experiment using the method of right and wrong cases, the value of h has to be estimated. Let the variable named t in Equation 6.1 take the value $(D/2)h$, that is, $(hD/2)$. That value represents an internal criterion against which the participant must decide whether Co exceeds $(hD/2)$. It should be noted that Link considers that Fechner created what is now known as signal detection theory because of Fechner's use of a "criterion" value of perceived heaviness.

Link (1994) then wrote:

> Therefore, given an experimentally fixed value of D, and an experimentally determined error probability [an obtained value derived from (r/n)], one could look up in Fechner's tables [based on the Gaussian distribution] the corresponding value of t. The values of t are similar to today's tables of z for the standard Gaussian ("normal") distribution.
>
> (p. 337)

Fechner (1860/1966, p. 90) devised a "Fundamental Table" in which hD-values are expressed as a function of (r/n), where (r/n) runs from 0.5 to 1.0. The table was reproduced by Titchener (1905a, p. 99). As (r/n) approaches 1.0, the value hD rises very rapidly, so rapidly, in fact, that Fechner (pp. 91–92) devised two Supplemental Tables, the first for (r/n)-values from 0.83 to 0.9725 in steps of 0.0025, and the second for (r/n)-values from 0.970 to 1.0 in steps of 0.001. One can take one's own estimated values of hD and find the predicted (r/n)-values that come closest to them in Fechner's Fundamental Table.

We know D; but how do we estimate h? On this question, Titchener (1905a, pp. 93–103) noted that, in practice, we know the range of D-values that occur in the study of a single standard weight. We also discover by experiment the proportion of correct "heavier" judgments, (r/n), with a given D-value. We also need to find the unknown values of two variables, h and t. Titchener used two simultaneous equations to estimate the values of h and t, as follows.

In an experiment on two-point thresholds on the skin, Titchener studied seven values of D_i = 0.5, 1, 1.5, 2, 3, 4 and 5 Paris lines. For each value, D_i, he determined the proportion, p_i, of responses of "I feel two sensations". For the n_i trials using D_i, the numerical value of p_i is given by that proportion. The obtained p_i-values were 0.10, 0.14, 0.40, 0.65, 0.80, 0.87 and 0.96 respectively. So, for each p_i, Fechner's Fundamental Table provided a corresponding value of t_i. From that t_i-value, Titchener used the identity $t_i = D_i h_i$ to estimate h_i.

Each equation yielded a different value of h_i. Titchener wished, instead, to find the *single* value of h that fitted all the response proportions obtained when a single location on the skin served as the standard. He also wished to estimate a *single* "two-point threshold" associated with that location. He named that two-point-threshold distance RL [standing for "stimulus (*Reiz*) limen"].

Titchener's values of h and RL were, however, obtained by using a "correction factor" or "weighting" in each of the seven equations. Originally, each equation had the form $t_i = D_i h_i$. Only the obtained proportions, p_i, and the prearranged values D_i, are known. It is also the case that when we look up, in Fechner's Fundamental Table, the value of t_i corresponding to an observed p_i-value, there is a certain error arising from the fact that a t_i-value cannot be predicted exactly from a known p_i-value. The amount of error will be less for p_i-values of 0.01 and 0.99 than it is for the p_i-value of 0.50.

According to G. E. Müller (1879), the error can be compensated for by "weighting" the p_i-values. Each of the seven equations of the form $t_i = D_i h_i$ is therefore slightly changed: Each p_i-value is multiplied by a weight w_i. The value of w_i associated with any given value of p_i was set out in G. E. Müller's Table of Coefficients of Weights, reproduced by Titchener (1905a, p. 101). For $p_i = 0.01$ and $p_i = 0.99$, the weight is 0.004. For $p_i = 0.50$ the weight is 1.000. Titchener's simultaneous equations below were therefore based on Fechner's Fundamental Table and on G. E. Müller's Table of Coefficients of Weights.

To estimate a single value of h, he used a method of least squares (the computations are given in detail on Titchener, 1905a, p. 102) to derive the following simultaneous equations:

$$16.05h - 6.37RLh = 1.96$$
$$-6.37h + 3.12RLh = 0.23$$

Solving these equations yields estimated values of $h = 0.80$ and $RL = 2.13$.[4]

Later, Urban (1912) suggested a further refinement based on statistical theory. Urban's weight for $p_i = 0.01$ and $p_i = 0.99$ is 0.1127, and for $p_i = 0.50$ it is 1.000 (Guilford, 1936, Table G, p. 543). Urban's (1912) table was corrected by Brown and Thompson (1925, p. 202) and these corrections were incorporated into Table G of Guilford (1936, p. 543). This table showed the weight, w_i, to be associated with a given proportion of correct responses, p_i. The table was easier to use when (Co – St) was measured in *h* units than when (Co – St) was measured in standard-deviation-units. Woodworth (1938, p. 414) therefore redesigned Urban's (1912) table in such a way as to facilitate a student's finding the weight, w_i, that could appropriately be applied when (Co – St) was measured in standard-deviation-units. Other changes adopted by Woodworth included the correction of a few more errors in Urban's table that had been unearthed by investigators in Titchener's laboratory at Cornell University. Moreover, Woodworth used *z*-scores calculated to the unusual length of six decimal places when estimating his w_i-values. He even gave his table a special name: it represented a set of "Müller-Urban weights".

This table of the Müller-Urban weights was published in Woodworth (1938, pp. 416–417). But it was not reported in Woodworth and Schlosberg's (1954) second edition of Woodworth's textbook. One justification for this omission was given by Woodworth and Schlosberg themselves. They contended that the arithmetic employed when the Müller-Urban weights were used was "laborious and tricky and scarcely worthwhile except for extensive data, for the Mean found by use of the weights is usually very close to that found by the simpler computations" (p. 207).

These standby calculations, that were so prized in laboratory classes in experimental psychology in the 1920s and 1930s, have probably vanished from most present-day classes. Nevertheless, for those interested in the use of psychometric functions, I particularly recommend Guilford's (1936) book titled, with a simplicity that belies its sophistication, *Psychometric Methods*. Because Gauss's measure of precision, *h*, was superseded in practical applications by the standard deviation, σ, from about the late nineteenth century, it is helpful to remember that $\sigma = [1/(\sqrt{2})h]$.

Other Estimations Used in Fechner's Psychophysics

Estimating the Numerical Value of an "Absolute" or "Differential" Threshold

Fechner's large experiment used the method of right and wrong cases to determine whether Weber's Law was valid for heaviness-judgments in experiments using lifted weights. Fechner made no attempt to estimate the value of the differential threshold for lifted weights, but, later, a great deal of emphasis was placed, in psychophysics teaching texts, on the need for students to know

4 Titchener's reported values were $h = 0.49$ and $RL = 1.88$, which are incorrect.

how to estimate both absolute and differential thresholds for any given stimulus-dimension.

Titchener's own contribution to the experimental literature was to create an estimate of an absolute threshold. Titchener (1905b, p. 104) made use of a variant of Fechner's "method of limits" to determine an absolute threshold. This variant was proposed by G. E. Müller (1878, pp. 63ff). A single participant made judgements to experimentally establish the frequency, in vibrations/sec., of the lowest-pitched tone that was only just audible against a background of silence. His table of data was reproduced by Titchener (1905b, p. 6), and was reprinted by Woodworth and Schlosberg (1954, p. 197), who followed it by a set of instructions. To calculate the threshold determined by those instructions, Titchener used the "method of limits". This involved presenting several series of tones *ascending* in pitch interspersed with several series of tones *descending* in pitch until the participant reliably claimed he or she could only *just* hear one particular tone, which was the "absolute-threshold" tone.

Because a differential threshold can be discovered using the same combination of ascending and descending series of stimuli, the differential threshold became identified with a just noticeable difference; an alternative name for the method of limits was therefore "the method of just noticeable differences" (as indicated in Table 6.2). Each series of trials was designed to ascertain whether a given comparison stimulus was judged as being "greater" or "smaller" than a given standard stimulus. In an ascending series of lifted weights, the value of the comparison stimulus at which the sequence of "lighter" responses shifts to a sequence of "heavier" responses will be called T_A. The equivalent value of the comparison stimulus in a descending series, where a sequence of "heavier" responses shifts to a sequence of "lighter" responses, will be called T_D.

According to Woodworth and Schlosberg (1954, p. 197), the following measures were given names which ran throughout the Fechnerian psychophysics adopted by Titchener (1905b) and his contemporaries:

$(T_D - T_A)$ is named the "interval of uncertainty" (IU);
$[(T_D - T_A)/2]$ is named the "differential threshold" or "differential limen" (DL);
$[(T_D + T_A)/2]$ is named the "point of subjective equality" (PSE).

Estimating the Numerical Value of the Proportion of Right Responses, (r/n)

A note may appropriately be added here concerning a dilemma faced by Fechner from the very outset of his large experiment. If a participant is asked to say which of two weights feels "heavier", then it can be inferred that the other weight feels "lighter".[5] Suppose the participant thinks the two weights feel

5 It may be asked whether, on a given series of 64 trials, the standard was always or only sometimes lifted before the comparison. Fechner (1860/1966) wrote "temporal and spatial conditions remain the same for a given series of trials" (p 75). By "temporal" condition Fechner was referring to whether the standard was lifted first or second.

equal, or is uncertain (for whatever reason) how to respond. Fechner (1860/1966) insisted on recording all such doubtful judgments. He wrote:

> Note that each judgment that remains in doubt should be counted half as belonging to the right and half to the wrong cases. In order to avoid half cases arising in this way, I count each right judgment as two right, each wrong judgment as two wrong, and each doubtful judgment as one right and one wrong, because only the ratios count in forming the fraction (*r*/*n*).
> (p. 178)

Unfortunately, Fechner made no further reference to this scheme of marking, nor, as Link (1992/2020) noted, did he "report the frequency with which these [doubtful] responses did occur, thus prohibiting the reanalysis of his data in the light of present-day theories" (p. 16fn).

An idea of Fechner to extend Weber's Law to his measures of probabilities, (*r*/*n*), was called "Fechner's Conjecture" by Stephen Link (1992/2020, pp. 12–13). The extension of Weber's Law to the method of right and wrong cases suggests that [(Co − St) /St] ought to be constant for any value of St that generate 75% of correct "heavier" judgments.

As was reported in Chapter 4, Link (1992/2020, pp. 12–13) tested the validity of Fechner's Conjecture by carrying out a chi-squared test for constant response frequencies. He concluded that the data from Fechner's large experiment did not satisfactorily confirm that those data were determined by Weber's Law.

This chapter closes by reproducing another listing from Ribot's (1886) book about contemporary German psychology. This listing is on page 159 and gives estimates of the absolute threshold values for the same sensory modalities as were listed, at the end of Chapter 3 in the present volume, in Ribot's table of Weber fractions.

For Touch	Pressure of 0.002 to 0.05 g
Muscular effort	Contraction of 0.004 mm of the right internal muscle of the eye
Temperature	(the heat of the skin being 18.4 degrees), (1/8) of a degree centigrade
Sound	Ball of cork of 1.001 g falling 0.001 m onto a plate of glass, the ear being distant 91 mm
Light	Cast on black velvet by a candle situated 8 ft 7 in distant

Summary

A survey was given of the contents of the four volumes of Titchener's (1901a, 1901b, 1905a, 1905b) *Experimental Psychology*. After an introduction to some of the psychophysical methods he discussed, the special case of the method of right and wrong cases was addressed. Fechner showed how the probability of correct "heavier" responses, in his large experiment, increased with the size of the difference in grams between the comparison weight (Co) and the standard weight (St). This difference is denoted by (Co – St). If St is an "absolute threshold" stimulus, (Co – St), can be written simply as *D*. Using Gauss's *h* as the measure of precision associated with a normal probability density function, Fechner prepared a "Fundamental Table" in which he gave a numerical value for the degree of precision, *hD*, associated with any proportion, from 0.5 to 1.0, of correct "heavier" responses. He prepared the table using an integral equation he himself had formulated. Link (personal communication, July 11, 2019) asserted that, by using the Gaussian probability distribution to represent variability in the nervous system, Fechner proposed a theory of choice that provided the first measure of the mind.

The cumulative Gaussian distribution of the probabilities of correct "heavier" responses to individual values of (Co – St) was called by Urban (1910) the "psychometric function". Gauss's *h* can be seen as being the slope of the straight line, the tangent, that best fits along a mid-section of the curved psychometric function. Discussed more briefly were the method of limits as used to estimate the numerical values of absolute and differential thresholds; and Fechner's handling of "doubtful" judgments in his large experiment.

7 Measuring Psychological Magnitudes

II. The Quantity Objection

Objections to Fechner's Psychophysics

The Meaning of "Quantity Objection"

Following the appearance of Fechner's (1860/1964) *Elemente der Psychophysik*, written criticisms of his views came surprisingly thick and fast. From 1860 until his death in 1887, at least three kinds of criticism were raised, so much so that Fechner felt obliged to reply to his critics in two books, Fechner's (1877) *The Case for Psychophysics* [*In Sachen der Psychophysik*] and Fechner's (1882) *Review of the Main Points of Psychophysics* [*Revision der Hauptpunkte der Psychophysik*], as well as in an article published only a year before his passing (Fechner, 1886).

The three kinds of objection were as follows. First, there was the objection that mental entities were not quantifiable in the way physical objects were (the "quantity objection"). Second, there was the objection that the use of just noticeable differences as measurement-units was unjustifiable. Third, there was the objection that it would be futile to found the discipline of experimental psychology on Fechner's psychophysics.

The present chapter concerns itself entirely with the quantity objection, its foes, and its friends. The literature ultimately influenced measurement theory in general, especially in physics. Chapter 8 will show how Plateau, Hering, and Delboeuf each played a role in replacing Fechner's Law with an alternative law (for Plateau and Hering, and, of course, their twentieth-century representative, S. S. Stevens, that alternative law was a power law). Chapter 9 will describe William James's concern that psychophysics rested on too fragile a theoretical foundation for it to deserve to be a "model" for any future psychology.

The "quantity objection" was the general name given to the belief that Fechner's efforts to found a new science of psychophysics were in vain because there were no scientifically acceptable parallels in Fechner's fledgling science, concerned with mental events, to the extensive (e.g., length, time, mass) and intensive (e.g., temperature) measurement-units used in the established sciences concerned with physical events.[1] This belief almost automatically relegates psychology to being the Cinderella of the sciences, working "in the kitchen" out of sight of the household upstairs, with nobody treating her claims seriously because those claims were not couched in the language of the exact sciences, namely, mathematics.[2]

Tannery's Importance in the History of the Quantity Objection

Jules Tannery (1848–1910), who may have come across Fechner's ideas in an article by Ribot (1874), did not just repeat the cliché that sensations could not be measured by using a ruler.[3] Tannery (1875a) claimed instead, according to Heidelberger (2004, pp. 208–209), that sensations are *so* different from, say, line lengths, that any kind of measuring device that could be applied to line lengths (e.g., a ruler) could not possibly be used to measure the sensation they aroused. Measurements made with a ruler can be concatenated (e.g., if two rulers are laid end-to-end) or subtracted; measurements of line lengths made with a ruler can lead to the conclusion that two lines are equal in length. But there is no evidence that measurements of a sensation can be obtained such that we can say that one sensation added to another equal in strength will provide a single sensation with twice the strength of the first sensations. Or that even two sensations can be equal in intensity.

More interesting, perhaps, is Tannery's (1875b) conclusion that, because a given extensive quantity (like a weight) can be predicted to yield a corresponding sensation (like a degree of "heaviness") according to a mathematical function (like a logarithmic function), it does not follow that we have "found" a "law" comparable to a law of physics. What we *can* do is *define* a sensation-magnitude as being the sum of a number of sensation units called "just noticeable differences", each of which is *defined* to be equal in magnitude to each of the others, and then relate that sensation-magnitude to the weight that constituted the stimulus.[4] This "relation" will be a mathematical function whose very nature

1 It is hard to pin down who first used the expression "quantity objection." In his review of the literature on the topic, Titchener (1905b, pp. l–li) noted that Delboeuf (1878) had written, referring to Fechner's views, that "it is impossible for anyone to have a clear idea of what might be meant by the quantity of sensation" (p. 61).

2 Apart from Fechner's controversial contributions, the first whisper of a reconciliation between psychology and the physical sciences might have been the finding of a common ground in probability theory. It was valuable both to the human sciences (as exemplified in Laplace's *Essai* described in Chapter 2) and to the physical sciences (as exemplified in the application of probability theory to the prediction of the movements of molecules in liquids that were being heated; on this, see Norwich, 1993, pp. 87–108). A broad overview about how probability theory came to influence science in general, with a weighting assigned to the physical and biological sciences that exceeded that assigned to the human sciences (e.g., economics, sociology, and psychology), was the compendious edited volume titled *The Probabilistic Revolution* (Krüger, Daston, & Heidelberger, 1987a, Vol. 1; Krüger, Gigerenzer, & Morgan, 1987b, Vol. 2).

3 Tannery was an eminent mathematician who spent his career in Paris. His PhD thesis of 1874 was about integrals in linear differential equations. He became an expert on elliptical functions.

4 Tannery was particularly upset by the way Fechner had talked of "sensation differentials," as if he imagined that greater credibility would accrue to his theory if he made a "magnitude" that was nothing more than a definition behave as if it were a genuine extensive magnitude (Heidelberger, 2004, p. 209).

will be an offshoot of how the sensation unit was *defined*. *Out* of the definition of a sensation-magnitude as being composed of equal-sized measurement-units, a logarithmic function *necessarily* falls. Let four stimulus intensities produce four sensations. These stimulus intensities equal 10, 100, 1,000, and 10,000. These can be written as 10^1, 10^2, 10^3, and 10^4 respectively. The logarithms to base 10 of 10, 100, 1,000, and 10,000 are numbers that increase in equal-sized steps of one unit, that is, they increase in the order 1, 2, 3, and 4, like sensations.

Perhaps the most scholarly history of the use of the quantity objection to argue against Fechner's psychophysics is that of Heidelberger (2004, Chapter 6, titled "Measuring the Mental", pp. 191–247). After describing Tannery's views in much more detail than given here, Heidelberger described, in roughly their chronological order of published appearance, many further criticisms of Fechner's psychophysics. I think that most subsequent expressions of the quantity objection arose directly from Tannery's initiative. Defenders of Fechner included, notably, Wundt. Attackers of Fechner came, to a surprising extent, from philosophers working within a neo-Kantian tradition. It is important to remember that, in his early writings (see Chapter 4), Fechner expressed his disagreement with Kant's notion that things that are real but unknowable, what Kant called "noumena", are hidden from our conscious awareness by the "phenomena" we call our sense-experiences. Fechner saw no need for such a "transcendental" assumption; putting it crudely, he believed that "what you see is what you see". Heidelberger (2004) summarized the dilemma for Fechnerians in the following words:

> For the physicists and the physiologists, Tannery's objection was a corollary of the mechanistic worldview of a governing science. For neo-Kantian philosophers fighting for dominance, Tannery's objection was also a consequence of their (historically rather questionable) interpretation of Kant, one that enabled them to go along with the physiologists, without sacrificing their own independence. For psychologists, the objection provided an opportunity to either take sides with the physiologists at the risk of losing their own scientific identity, or to pursue an independent third way between neo-Kantian philosophy and established natural science.
>
> (p. 211)[5]

With Heidelberger (2004, pp. 208–209), let us summarize Tannery's criticism as being based on the three notions (i) that the measurement-units used to quantify the entities-to-be-measured can be characterized as potentially "equal" in magnitude; (ii) that the entities-to-be-measured are homogeneous; and (iii)

5 The reader may be reminded here that the "mechanistic worldview" presumably upheld by Tannery in 1875 was based largely on the force of gravity. This viewpoint was in the course of being replaced by a model of physics according to which gravitational forces were supplemented by the forces associated with a field determined by electromagnetic waves. Maxwell's "electromagnetic spectrum" was first announced in a paper presented to the Royal Society in London on December 8, 1864.

that how their measurement-units are defined determines the mathematical function postulated to relate the magnitude of one to the other entity.

Von Kries (1882) on the "Equality" of Measurement-Units

With respect to the condition that one magnitude can be said to "equal" another magnitude taken from the same scale of magnitudes, particular attention must be paid to the views of Johannes von Kries (1853–1923).[6] Von Kries (1882) stated, with respect to the development of his own ideas, that

> it became clear what physical measurement means. It became evident that the *concept of equality*, with its full mathematical stringency, is a part of the quantitative statements about all kinds of empirical circumstances. If only values of the same dimension can be considered equal, then all such statements can be understood as statements about relations of spatial and temporal distances and sizes of mass or as statements about unnamed numbers.
>
> (as cited by Heidelberger, 2004, p. 226)

Von Kries did not have at his disposal the tables of measurement-units formulated by Krantz et al. (1971/2007, Vol. 2, pp. 539–544), but would probably have been gratified to see how all those measurements contained a reference to distance (length), time, and/or mass.

In von Kries's (1882) own article, he presented a list of measurement-units used by physicists (pp. 248–262). For example, the simplest unit, speed (*Geschwindigkeit*), was given as (L/T), where L refers to length (*Länge*), that is, distance, and T refers to time. Next comes acceleration = (L/T^2). And then comes Newton's second law, namely, that force (*Kraft*) = mass times acceleration = $[(M)(L/T^2)]$, where M refers to mass. Von Kries provided four more examples from classical mechanics, and ended this passage by showing that measurements of electrical charge can also be derived from L, T, and M.

Von Kries was then led naturally to switch from the discussion of extensive measurement-units to an assessment of the value of intensive measurement-units in physics, including those concerned with temperature (see Chapter 2 of the present volume). He also confessed that the task of stipulating the characteristics of intensive measurement-units can be surprisingly difficult. His example concerned the measurement of the intensity of a light-source. Here von Kries (1882) made the following astute remark about "equality" in this particular

6 Von Kries studied physiology and medicine at Halle, Leipzig, and Zürich before working for a year with Helmholtz in Berlin. He was then given his first teaching position at Leipzig, but moved to Freiburg in 1880 as chair of physiology. He became famous for his version of a "duplicity theory" of the workings of the rods and cones in the retina (Von Kries, 1895). He also wrote an important book that tried to pin down what was "subjective" in probability theory (Von Kries, 1886). Heidelberger (2004, p. 229) stated that von Kries's contributions to probability theory were strongly influenced by his 1882 essay on the merits of intensive measurements in physics and the more subjective use of intensive measurements in psychophysics.

context. If one wishes to assert that two light intensities, say, are "equal" if they appear equally bright to the eye, then *one* of the necessary preconditions that would make the assertion valid is that "two lights that appear equal in brightness to that of a third light must also appear equal in brightness to each other" (p. 269). Apart from the intensive measurement of light intensity, von Kries acknowledged that other intensive measurements to do with physics, including the measurement-units suited to denote the intensity of an electric current that can activate the firing of a nerve impulse, remained to be determined. Despite such difficulties, von Kries believed that any derived intensive measurement-units that are found to be useful in physics would ultimately incorporate spatial and temporal extensive measurement-units, and sometimes, measurements of numerosity as well.[7] Within the same paragraph, von Kries wrote:

> We now turn to confronting a completely new task (*Versuch*), namely, the measurement *of intensive magnitudes in the realm of psychology*, for example, sensations. It is obvious that we can no longer rely on space- and time-magnitudes to help us here.
>
> (p. 273)

Von Kries (1882) went on to say that it makes no sense to try to equate a growth from *a* to *b* in sensation-magnitude with a physical growth from *p* to *q*. This is because, with sensations, one can only rarely assume that a large sensation-magnitude is composed in such a way that we can think of a small sensation-magnitude as being part of that large sensation-magnitude. With respect to spatial extent, a part of one foot is one inch (of which there are 12 in one foot); with respect to temporal durations, a part of one minute is one second (of which there 60 in one minute). But with respect to sensations, one cannot say that one loud tone is so-and-so many units stronger than a quiet tone. One cannot just jump from a theory of measurement-units that might be useful and applicable in physics to an analogous theory that is comparably applicable and useful in psychology.

This is not to deny that some kind of quantification might be found useful with respect to sensations. According to von Kries, there is a "null point" at which the intensity of a stimulus is such as to fail to arouse a corresponding sensation. When comparing sensations one can be judged to be more intense than another. There is no specification of a sensation measurement-unit that can be said to be "equal" in magnitude to one (or more) measurement-units of the same kind. As an example, von Kries (1882, p. 281) described how an attempt to "equate" the level of perceived brightness of a red stimulus to that of a blue stimulus turned out to "go nowhere" when a test was applied concerning the robustness of this so-called "equality". Suppose the luminosities of the red and blue lights were incremented in such a way that the resulting perceived

7 Here von Kries (1882, p. 273) had in mind the "intensive" measure of population density (the *number* of people living within a given geographical surface area during a given time period).

brightness of the red light was associated with *m* just noticeable differences in perceived brightness. If blue light was also incremented by *m* just noticeable differences in perceived brightness, the brightnesses of the red and blue lights proved not to be identical.

Von Kries (1882) asserted that, although we can arbitrarily equate two sensation differences so that, say, $(a–b) = (p–q)$, this has no specific (*bestimmt*) or comprehensible (*verständlich*) meaning from a scientific point of view. The difference between yellow and red can be perceived as "greater than" the difference between orange and red. Assuming that $c < d < e$ are sensations, red, orange, and yellow, the difference between *c* and *d* may be "smaller than" the difference between *c* and *e*. "Is the difference between red and yellow larger or smaller than the difference between *c* and *d*? Nobody will consider that an answer to that question is itself permissible [*zulässig*]" (pp. 285–286). Von Kries (1882) went on to add:

> A difference between sensations that is only detectable if we devote considerable attention to them will be assessed as being smaller than a difference between sensations that is so large that it is impossible not to notice it. Individual intensities, quite as much as differences between sensations, are frequently judged, in the course of everyday unrestricted thinking, in terms of the roles they play in the ongoing flow of *Vorstellungen*. Does it then follow, given this basic rule [*Maassstab*], that there is a countable degree of comparability between them? Absolutely not!
>
> (pp. 291–292)

Von Kries's (1882) final remark is to the effect that any contest as to which of the following is correct, a logarithmic or a power function relating sensation-magnitude to stimulus intensity, is not a question that can be treated as a scientifically meaningful (*sachlich*) one. The question is actually a dispute over what vocabulary to use, given that there was a misunderstanding about the meanings of these individual words (p. 294). One such word, if von Kries is correct, is "equal".

Stadler (1878) on the Lack of "Homogeneity" between Stimulus and Sensation

1877–1878 were crucial years in the history of psychophysics because of four publications published in that year. First, there was G. E. Müller's (1878) first book on psychophysics, *On the Foundations of Psychophysics* [*Zur Grundlegung der Psychophysik*]. While much of the book concerned Weber's Law and the reliability of Fechner's use of *h* as a measure of precision, Müller tried to pull Fechner's Law in the direction of greater generality by relating it to physiological events, in part by refining what was meant by "stimulus". Second, there was Fechner's (1877) second book on psychophysics, *The Case for Psychophysics* [*In Sachen der Psychophysik*]. Third, Delboeuf (1878) published a monograph titled *A Critical*

Examination of the Psychophysical Law, its Foundation, and its Importance [*Examin Critique de la loi Psychophysique, sa Base et sa Signification*].[8] Fourth, August Stadler (1850–1910) followed up on Delboeuf's (1878) monograph with an article in a philosophy journal, an article that zoomed in on what was essentially a mathematically anomalous prediction derived from Fechner's Law (Stadler, 1878).[9] This anomaly can be directly attributed to the fact that sensation-magnitude and stimulus intensity are magnitudes associated with disparate dimensions, that is, dimensions that are not homogeneous with respect *to each other*.

The gist of Stadler's argument was communicated by Heidelberger (2004, pp. 213–217). Heidelberger's account also discussed an extended examination of Stadler's argument, written in 1882 by Ferdinand August Müller (1858–1888). Because F.A. Müller was supervised by Hermann Cohen, his dissertation represents one of the "purest" examples of a neo-Kantian attack on Fechner's psychophysics.

The anomaly—or, rather, self-contradiction—in Fechner's Law arises as follows. Assume that "stimulus intensity" is a variable whose values, starting at a null point, increase *continuously*, at least in theory. In practice, one must necessarily preselect a discrete number of those values in order to carry out an experiment in which stimulus intensity is to serve as the *independent* variable. According to Fechner's Law,

$$S = K \log_e(I/I_0) \qquad (4.6)$$

In Chapter 4, it was stated that the null point of the stimulus range can be taken to be either I_0 or I_{NULL}. This choice was discussed in the context of the hypothetical calculation, in Table 4.3, of the S-values predicted by Fechner's Law given a range of increasing I-values. No matter whether that choice be I_0 or I_{NULL}, it is indubitable that S, the sensation-magnitude, is the *dependent* variable in Fechner's Law.

Now let us take Fechner's assumption that S can be measured in terms of equal-sized just noticeable differences. Let us focus on a stimulus intensity we denote I_1. Let us denote a single just noticeable difference as ΔI_1. And let us assert that, corresponding to the initial and smaller intensity I_1, the corresponding sensation-magnitude can be labelled S_1 and that the sensation-magnitude corresponding to the larger stimulus intensity, $(I_1 + \Delta I_1)$, can be labelled S_2.

8 Fechner (1877) actually devoted space to some earlier research findings obtained by Delboeuf (1873). These experimental findings are so important that special space will be devoted to them in Chapter 8. Delboeuf's (1883a) assembly of two monographs published together (Delboeuf, 1877, 1878) was more of a theoretical dissection of psychophysical theory as a whole.

9 Stadler was born in Zürich, Switzerland; he eventually became Professor of Philosophy and Pedagogy at the Polytechnic Institute there. He had also studied with Helmholtz in Berlin in 1872. Here he made the acquaintance of an eminent neo-Kantian philosopher, Hermann Cohen (1842–1918). Cohen became the founder of the so-called Marburg School, which was notable for applying Kant's verbally expressed views on epistemology to some problems in applied mathematics. More will be said soon about Cohen's negative attitude towards Fechnerian psychophysics. Stadler himself became a noted expert on Kant.

What happens if we take literally the pronouncement that the values of stimulus intensity, I, increase *continuously* from the null point? If I-values are continuous, then a stimulus intensity *could* have a value intermediate between I_1 and $(I_1 + \Delta I_1)$. For example, such a stimulus intensity could have a value $[I_1 + (1/2)\Delta I_1]$ using fractions or $[I_1 + 0.5\Delta I_1]$ using decimals.

So let us introduce the following proposition, P1. Let sensation-magnitude S, *if* S increases continuously in the way the stimulus intensity I does, be predicted to have a value somewhere between S_1 and S_2. Fechner's Law says that a sensation-magnitude can only increase by whole-unit steps, from S_1 to S_2, if I_1 increases to $(I_1 + \Delta I_1)$. When I_1 increases by less than $(I_1 + \Delta I_1)$, this difference in stimulus intensity will *not* be noticed because, by definition, S_1 can only increase by one whole step to S_2. S_1 cannot increase by half-a-step even though it is no problem for an experimenter to increase I_1 by half of ΔI_1. So, if S_1 can only increase to S_2 and not to an S-value somewhere between S_1 and S_2, then sensation-magnitude must increase discontinuously. But proposition P1 above asserted that sensation-magnitude could increase continuously. Therefore, P1 must be false.

Heidelberger (2004) phrases Stadler's outcome as follows:

> Sensation does not increase when the increase in stimulus is smaller than $[\Delta I]$; put in modern terms, it follows from this that sensation is a discontinuous non-monotone function of the stimulus … Fechner's fundamental formula employs a continuous and monotone function. Therefore [Fechner's fundamental formula] is incompatible with Fechner's Law.
>
> (p. 214)

Following Tannery and others, Stadler (1878) wrote that "the intensity of a sensation cannot be understood as the sum of this or that many simple degrees of sensation" (as quoted by Heidelberger, 2004, p. 214).

Four years later, F. A. Müller (1882) used another rather sophisticated argument. We quote in full Klohr's translation of Heidelberger's summary of F. A. Müller's argument:

> As Fechner himself [1860/1964, Vol. 2, Chapter 31] had shown, we can think of the general problem that Weber's Law is meant to solve, as a function having the following form:
>
> $$f(R) \cdot \Delta R = \text{const.},$$
>
> where R stands for stimulus (*Reiz*) and ΔR corresponds to the just noticeable difference (j.n.d.) of sensation. If $f(R) = k/R$ results in an empirically determined function, we get Weber's Law by inserting it. If experience should prove that Weber's Law is invalid, we can always find another function adapted to experience and that can take the place of Weber's Law by

> "using one of the well-known formulas for interpolation". Weber's Law can be substituted in this way, but [Fechner's] fundamental formula, and therefore psychophysics, cannot. For if we set
>
> $$f'(E)\cdot\Delta E = f(R)\Delta R$$
>
> [where E stands for sensation (*Empfindung*)], which would be the general case of the measurement formula, then f' is an entirely arbitrarily selected function that cannot be determined empirically. It is a hypothesis that cannot be tested empirically. If we make f' a constant, as Fechner does, such that ΔE is constant (hypothesis of difference), then it is true that we can derive Weber's Law. But if we make $\Delta E/E$ constant, as Plateau and Brentano do (hypothesis of relation), then experience expressed in Weber's Law is equally deducible. But only one of the two hypotheses can be correct.
>
> (Heidelberger, 2004, pp. 215–216)[10]

F. A. Müller also marshalled the forces of Kantian metaphysics in order to prove that Fechnerian psychophysics was, for him, a non-starter in the application of mathematics to psychology. Applied mechanics is only possible given that we have pure intuitions in space and time that, when synthesized with the aid of our imagination, give rise to our concepts of "objects". And only "objects" can be associated with numerical magnitudes. So, F. A. Müller (1882) adopted the position that:

> Sensation is not a function of the stimulus, but instead, the stimulus is the object of the sensation, therefore, according to the findings of our transcendental exposition, sensation cannot be represented in the form of number at all, because we can only have knowledge of objects.
>
> (as cited by Heidelberger, 2004, p. 216)

This downplaying of sensation, and the favouring of (Kantian) intuitions, as sources of knowledge were propagated, to an extreme extent, by Stadler's supervisor, Hermann Cohen (1883). Cohen found a conceptual link between the "formal intuition of objects" and the "material knowledge of objects", not in the usual mathematical concepts of points, lines, or numbers, but in differentials. With respect to Fechner's Law, however, Cohen did not deny that magnitudes could ever be allotted to sensations. In fact, he argued that one could estimate the similarity of one sensation to another which, for Cohen, *meant* comparing one intensive sensation-magnitude with another. But Fechner's fundamental formula, namely, $\Delta S = (\Delta I/I)$ times a constant, was assumed by Cohen to be an attempt to equate an intensive magnitude, ΔS, with an extensive magnitude, ΔI, which was, for Cohen, not permissible (Heidelberger, 2004, p. 222).

10 This work by Plateau and Brentano will be discussed in Chapter 8.

The Arbitrary Aspects of Assigning Magnitudes to Sensations

Perhaps the most dismissive passage about Fechnerian psychophysics that can be found in Heidelberger's (2004) account is the following quotation from Elsas (1886, p. 70):

> Mathematical psychology, psychophysics and physiological psychology—three absurd names! Metaphysics cannot be applied any more than the concepts of movement and force can be applied; physics ends where causality no longer rules; and physiology has no further purpose once it has finished measuring an organism.
>
> (as cited by Heidelberger, 2004, p. 230)

There is little new in the first part of this passage; it repeats the dictum that all numerical measurements must ultimately fall back on measurements of space and time. There is now a new authoritarian slant to its expression because Adolf Elsas (1855–1895) was a physicist at the University of Marburg where Cohen reigned over the philosophy department. Elsas had already won a prize for an essay on how far Kantian views could be usefully applied to the evaluation of psychophysics as a science.[11] In his introduction to his *On Psychophysics* [*Über die Psychophysik*], Elsas (1886, p. vi) also wrote a passage that I here translate as follows:

> In general, then, is it possible that a science of psychophysics, as defined by Fechner, can even exist? I answer: No. If one conceives of a sensation as being something psychological, then a sensation is a psychological counterpart to something physical [a stimulus]. But the application of mathematics is restricted exclusively to what is physical.
>
> (as cited in Heidelberger, 1993, p. 265)

Elsas was adamant about the importance of another issue in the philosophy of science, an issue he believed was crucial if we were to evaluate psychophysics as a science. This issue exemplifies the distinction between the assertions that an event A *causes* event B to happen and the assertion that the occurrence of an event A can be *correlated* with the occurrence of an event B. A good old-fashioned example is the controversy over whether cigarette-smoking (event A) actually *causes* lung cancer (event B) or whether the number of people who smoke and acquire lung cancer is *correlated* with the number of people who get lung cancer. To revert to Fechner's Law: Elsas (1886) was asking whether stimuli of intensities $I_1, I_2, I_3, \ldots$ *caused* their corresponding sensations to have magnitudes $S_1, S_2, S_3, \ldots$, or whether the monotonic function relating the stimulus intensities $I_1, I_2, I_3, \ldots$ to sensation-magnitudes $S_1, S_2, S_3, \ldots$, reflected only a statistical *correlation* between I and S.

11 Elsas was also a good friend of Helmholtz and Hertz.

Elsas's point was that physics is only interested in functions relating the successive values of a variable V_1 to the corresponding successive values of V_2 if those functions reflect *causes* rather than correlations and/or coincidences. And here is my punchline: IF a psychophysical function like Fechner's Law is only a correlation and IF psychological functions are interpreted as correlations, THEN causal mathematics could not be applied to Fechnerian psychophysics.[12]

Fechner, of course, responded to his critics as best he could. Fechner (1886) gave to his final major article on psychophysics the title "On the Principles of Psychophysical Measurement and Weber's Law: A Discussion with Elsas and Köhler". Alfred Köhler (1886) wrote a review of various alternative "psychophysical laws" that were proposed following the appearance, in 1860, of Fechner's Law. Elsas (1886), we have just seen, adopted a hard-line approach by denying that mental entities like sensations could be quantified. These alternatives included Helmholtz's revision of Fechner's Law that had included the addition of intrinsic neural noise, as well as the psychophysical laws attributed to Plateau and Delboeuf. Fechner, in other words, had his back to the wall, fending off his intellectual rivals. Then, unexpectedly, a physicist appeared whose ideas would cause *physicists* to revise their attitudes towards scientific data *as such*. Fechner was thereby offered scientific support that, I think, helped to ensure that his ideas would survive to the present day and not be snuffed out after his death in 1887.

Ernst Mach (1838–1916) on Why *Sensations* Matter in Physics

Mach's Career

The Austro-Hungarian Empire, in the middle of the nineteenth century, included Austria (capital, Vienna), Hungary (capital, Budapest), Czechoslovakia (capital, Prague), as well as some of the other smaller Balkan countries, including Serbia and Croatia. Mach was born on February 18, 1838, in a small village in Czechoslovakia. In 1855, he went to the University of Vienna where he studied medical physiology as well as physics. He obtained his PhD in physics in 1860 with a thesis on electricity. His first teaching position was at the University of Graz (Austria) where he was Professor of Mathematics from 1864 to 1865 and Professor of Physics from 1866 to 1867. Then, from 1867 to 1895, he was Professor of Physics at the Charles University in Prague, before returning, for his final years as an academic, to the University of Vienna, where he had been a student. His famous work on projectiles moving at a speed greater than sound belonged to his later years.[13]

12 Elsas's view is exactly the opposite of what Link (1994) wrote about Fechner's creation of a *causal* relation between the internal variability of sensation and the variability of judgments of "heaviness."

13 One Mach is the ratio of the speed of an object to the speed of sound in the surrounding atmosphere; just as units in terms of "horse-power" have persisted in automotive engineering, "Mach units" have persisted in aeronautical engineering.

One of his major discoveries about sensory physiology, namely, the fact that the semi-circular canals that adjoin the auditory apparatus mediate our sense of balance, was made early in his career—he published it in 1873. It was in that same year that Josef Breuer (1842–1925), with whom Freud later collaborated in the first book to broach psychoanalysis (Breuer & Freud, 1895/1955), provided evidence independently of Mach of the importance of the semi-circular canals in mediating one's sense of one's bodily position. Also early in his career, Mach conducted experiments that led to his discovery of "Mach bands", light or dark stripes that seemed to come "out of nowhere" when one views a complex pattern involving closely adjacent patterns differing in lightness.

Mach's contributions to psychophysics have ensured that Fechner's views persisted despite their endless criticism on the grounds that sensations cannot be viewed as extensive entities. Mach argued that most physicists since Newton—or Aristotle, for that matter—made the mistake of ignoring *how* they "know" that a triangle has three sides whose internal angles add up to 180 degrees, or that a cannonball flies with a parabolic trajectory before it lands to wreak its mischief. Physicists know these things because physicists possess sensations.

The fact that almost everything that we know is given to us by way of sensations was, of course, interpreted by past philosophers in a variety of ways. Challenging one's common sense or intuition, we have Berkeley's solipsism. This is the view that all that we know consists of sensations. We can, therefore, only "infer" or "guess" that there is a "real" world out there. At a less controversial level, we can point to Kant, who gave separate names to sensations that themselves had "contents" (*phenomena*) from which we could, thanks to our possession of certain "intuitions", validly infer that there was a world out there. Kant, however, also maintained that the things that *were* out there were never knowable "directly" as things-in-themselves (*noumena*). At the other end of this epistemological spectrum, so to speak, is the conventional modern view that there *is* a world of things out there, many of which could radiate light waves, sound waves, etc., through a medium like air or water, until they activated specialized nerve cells called "receptors". These sensory receptors then transmitted encoded versions of those activation-events to a central nervous system.

Mach's View that Sensations Precede the Mechanical Sciences

Mach more or less repeated Kant's belief that we explain how events happen out there in the world on the basis of our personal sensory experience. There is no mention of Kant in the index of Mach's (1875/1959) *The Analysis of Sensations*. Mach did not lay great stress on the fact that sensations differ in apparent intensity. He claimed, instead, that the way we *choose* to discuss events in the external world depends on our seeing similarities between objects in the external world with respect to their resemblances to each other in spatial extent, spatial shape, temporal duration, and gravitational inertia. That is to say, we *choose* our measurement-units on the basis of what our sensations concerning external objects *suggest* will be pragmatically useful. This being so, there is nothing that need prevent us from assigning (extensive) magnitudes to objects moving through space, nor from assigning (intensive) magnitudes to qualities inherent in objects but that are not consistent with the concatenation criterion. So, in Mach's system, the fact that the events of physics need *not* be interpreted as being ball-and-chain devices limiting us to talking about Newtonian mechanics means that magnitudes *can* be assigned to non-physical entities (such as sensations).

These ideas would also turn out to be consistent with the revolutionary opinion that the traditional three-dimensional coordinates typical of Newtonian mechanics (the x-axis, the y-axis, the z-axis) is not the only possible coordinate system. Einstein and Infeld (1938, pp. 129–255) make it clear that the path that led from the gravitation-centred Newtonian mechanics through the world of "fields" determined by electromagnetic waves to the special, and then the general, relativity theory can also be delineated as a path from one coordinate system to another. The three Cartesian coordinates of Newtonian physics were applied to a world where two separate three-dimensional Cartesian coordinate systems can be applied to one and the same event, as in special relativity theory. In Einstein's general relativity theory, a four-dimensional coordinate system is applied, where the dimension of time is added to the three dimensions of space. In this last world, an object can move in a curved trajectory in four dimensions rather than in a straight line in three dimensions.

It is not too difficult for someone in the twenty-first century to look back to the years from about 1890 to 1910 and see Mach as having switched our perspective on mechanical events from a concentration on those movements in themselves to a concentration on our *sensations* of those movements. This switch allowed Einstein to gracefully assert that, IF the sensations experienced by a person A standing *inside* an elevator travelling at such and such a velocity will be different from those experienced by a person B standing *outside* that same elevator, THEN the coordinate system employed by A to describe his or her movements *inside* the elevator may differ from the coordinate system employed by B to describe how he or she perceives, from *outside* the elevator, the movements of the elevator itself.[14]

Mach's restructuring of the perspective from which physical events are viewed led to a re-evaluation of Fechner's efforts to quantify non-physical (mental) events. More details will be found in Heidelberger (2004, pp. 234–244). Heidelberger's chapter on psychophysics provides a table showing six ways in which a mechanistic perspective of the world can be contrasted with the

14 Einstein laid great store on the value of "thought-experiments" that appear to demand that the reader possesses good visual imagery. Some are described by Einstein and Infeld (1938), but experimental psychologists can get a good idea of how Einstein arrived at his special relativity theory, first described by Einstein (1905/2002), from an interview held with Einstein by the Gestalt psychologist Max Wertheimer and reported by Wertheimer (1945, pp. 168–188).

Fechner-Mach perspective of the world. Summarizing briefly, but, I hope, comprehensibly, these six differences are:

1. Mechanistic perspective: extensive measurements only. Fechner-Mach perspective: measurements involve *ordering* a set of physical characteristics.
2. Mechanistic perspective: intensive magnitudes ultimately depend on extensive magnitudes. Fechner-Mach perspective: we first determine what physical measurements are compatible with our own sensations, and then we can measure sensations.
3. Mechanistic perspective: sensations cannot be measured. Fechner-Mach perspective: sensations *can* be measured.
4. Mechanistic perspective: all physics rests on space, time, and mass. Fechner-Mach perspective: you can choose whether or not to add extra physical measurements to those already established (space, time, or mass).
5. Mechanistic perspective: measuring instruments allow us to ignore our personal sensations about magnitudes. Fechner-Mach perspective: measuring instruments refine and extend what we learn from our sensations.[15]
6. Mechanistic perspective: physics, over time, expands on earlier discoveries made with the aid of measurements. Fechner-Mach perspective: because measurement depends on human objectives (goals, aims, intentions), the structure of physics can be expected to change as those goals (e.g., biological, cultural, economic) change.

In a word, Mach stressed that, *because* all that we experience directly comes from sensations, the measurements we choose to use in physics are selections made on the basis of their usefulness and tractability. All measurement-units are human-made. Einstein acknowledged his indebtedness to Mach, though more so at the start of Einstein's career than late in his career (Szasz, 1959). For example, in an obituary notice of Mach's death, in 1916, Einstein wrote: "Mach recognized the weak spots of classical mechanics and was not very far from requiring a general theory of relativity half a century ago" (as cited by Szasz, 1959, p. xiii). I see no reason why Fechner, had he lived beyond 1887 and survived to 1916, might not have written: "Mach recognized the weak spots of classical mechanics and was not very far from providing a convincing rationale for my psychophysical dictum that sensations *can* indeed be measured".

Summary

Although it is unclear who invented the term "quantity objection" (Titchener suggested it might be attributable to Delboeuf), there is no doubt that Fechner, between 1860 and his death in 1887, was assailed both by physicists and

15 Heidelberger (2004) wrote expressly that, in the Fechner-Mach perspective, "The observer and his sensations cannot be eliminated. Instead, sensations constitute the foundations from which physics proceeds" (p. 247).

philosophers for trying to accomplish what seemed, at that time, an impossible task. The task was to take the extensive measurements that had been so successfully applied to Newtonian physics and somehow apply them to mental experiences, especially sensations. Fechner's idea was to reify a "just noticeable difference" as being a measurement-unit within psychophysics. Mathematicians, including Tannery and Von Kries, argued that sensations simply could not be designated as "equal" to each other with the confidence that mathematicians could say two lines were of "equal" length to each other. As a general principle, one could justifiably say that one sound was sensed as being louder than another. Nevertheless, discrete magnitudes could not be assigned to such sensations even though discrete numbers could be assigned to physical measures of sound intensity.

Stadler and F. A. Müller went further and claimed that stimulus intensity and sensation-magnitude were not sufficiently "homogeneous" to permit a researcher to take a stimulus intensity and transform that stimulus intensity compellingly into a sensation-magnitude. The paradox that just noticeable differences increased discontinuously while stimulus-magnitudes could increase continuously was also highlighted (there is more on this in Chapter 8). Elsas raised several criticisms to the effect that there is an arbitrary element to the definition of "sensation-magnitudes" that pushed them "out of court" when it came to comparing them to the established (and less arbitrary) extensive measurement-units of physics. Moreover, Elsas stressed that physics was only concerned with causal explanations of events in nature, whereas psychophysical events might only be correlational.

Ernst Mach provided a scientist's support for Fechner by insisting that physics itself depended on the sensations felt and interpreted by physicists. In Chapter 1, a broad reading of Kant's delineation of an "intensive" magnitude as representing a "filling-in" of a physical object's characteristics was claimed to assist us to say more about that object's behaviour in a Newtonian universe than was provided by "extensive" magnitudes alone. Kant's thinking was a precursor to Mach's insistence that physics *incorporates* dicta about how objects are sensed. There is little doubt that relativity theory stemmed indirectly from the Fechner-Mach perspective outlined so well in Chapter 6 of Heidelberger's (2004) biography of Fechner.

8 The Power Law in Early Psychophysics

A Question in Visual Psychophysics

The present chapter will focus on visual psychophysics in the nineteenth century. In particular, a specific question about visual experiences was barely touched on by Fechner himself in the *Elemente*, although simultaneous contrast was discussed in earlier papers (Fechner, 1838, 1840, 1860b). Fechner (1860/1964, Vol. II, pp. 198–311 and 1860/1966, pp. 110–146) wrote at considerable length about the need to obtain more evidence as to whether Weber's Law could always be applied to the perception of small differences in stimulus intensity when the stimuli were *visual*. He could only find a handful of studies, carried out prior to 1860, that were concerned with lightness-discrimination and/or colour-discrimination.[1]

The literature to be discussed in this chapter concerns attempts to answer the following question. Let us construct a display of concentric circular bands gradated in greyness from a light grey central band to a dark grey outermost band. The intermediate bands look to have equal steps in greyness from one band to the next. Would such a display continue to *look* equally gradated if the overall level of illumination changed?

J. A. F. Plateau (1801–1883)

Plateau's (1872) Experiments

Plateau was born into a French-speaking Belgian family. His father was an expert at painting flowers, which may have led Plateau to develop a curiosity about visual experiences. His dissertation of 1829, on visual science, was presented at the University of Liège in north-eastern Belgium (Koppelman, 1970). An early position as professor of physics at the prestigious Institut Goggia in Liège was followed by his employment as extraordinary professor of experimental physics at the University of Ghent in 1835. In 1842, he was later promoted to ordinary professor, a rank he held until 1872.

1 I have chosen not to review this early literature, which included the measurement of the brightness of stars. It may also be mentioned that, because light and sound are transmitted by undulations (waves, vibrations) through the air to the eye and the ear respectively, the most sophisticated mathematics in the second volume of the *Elemente* are to be found on pages 198–391.

As part of an experiment in 1829, he stared into the sun for 25 seconds. This led to a temporary blindness for about a week, from which he partially recovered. In 1841, however, he suffered from a disease of the cornea, which led to complete blindness. Whether his staring at the sun was related to the permanent blindness that came on 13 years later, is not clear (De Laey, 2002).

Prior to his blindness, much of his research was on retinal processes. He asked how quickly a retinal image would fade. He showed it took about one-third of a second. His research included the discovery of the Talbot-Plateau Law (relating the intensity of a colour sensation to the intensity and the duration of the colour stimulus). He also invented an early form of stroboscope, in which standing human figures, each one slightly different from the previous, seemed to "dance" when presented in rapid succession. He performed experiments on the "bisection" of levels of lightness/greyness; these are presented below.

After his blindness, he made fundamental discoveries about surface tension in liquids. He demonstrated that a thin film of soapy liquid formed a surface of minimal area when stretched across a wire that had the shape of a loop or other closed form. He also completed an annotated bibliography, from ancient times to the 1870s, of quotations about visually perceived phenomena, including lightness contrast (Plateau, 1878). His study on the bisection of levels of lightness in order to find a mid-grey that looked halfway in lightness between white and black was actually carried out in the 1830s, prior to his blindness, but not published until Plateau read Fechner's (1860/1964) *Elemente der Psychophysik.*[2]

Plateau is remembered for a classic experiment. He asked eight experts in oil painting to paint a grey square that *looked* halfway between white and black. They were asked to do this in "natural light", which is a vague enough term for us to accept that each individual painter would have worked in a "light" determined by himself. Despite this source of variability, the eight greys *looked* remarkably similar to each other; and when the eight greys were viewed in bright daylight, the eight greys continued to *look* remarkably similar to each other. Later, the experiment was extended to the creation of a grey that looked halfway between the above grey and black, or between the above grey and white. This procedure led to Plateau's assertion that the "intensity of the sensations corresponding to these five shades from black to white would be 0, 1, 2, 3, 4" (Laming & Laming, 1996, p. 137).

Then Plateau (1872a) argued that "if the ratios of the intensities produced by two different shades of grey is independent of the degree of common lighting, one arrives at a formula which does not coincide with Fechner's" (Laming & Laming, 1996, p. 138). Plateau proved this formula was a power law.[3] Matters did

2 Plateau (1872a) reported that he carried out the first of these experiments "about twenty years earlier," that is, in the 1850s. But Laming and Laming (1996, p. 143, note c) convincingly argue that the experiments must have been carried out in the 1830s, before Plateau went permanently blind.

3 Plateau (1872a) provided a mathematical proof that a power function could predict that the black minus the mid-grey would equal the mid-grey minus the white. Laming and Laming (1996), however, claimed that Plateau's proof was mathematically flawed.

not rest there. Delboeuf (1873) argued that a logarithmic law based on intrinsic nervous activity could fit a pattern of equal-looking steps of lightness-level that had 13 shades of grey, just as well as could a power law.

In his reply to Plateau, Fechner (1877, pp. 21–23) himself argued that his own derivation of his logarithmic law could be modified at its very outset in such a way as to yield a power law. This would happen if, in the "fundamental formula", the left side was changed from

$$\Delta S = K(\Delta I/I) \tag{8.1}$$

to

$$\Delta S/S = K(\Delta I/I). \tag{8.2}$$

Instead of assuming that an increment in sensation strength, *S*, was a constant, assume that the increment in sensation strength, *relative to its present sensation strength*, was a variable. Fechner showed that this assumption led to a power law.[4] As first suggested by Plateau, the psychophysical power law was then:

$$S = kI^c. \tag{8.3}$$

The value c is a numerical value that varies with the type of stimulus. The value k is a constant whose value varies with the measurement-unit associated with the stimulus.

No matter what its base, a logarithmic function of I is always negatively accelerated and increases towards an asymptote as I increases. Often, a power function of I is also negatively accelerated and increases towards an asymptote. This is found when the value of the power is less than 1.0. Estimated values of the power are indeed often less than one. Therefore, a negatively accelerated function could be either a logarithmic function or a power function.

Hering's (1875) Criticism of Fechner's Psychophysics

Ewald Hering (1834–1918), like his almost exact contemporary Ernst Mach (1838–1916), spent most of his career in the Austro-Hungarian Empire. He taught, in German, at the University of Prague as well as at the University of Vienna. Hering studied with Fechner at Leipzig for a while and acknowledged his indebtedness to Fechner as a mentor. But Hering's (1875) article was an exceptionally blistering attack on his mentor's psychophysics.

4 Somebody strongly attracted to a psychophysical power law could surely claim that this is an example *par excellence* of the improvement of a theory (here, Fechner's) by exchanging an absolute value (here, ΔS) for a relative value (here, $\Delta S/S$).

Hering's Experimental Contributions

One underpinning of Hering's criticisms of Fechner's development of psychophysics was Hering's belief that Fechner's deduction of Fechner's Law from Weber's Law was faulty. Another was Hering's insistence that Weber's Law was not shown, in Fechner's large experiment using weights, to be valid for lifted weights. Hering's argument was three-pronged.

First, Fechner's own data (as shown in the section on Fechner's Large Experiment in Chapter 4 of the present volume) did not succeed in confirming that Weber's Law was upheld for the case of lifted weights (a thesis confirmed by Link's, 1992, p. 15, chi-squared analysis of Fechner's data).

Second, for Hering, the reliability of the visual sense was due to the presentation of visual information in parallel. For example, we can look simultaneously at a small triangle and at a large triangle and judge that those triangles differ in area, and whether or not they are congruent. In the context of weight-lifting studies, Hering insisted that this perspicuity of inner judgment is almost nullified by the facts that, usually, weights have to be lifted successively and can involve muscular sensations of the arms, fingers, etc. that vary from body-part to body-part. In a word, if one is going to do psychophysics, one should use visual displays rather than lifted weights as one's stimulus material.[5]

Third, Hering asked two of his students to test Weber's Law for lifted weights by starting with a *Hauptgewicht* (which is better translated as a "main weight" than as a "standard weight") and then finding the extra weight needed to be added to the main weight in order for the new weight to feel just noticeably heavier. In one study (Hering, 1875, pp. 342–344), main weights ranged from 250 to 2,750 g. According to Fechner (1877) "a towel (*Handtuch*) was held by tying its two ends together. In the sling so formed, a wooden plate was suspended by one to three cords. The wooden plate carried the weight. Towel, cords and plate altogether weighed 250 gm" (p. 192). The apparatus holding the main weight will here be called the "sling-apparatus".

Table 8.1 is a reproduction of Hering's (1875, p. 343) first table, with the addition of Fechner's (1877, p. 193) calculations on arm-weight. The first column shows the row-numbers associated with each weight. These main weights, W, are shown in the second column. The smallest main weight was 250 g. The largest was given by Fechner as 3,000, rather than 2,750 g. The third column shows, for each main weight, a small increase in grams, ΔW, needed to be added to the main weight to make it feel just noticeably heavier. The fourth column shows a psychophysicist's preferred expression of Weber's constant ($\Delta W/W$), as $[1/(W/\Delta W)]$. The values shown in the fourth column generally decrease as W increases. The fifth column shows Fechner's recalculation of these values when, instead of using W, he used ($W + 2{,}273$). Here, 2,273 g is Fechner's estimated weight of a participant's arm.[6] The sixth column shows how Fechner adjusted these values in the

5 Later, a similar opinion was expressed by T. Lipps (1905/1926). His views were discussed by Murray and Barnes (2014).

6 Fechner (1877, p. 192fn) obtained the value of 2,273 g by a rather ingenious analysis of Hering's data.

Table 8.1 How Fechner (1877, p. 193) Used Hering's (1875, p. 343) Data to Show the Influence of Adding an Arm-Weight of 2,273 g on the Resulting Weber Fraction

Row	*Main weight*	*JND*	*Weber fraction*	*Weber fraction (arm-weight included)*	*Fechner's adjustment*★
	W	ΔW	$1/(W/\Delta W)$	$1/[(W + 2273)/\Delta W]$	
1	250	12	1/21	1/210	1/21.0
2	500	13	1/38	1/213	1/21.3
3	750	13	1/58	1/233	1/23.3
4	1,000	15	1/67	1/218	1/21.8
5	1,250	16	1/78	1/220	1/22.0
6	1,500	17	1/88	1/222	1/22.2
7	1,750	19	1/92	1/212	1/21.2
8	2,000	20	1/100	1/214	1/21.4
9	2,250	22	1/102	1/206	1/20.6
10	2,500	22	1/114	1/217	1/21.7
11	2,750	28	1/98	1/179	1/17.9
12★★	3,000	28	1/98	1/188	1/18.8

★ Row 1 shows that, when W was 250 gm, the observed JND, ΔW, was 12 gm. The associated Weber fraction can be written as $(\Delta W/W) = (12/250) = 0.048$. In this case, the expression of Weber's constant is $[1/(W/\Delta W)] = [1/(250/12)] = 1/21$, as shown in Column 4. Adding the arm-weight (2,273 gm) to the main weight (250 gm) gave 2,523 gm. The expression of Weber's constant is $[1/(2{,}523/12)] = 1/210$, as shown in Column 5. Fechner divided 210 by 10. This gives (1/21.0) as shown in Column 6.

★★ In Row 12, $W = 3{,}000$ in Fechner's table, but does not appear in Hering's table. The editor and author calculated the value 1/17.9 in the final column of Row 11.

fifth column by dividing each denominator by 10. This created a range of values that should not change if Weber's constant is, indeed, constant.

In a second study (pp. 344–345), the main weights ranged from 10 to 500 g, and were lifted by a wooden handle held between the thumb and forefinger. When the main weight was increased, in seven unequal steps, from 10 to 500 g, the values $[1/(W/\Delta W)]$ decreased just as in the first study. A third study was carried out (p. 345), which was not reported but yielded the same finding as the others, namely that Weber's constant was *not* constant as W increased.

Nevertheless, there is a problem concerning Table 8.1. Neither Hering (1875) nor Fechner (1877) mentioned the role played by the weight of the sling-apparatus in determining a Weber fraction. The Appendix to this chapter recalculates the Weber fractions when the sling-apparatus is included in the calculations.

The above narrative well exemplifies Fechner's continual concern with answering his critics. Traditionally, however, when psychophysicists thought about Hering's criticism of Fechner's logarithmic law, it was not about the above experiments. Instead, they were referring to a *thought*-experiment described by Hering (1875, pp. 323–325), near the beginning of his article, as follows.

Hering's Thought-Experiment

Despite his disapproval of weight-lifting experiments as potentially providing evidence for Weber's Law or Fechner's Law, Hering was convinced that a particular prediction made by Fechner's Law was almost certainly erroneous. IF it is true (a) that sensation-magnitudes can be portrayed as a scale in which the units are just noticeable differences (JNDs), and (b) that the step from a sensation-magnitude, S_2 (which equals 2 JNDs), to an S_3 (which equals 3 JNDs), counts as "one step", and (c) that therefore the step from a sensation-magnitude, S_{12} (which equals 12 JNDs) to an S_{13} (which equals 13 JNDs), also comprises "one step", THEN the sense-distance ($S_3 - S_2$) should be experienced subjectively as equal in sensation-magnitude to the sense-distance ($S_{13} - S_{12}$).

Hering (1875) not only refused to believe that this could be true, he suggested that one imagine, or even try out in practice, the following thought-experiment:

> If I take a weight of 100 grams in one hand, I will feel it as having a certain heaviness. If I take a weight of 1,000 grams in the other hand, I will feel this as having a much greater heaviness. Now let me add another 100 grams to the 100 grams already in the one hand, and add another 1,000 to the 1,000 grams already in the other hand. The relative stimulus increase on both sides is equally large. As a consequence, according to Fechner, the sensation of increase yielded by the addition of 1,000 grams to one side must feel identical to the sensation of increase yielded by the addition of 100 grams to the other side, and I ought therefore to succumb to the illusion that the increase in the [perceived] heaviness of the load is identical on both sides. But everybody will admit from the outset, and easily confirm by experiment, that this is not even remotely the case. It is much more likely that the increase is small on one side, but very large on the other side.
>
> (pp. 323–324) (my translation)

To Fechner's probable objection that this argument ignores the weight of the arm, Hering made the riposte that the same outcome would be obtained if the participant, instead of lifting the weight, had the weight placed "passively" on his outstretched palm with his arm lying on the table. The left palm initially holds one metal plate of the kind used in a Voltaic pile, and the right palm initially holds five metal plates of this kind. Then, rapidly, the experimenter places one more plate on the left palm and five more plates on the right palm. According to Hering (1875): "the increase in heaviness, even if the participant's eyes are closed and he does not know from the outset what extra weights are to be placed on his palms, would appear to be very much greater on the right palm than on the left palm" (p. 324).

No data supporting these opinions were presented by Hering (1875). He assumed that it would be obvious to anybody that, IF you have a light weight, W, and double it, and that, IF you have a heavy weight $W+$ and double it, THEN the experienced increase in heaviness will *not* be identical for the two weights.

Delboeuf's Contributions to Psychophysics

Now is the time to look at Delboeuf's work on lightness discrimination. Delboeuf was a student of Plateau's. Plateau suggested a clever way to manufacture surfaces varying in greyness without needing to mix pigments.

Delboeuf's Career

Joseph-Rémi-Léopold Delboeuf (1831–1896) was born into a family of modest means in the Belgian city of Liège.[7] He attended university by undertaking tutoring jobs during his teens. He obtained a doctorate in philosophy in 1855 and a doctorate in physical and mathematical science in 1858. After some postdoctoral research at the University of Bonn in Germany, and some teaching (of Greek, among other subjects!) in Liège, he was offered the Chair of Philosophy at the University of Ghent in 1863, where he also taught psychology at the École Normale des Sciences. While preparing his psychology course, he read the first edition of Wundt's (1863) *Lectures on Human and Animal Psychology* [*Vorlesungen über die Menschen- und Thierseele*], from which he learned about Fechner's (1860/1964) *Elemente der Psychophysik*.

In 1864, Delboeuf began a long career of experimentation in psychology, including studies of memory (summarized by Nicolas, 1995a), visual illusions (reviewed by Nicolas, 1995b), and, towards the end of his career, hypnotism (reviewed by Duyckaerts, 1992). His three most important monographs on psychophysics were: *Theoretical and Experimental Research on the Measurement of Sensations, Particularly Sensations of Light and Fatigue* [*Étude Psychophysique. Recherches Théoriques et Expérimentales sur la Mesure des Sensations et Spécialement des Sensations de la Lumière et de Fatigue*] (Delboeuf, 1873); a theoretical study titled *Critical Examination of the Psychophysical Law: Its Basis and its Significance* [*Examen Critique de la loi Psychophysique: Sa Base et sa Signification*] (Delboeuf, 1883a); and *Elements of Psychophysics, Both General and Specific* [*Éléments de Psychophysique Générale et Spéciale*] (Delboeuf, 1883b).

Recent writings on Delboeuf include the following. A table of data reported by Delboeuf (1873, Table 1, p. 54) was reproduced on page 141 of Laming and Laming's (1996) translation of Plateau (1872b). Delboeuf's original table had included 14 columns. Plateau's version shortened it to six columns. Plateau's (1872b) summary detailed Delboeuf's mathematics, as did an article on Delboeuf's psychophysics written over 100 years later by Nicolas, Murray, & Farahmand (1997). What follows is largely based on this article.

7 Belgium has two official languages, Flemish (spoken mainly in the North) and French (spoken mainly in the South). Many cities in Belgium therefore have two names. The capital is Brussel (Bruxelles) [Brussels in English]; major universities are found at Leuven (Louvain), Brugge (Bruges), Gent (Gand) [Ghent in English], and Liège.

Delboeuf's (1883) Ideas About Psychophysics

Delboeuf (1883a, p. 129 ff.) raised the question of how two viewpoints concerning sensation-magnitude could be reconciled. According to the first point of view, a sensation-magnitude was a variable that increased monotonically and continuously with stimulus intensity. Whether the increase was determined by a power or by a logarithmic function is not the question here. The question concerns only the idea that sensation-magnitude will always rise as stimulus intensity rises, or always fall as stimulus intensity falls.

According to the second point of view, sensation-magnitude could be regarded as increasing in units called JNDs. A power function of stimulus intensity was consistent with the finding that psychological sizes of the JNDs increased as stimulus intensity increased. A logarithmic function was consistent with the finding that the psychological sizes of the JNDs remained identical as stimulus intensity increased. The first point of view specifies that a JND between two stimulus intensities, I_1 and I_2, results from a rise in sensation-magnitude from that associated with I_1 to that associated with I_2. What happens if a stimulus with a value of $I_{1.5}$ is presented midway in intensity between I_1 and I_2? Will $I_{1.5}$ be sensed? If I_1 and I_2 provide a context in which any intensity between 1 and 2 JNDs is "*not* just noticeable", then $I_{1.5}$ will *not* be sensed. If there is no such context, however, $I_{1.5}$ *would* be sensed because $I_{1.5}$ is not contained within that context.

Delboeuf (1883a, p. 104), using an analogy, argued that $I_{1.5}$ would be sensed. He compared the arousal of a sensation by the presentation of an appropriate stimulus with the behaviour of a compass needle hanging from the middle of a loop of wire when the needle is set into motion by sending an electric current through the wire. The needle moves further and further as the strength of the current increases. The *monotonic* relation between sensation-magnitude and stimulus intensity is paralleled by the monotonic relation between the distance moved by the needle and the strength of the electric current.[8]

There is more to this story. When the electric current is *first* sent through the wire, the needle does not instantaneously begin to move because friction prevents its moving at first. There is a delay before the needle starts to move, but when it does, Titchener (1905b, p. xxix) described it as going "with a little jump to the position which the law of correlation requires". For Delboeuf, the delay had its parallel in the nervous system. A stimulus has to attain a certain intensity before the neural processes underlying the arousal of a sensation-experience could be initiated. Delboeuf particularly liked this analogy, because *his* version of the psychophysical law (described below) assumed that there was indeed a resistance at the receptor level to the initiation of activity strong enough to yield a sensation. Delboeuf (1873, p. 28) argued that this resistance

8 Please note that the relation is not linear because, as current strength increases regularly by equal amounts, the needle is deflected by smaller and smaller amounts before coming to rest. If d is the angle of deflection, $\tan d = a/k$, where a is the number of amperes in the current and k is a constant.

at the receptor level to the initiation of processes leading to a sensation could be quantified by a variable he named *c*.[9]

Helmholtz on Psychophysics

A decade earlier, factors indigenous to receptor physiology were also invoked when von Helmholtz (1860/1962, pp. 172–181) described Fechner's Law during Helmholtz's discussion of the intensity of sensations of light. Fechner (1860/1966, pp. 116–146) described just how far earlier research on just noticeable differences in luminosity obeyed Weber's Law. von Helmholtz (1860/1962, pp. 173–175) reviewed the same literature more briefly, but went on to add that:

> The fact that within a wide range of luminosity the smallest perceptible differences of the light sensation correspond to (nearly) constant fractions of luminosity was used by FECHNER in formulating a more general, so-called *psycho-physical* law, which is found to be true also in other regions of the sensations ... According to E. H. Weber's investigations, the case is similar also with the ability to recognize differences between weights and linear magnitudes.
>
> (p. 175)

Fechner also pointed out that Weber's Law is often not obeyed either at very low or at very high stimulus luminosities. Helmholtz (1860/1962) noted that, at very low luminosities, the intrinsic light of the eye must make itself felt. Together with the stimulation due to external light (denoted by Helmholtz as *H*) there is always, in addition, a stimulation due to internal causes, the amount of which may be considered as being equivalent to the stimulation by a light of luminosity H_0.

If, for narrative continuity, we replace Helmholtz's *H* by our *I*, Helmholtz therefore suggested that Fechner's "fundamental formula" be changed from

$$\Delta S = K\left(\Delta I / I_0\right). \tag{8.1}$$

to

$$\Delta S = K\left[\Delta I / \left(I + H_0\right)\right] \tag{8.4}$$

Helmholtz's amendment of Fechner's fundamental formula did not lie buried in the hundreds of pages of the *Physiological Optics*. It was taken up by Wundt,

9 For Delboeuf, *c* was defined as an "interior excitation" as contrasted with a level of "exterior excitation" here named *d* [Delboeuf used δ]. This dichotomy was applied to all the senses. With particular reference to the eye, Delboeuf wrote that "*d* is a cause that is usually of a luminance kind, *c* is a physiological cause ... *d* and *c* together set the [nerve]-fibres of the retina into a particular state of vibration. ... We admit that no corresponding sensation can be effectively ascribed to *c*. Sensation begins at the moment when to *c* is added some kind of *d*" (my translation of Delboeuf, 1873, pp. 28–29). Nevertheless, some unusual experiences might reflect the activity of *c*. Examples include phosphenes when the eyeball is pressed, "seeing stars" when one is "knocked out," and sensations of light when the optic nerve is sectioned (p. 30).

who included it in his *Principles of Physiological Psychology* [*Grundzüge der Physiologische Psychologie*], (e.g., Wundt, 1887, pp. 387–388). Wundt demonstrated that, starting from Equation 8.4, it can be predicted mathematically that Weber's Law will break down at very low and at very high values of luminosity.

In his *Étude Psychophysique*, Delboeuf (1873) assumed that *c* stayed constant during, let's say, a typical psychophysical experiment such as finding a grey midway between two other greys. By the time of publication of his *Examen Critique*, Delboeuf (1883a) came to view *c* as continuously varying rather than as a constant. Now think of the resistance of a receptor to initiating processes that would lead to a sensation as constituting a "threshold" that had to be crossed. In Delboeuf's earlier psychophysics, the assumption that *c* had a fixed value is consistent with the notion that there is indeed a fixed sensory threshold analogous to the Fechnerian absolute threshold. In Delboeuf's late psychophysics, however, where *c* is variable due to contextual changes in the execution of an experiment, it is hard to see how this is compatible with a "fixed" threshold.

Delboeuf's (1873) Experiments on Psychophysics

Plateau (1872a) suggested that the greyness-level of a stimulus could be quantitatively controlled by taking a black disc, adding a slice-of-pie-shaped sector of white to the expanse of black, then rapidly rotating the disc. The eye-brain system of the participant would fuse the sensations aroused by the white sector with the sensations aroused by the expanse of black not covered by the white sector. The result would be a uniform grey. The greater the proportion of black expanse that was occupied by the white sector, the lighter-looking was the uniform grey that was perceived, provided that the rotation was sufficiently rapid that no trace of the contours of the white sector were preserved in the uniform greyness.

In Delboeuf's first study, from which his famous Table 1 was derived, he used four concentric discs, the smallest of which was white, the next largest had a grey that was selected by the participant, the third largest had a darker grey selected by the experimenter, and the largest—the outermost—had a very dark grey that was also selected by the experimenter. The whole display appeared against a black background. To vary the greyness of a band, a removable white sector of a given angular width was pushed into a gap in front of a disc so as to provide the greyness required of that disc.

On any single trial, the experimenter would pre-set the outer ring, R_1, to a dark grey, the next-to-outer ring, R_2, to a lighter grey and leave the centre circle all white. The participant's task was to choose a grey for the next-to-inner circle, R_3, so that R_2 looked intermediate in greyness between R_3 and the outer ring R_1.[10]

10 In describing Delboeuf's experiment, Titchener (1905b, p. 212, fn. 1) wondered why it was R_3, and not R_2, that was variable; after all, in Plateau's early bisection study, painters had to paint a greyness R_2 that looked halfway between R_1 (painted black) and R_3 (painted white). Titchener suggested that "the sectors to be varied (pulled out and pushed in) should be short and broad (p. 211), which would make it easier [for the participant] to manipulate the greyness of R_3 than it was to manipulate R_2 or R_1." Titchener (1905a, pp. 88–91) also illustrated Delboeuf's apparatus.

The greyness of a disc itself was given in units that represented the angular width subtended by the white sector in an otherwise black disc. The lower the number, the darker the grey associated with that disc. Delboeuf's aim was to find a psychophysical function (for which Fechner's logarithmic law and Plateau's power law were both potential candidates) that would allow Delboeuf to *predict* the numerical value of R_3 that would make R_2 *look* halfway in greyness between R_3 and R_1.

Delboeuf, in fact, derived his own psychophysical function. The function depends in part on the value, c, introduced by Delboeuf, the resistance offered by a receptor to being stimulated intensely enough to arouse the relevant sensation.[11]

We now present Delboeuf's psychophysical function. From a remark he made in his monograph titled "Hering versus Fechner" (Delboeuf, 1877) we learn that, when he first read Fechner's (1860/1964) *Elemente der Psychophysik*, he was struck by a need to correct Fechner's Law. To do so, he would take into account physiological events associated with the successful arousal, via the central nervous system, of a sensation evoked by the stimulus that was presented in a trial in a psychophysical discrimination task. He started with Fechner's Law in the form $S = K\log_e I$, but replaced the stimulus intensity, I, by the term $(p' - p)$, where p' is the extra excitation added by the presentation of a stimulus to a resting level of neural excitation represented by p. According to Nicolas, Murray, and Farahmand (1997, p. 1299), Delboeuf also assumed that there was a value c which represented the state of excitation possessed uniquely by a sense organ, and which was in turn due to [intrinsic nervous activity] quite distinct from any source of excitation... This value c was added to the value representing external excitation, namely $(p' - p)$, equal to I, and the equation [was amended].

The amended equation was

$$S = K\log_e\left[\left(I + c\right)/c\right]. \tag{8.5}$$

In Equation 8.5, I can be identified with R, the proportion a white sector constitutes of a black disc. No specific numerical values were initially assigned to K and c. One reason was that the values of K and c in Equation 8.5 were not determined enough to allow the prediction of the greyness-level R_3 that would make the greyness-level R_2 look halfway between R_3 and R_1. To make this prediction, Equation 8.5 would have to use known values of K and c.

Let us denote the greyness-level of R_1 (the outermost ring with the darkest grey) by d, the greyness-level of R_2 by d', and the greyness-level of R_3 by d''.

11 His original Table 1 (Delboeuf, 1873, p. 54) consisted of no fewer than 14 columns. Plateau (1872b) reduced Delboeuf's Table 1 to six columns; Titchener (1905b, p. 211) reduced it to seven; and Murray (1993, p. 120) reduced it to five columns, namely, the greyness-level of R_1, the greyness-level of R_2, the predicted greyness-level of R_3 when $c = 0.5$, the median obtained greyness-level of R_3 as set by the participant, and the mean obtained greyness-level of R_3 also as set by the participant.

Let the corresponding sensation-magnitudes be denoted by S, S', and S'' (Delboeuf used s). Let $K = 1$ in Equation 8.5. Then, from Equation 8.5, we can infer that

$$S = \log_e\left[(d + c) / c\right] \tag{8.6a}$$

$$S' = \log_e\left[(d' + c) / c\right] \tag{8.6b}$$

$$S'' = \log_e\left[(d'' + c) / c\right] \tag{8.6c}$$

By the definition of S, we know that $S' - S = S'' - S'$. After algebraic manipulation, Delboeuf concludes that

$$c = \left[(d')^2 - dd''\right] / (d + d'' - 2d') \tag{8.7}$$

and that

$$d'' = \left[(d')^2 - cd + 2cd'\right] / (c + d). \tag{8.8}$$

These derivations are found on page 58 of Delboeuf (1873).

Equation 8.8 says that, if we know the numerical values of d' and of d (which we do, because both were pre-set by the experimenter), and if we know the numerical value of c, which we don't, so Delboeuf used both $c = 0.5$ and $c = 0.12$ in deriving his Table 1 (Table 8.2 here), then we can use Equation 8.8 to estimate the *predicted* value of d'' (i.e., the greyness-level of R_3 that will be chosen by the participant so that R_2 *looks* halfway between R_3 and R_1).[12]

Table 8.2 shows the corrected table as originally presented by Delboeuf (1873, p. 54). One single participant undertook a total of 14 blocks of 5 trials each. Delboeuf included, in the original table, the participant's greyness-setting on each *trial*. Some errors were found in Delboeuf's Table 1. In Table 8.2 the corrected numbers are indicated in **bold** typeface adjacent to the erroneous numbers.[13]

Table 8.2 shows the full Table 1 from Delboeuf (1873, p. 54). The units represent the angular width subtended by a white sector in an otherwise black circle. The lower the number, the darker the appearance of the associated ring. The greyness allotted by the participant to R_3, d'', is such that R_2 looks intermediate between R_3 and R_1. Column 1 numbers the 14 blocks of five trials each. Columns 2 and 3 show the greyness (set by the experimenter) of R_1 and R_2

12 The *final* experiment carried out by Delboeuf (1873) allowed him to estimate a value $c = 0.12$, so the addition of predicted R_3-settings when $c = 0.12$ in *his* Table 1 was added as an afterthought when Delboeuf was writing up his work for presentation to the Royal Academy of Sciences of Belgium.

13 Numbers corrected by editor and author.

Table 8.2 Results of Delboeuf's Bisection Experiment

1	*2*	*3*	*4*	*5*	*6*	*7*	*8*	*9*	*10*	*11*	*12*	*13*	*14*
Block of 5 trials	Greyness of outer ring (R_1), d	Greyness of middle ring (R_2), d'	Predicted greyness of inner ring (R_3) for $c = 0.5$, d''	Predicted greyness of inner ring (R_3) for $c = 0.12$, d''	Obtained greyness of inner ring (R_3)					Obtained min. of the 5 trials	Observed max. of the 5 trials	Obtained average of min. and max.	Obtained average of all 5 trials
					Trial 1	Trial 2	Trial 3	Trial 4	Trial 5				
1	9	47	237	242.2	287	247	272	205	177	177	287	232	237.6
2	13	27	55.5	55.9	53	54	54	56	55	53	56	55.5 **54.5**	54.4
3	13	36	98.3	99.3	102	98	93	112	89	89	112	105 **100.5**	98.8
4	13	41	127	128.7	105	141	151	126	123	105	151	128	129.2
5	13	56	236	239.9	316	238	241	222	222	222	316	274 **269**	247.8
6	21	60	169.7	171	169	181	153	168	176	153	181	167	163.4 **169.4**
7	21	64	193	202	196	200	213	184	207	184	213	198.5	200
8	22	36	58.7	58.9	59	60	55	55	59	55	60	57.5	57.6
9	22	51	117.4	117.8	134	114	96	128	127	96	134	115	119.8
10	22	58	151.6	152.5	156	150	144	158	158	144	158	151	152.2 **153.2**
11	22	66	196	197.5	224	233	166	179	172	160 **166**	233	199.5	194.8
12	43	64	97.4	98.1	98	104	100	91	94	91	104	97.5	97.4
13	43	72	119.5	120.05	147	125	144	118	116	116	147	131.5	130
14	43	87	175.5	178.2	177	195	142	170	200	142	200	171	176.8

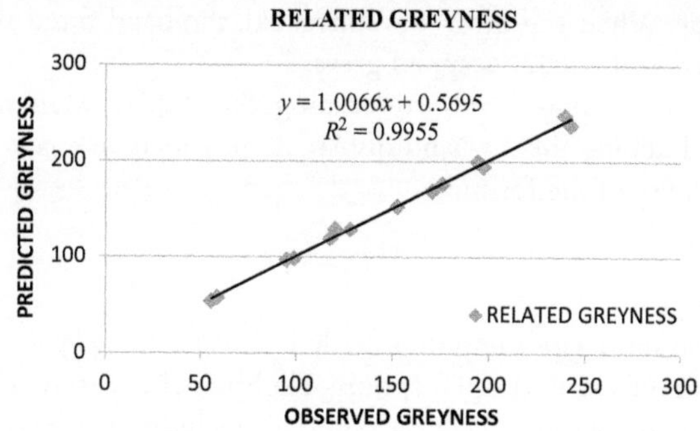

Figure 8.1 The predicted greyness-value for R_3 as a function of its observed value.

respectively. Columns 4 and 5 show the *predicted* greyness of R_3, according to Equation 8.8, when $c = 0.5$ and $c = 0.12$ respectively. Columns 6 to 10 show the participant's *obtained* greyness settings of R_3 on trials 1 to 5 of that block of trials. Columns 11 and 12 show, respectively, the minimum and maximum settings obtained on those five trials. Column 13 shows the obtained average of the minimum and maximum settings only. Column 14 shows the obtained average of all five greyness settings.

There is a good match between the entries on the fifth and fourteenth column on any row of Table 8.2. One test of the goodness-of-fit is to determine the linear equation which best fits a plot of the predicted d''-values as a function of the observed d''-values. A perfect fit would yield a linear equation with a slope of 1.0, and an intercept on the ordinate of zero. The following equation, shown in Figure 8.1, provides the best fit of a straight line to the 14 values reported in columns 14 and 5 respectively of Table 8.2:

$$\text{predicted greyness} = 1.01\left(\text{observed greyness}\right) \tag{8.9}$$

The percentage of variance accounted for by Equation 8.9 was 99.55%. There is no doubt that Delboeuf's change to Fechner's equation successfully predicted how a participant will set greyness-level R_3 in such a way that greyness-level R_2 will look halfway between greyness-level R_3 and greyness-level R_1.

Delboeuf also brought his *Étude Psychophysique* to an extraordinary ending. He proved that as many as 14 discs can be so arranged that the innermost looks white, the outermost looks black, and all the intermediate greys are such that the whole display appears to present a smooth, equal-stepped gradation from white in the centre to black at the periphery. If this could be achieved, Delboeuf would have concrete—incontrovertible?—evidence that Equation 8.8 could serve as a basis for the construction of a visual display whose lightness varied in 13 equal-looking steps of grey from white to black.

Delboeuf and his colleagues actually constructed such a display. When one of the bands looked "out of place", it was discovered that an error in calculation had been made. When the error was corrected, the band fitted neatly into its place in the series of equally-stepped greys.[14]

Delboeuf's concluding words concerning the display were simply to the effect that, by building the 13-band display, he provided an *a posteriori* verification of the validity of the formula

$$S = \log_e\left[(d + c)/c\right]. \tag{8.6a}$$

The above account details the points made in *Étude Psychophysique*. The monograph deals, not only with the perception of lightness, but also with the development of fatigue in a sensory receptor system. It includes six theorems. Theorem 4 contends that, if d' looks halfway between d and d'', then the numerical value of d' will be less than the arithmetic mean of d and d'', while Theorem 5 asserts that d' will be greater than the geometric mean of d and d''.

The problems experienced by Delboeuf in putting together his discs, so that the white sector associated with any particular disc can be easily detached or added to that disc without affecting the discs adjacent to that disc, were clearly spelled out.

The most important of Delboeuf's discoveries takes us back to the question with which this chapter opened. If the triple d, d', and d'' are three greys such that d' *looks* halfway between d and d'', will d' continue to *look* halfway between d and d'' when the overall illumination of the display is changed to brighter or dimmer?

Delboeuf claimed that d' would *not* look halfway between d and d'' if a bright light were shone on the display. He argued that if the overall illumination increased, d' would lose its apparent greyness-level relative to the combined greyness-level of d and d''. He demonstrated experimentally that when d' looks halfway between d and d'' with a candle at a particular distance from the display, and IF one wishes to keep d' looking halfway between d and d'' when the candle is moved towards or away from the display, THEN d' must be increased when the candle is moved towards the display or decreased when the candle is moved away from the display (pp. 67–69). Let a candle be moved towards or away from the 14-disc array, after the display is set so the 13 bands are gradated in equal-appearing steps. Then moving the candle towards the display causes the outermost greys to look relatively lighter than the innermost greys, while moving the candle away from the display causes the outermost greys to look relatively darker than the innermost greys.[15]

14 The mathematics required in order to predict the correct mix of white-added-to-black for each individual band was described in exemplary detail by Delboeuf (1873, pp. 91–95). The construction of the display by the attachment of white sectors of predicted angular widths to each of the 14 black discs was described on pages 95 to 99.

15 These findings depend on the premise that when $d - x = d'$ and $d' - x = d''$, THEN the casting of a brighter or dimmer light over the whole display will change the values of $\log_e [(d + c)/c]$, $\log_e [(d' + c)/c]$, and $\log_e [(d'' + c)/c]$ so that it would no longer be true that $d - x = d'$ and that $d' - x = d''$. The change in overall illumination might conserve $d - x = d'$, but would change the second identity to $d' - y = d''$ where y is unequal to x. It can be added that C. Lloyd Morgan (1900) carried out an experiment very similar to Delboeuf's and also concluded that "a black and white disc which shows good shading for a medium illumination fails to grade smoothly in a strong light" (p. 224).

In his section on Delboeuf in his *The Case for Psychophysics* [*In Sachen der Psychophysik*], Fechner (1877) discussed the *Étude* (Delboeuf, 1873), another book by Delboeuf (1876), and the article on Hering versus Fechner (Delboeuf, 1877). Essentially, Fechner considered that the *Étude*, because it supported the validity both of Weber's Law and made sensation-magnitude a logarithmic function of stimulus intensity, was not an opposition to Fechner's idea. Rather, the *Étude* showed that Fechner's Law could be adapted to account for the case of equal-appearing greyness-levels (lightnesses). As such, the *Étude* permitted Fechner's Law to be extended to sensations of visual lightness in a manner that was not previously achieved by any other experimenter. Fechner complained that Delboeuf, in postulating a variable, *c*, that referred to the resistance to excitation of a visual receptor organ, had not referred to the *Augengrau*, the field of darkish grey that one sees if one closes one's eyes in a darkened room. Both Fechner and G. E. Müller mentioned it in their writings on psychophysics.

Fechner (1877) felt that, in Delboeuf's later books, he became more negative. In Delboeuf's (1876) book and his 1877 article titled "Hering versus Fechner", Delboeuf was critical of Fechner's inner psychophysics. Delboeuf had only touched on this matter briefly in the *Étude*. Delboeuf also became increasingly critical of Fechner's predictions of negative sensations when, in Fechner's Law, I had a value less than one. Because the value of $[(d + c)/c]$ would always exceed one, assuming c and d to be positive, these negative values did not arise in Delboeuf's psychophysical law.

Delboeuf's Influence on Titchener

Let us distinguish between the influences on the history of psychophysics exerted by Delboeuf's (1873) monograph, with its extensive experimental evidence, and that of Delboeuf's (1883a, 1883b) two compendia of arguments for and against the validity of Fechner's psychophysical law. Starting with the latter, Titchener (1905b, pp. cxvi–cxxii) explicitly stated that it was because of Delboeuf's (1883a) close examination of what was meant by a "sensation-magnitude" that Titchener adopted the language of "sense-distance". Psychophysicists in general were forced to consider the possibility that a so-called "sensation-magnitude" could be considered an indirect way of referring to a "sensation of contrast" between a stimulus of intensity I and the stimuli that combined to form the background against which stimulus I was exposed.

Delboeuf's (1873) experiments led to Delboeuf's (1883a) innovative idea that a sensation-threshold need not be "fixed" but could vary.

Summary

The pioneering work by Plateau in the late 1830s on the task of finding a grey midway between black and white, led Plateau himself to suggest that his own early research on the bisection method was consistent with a power function relating sensation-magnitude to stimulus intensity. Moreover, the thought-experiment by Hering (1875) indicated that the "psychological size" of a just noticeable difference associated with a stimulus of intensity I_1 did not stay constant, but increased as I increased. This, Hering maintained, was also consistent with his psychophysical power law.

Delboeuf, however, claimed that the sensation-magnitude of a grey stimulus that looked halfway between a white and black could be predicted by an elaborated version of Fechner's Law, in which that sensation of mid-grey could be predicted from a knowledge of the greyness-levels of that white, that mid-grey, and that black. In turn, each of these greyness-levels was contended to be a logarithmic function of a new measure of stimulus intensity. This new logarithmic function used a variable c to represent the intrinsic nervous activity required to activate the flow of sensory excitation.

A more compelling demonstration that Delboeuf was on the right track when he redefined stimulus intensity in terms of the physiological variable, c, was provided when Delboeuf succeeded in predicting exactly what greyness-levels were required if a set of 13 concentric bands were to look equidistant from each other in greyness-level as they increased in darkness from white to black. When the overall illumination of the display was changed, the equal-stepped gradation from white at the centre to black at the outer edge of the display no longer looked "equal-stepped" but imbalanced. Delboeuf predicted this phenomenon from his equations.

Table 8A Table 8.1 modified so as to include W_H, the weight of the sling-apparatus. $W_H = 250$ g

Row	*Main weight*	*JND*	*Weber fraction*	*Weber fraction (arm-weight included)*
	$W_H + W$	ΔW	$1/[(W_H + W)/\Delta W]$	$1/[(W_H + W + 2{,}273)/\Delta W]$
0	250 + 0	11	1/23	1/22.9*
1	250 + 250	12	1/42	1/23.1
2	250 + 500	13	1/58	1/23.3
3	250 + 750	13	1/77	1/25.2
4	250 + 1,000	15	1/83	1/23.5
5	250 + 1,250	16	1/94	1/23.6
6	250 + 1,500	17	1/103	1/23.7
7	250 + 1,750	19	1/118	1/22.5
8	250 + 2,000	20	1/112	1/23.9
9	250 + 2,250	22	1/114	1/21.7
10	250 + 2,500	22	1/125	1/22.8
11	250 + 2,750	28	1/107	1/18.8
12	250 + 3,000	28	1/116	1/19.8

* In Row 0, $(W_H + W) = 250+0 = 250$ and $\Delta W = 11$. The Weber fraction (arm-weight included) expressed as $1/[(250+0+2{,}273)/11] = 1/229.36$. Dividing 229.36 by 10 gives 1/22.9, as shown in Column 5 of Row 0.

APPENDIX

The Role of the Weight of the Apparatus Itself in Determining Hering's (1875) Weber Fractions

Denote the 250 g weight of the sling-apparatus itself as W_H g. Table 8A is a modification of Table 8.1 when W_H is included in the calculations. Four changes to Table 8.1 were introduced into Table 8A. First, a new row, labelled Row 0, precedes Rows 1 to 12 of Table 8.1. Second, in Column 2 of Table 8A, the term W is replaced by $(W_H + W)$. Third, in Column 3 of Table 8A, the value ΔW on Row 0 was determined by Hering to be 11 g. Fourth, the two final columns in Table 8A show Weber fractions without the arm-weight (Column 4) or with the arm-weight (Column 5). In both columns, the term W is replaced by $(W_H + W)$. The Weber fractions in Column 5 were calculated using Fechner's adjustment explained in the context of Table 8.1. Even when the weight of the sling apparatus formed part of the calculations, Table 8A shows that Weber's constant did indeed remain essentially constant when the participant's arm-weight was included.

9 William James and Psychophysics

What James's *Principles of Psychology* Said about Fechner

James's Chapter 13 on "Discrimination and Comparison"

According to Burke-Gaffney (1963), the English word "psychophysics" made its first appearance in Lewes (1879, p. 184). This was nearly 20 years after Fechner (1860a) had introduced the word in German. He had first used it to "mean … an exact theory of the relation of body and mind" (Fechner, 1860/1966, p. xxvii). In the history of nineteenth-century psychophysics, Britain took a back seat to Germany and Belgium in particular. Two well-known histories of British psychology, those of Hearnshaw (1964) and Bunn, Lovie, and Richards (2001), had no index references to Weber, Fechner, or, psychophysics. Johnson (1987) gave a detailed account of the lack of impact of psychophysics on late nineteenth-century British psychology.[1]

William James (1890/1950, Vol. 1, Chapter 13, p. 549), in describing Fechner's work, wrote that "it would be terrible that even such a dear old man as this could saddle our Science forever with his patient whimsies". James famously prognosticated a dull future for psychology if psychophysics were to continue to dominate university-based research as much as it had in the previous 30 years. Let us describe the reasons for James's anxieties and evaluate the degree to which his fears were justified. To be fair, let us place his remarks in their context.

James's remarks on psychophysics come at the end of Chapter 13 (Vol. 1, pp. 483–549). The chapter has 66 pages of quite small print. The two-volume *Principles of Psychology* (1890/1950) played in English-language psychological circles a role similar to that played in German-language psychological circles by Wundt's *Principles of Physiological Psychology* [*Grundzüge der physiologischen Psychologie*]. Both were compendious and aimed to cover the wealth of experiments carried out, for the most part, between about 1860 and 1890. These experiments concerned the realms of what we now call physiological

1 Whittle (1997), however, discussed an attempt to set up a psychophysics laboratory at the University of Cambridge in the 1890s.

psychology, cognitive psychology and the psychology of sensation and perception.[2] I divided James's Chapter 13, titled "Discrimination and Comparison", into four sections.

The Four Sections of Chapter 13

The first section, pages 482–502, deals with the fact that individuals differ, not only in their ability to detect small differences between stimuli, but also in their ability to see likenesses between several stimuli. Discriminations of differences always involve feelings that one difference is greater or less than another, and it is easy for us to arrange a "string" (James's word) of differences serially, so that each difference is equal to the difference that preceded it on the string. Whether or not the existence of such a string is convincing depends on the stimulus-contents involved in the string.

James (1890/1950) asked, "is blue [equal to] yellow *plus* something, if so, *plus* what?" (p. 493). When, however, we do cognize a difference between two stimuli, that cognition is more readily arrived at if the stimuli appear successively, rather than simultaneously. This occurs, says James, because so many stimuli are perceived simultaneously, that the only way we can single out two individual stimuli as being different from each other is when those two stimuli were viewed separately at earlier times. When a difference *is* cognized, that cognition is a "direct intuition of difference somewhere" (p. 497). If the stimuli are now presented one immediately after the other, "the shock of their difference was *felt*" (p. 498). James postulated that this feeling of shock on seeing that stimulus M was different from a stimulus N entailed that N was not thought about as simply being N, but as N-as-different-from-M. He admitted that no explanation (for example, in terms of cerebral conditions) had yet been offered.

In the second section, pages 502–522, discrimination between objects less simple than M and/or N are discussed. As hinted at in the previous section "only such elements as we are acquainted with, and can imagine, separately, can be discriminated *within* a total sense-impression" (James, 1890/1950, pp. 504–505). Helmholtz (1863/1954) is quoted as asserting that we never notice overtones when listening to a piece of music played by several instruments, unless we actually had prior experience to that one tone when played on that same instrument. Moving to sequences of sensory events, labelled by James *abcd* or *aefg*, we naturally "abstract" the common event *a* from the two sequences. With repeated thinking about *a*, *a* comes to be dissociated from *abcd* and *aefg* and becomes an object that can be thought about as an independent object of abstraction, a "conception".

2 Among superficial differences between the two books were: Wundt's textbook went into six editions, whereas James's had only one edition; and Wundt's textbook was far more profusely illustrated than was James's. Thomas (2016) has claimed that Wundt had a greater influence on later experimental psychology than did James.

James (1890/1950) then turned to the question of whether one can be trained to improve one's skills of discrimination. An experiment conducted by Volkmann (1858) with Fechner's assistance showed that practice could reduce the two-point threshold associated with a given skin-region (as cited in James, 1890/1950, Vol. 1, p. 514). James noted that "the blind deaf-mute, Laura Bridgman, has so improved her touch as to recognize, after a year's interval, the hand of a person who once had shaken hers" (p. 509). Learning to distinguish, by taste alone, claret from burgundy can be facilitated if claret and burgundy are regularly tasted in different environments (e.g., different restaurants).[3]

In the third section, pages 523–533, James reviewed evidence that reaction times measure the ease or difficulty of discrimination. He reviewed results obtained by Tischer (1883) and by J. M. Cattell (1886a, 1886b) in Wundt's laboratory that support this idea.[4] James queried the logic behind the idea that reaction time measures the ease of discrimination. He claimed that all this experimental evidence focussed on the *minimal* reaction time required in a particular test of discrimination. James (1890/1950) argued that

> this minimum time by no means measures what we consciously know as discrimination. It only measures something which, under the experimental conditions, leads to a similar result. But it is the bane of psychology to suppose that, where results are similar, processes must be the same. Psychologists are apt to reason as geometers would, if the latter were to say that the diameter of a circle is the same thing as its semi-circumference [which it isn't!], because, forsooth, they terminate in the same two points.
>
> (p. 528)

In a footnote, James remarked that G. F. Lipps (1883) said much the same in an "excellent passage". James then noted that Stumpf (1883) claimed that the magnitudes of differences arranged in a series could be aptly described as "distances". James noted that linear magnitudes and musical notes are particularly easy to arrange in terms of (sense)-distances. But so can shades of lightness. In his words, "Messrs Plateau and Delboeuf have found it fairly easy to determine what shade of gray will be judged by every one to hit the exact middle between a darker and a lighter shade" (p. 531). James expressed his agreement with Stumpf that our judgement of the *magnitude* of a sensation is not given by some sort of unconscious "counting" process, but by an "unanalyzable endowment of the

3 In a footnote, James describes another example reported by Helmholtz. Using stereoscopic displays, it is possible to distinguish a spot A from spot B when A and B are presented separately to the two eyes and A seems to look further away than does B. But A and B are indistinguishable if both fall on corresponding foveal areas in each eye. James draws the interesting conclusion that "two processes which occasion feelings quite indistinguishable to direct consciousness may nevertheless be each allied with disparate associates both of a sensorial and of a motor kind" (p. 513). Helmholtz (1863/1954) is quoted at length on how experience can influence "unconscious inference" in perception.

4 That Tischer worked in Wundt's laboratory is confirmed by Boring (1942, p. 343).

mind", thus mirroring what James said earlier about how our noticing of a difference occurs "intuitively" (p. 531).

In the fourth section, pages 533–549, James (1890/1950) came to grips with Fechner's theory of discriminative sensibility, that is, Fechner's psychophysics. Fechner's Law was expressed in the following words: "when we pass from one sensation to a stronger one of the same kind, the sensations increase proportionally to the logarithms of their exciting causes" (p. 534). But then James described the *literature* on psychophysics as follows: "it would be perhaps impossible to match [this literature] for the qualities of thoroughness and subtlety, but of which, in the humble opinion of the present writer, the proper psychological outcome is just *nothing*" (p. 534).

Fechner's logic was explained by a direct translation of a long passage from Wundt (1863), which necessarily included an account of Weber's Law (pp. 534–537).[5] James (1890/1950, p. 539) expressed Fechner's Law mathematically as $S = C \log R$, where S is sensation-magnitude measured in units of the "just noticeable increment above zero", C is a constant and R is the stimulus intensity (from *Reiz*, the German for stimulus). If Sensation 0 equals stimulus A, then Sensation 1 equals $A(1 + r)$ where "r is the percentage of itself which must be added to it to get a sensation which is barely perceptible", Sensation 2 equals $A(1 + r)^2$ … and Sensation $n = A(1 + r)^n$. The sensations form an arithmetical series and the stimuli a geometric series. For James, Fechner's Law was improved upon by Delboeuf (1873) and Elsas (1886).

James listed the following among the facts which might lead us to think twice about the scientific validity of Fechner's Law. First, there are so many "accidental errors" that can take place when trying to establish a just perceptible difference, that the "normal sensibility" can only be revealed by experiments involving large numbers of trials from which an average score might be assumed to represent that normal sensibility. It was with this in mind that Fechner had devised the first of three psychophysical methods described by James as "The Method of Just-discernible-Differences". Larger differences, James pointed out, were studied using "The Method of True and False Cases", and "The Method of Average Errors". James (1890/1950) pointed out that

> Delboeuf and Wundt have experimented with larger differences by means of [a fourth method that] Wundt called the *Methode der mittleren Abstufungen* [Method of Mean Gradations] and what we may call "The Method of Equal-appearing Intervals."
>
> (pp. 541–542)

James also mentioned, very briefly, a fifth method involving the doubling of a stimulus (Merkel, 1888).

5 Wundt (1863) also gave one of the earliest lists of Weber fractions as follows: sensation of light, 1/100; muscular sensation, 1/17; feeling of pressure, warmth, sound, 1/3. This list was reproduced by Delboeuf (1873, p. 12).

James (1890/1950) then summarized evidence concerning the validity of Weber's Law for the discriminative sensibility of light, sound, pressure, muscular sense (including Hering's experiment on lifted weights), and line-lengths. He took this evidence, which included the fact that Weber's Law held only for the middle region of a scale of intensities, as attesting that "Weber's law … expresses an empirical generalization of practical importance, without involving any theory whatever or seeking any absolute measures of the sensations themselves" (p. 545). James then provided an argument supporting the view that Weber's Law was a by-product of the possibility that "If our feelings resulted from a condition of the nerve-molecules which it grew ever more difficult for the stimulus to increase, our feelings would naturally grow at the slower rate than the stimulus itself" (p. 548).

James on Fechner's Originality

James (1890/1950, Chapter 13) now contended that Fechner's originality consisted mainly in his *theoretical interpretation* of Weber's Law. James claimed that Fechner assumed that a just-perceptible increment was a sensation-unit that was equal in magnitude on all parts of the sensation scale (i.e., ΔS was constant). Fechner also assumed that a sensation consists of a sum of these units; and that the logarithmic law is "an ultimate law of the connection of mind with matter" (p. 545). James added that "Fechner seems to find something inscrutably sublime in the existence of an ultimate 'psychophysics' law of this form" (p. 545).

James had a major concern with Fechner's argument that ΔS was constant. James, on the other hand, believed that sensations should not be thought of as things that have specific magnitudes ("a feeling of pink is surely not a portion of our feeling of scarlet", p. 546) but as objects that can be arranged in a serial string in which the "distance" or "interval" or "difference" between sensations A and B on the scale does *not* necessarily have to equal the distance between sensations B and C.

To be more precise, Fechner made a testable assumption, namely, that all *equally perceptible* additions to a sensation are "*equally great* additions" (p. 547). This led James (1890/1950) to suggest the following:

> If Δ stand for the smallest difference which *we perceive*, then we should have, instead of the formula Δs = const., which is Fechner's, the formula $(\Delta s/s)$ = const., a formula which interprets all the *facts* of Weber's Law, in an entirely different theoretic way from that adopted by Fechner.
>
> (p. 547)

James went on to say what he thought of Fechner when Fechner found all sorts of excuses to explain why Weber's Law did *not* fit the data obtained in his large experiment. James, who did not explicitly mention the issue of arm weight, wrote:

> As if *any* laws could not be found in *any* set of phenomena, provided one have the wit to invent enough other existing laws to overlap and to

neutralize it! The whole outcome of the discussion, so far as Fechner's theories are concerned, is indeed *nil. Weber's law alone remains true as an empirical generalization of fair extent*: What we add to a large stimulus we notice less than what we add to a small one, unless it happen *relatively to the stimulus* to be as great.

(p. 548)

An Evaluation of the Final Paragraph of Chapter 13

And so it is that we come to the final paragraph of James's (1890/1950) chapter on discrimination and comparison. The bulk of its middle portion reads:

> Fechner himself indeed was a German *Gelehrter* of the ideal type, at once simple and shrewd, a mystic and an experimentalist, homely and daring, and as loyal to his facts as to his theories. But it would be terrible if even such a dear old man as this could saddle our Science forever with his patient whimsies, and, in a world so full of more nutritious objects of attention, compel all future students to plough through the difficulties, not only of his own works, but of the still drier ones written in his refutation. Those who desire this dreadful literature can find it; but I will not even enumerate it in a footnote. The only amusing point of it is that Fechner's critics should always feel bound, after smiting his theories hip and thigh and leaving not a stick of them standing, to wind up saying that nevertheless to him belongs the *imperishable glory* of first formulating them and thereby turning psychology into an *exact science* (!).
>
> (p. 549)

Let us quickly go through this paragraph sentence-by-sentence and evaluate its acceptability by way of a question/answer format.

1. Question: Was Fechner a "German *Gelehrte* of the ideal type?"
   Answer: Fechner's publishing career included tongue-in-cheek satires (by "Dr Mises"); important original works about Ohm's Law and about visual brightness contrast; three books and several articles about psychophysics; one book (Fechner, 1876) and some research articles that created the field of experimental aesthetics; several articles or monographs that anticipated such modern topics as self-organizing systems (Perruchet & Vinter, 2002) and atomism; the semi-mystical books such as the *Zend-Avesta* and *Nanna*; and a book (published posthumously) on nonparametric statistics (Fechner, 1897); this book was usefully summarized by Heidelberger (1987). A comprehensive list of Fechner's works will be found in Heidelberger's (2004, "Bibliography", pp. 381–385).

   "*Gelehrte*" means "learned" as an adjective, or a "learned person" as a noun. Fechner's extraordinary ability to write about so many topics makes him indeed a polymath, that is, an ideal scholar of the kind who found their métier in the German university system from the seventeenth to the nineteenth century. The first well-known *Gelehrte*, Leibniz, worked as the librarian and secretary of an aristocratic household but the list of university faculty *Gelehrten* included Thomasius,[6] Wolff, Kant, Herbart, Fechner, and Wundt.

2. Question: Was Fechner really such a "dear old man" as James makes him out to be?
Answer: Yes, I think so. Following his breakdown in his late 40s, he did little teaching compared with his contemporaries such as E. H. Weber, Wilhelm Weber, Helmholtz, Wundt, Hering, and G. E. Müller. The *Elements of Psychophysics* [*Elemente der Psychophysik*] (Fechner, 1860/1964) was published when he was 59. In the years 1860–1887, he was devoted almost exclusively to writing about psychophysics and to creating the field of experimental aesthetics. In my reading about Fechner, I have come across no evidence that he was authoritarian or unpleasant in his social conduct.

3. Question: Is it fair to call the literature for or against Fechner's psychophysics "difficult", "dry", or "dreadful?"
Answer: Here the answer must be "yes" *and* "no". Readers of Fechner in the original German will find it wearisome if they know only some German, but elegant and even moving if they can read German fluently. When translated into English, Fechner's own writings are clear and punctilious, but, nevertheless, seem wordy in a way some people would call "expansive" and others, less polite, might call "prolix". One of my aims when I started to write this book was to make psychophysics thought-provoking rather than "dreadful", given that its mathematical content can be off-putting to non-mathematical readers. I think, however, that the ambiguities (*what* is a threshold? *can* sensations be measured?) have indeed given rise to a literature that is larger than would be the case had those ambiguities been absent. If all late-nineteenth-century psychophysics consisted of Delboeuf's (1873) monograph only, many of these "dry" and "difficult" monographs may possibly never have been written. On the other hand, as indicated in Chapter 6, Stephen Link made a convincing case that Fechner's theoretical approach allowed Fechner to estimate the quantitative values of *mental* entities in such a way that he may truly be credited with having made psychology a science (Link, 1994, p. 337).

4. Question: Who were those critics who "[smote] his theories hip and thigh and [left] not a stick of them standing?"
Answer: The table of contents of Fechner's (1877) *The Case for Psychophysics* [*In Sachen der Psychophysik*] lists the following persons, among others, as *Gegner* [opponents] of Fechner's theories: Helmholtz, Mach, Plateau, Brentano,

6 In 1692, Christian Thomasius (1655–1728) offered a theory of personality, according to which a person's character could be described in terms of four desires ("passions"), each of which was possessed to a different (quantifiable) degree, by that person. More information is provided by McReynolds (1975).

Delboeuf, and Hering. The table of contents of Fechner's (1882) *Review of the Main Points of Psychophysics* [*Revision der Hauptpunkte der Psychophysik*] includes criticisms made by the psychologists G. E. Müller and Wundt, as well as by the philosophers Von Kries and F. A. Müller. Fechner's (1886) article replied to criticisms made by Elsas and A. Köhler. In Chapter 7, we discussed the criticisms of Fechner's ideas made by Hermann Cohen as outlined by Heidelberger (2004, pp. 217–224).

5. Question: Well, was it so wrong of me to follow the establishment line of praising Fechner's psychophysics as a stepping-stone to making psychology as mathematically rigorous as physics?
   Answer: If truth be told, I think of Herbart as being the person deserving the "imperishable glory" of having been the first to try to base psychology on a mathematical foundation as sturdy as that provided for physics by Sir Isaac Newton. At first sight, Fechner's failure to confirm Weber's Law in his large experiment suggests that Herbart's scepticism about experimentation in psychology was justified. Yet, the reliability of Fechner's results, based on 24,576 individual trials, is an example of the new psychological science. I am also aware, moreover, that some isolated nineteenth-century studies—I am thinking of Delboeuf's (1873) concentric circles equally gradated in lightness from white to black, and Müller and Schumann's (1889) demonstrations of "set" effects in weight-lifting experiments—were so successful as to make me wonder whether Herbart had been too pessimistic in his rejection of experimentation as a means for adding to knowledge about psychology.

6. Question: Has "our Science", in fact, been "saddled" over the *twentieth* century with Fechner's "patient whimsies?"
   Answer: Speaking for myself, while I think that James was right to warn us of the potential fancies (and potential for dullness!) of psychophysics, I also think, for the following reason, that James spoke too soon. When I started to write this book, I had no idea that I would conclude the main body of the text by referring to Delboeuf's (1873) construction of a set of concentric grey circles progressing upwards from white at the centre to black at the circumference in 13 equal-*looking* steps of greyness. Yet, it seems to me now, in retrospect, that this is indeed a fitting ending—something solid and tangible to the mind, so to speak—to one of the most controversial sets of polemics in the history of science. This fuss was engendered, both in the established academic world of the physicists and philosophers, and in the grasping-in-the-dark world of would-be academic psychologists, by the two volumes of Fechner's (1860/1964) *Elemente der Psychophysik*. One striking aspect of the late-nineteenth-century literature for and against Fechner's Law was how much of that literature was generated in German (Fechner, G. E. Müller) and in French (Plateau, Delboeuf). Despite the competence of English-speaking physicists in that same period, notably James Clerk Maxwell, whose insights

led to the discovery of the electromagnetic spectrum and its application to telegraph, radio, and television, only a handful of the early writings on psychophysics came from English-speaking countries like Britain, its former colonies, Ireland, and the United States.

Exactly the opposite held for the twentieth century. Psychophysics joined experimental studies of human memory and of animal learning as focal research topics in the American, Australian, British, Canadian, New Zealand, and South African psychology laboratories of the early twentieth century. It is fitting that one of the major transitional works in this transfer of academic power vis-à-vis the history of psychophysics, namely, Peirce and Jastrow's (1884) paper, should have been published in the *Memoirs of the National Academy of Sciences* in the United States.[7]

Late Nineteenth-Century Research on Confidence Ratings and Response Times in Psychophysics

Both Peirce and Jastrow would go on to become famous, but for different reasons. Charles Sanders Peirce (1839–1914) became an eminent philosopher of science and Jacob Jastrow (1864–1955) became a leading experimental psychologist at the University of Wisconsin.

According to Heidelberger (2004, p. 268), Peirce and Jastrow were the first to introduce Fechner's psychophysics to the United States. According to Danziger (1990), Jastrow was "the first psychologist who was never anything else but a psychologist" (p. 223, fn13). And according to Hacking (1990), one of the consequences of the adoption of probability theory into nineteenth-century science was a shift away from Laplace's determinism to a general indeterminism. Hacking suggested that: "Somebody had to make a first leap to indeterminism. Maybe it was Peirce, perhaps a predecessor" (p. 201). Perhaps Fechner was the predecessor. Furthermore, Hacking stressed that Peirce and Jastrow designed experiments using the randomization, over successive trials, of experimental conditions.

Peirce started his career as a geodesist (it will be recalled from Chapter 2 that Gauss and Hagen, both pioneers in the practical use made of the Gaussian distribution, were themselves experts in land measuring, that is, geodesy). Peirce ended his career as one of the most respected thinkers of his time about probability theory, inductive reasoning, and the philosophy of science generally. He played a part in the growing approval, among academics, of a "pragmatic" approach to what we mean when we use the word "truth". His domicile was Cambridge, Massachusetts, where he was a colleague of William James. James lectured regularly, and Peirce occasionally, at Harvard University.

7 This Academy was founded by an act of the United States Congress in 1863 and is located in Washington, DC. The oldest learned society in the United States is the American Philosophical Society, founded by Benjamin Franklin in 1743, located in Philadelphia.

Peirce and Jastrow (1884) attempted to improve on Fechner's methodology for establishing that a Gaussian distribution determined the variability of erroneous "heavier" responses in a weight-lifting task. Peirce and Jastrow did not try to do this by predicting that their response-data would be fit by Weber's Law (as Fechner had done). Instead, on each trial, one of three comparison weights (1,015, 1,030, and 1,060 g) was mechanically pressed onto the pad of a blindfolded participant's forefinger. That pressure was either followed by, or preceded by, a pressure from a standard weight of 1,000 g.

Peirce and Jastrow (1884) claimed that the effect of this procedure was to introduce an error into the participant's sensation of the standard. The error would cause occasional failures to judge that the comparison weight was heavier than the standard weight, especially if the difference in weight was small rather than large. In his description of Peirce and Jastrow's study, Link (1992, pp. 18–25) carefully spelled out how their technique yielded more clear-cut evidence than had Fechner's experiment that the errors in this task follow a Gaussian distribution. Link showed how the fit of the obtained error probabilities to those predicted by the Gaussian distribution was very close as judged by the Method of Least Squares. Finally, Peirce and Jastrow determined from the least squares fit the weight of a comparison stimulus leading to 25% of the comparison stimuli being judged just noticeably heavier than the standard. This weight was estimated to be 1,023.5 g. Although Peirce and Jastrow started by criticizing Fechner, their findings can readily be interpreted as supporting his views about the role of the Gaussian distribution in determining psychophysical judgements.

In that study, Jastrow served as the sole participant. An incidental finding was that, when Jastrow rated his confidence in a judgement on a four-point scale, the confidence rating increased monotonically with response accuracy. This was the first psychophysical study to incorporate confidence ratings as an accessory measure of response efficiency that could be used to supplement the conventional measure of response accuracy. Peirce and Jastrow's (1884) findings on confidence ratings were later confirmed by Fullerton and Cattell (1892). Link (2003) showed that, earlier, Peirce (1877) provided a rationale for believing that confidence ratings could be used to further our understanding of the processes underlying decision-making.

Cattell (1886a, 1886b) provided evidence, using light intensities as stimuli, that correct "brighter" response times became shorter as stimulus intensity increased. This finding was substantiated in many later studies (Link, 1992, pp. 27–34, 82–84, 163–167). But its replicability can be reduced by even a small change in experimental procedure (Murray, 1993, pp. 176–177). James McKeen Cattell (1860–1944) was Wundt's first American student. His 1886 studies on response times were carried out with the help of G. O. Berger of Wundt's laboratory in Leipzig. When Cattell returned to America, he founded a laboratory of experimental psychology at the University of Pennsylvania. There he collaborated with G. S. Fullerton (1859–1925) in Fullerton and Cattell's 1892 study of confidence ratings in psychophysical tasks.

By 1900, the scope of psychophysical experimentation was already undergoing substantial modifications. To responses indicative of a participant's *accuracy* at judging that one weight was heavier than another, there were added responses indicative of a participant's *confidence* in his or her judgements, and *response times* indicative of the rapidity with which such judgements were arrived at. At the end of the nineteenth century, both of these new measures, confidence ratings and response times, were introduced to psychophysicists in America by Peirce, Jastrow, and Fullerton (on confidence ratings) and by Cattell (on response times). Both measures provided material for prolific experimentation and theorizing during the twentieth century (see e.g., Luce, 1986, on response times). Hence, no matter what James said about the usefulness of response times for psychology in general—we recall the scepticism about their value that he had expressed in the third section of Chapter 13 of his *Principles of Psychology*—*experiments* on psychophysics continued to be carried out throughout the entire twentieth century.

It was for this reason that I claimed above, that James spoke "too soon" when he derided the idea that Fechnerian psychophysics could serve as a theoretical basis for psychology in general. I would also observe that my claim is justified here in the context of Fechnerian psychophysics. I avoided reference to cases where the word "psychophysics" has come to denote, loosely, the subject matter of visual science and auditory science in particular, and of sensory science in general. An interesting account of how the word "psychophysics" had its domain of reference extended from "Fechnerian psychophysics" to "sensory science in general" was provided by Whittle (1993). His review of his own research on brightness contrast (Whittle, 1994a, 1994b) indicates ways in which Fechner's Law can still be held to be valid in psychophysical tasks in which the background is presented to one eye and the contrasting figure to the other eye.

Summary

William James (1890/1950, Vol. 1, Chapter 13 on "Discrimination and Comparison") attained a certain notoriety among psychophysicists for his claim that Fechner, a "dear old man" and learned scholar, had, nevertheless, been unduly overpraised for his assertion that the magnitude of a sensation was a natural logarithmic function of the intensity of the stimulus. He was overpraised because some of the many objections raised against his theory were, in James's opinion, dismissed too cavalierly. This is in spite of the fact that Fechner (1877, 1882) felt obliged to write two books, attempting to answer his critics, not to mention the long article that Fechner (1886) published just before his death. James emphasized, in particular, that the apparent "size of a difference" between sensations does not necessarily remain constant as stimulus intensity increases (as Fechner's logarithmic law claimed it should), but can grow as stimulus intensity increases (as Plateau's and Hering's power laws claimed it should). In this respect, James was a forerunner of the emphasis, in the twentieth century, on Stevens' power law.

Also, in the United States, James's contemporaries, Peirce and Jastrow (1884) and Fullerton and Cattell (1892), published early research on how far confidence ratings can supplement accuracy measures in informing us how sensory discrimination judgements are made. Cattell (1886a, 1886b), working with Wundt, also established that response times could be inversely related to measures of accuracy obtained in psychophysical tasks. Twentieth-century studies of confidence ratings and of response times add to our understanding of the cognitive processes involved in the kind of decision-making these tasks require.

Passing the Torch

Prior to Herbart, the psychological writings that included mathematics were sporadic. Four such writings are mentioned in the present volume. In chronological order, they were: Christian Thomasius's (1692) theory of personality (in Chapter 9); Robert Hooke's (1705/1971) account of human memory (in Chapter 1); Daniel Bernoulli's (1738/1954) analysis of the subjective value of monetary gains (in Chapter 4, Appendix 1); and Körber's (1746) underknown monograph on the quantification of mental processes (in Chapter 2).

Fechner (1860/1966, p. 46) criticized Herbart for not having attempted to measure, in a laboratory setting, the strength of a sensation-*Vorstellung*. Otherwise, Fechner was impressed by Herbart's theory, and adopted Herbart's word *Schwelle* ("threshold") into his psychophysics. If Fechner's Law were to be compellingly demonstrated by a numerical example, the term "absolute threshold" requires two denotations. These I introduced in Chapter 4. One kind of absolute threshold (labelled W_{NULL} in Table 4.3) was exceeded when a stimulus was intense enough to arouse a neural response, presumably at the receptor level. A second kind of absolute threshold (labelled W_1 in Table 4.3) was exceeded when a stimulus was intense enough to arouse conscious feelings.

Fechner (1860/1966) proposed that a Gaussian distribution of individual neural response intensities underlay a participant's judgment about a sensation-magnitude. Prior to Gauss, De Moivre and Laplace made substantial inroads in determining a mathematical expression for what we now call the bell-shaped Gaussian probability density function. Their work was described in Chapter 2. Fechner also acknowledged that his theory had parallels in David Bernoulli's (1738/1954) logarithmic function relating the utility of a gain, for a player in a betting game, to the wealth of that player at the start of the game.

Fechner's concepts concerning inner psychophysics may be seen to apply to the distinction between W_{NULL} and W_1. According to Fechner, if W_{NULL} was exceeded, then excitation was transformed logarithmically into a neural response associated with a consciously experienced sensation-magnitude only when threshold W_1 was also exceeded. Fechner's inner psychophysics also shared several features with Herbart's statics. Fechner's inner psychophysics anticipated Freud's (1895/1966) later division of nerve cells into three kinds, one of which mediated conscious experiencing.

Fechner (1860/1964, 1860/1966) was inspired by E. H. Weber's monographs on touch [*De Tactu*, Weber (1834/1996a); *Der Tastsinn*, Weber (1846/1996b)] in two major ways. First, by assuming that Weber's constant, $\Delta I/I$, could be identified with the differential (dI/I), he derived Fechner's Law. This law stipulated that sensation-magnitude was a natural logarithmic function of stimulus intensity. Sensation-magnitude would increase in equal-appearing steps as sensation intensity increased in ever-widening steps. More precisely, sensation-magnitude increased arithmetically as stimulus intensity increased geometrically.

Second, Fechner's large experiment on lifted weights, described in Chapter 4, was designed to test the validity of Weber's Law. In that experiment, Fechner judged whether a comparison weight, Co (the weight of which in grams varied over a range chosen by Fechner) felt heavier than a standard weight, St. He made his judgments under varying circumstances. The experimental design, shown in Figure 4.1, represented an early use of a factorial design in order to maintain the effects of constant errors.

Fechner defined constant errors as being mainly of two kinds. There was a "temporal" constant error when there was a tendency to respond that the second weight picked up on a trial felt heavier than the first weight. When the two weights were presented side by side, a "spatial" constant error produced a tendency to respond that the weight located on one side felt "heavier" than the weight located on the other side.

Fechner postulated that there were other errors beside constant errors. He distinguished himself by asserting that some errors arose because sensation-magnitudes were Gaussian distributed. He claimed that random variations in the magnitude of response of those nerve cells that were activated during the decision process could lead to *incorrect* responses. This was because the sensation-magnitude of the larger comparison stimulus could be smaller than the criterion for judging that the comparison stimulus was "heavier" than the standard stimulus, and the participant made the incorrect judgement "lighter".

E. H. Weber and Fechner both held professorial positions at the University of Leipzig. Twenty-nine years after the publication of Weber's *Der Tastsinn* and 15 years after the publication of Fechner's *Elemente der Psychophysik*, Wilhelm Wundt was offered a Chair of Philosophy at Leipzig in 1875.[1] His mandate was

1 Wilhelm Weber and Fechner were both at Leipzig in 1879, but E. H. Weber had died a year earlier. Wilhelm Weber was aged 87 and Fechner was aged 86. When Wundt was called to Leipzig, he reported being taken by surprise. In his posthumously published autobiography (Wundt, 1920), he wrote: "the puzzle behind this call was only solved for me much later. It was not the faculty [of philosophy], or some considerable proportion thereof, who stood behind the call. It was one single individual, none other than Friedrich Zöllner [1834–1882] the astrophysicist" (my translation of a passage cited by Meischner & Eschler, 1979, pp. 60–61). Boring (1950, p. 306) also attributed Wundt's call to Zöllner. Boring added, however, that Zöllner had participated, in 1877–1878, with Wilhelm Weber and Fechner in investigations of a spiritistic medium named Henry Slade (1840–1904). More details of this investigation were provided by Bringmann, Bringmann, and Medway (1987). I have found no documentary evidence that E. H. Weber and Fechner were somehow directly involved in Leipzig's call to Wundt. Meischner and Eschler (1979, pp. 58–60), however, reproduce a letter from Helmholtz, written on December 16, 1872, strongly endorsing Wundt's suitability to be a professor of philosophy at any interested German university.

to demonstrate the relevance of new psychophysiological research to the philosophy of mind. He had already published (in 1874) the first of six editions of his *Principles of Physiological Psychology* (1874, 1880, 1887, 1893, 1902–1903, and 1908–1911). Titchener translated some of these editions into English, but the only translation he actually published was Part I of the 1902–1903 edition (Wundt, 1904). In all six editions, Fechner's psychophysical contributions were described in detail. Fechner's psychophysical views, however, were publicized, not only in Wundt's book, but also because they formed the topic of doctoral dissertations in Wundt's own laboratory between 1886 and 1919.

In 1879, Wundt obtained funding for a Psychological Institute on the Leipzig campus. Its physical layout, its changes in location over Wundt's lifetime, and its facilities for teaching and research are described in splendid detail, along with photographs, by Bringmann, Bringmann, and Ungerer (1980). A large number of foreign visitors came to the Institute to obtain doctoral degrees under Wundt's supervision. Tinker (1932/1960) gave the authors and titles of 184 doctoral dissertations accepted by the Institute. Students of German or Austrian ancestry wrote 136 of these. There were also 14 Americans, most of whose dissertations were submitted between 1886 and 1900; 10 English; 13 Balkan; 6 Polish; 2 French; 2 Danish; and 3 Russian. Wundt's English students included Titchener, who wrote a thesis on binocular vision (Titchener, 1892). They also included Carl Spearman (1863–1945), a pioneer in the quantitative investigation of adult human "intelligence".

Hilgard (1987, pp. 31–36) listed those American students of Wundt who, on returning to the United States, helped to found Departments of Psychology at their universities. Here is that list, in an order determined by the year the candidate obtained his doctoral degree with Wundt. There was:

- J. McKeen Cattell (who founded the Department of Psychology at the University of Pennsylvania in 1888, and at Columbia University in New York City in 1889)
- H. K. Wolfe (at the University of Nebraska in 1889)
- Frank Angell (at Cornell University in 1891 and at Stanford University in 1892)
- E. A. Pace (at Catholic University of America, Washington, DC, in 1892)
- E. W. Scripture (at Yale University in 1892)
- W. G. Smith (at Smith College in 1895)
- G. M. Stratton (at New York University, Washington Square, in 1900)
- Walter Dill Scott (at Northwestern University in 1900).

The first *laboratory* of psychology in Canada was at the University of Toronto. It was founded in 1889 by James Mark Baldwin (1861–1934). Wright and Myers (1982) wrote that:

> Baldwin had received part of his advanced training at Leipzig and he taught in the Wundtian tradition. He established at Toronto a psychological

> laboratory, the first such laboratory on British soil and he initiated a program of experimental research. … In 1893 he accepted an invitation to return to Princeton, which had been his original Alma Mater. … at his instigation, the University [of Toronto] had decided to import another student of Wundt's to assist in their management. This student was a German named August Kirschmann [1860–1932]. He arrived in 1893, and, after Baldwin's departure was put in charge of the laboratory.
>
> (p. 12)

Kirschmann stayed there until 1917, when he returned to Germany to teach psychology at the University of Leipzig. As narrated by Wright and Myers (1982, p. 84) and Slater (2005, Chapter 5), the *Department* of Psychology at Toronto was not officially founded until 1927.

When Titchener (1901a, 1901b, 1905a, 1905b) wrote his manual of experimental psychology, the target readerships were instructors with students taking laboratory classes in these and other departments. Titchener did not confine his remarks on psychophysics to Fechner's works only. He also gave plenty of space to the "method of equal-appearing intervals" associated with the work of Plateau and Delboeuf in Belgium. As described in Chapter 8, the work of Hering and Plateau gave reasons for believing that Fechner's logarithmic law should be replaced by a power law. The evidence favouring a power law was sufficiently compelling for William James (1890/1950, Chapter 13) to cast his vote in favour of Hering's views rather than those of Fechner.

Plateau, Hering, Delboeuf and Later Psychophysics

The views of each of these scientists influenced later psychophysics in several ways. With respect to the power law, Franz Brentano (1838–1917) wrote a book in 1874 titled *Psychology From an Empirical Standpoint* [*Psychologie vom empirischen Standpunkte*]. It was mainly concerned with defining what is implied when we talk of a "psychological event" (Murray, 1988, pp. 272–273). But on pages 62–68, Brentano discussed psychophysics. He argued that the just noticeable differences associated with a particular scale of sensation-magnitude are not necessarily equally sized, but are only equally noticeable. He is therefore considered to have been one of the earliest proponents of a psychophysical power law.

Plateau's Influence

Plateau was the first to indicate how a power law might be a better predictor of psychophysical judgments than Fechner's logarithmic law. Later, S. S. Stevens (1906–1973) started what might almost be called a "movement", within the psychophysical community, to encourage the adoption of a psychophysical "power law" instead of Fechner's "logarithmic law". Stevens presented theoretical reasons for thinking that the "psychophysical function" that ought generally to be preferred gave S as a power function (Equation 8.3), rather than as a logarithmic function, of *I*. Stevens (1975, Table 1, p. 15) compiled tables of estimated values of the exponent *c*, for 33 kinds of sensory stimulus in much the same way as Boring, Langfeld, and Weld (1948, p. 268) had compiled tables of estimated values of Weber fractions. Thirteen of Stevens's estimated *c*-values were less than 1.0. It was noted in Chapter 8 that when $c < 1.0$, the associated power function is negatively accelerated, and may need to be distinguished from a natural logarithmic function.

One indication that Stevens' power law took over from Fechner's logarithmic law is illustrated in Gescheider's (1997) textbook of psychophysics. He not only reprints Stevens' table of exponents (p. 303), offering no comparable table of Weber fractions, but refers to Stevens on 54 pages of his book, and to Fechner on only four pages. Another indication is the fact than an important target article in the journal *Behavioral and Brain Sciences* had the title "Reconciling Fechner and Stevens: Toward a Unified Psychophysical Law" (Krueger, 1989).

In Chapter 4, we saw that Fechner described three psychophysical "methods" for establishing differential thresholds. Stevens devised yet another, the method of magnitude estimation, which is easier to administer in practice than are any of Fechner's three methods, and has "caught on" as a method widely used in twentieth century and twenty-first-century psychophysical laboratories.

It is appropriate, here, I think, to add that this question was also addressed by other twentieth-century psychophysicists. Falmagne (1985, pp. 76–77) supposed that, in a threefold display of white-grey-black, the "grey-white" difference *looked* equal to the "black-grey" difference. IF this appearance of equal-steppedness remained unchanged when the level of illumination cast over the display was made brighter or dimmer, THEN only two possible *functions* were consistent with that phenomenon, a power function and a logarithmic function. This conjecture was not supported by Delboeuf's (1873) experiments.

Laming and Laming (1996), in their introduction to their translation of Plateau (1872a), proved that IF a power law held, such that luminances of the white, grey, and black squares in Plateau's study *looked* equal-stepped under two different levels of luminance, and IF a logarithmic law also held, THEN, in both cases, the luminances must be raised by a multiple. The difference between the power function and the logarithmic function lay in the multiple itself, which, according to Laming and Laming (p. 135) can be represented as a stand-alone number in the case of the logarithmic law (e.g., the number could be 0.5) and that same stand-alone number raised to a power in the case of the power law (e.g., the number could be 0.5^2).

Hering's Influence

Hering (1875) added fuel to the fire. His previous experimental evidence showed that Fechner's logarithmic law was inconsistent with the observation that the *difference* between sensation-magnitudes associated with stimuli I_2 and I_1 *did not look* equal to the difference between the sensation-magnitudes created by multiplying I_2 and I_1 by a constant.

The concept of a "just noticeable difference" is applicable both to a logarithmic law and to a power law. A logarithmic law has units of sensation-magnitude that are psychologically equal as stimulus intensity increases geometrically. A power law has units of sensation-magnitudes that are unequal in "psychological size" as stimulus intensity increases linearly. In fact, experimental evidence obtained in the mid-twentieth century suggests that the difference in sensation-magnitude resulting in a "just noticeable difference" is not constant as stimulus intensity increases. It was shown that ΔS can increase linearly as S increases. Gösta Ekman (1920–1971) proposed that, when ΔS is a JND in a psychological magnitude, S is the psychological size of a stimulus, and k is a constant, then:

$$\Delta S = kS. \tag{PT.1}$$

This is a move of Weber's Law to the domain of psychological experience. Ekman reanalysed some psychophysical data from Stevens's laboratory at Harvard gathered by Harper and Stevens (1948). The stimuli consisted of lifted weights. Ekman (1956, 1959) concluded that, just as Weber's Law can be represented as a description of how judgments about sensory differences can increase as the *stimulus intensity* increases, then Equation PT.1 can be interpreted as describing how sensation-magnitudes experienced by humans can also increase as the *sensation-magnitude* increases (on this, see Gescheider, 1997, p. 351).

Stevens (1975, pp. 234–235) liked Ekman's generalization so much that he proposed that Equation PT.1 be called "Ekman's Law". Its most appealing points, according to Stevens, were that the Law not only was consistent with a power law rather than with a logarithmic law, but that it also dovetailed neatly with many twentieth-century findings, including the finding that Fechner's Law is often found to apply to continua such as loudness, lightness, and heaviness, but not to continua such as colour and pitch. On the other hand, Ekman's Law can be found to hold true for both continua.[2]

We seem to have come a long way from discussing Hering's thought-experiment about how much heavier the doubling of a heavy weight feels, to somebody lifting it, as compared with the doubling of a light weight. Yet, if I had to make a forced choice as to where, in the nineteenth-century literature on Fechner, an anticipation can be found of Ekman's Law, I can't really think of an alternative to Hering's (1875) diatribe against Fechner.

Delboeuf (1873), influenced by Helmholtz, still opted for a logarithmic law, but Delboeuf's version of Fechner's Law contained a twist. Sensation-magnitude increased differently as the logarithm of stimulus intensity increased. This was because stimulus intensity itself was expressed as a ratio, namely $[(I + c) / c]$. Here

2 Because a proper coverage of the applications of power functions and of Ekman's Law to psychophysical judgments of preferences (e.g., for favourite composers, or for the prestige-values associated with certain professions) demands going into twentieth-century theories such as Thurstonian scaling, we will not here discuss these historically relatively recent applications of psychophysical methods to non-sensory stimuli. Many of these studies were carried out under Stevens at Harvard and under Ekman at Stockholm. This literature has been reviewed by Stevens (1975) and Gescheider (1997).

c refers to a resting-level of neural activity associated with the sensory receptor being investigated. Later, Delboeuf (1883a, 1883b) postulated that the value of *c* was not fixed but could vary. Delboeuf himself focussed on fatigue as a variable determining the degree to which the value of *c* fluctuated.

According to Laming (1993), the removal of the notion that thresholds had to be "fixed" in psychophysical tasks was associated with the rise of signal detection theory. Laming specified articles by Peterson, Birdsall, and Fox (1954) and Tanner and Swets (1954) as pioneering that approach. As noted in Chapter 4, Appendix 2, Link (1994) showed that Fechner's forgotten creation of psychological decision theory was later known as "ideal observer theory", a form of signal detection theory. When Fechner's criterion moves from the optimal decision position, the theory is known as "signal detection theory".

Fechner's theory was also assailed by investigators who refused to believe that intangible entities such as sensations could be quantified as successfully as entities capable of being added together, such as length, duration, and mass. My account of the "quantity objection" in Chapter 7 was indebted to Heidelberger's (2004, Chapter 6) exposition of the topic. But in Ernst Mach's (1875/1959) new perspective on physics, a prominent role was ascribed to sensations experienced by physicists themselves. Mach's perspective undermined the supremacy of classical Newtonian physics. For example, as was outlined in Chapter 7, Mach anticipated Einstein's relativistic perspective on physics.

I now quote a passage from Norton Wise's (1987) discussion of Einstein's contribution to our understanding of the photoelectric effect. Wise wrote:

> Einstein has emphasized that the photoelectric effect involved not a gradual buildup of energy in an oscillating electron followed by its escape from the atom, but a sudden transition. He had shown, furthermore, that the electromagnetic energy had to be taken up by the electron as a single localized light quantum, a photon. Either one had to give up continuous electromagnetic field energy, and along with it the wave picture of light, or give up conservation of energy and momentum.
>
> (p. 419)

The idea that some continuous psychophysical functions might be the outcome of prior discrete processes involving entities called "quanta" (of which Einstein's photons are examples) was successfully introduced into sensory physiology in the early twentieth century. von Békésy (1930/1960) created neural quantum theory applied to auditory loudness thresholds. Stevens and Volkmann (1940) introduced neural quantum theory to the English reader. According to Stevens (1975): "Curiously enough what appears to [have motivated] Békésy's experiment was the search for the basis of Fechner's logarithmic laws" (p. 186). Later, von Békésy (1967, Chapter 6) proposed the existence of "temporal quanta", discrete successive short-duration time-intervals, each of which had to elapse before one sensory experience could be replaced by another.

Stevens (1975, Chapter 6) summarized his own work on this topic. At present, neural and temporal quanta are hypothetical entities that might indeed improve our understanding of sensory science in general and possibly of Fechnerian psychophysics as well. In fact, Cervantes and Dzhafarov (2018) and other psychophysicists are exploring the possible relevance of quantum mechanics to psychophysics.

The second half of the twentieth century included efforts to incorporate information theory into psychophysics. Baird (1970a, 1970b) argued that the interpretation of a psychophysical law depended on an understanding of a participant's cognitive encoding processes. In order to understand a psychophysical law, one needed to define the "perceptual channel capacity" and the "cognitive channel capacity" of a participant. One also needed to define the measure of "stimulus information" used by an experimenter.

Norwich (1993, pp. 87–107) showed how modern information theory, as applied to communication systems by Shannon and Weaver (1949), had its origins in the statistical mechanics used by Boltzmann and other nineteenth-century physicists to elucidate the laws of thermodynamics. On pages 133 to 150, Norwich showed how an estimate of sensation-magnitude can be derived from an estimate of the information, H, created by a participant from a stimulus.

On pages 151 to 153, Norwich (1993) showed how his very complicated Equation 10.3 stipulated that not only H, but also sensation-magnitude, was a function of three constants. He demonstrated how his Equation 10.3 was related to Fechner's Law and to Stevens' Law. He wrote that "by and large, both the logarithmic law and the power law (Weber-Fechner and Plateau-Brentano-Stevens laws) provide good approximations to the data" (p. 153).

In Link's (1992/2020) book titled *A Wave Theory of Difference and Similarity*, he assumed that a receptor neuron was activated when a discrete quantum of energy from the physical stimulus excited one of several individual transceiver units located on that receptor neuron (pp. 185–212). The activation of a transceiver unit would then be a discrete "event". The probability of this event followed from a Poisson probability distribution.

The Wave Theory also assumed that the level of activation transmitted to the brain had to accumulate to a certain level before a judgement of "larger than" could be given. The time elapsing during this accumulation could be influenced by two variables not discussed by Fechner. One variable, A, was a "resistance to respond". Its importance can be demonstrated in experiments where a participant either has unlimited time to come to a judgment, or is constrained to respond within a rather short timeframe such as 260 or 460 msec. Such rapid responding usually leads to more incorrect judgments. The second variable was named theta. Link (1992/2020, pp. 193–196) proved that a stimulus with intensity I resulted in a value

$$\theta = \log_e\left[(I + \Delta I) / I\right].$$

Therefore $A\theta = A\log_e [(I + \Delta I)/I]$, which is Fechner's Law—a derivation from Wave Theory.

Fechner's large experiment (Table 4.1) was designed to demonstrate that, when a comparison weight was a constant fraction of a standard weight, over a range of standard weights, the probability of a correct "heavier" response should remain constant as the weight of the standard increased. His demonstration failed because the proportion of correct responses steadily rose as the weight of the standard increased. Using Fechner's data, Link (1992/2020, Figure 14.9) showed that the value of theta remained constant. Therefore, the changes in response probability were due to increases in *A*, the amount of difference needed to respond as stimulus magnitudes increased. Then, using data from an experiment by Link and Tindall (1971), Link (1992/2020, pp. 213–222, Figure 14.6) confirmed the variable *A*, the "resistance to respond", caused response time to change due to instructions to respond more or less quickly.

The word "psychophysics" might lead a newcomer to conclude that there exists a discipline whose theory and data were absorbed into a psychological "canon" of widely accepted findings. This conclusion is questionable. One of the reasons for this was a shortage of researchers. Most professional psychologists with doctorates in psychology entered their undergraduate years without academic qualifications in mathematics, physics, or engineering. Another reason was the sheer difficulty of developing a science in which "consciousness" plays a part. Nobody has yet given a scientifically accepted account of how "conscious experience" can emerge from the activities of billions of neurons in human brains. A third reason was because some philosophical problems dominated psychophysical discourse more than they did for physics. Examples of such problems include measuring the magnitude of sensations and the need to distinguish between causal and correlational accounts of psychophysical phenomena (Chapter 7).

Nevertheless, by the first decades of the twenty-first century, neuroscientists and psychologists amassed an enormous database of knowledge concerning mind/brain interactions. Most of this knowledge was unknown to Fechner and his contemporaries. I am convinced that the existence of this database owes an incalculable historical debt to the concepts and methodologies explored by the pioneering psychophysicists of the nineteenth century.

References

Alvarez, W. C. (1961). *Minds that came back*. New York, NY: D. Lippincott.

Angell, F. (1899). [Review of] *Zur Analyse des Unterschiedsempfindlichkeit. Experimentelle Beiträge* by Lillien J. Martin and G. E. Mueller. *American Journal of Psychology, 11*, 266–271.

Asimov, I. (1972). *Asimov's biographical encyclopedia of science and technology: The lives and achievement of 1195 great scientists from ancient times to the present chronologically arranged* (New rev. ed.). New York, NY: Avon Books.

Asmus, W. (1968/1970). *Johann Friedrich Herbart. Eine pädagogische Biographie* [Johann Friedrich Herbart. A pedagogical biography]. (2 vols.). Heidelberg, Germany: Quelle & Meyer.

Baird, J. C. (1970a). A cognitive theory of psychophysics: I. Information transmission, partitioning, and Weber's Law. *Scandinavian Journal of Psychology, 11*, 35–46.

Baird, J. C. (1970b). A cognitive theory of psychophysics: II. Fechner's Law and Stevens' Law. *Scandinavian Journal of Psychology, 11*, 89–102.

Bakewell, S. (2016). *At the existentialist café: Freedom, being, and apricot cocktails*. London, UK: Chatto & Windus.

Bardi, J. S. (2006). *The calculus wars: Newton, Leibniz, and the greatest mathematical clash of all time*. New York, NY: Thunder's Mouth Press.

Békésy, G. von. (1960). On Fechner's Law and its significance for errors in acoustic observations and the theory of hearing. In *Experiments in hearing* (pp. 238–267). New York, NY: McGraw-Hill. (Original work published 1930)

Békésy, G. von. (1967). *Sensory inhibition*. Princeton, NJ: Princeton University Press.

Bernoulli, D. (1954). Exposition of a new theory on the measurement of risk (L. Sommer, Trans.). *Econometrica, 22*, 23–36. (Original work published 1738)

Biot, J.-B. (1824). *Précis elementaire de physique expérimentale* [An elementary introduction to experimental physics] (2 vols., 3rd. ed). Paris, France: Deferville. Fechner's 1824 translation of this edition appeared as: *Lehrbuch der Experimentelle Physik oder Erfahrungs-Naturlehre* [A textbook of experimental physics or learning to understand nature by experience] (4 vols.). Leipzig, Germany: Leopold Voss.

Boring, E. G. (1942). *Sensation and perception in the history of experimental psychology*. New York, NY: Appleton-Century-Crofts.

Boring, E. G. (1950). *A history of experimental psychology* (2nd ed.). New York, NY: Appleton-Century-Crofts.

Boring, E. G., Langfeld, M. S., & Weld, H. P. (1948). *Foundations of psychology*. New York, NY: Wiley.

Boudewijnse, G.-J. A., Murray, D. J., & Bandomir, C. A. (1999). Herbart's mathematical psychology. *History of Psychology, 2*, 163–193.

Boudewijnse, G.-J. A., Murray, D. J., & Bandomir, C. A. (2001). The fate of Herbart's mathematical psychology. *History of Psychology, 4*, 107–132.

Brentano, F. (1973). *Psychology from an empirical standpoint* (A. C. Rancurello, A. S. Terrell, & L. L. McAlister, Trans.). London, UK: Routledge. (Original work published 1874)

Breuer, J., & Freud, S. (1955). Studies in hysteria. In J. Strachey (Ed. & Trans.), *The standard edition of the complete psychological works of Sigmund Freud* (Vol. 2, pp. 1–306). London, UK: Hogarth Press. (Original work published 1895)

Breul, K. (Ed.). (1940). *Cassell's German and English dictionary* (Rev. and enlarged by J. H. Lepper & R. Kottenhahn). London, UK: Cassell.

Bringmann, W. G., Bringmann, N. J., & Medway, N. I. (1987). Fechner and psychical research. In J. Brožek & H. Gundlach (Eds.), *G. T. Fechner and psychology* (pp. 243–256). Passau, Germany: Passavia Universitätsverlag.

Bringmann, W. G., Bringmann, N. J., & Ungerer, G. A. (1980). The establishment of Wundt's laboratory: An archival and documentary study. In W. G. Bringmann & R. Tweney (Eds.), *Wundt studies* (pp. 123–157). Toronto, Canada: C. J. Hogrefe.

Brodie, E. C. (1995). Direct and indirect perception in weight discrimination and other manual tasks. In C.-A. Possamai (Ed.), *Fechner day 95. Proceedings of the eleventh annual meeting of the International Society for Psychophysics* (pp. 35–40). Cassis, France: The International Society for Psychophysics.

Brown, W. (1910). The judgment of difference with special reference to the doctrine of the threshold, in the case of lifted weights. *University of California Publications in Psychology, 1*, 199–268.

Brown, W., & Thompson, J. H. (1925). *The essentials of mental measurement*. London, UK: Cambridge University Press.

Bunn, G. C., Lovie, A. D., & Richards, G. D. (Eds.). (2001). *Psychology in Britain: Historical essays and personal reflections*. London, UK: The British Psychological Society in association with the Science Museum.

Burke-Gaffney, M. W. (1963). Pogson's Scale and Fechner's Law. *Journal of the Royal Astronomical Society of Canada, 57*, 3–7.

Calinger, R. S. (2015). *Leonhard Euler: Mathematical genius in the enlightenment*. Princeton, NJ: Princeton University Press.

Calkins, M. W. (1894a). Association. *Psychological Review, 1*, 152–158.

Calkins, M. W. (1894b). Association (Part I). *Psychological Review, 1*, 476–483.

Cannon, W. B. (1963). *Bodily changes in pain, hunger, fear, and rage*. New York, NY: Harper & Row. (Original work published 1929)

Cattell, J. M. (1886a). The time taken up by the cerebral operations. *Mind, 11*, 220–242, 377–392, 524–538.

Cattell, J. M. (1886b). The influence of the intensity of a stimulus on the length of the reaction time. *Brain, 8*, 512–515.

Cervantes, V., & Dzhafarov, E. (2018). *True contextuality in a psychophysical experiment* [Abstract]. Retrieved from www.researchgate.net/publication/329388439

Cohen, H. (1883). *Das Princip der Infinitesimal-Methode und seine Geschichte* [The principle of the infinitesimal method and its history]. Berlin, Germany: Dümmler.

Cohn, T. E., & Lasky, D. J. (1986). Visual sensitivity. *Annual Review of Psychology, 37*, 495–521.

Collins, W. (1982). *Collins Gem German-English English-German dictionary*. London and Glasgow, UK: Collins. (Original work published 1953)

Conrad, R. (1959). Errors of immediate memory. *British Journal of Psychology, 50*, 349–359.

Corbet, H., & Marshall, M. E. (1969). The comparative anatomy of angels: A sketch by Dr. Mises: 1825. *Journal of the History of the Behavioral Sciences, 5*, 135–151.

Cowles, M. (1989). *Statistics in psychology: An historical perspective*. Hillsdale, NJ: Lawrence Erlbaum Associates.

Curtis, S. J., & Boultwood, M. E. A. (1963). *A short history of educational ideas* (3rd ed.). London, UK: University Tutorial Press Ltd.

Damm, S. (1998). *Christiane und Goethe: Eine Recherche* [Christiane and Goethe: An investigation]. Frankfurt am Main and Leipzig, Germany: Insel Verlag.

Danziger, K. (1990). *Constructing the subject: Historical origins of psychological research*. Cambridge, UK: Cambridge University Press.

Darwin, C. (2004). *On the origin of species by means of natural selection: Or, The preservation of favored races in the struggle for survival*. London, UK: Collector's Library, CRW. (Original work published 1859)

De Ford, M. A. (1948). *Psychologist unretired: The life pattern of Lillien J. Martin*. Palo Alto, CA: Stanford University Press.

De Garmo, C. (Ed.). (1894). *Apperception: A monograph on psychology and pedagogy by Dr. Karl Lange* (Translated by thirteen members of the Herbart Club). Boston, MA: D. C. Heath & Co.

De Garmo, C. (1896). *Herbart and the Herbartians*. New York, NY: Charles Scribner's Sons.

De Laey, J. J. (2002). De Blindheid van Joseph Plateau. Myth en realitet [The blindness of Joseph Plateau. Myth and reality]. *Tijdschrift voor Geneeskunde, 58*, 915–920.

De Moivre, A. (1967). *The doctrine of chances: Or, a METHOD for calculating the probabilities of events in PLAY* (3rd ed.). New York, NY: Chelsea. (Original work published 1756)

Defoe, D. (2003). *The life and adventures of Robinson Crusoe*. London, UK: Penguin Classics. (Original work published 1719)

Delboeuf, J. (1873). Étude psychophysique. Recherches théoriques et expérimentales sur la mesure des sensations et spécialement des sensations de la lumière et de fatigue [Theoretical and experimental research on the measurement of sensations, particularly sensations of light and fatigue]. In *Mémoires couronnés et autres mémoires publiés par l'Académie Royale des Sciences, des Lettres, et des Beaux-Arts de Belgique* (Vol. 23). Bruxelles, Belgium: Hayez.

Delboeuf, J. (1876). Théorie générale de la sensibilité [A general theory of sensitivity]. In *Mémoires couronnés et autres mémoires publiés par l'Académie Royale des Sciences, des Lettres et des Beaux-Arts de Belgique* (Vol. 26). Bruxelles, Belgium: Hayez.

Delboeuf, J. (1877). La loi psychophysique: Hering contre Fechner [The psychophysical law: Hering versus Fechner]. *Revue Philosophique, 3*, 225–263.

Delboeuf, J. (1878). La loi psychophysique et le nouveau livre de Fechner [The psychophysical law and the new book by Fechner]. *Revue Philosophique, 5*, 34–65, 127–157.

Delboeuf, J. (1883a). *Examen critique de la loi psychophysique: Sa base et sa signification* [Critical examination of the psychophysical law: Its basis and its significance]. Paris, France: Baillière. [Combines Delboeuf, 1877 and Delboeuf, 1878]

Delboeuf, J. (1883b). *Éléments de psychophysique générale et spéciale* [Elements of psychophysics, both general and specific]. Paris, France: Baillière.

Donders, F. C. (1969). On the speed of mental processes. *Acta Psychologica, 24*, 412–431. (Original work published 1868)

Drobisch, M. W. (1972). *Erste Grundlehren der mathematischen Psychologie* [First principles of mathematical psychology]. Zandervoort, Netherlands: E. J. Bonset. (Original work published 1850)

Duijker, H. C. J., & van Rijswijk, M. J. (1975). *Dreisprachiges Psychologiches Wörterbuch. Band 3: Deutsch/Englisch/Französisch* [Trilingual psychological dictionary. Vol. 3: German/ English/French]. Bern, Switzerland: Hans Huber.
Dunkel, H. B. (1970). *Herbart and Herbartianism: An educational ghost story*. Chicago, IL: University of Chicago Press.
Duyckaerts, F. (1992). *Joseph Delboeuf: Philosophe et hypnotiseur* [Joseph Delboeuf: Philosopher and hypnotist]. Paris, France: Delagrance.
Dzhafarov, E. N., & Colonius, H. (2011). The Fechnerian idea. *American Journal of Psychology, 124*, 127–140.
Ebbinghaus, H. (1964). *Memory: A contribution to experimental psychology* (H. A. Ruger & C. E. Bussenius, Trans.). New York, NY: Dover. (Original work published 1885)
Einstein, A. (2002). On the electrodynamics of moving bodies (W. Perrett & G. B. Jeffery, Trans.). In S. Hawking (Ed.), *On the shoulders of giants: The great works of physics and astronomy* (pp. 1167–1190). Philadelphia, PA: Running Press. (Original work published 1905)
Einstein, A., & Infeld, L. (1938). *The evolution of physics: The growth of ideas from early concepts to relativity and quanta*. New York, NY: Simon & Shuster.
Ekman, G. (1956). Discriminal sensitivity on the subjective continuum. *Acta Psychologica, 12*, 233–243.
Ekman, G. (1959). Weber's Law and related functions. *Journal of Psychology, 47*, 343–352.
Ellenberger, H. (1970). *The discovery of the unconscious*. New York, NY: Basic Books.
Elsas, A. (1886). *Über die Psychophysik. Physikalische und erkenntnistheoretische Betrachtungen* [On psychophysics. Physical and theory-of-knowledge considerations]. Marburg, Germany: Elwert.
Ertle, J. E., Bushong, R. C., & Hillix, W. A. (1977). The real F. M. Urban. *Journal of the History of the Behavioral Sciences, 13*, 379–383.
Euclid. (2013). *Euclid's elements* (T. L. Heath, Trans., & D. Densmore, Ed.). Santa Fe, NM: Green Lion Press. (Original work published about 300 BCE)
Falmagne, J.-C. (1985). *Elements of psychophysical theory*. New York, NY: Oxford University Press.
Fechner, G. T. (1823). *Premissae ad theoriam organismi generalem* [Premises toward a general theory of organisms]. Leipzig, Germany: Staritz.
Fechner, G. T. (1825). *Vergleichende Anatomie der Engel: Eine Skizze* [Comparative anatomy of angels: A sketch]. Leipzig, Germany: Baumgärtner.
Fechner, G. T. (1830). *Elementarbuch des Elektromagnetismus nebst Beschreibung der hauptsächlichen elektromagnetische Apparate* [An elementary book on electromagnetism together with a description of the principal electromagnetic apparatus]. Leipzig, Germany: Leopold Voss.
Fechner, G. T. (1832). *Beweis, dass der Mond aus Iodine bestehe* [A proof that the moon consists of iodine] (2nd ed.). Leipzig, Germany: Voss. (Original work published 1821)
Fechner, G. T. (1836). *Das Büchlein vom Leben nach der Tode* [A little book about life after death]. Dresden, Germany: Grimmer.
Fechner, G. T. (1838). Über die subjektiven Complementarfarben [On subjective complementary colours]. *Annalen der Physik und Chemie, 44*, 221–245, 513–535.
Fechner, G. T. (1840). Über die subjektiven Nachbilder und Nebenbilder [On subjective after-images and simultaneous contrast]. *Annalen der Physik und Chemie, 50*, 193–221, 427–470.
Fechner, G. T. (1846). *Über das höchste Gut* [On the highest good]. Leipzig, Germany: Breitkopf und Härtel.

Fechner, G. T. (1848). *Nanna oder über das Seelenleben der Pflanzen* [Nanna, or on the soul life of plants]. Leipzig, Germany: Breitkopf und Härtel.

Fechner, G. T. (1851). *Zend-Avesta oder über die Dinge des Himmels und des Jenseits. Vom Standpunkt der Naturbetrachtung* [Zend-Avesta, or on matters of Heaven and beyond. From the standpoint of a spectator of nature] (3 parts). Leipzig, Germany: Leopold Voss.

Fechner, G. T. (1860a). *Elemente der Psychophysik* [Elements of psychophysics] (2 vols.). Leipzig, Germany: Breitkopf und Härtel.

Fechner, G. T. (1860b). Über die Contrastempfindung [On the sensation of contrast]. *Berichte über die Verhandlungen der Königlich Sächsische Gesellschaft der Wissenschaften zu Leipzig, Mathematisch-physische Klasse, 12*, 71–145.

Fechner, G. T. (1876). *Vorschule der Aesthetik* [A primer on aesthetics] (2 parts). Leipzig, Germany: Breitkopf und Härtel.

Fechner, G. T. (1877). *In Sachen der Psychophysik* [The case for psychophysics]. Leipzig, Germany: Breitkopf und Härtel.

Fechner, G. T. (1882). *Revision der Hauptpunkte der Psychophysik* [Review of the main points of psychophysics]. Leipzig, Germany: Breitkopf und Härtel.

Fechner, G. T. (1886). Ueber die psychischen Massprincipien und das Weber'sche Gesetz. Discussion mit Elsas und Köhler [On the principles of psychological measurement and Weber's Law. Discussion with Elsas and Köhler]. *Philosophische Studien, 4*, 161–230.

Fechner, G. T. (1892). Krankheitsgeschichte [A history of my illness]. In J. E. Kuntze, *Gustav Theodor Fechner (Dr. Mises). Ein deutsches Gelehrtenleben* [Gustav Theodor Fechner (Dr. Mises). The life of a German man of learning] (pp. 105–126). Leipzig, Germany: Breitkopf und Härtel. (Original work written 1845)

Fechner, G. T. (1897). *Kollektivmasslehre* [A treatise on the measurement of collectives] (G. F. Lipps, Ed.). Posthumously published on behalf of the Royal Saxon Society of Sciences. Leipzig, Germany: W. Engelmann.

Fechner, G. T. (1946). Conclusion of *Nanna*. In W. Lowrie, *Religion of a scientist: Selections from Gustav Th. Fechner edited and translated by Walker Lowrie* (pp. 211–212). New York, NY: Pantheon. (Original work published 1848)

Fechner, G. T. (1964). *Elemente der Psychophysik* [Elements of psychophysics] (2 vols.). Amsterdam, Netherlands: E. J. Bonset. (Original work published 1860)

Fechner, G. T. (1966). *Elements of psychophysics, Volume 1* (H. E. Adler, Trans., D. H. Howes & E. G. Boring, Eds.). New York, NY: Holt, Rinehart & Winston. (Original work published 1860)

Fechner, G. T. (1987a). Outline of a new principle of mathematical psychology (1851). In G. T. Fechner, *Zend-Avesta oder über die Dinge des Himmels und des Jenseits* (Vol. 2, pp. 373–386) (E. Scheerer, Trans.). *Psychological Research, 49*, 203–207.

Fechner, G. T. (1987b). Some thoughts on the psychophysical representation of memories (1882). In G. T. Fechner, *Revision der Hauptpunkte der Psychophysik* (pp. 290–299) (E. Scheerer, Trans.). *Psychological Research, 49*, 209–212.

Fechner, G. T. (2001). From Fechner's Diary in 1850. In *From Fechner's Diary October 22nd, 1850 etc.* [Brochure circulated at the 17th annual meeting of the International Society for Psychophysics, University of Leipzig, Germany (pp. 1–2)]. (Original work published 1850)

Fechner, G. T. (2004). Handwritten biography (C. Klohr, Trans.). In M. Heidelberger, *Nature from within: Gustav Theodor Fechner and his psychophysical worldview* (pp. 321–323). Pittsburgh, PA: University of Pittsburgh Press. (Original work published 1885)

Flügel, D. (1905). *Der Philosoph J. F. Herbart* [The philosopher J. F. Herbart]. (Paperbound book on file in pamphlet box in the Joseph L. Stauffer Library at Queen's University at Kingston, Ontario, Canada; Call No. B3048)

Ford, B. J. (1973). *The revealing lens: Mankind and the microscope*. London, UK: Harrap.

Freud, S. (1958). Psycho-analytic notes on an autobiographical account of a case of paranoia (dementia paranoides). In J. Strachey (Ed. & Trans.), *The standard edition of the complete psychological works of Sigmund Freud* (Vol. 12, pp. 1–79). London, UK: Hogarth Press. (Original work published 1911)

Freud, S. (1966). Project for a scientific psychology. In J. Strachey (Ed. & Trans.), *The standard edition of the complete psychological works of Sigmund Freud* (Vol. 1, pp. 281–392). London, UK: Hogarth Press. (Original work published 1950 [written 1895])

Fullerton, G. S., & Cattell, J. M. (1892). On the perception of small differences with special reference to the extent force and time of movement. *Publications of the University of Pennsylvania. Philosophical Series #2*. Philadelphia, PA: University of Pennsylvania Press.

Gauss, C. F. (1963). *Theory of the motion of heavenly bodies moving about the sun in conic sections* (C. H. Davis, Trans.). New York, NY: Dover. (Original work published 1809)

Gauss, C. F. (1986). *Disquisitiones arithmeticae* [A treatise on arithmetic] (2nd corrected ed.) (A. A. Clarke, Trans.). New York, NY: Springer. (Original work published 1801)

Gescheider, G. A. (1997). *Psychophysics: The fundamentals* (3rd ed.). Mahwah, NJ: Lawrence Erlbaum Associates.

Gibbon, E. (2005). *The history of the decline and fall of the Roman empire* (D. Womersley, Ed.) (3 vols.). New York, NY: Penguin. (Original work published 1776–1789)

Glendinning, P. (2013). *Math in minutes: 200 key concepts explained in an instant*. New York, NY and London, UK: Quercus.

Green, D. M. (1995). Weber's Law in auditory intensity discrimination. In C.-A. Possamai (Ed.), *Fechner day 95. Proceedings of the eleventh annual meeting of the International Society for Psychophysics* (pp. 1–20). Cassis, France: The International Society for Psychophysics.

Greenblatt, S. (2011). *The swerve: How the world became modern*. New York, NY: W. W. Norton & Co.

Gregory, R. L. (1966). *Eye and brain: The psychology of seeing*. New York, NY: McGraw-Hill.

Gregory, R. L. (1984). *Mind in science: A history of explanations in psychology and physics*. London, UK: Peregrine. (Original work published 1981)

Gregory, R. L., & Ross, H. E. (1967). Arm weight, adaptation and weight discrimination. *Perceptual and Motor Skills*, *24*, 1127–1130.

Gregson, R. A. M. (1993). The head and tail of psychophysical algebra. *Behavioral and Brain Sciences*, *16*, 141–142.

Gribbin, J. (Ed.). (2008). *The Britannica guide to the 100 most influential scientists*. London, UK: Robinson.

Guilford, J. P. (1936). *Psychometric methods*. New York, NY: McGraw-Hill.

Hacking, I. (1975). *The emergence of probability: A philosophical study of early ideas about probability, induction and scientific inference*. Cambridge, UK: Cambridge University Press.

Hacking, I. (1990). *The taming of chance*. Cambridge, UK: Cambridge University Press.

Hagen, G. H. L. (1867). *Grundzüge der Wahrscheinlichskeitrechnung* [Principles of the calculation of probabilities] (2nd ed.). Berlin, Germany: Ernst & Korn.

Hand, D. J. (2016). *Measurement: A very short introduction*. Oxford, UK: Oxford University Press.

Harper, R. S., & Stevens, S. S. (1948). A psychological scale for weight and a formula for its derivation. *American Journal of Psychology*, *61*, 343–351.

Haupt, E. J. (1998). Origins of American psychology in the work of G. E. Müller: Classical psychophysics and serial learning. In R. W. Rieber & K. Salzinger (Eds.), *Psychology: Theoretical-historical perspectives* (2nd ed., pp. 17–75). Washington, DC: American Psychological Association.

Hearnshaw, L. S. (1964). *A short history of British psychology, 1840–1940*. London, UK: Methuen.

Hegelmaier, F. (1852). Über das Gedächtniss für Linearanschauungen [On the memory for the length of a line]. *Archiv für physiologische Heilkunde, 11*, 844–853.

Heidelberger, M. (1987). Fechner's indeterminism: From freedom to laws of chance. In L. Krüger, L. J. Daston, & M. Heidelberger (Eds.), *The probabilistic revolution. Vol. 1: Ideas in history* (pp. 117–156). Cambridge, MA: MIT Press (Bradford Books).

Heidelberger, M. (1993). *Die innere Seite der Natur: Gustav Theodor Fechners wissenschaftlich-philosophische Weltauffassung* [The inner side of nature: Gustav Theodor Fechner's scientific-philosophical worldview]. Frankfurt am Main, Germany: Vittorio Klostermann.

Heidelberger, M. (2004). *Nature from within: Gustav Theodor Fechner and his psychophysical worldview* (C. Klohr, Trans.). Pittsburgh, PA: University of Pittsburgh Press.

Heidelberger, M., & Thiessen, S. (1981). *Natur und Erfahrung: Von der mittelalterlichen zur neuzeitlichen Naturwissenschaft* [Nature and experience: From mediaeval to modern science]. Reibeck bei Hamburg, Germany: Rowohlt Taschenbuch Verlag GmbH.

Helmholtz, H. von. (1954). *On the sensations of tone*. New York, NY: Dover. (Original work published 1863; English translation of the 4th edition of 1877 with additional notes by A. J. Ellis, 1885)

Helmholtz, H. von. (1962). *A treatise on physiological optics* (J. R. Southall, Trans.). New York, NY: Dover. (Original Vol. 1 published 1856; original Vol. 2 published 1860; original Vol. 3 published 1866)

Herbart, J. F. (1851). Ueber die Messbarkeit einer Vorstellung [On the measurability of a Vorstellung]. In G. Hartenstein (Ed.), *Johann Friedrich Herbart's saemmtliche Werke* (Vol. 7, pp. 50–57). Leipzig, Germany: Voss. (Original work published 1837)

Herbart, J. F. (1877). Possibility and necessity of applying mathematics in psychology (H. Haanel, Trans.). *Journal of Speculative Philosophy, 11*, 251–264. Retrieved from http://psychclassics.yorku.ca/Herbart/mathpsych.htm. (Original work published 1822)

Herbart, J. F. (1888a). Über die dunkle Seite der Pädagogik [On the dark side of pedagogy]. In K. Kehrbach & O. Flügel (Eds.), *Joh. Fr. Herbart's sämtliche Werke. In chronologischer Reihenfolge* (Vol. 3, pp. 147–154). Langensalza, Germany: Hermann Beyer und Söhne. (Original work published 1812)

Herbart, J. F. (1888b). Psychologische Untersuchung über die Stärke einer gegebener Vorstellung als Function ihrer Dauer betrachtet [Psychological investigation into the strength of a given Vorstellung considered as a function of its duration]. In K. Kehrbach & O. Flügel (Eds.), *Joh. Fr. Herbart's sämtliche Werke. In chronologischer Reihenfolge* (Vol. 3, pp. 119–145). Langensalza, Germany: Hermann Beyer und Söhne. (Original work published 1812)

Herbart, J. F. (1890a). Psychologie als Wissenschaft [Psychology as science]. In K. Kehrbach & O. Flügel (Eds.), *Joh. Fr. Herbart's sämtliche Werke. In chronologischer Reihenfolge* (Part 1, Vol. 5, pp. 177–434). Langensalza, Germany: Hermann Beyer und Söhne. (Original work published 1824)

Herbart, J. F. (1890b). Ueber die Moeglichkeit und Nothwendigkeit, Mathematik auf Psychologie anzuwenden [On the possibility and necessity of applying mathematics to psychology]. In K. Kehrbach & O. Flügel (Eds.), *Joh. Fr. Herbart's sämtliche Werke. In chronologischer Reihenfolge* (Vol. 5, pp. 81–122). Langensalza, Germany: Hermann Beyer und Söhne. (Original work published 1822)

Herbart, J. F. (1890c). De attentionis mensura causisque primariis [On the primary causes and measurement of attention]. In K. Kehrbach & O. Flügel (Eds.), *Joh. Fr. Herbart's sämtliche Werke: In chronologischer Reihenfolge* (Vol. 5, pp. 41–89). Langensalza, Germany: Hermann Beyer und Söhne. (Original work published 1822)

Herbart, J. F. (1891). *A text-book in psychology* (M. K. Smith, Trans.). New York, NY: D. Appleton. (Original work published 1834)

Herbart, J. F. (1892). Psychologie als Wissenschaft [Psychology as science]. In K. Kehrbach & O. Flügel (Eds.), *Joh. Fr. Herbart's sämtliche Werke. In chronologischer Reihenfolge* (Part 2, Vol. 6, pp. 1–340). Langensalza, Germany: Hermann Beyer und Söhne. (Original work published 1825)

Herbart, J. F. (1906a). Psychologische Untersuchungen [Psychological investigations]. In K. Kehrbach & O. Flügel (Eds.), *Joh. Fr. Herbart's sämtliche Werke. In chronologischer Reihenfolge* (Part 1, Vol. 11, pp. 45–176). Langensalza, Germany: Hermann Beyer und Söhne (Beyer & Mann). (Original work published 1839)

Herbart, J. F. (1906b). Psychologische Untersuchungen [Psychological investigations]. In K. Kehrbach (Ed.), *Joh. Fr. Herbart's sämtliche Werke. In chronologischer Reihenfolge* (Part 2, Vol. 11, pp. 177–343). Langensalza, Germany: Hermann Beyer und Söhne (Beyer & Mann). (Original work published 1840)

Herbart, J. F. (1968). *Psychologie als Wissenschaft* [Psychology as science]. Amsterdam, Netherlands: E. J. Bonset. (Original work published 1824)

Hering, E. (1875). Zur Lehre von der Beziehung zwischen Leib und Seele. I. Mitteilung, Über Fechner's psychophysisches Gesetz [On the doctrine of the relationship between body and soul. Communication I. On Fechner's psychophysical law]. *Sitzungsberichte der Kaiserlichen Akademie der Wissenschaften (Wien), math.-natur. Klasse, 72* (III Abt.), 310–348.

Hickok, L. P. (1854). *Empirical psychology: Or, the human mind as given in consciousness.* New York, NY: Ivison & Phinney.

Hilgard, E. R. (1987). *Psychology in America: A historical survey.* New York, NY: Harcourt, Brace, Jovanovich.

Holway, H., Goldring, L. E., & Zigler, M. J. (1938). On the discrimination of minimal differences in weight: IV. Kinesthetic adaptation for exposure intensity as variant. *Journal of Experimental Psychology, 23*, 536–544.

Hooke, R. (1971). *An hypothetical explication of memory: How the organs made use of by the mind in its operation may be mechanically understood.* Lecture given to the Royal Society on June 21 and again on June 28, 1682. In R. Waller (Ed.), *The posthumous works of Robert Hooke, containing his Cutlerian Lectures and other discourses, read at the meetings of the illustrious Royal Society* (2nd ed., pp. 138–148). With a new introduction by T. M. Brown. London, UK: Frank Cass & Co. Ltd. (First edition of original work published 1705)

Husserl, E. (1900–1901). *Logische Untersuchungen* [Logical investigations]. Halle, Germany: M. Niemeyer.

Jacyna, L. S. (1994). *Philosophic whigs: Medicine, science and citizenship in Edinburgh, 1789–1848.* London, UK: Routledge.

James, W. (1950). *Principles of psychology* (2 vols.). New York, NY: Dover Press. (Original work published 1890)

Jankowiak, T. (2013). Kant's argument for the principle of intensive magnitudes. *Kantian Review, 18*, 387–412.

Jardine, L. (2003). *The curious life of Robert Hooke: The man who measured London.* London, UK: HarperCollins.

Johnson, D. F. (1987). Early responses to psychophysics in Great Britain—James Sully and James Ward. In J. Brožek & H. Gundlach (Eds.), *G. T. Fechner and psychology* (pp. 157–167). Passau, Germany: Passavia Universitätsverlag.

Jorland, G. (1987). The Saint Petersburg paradox 1713–1937. In L. Krüger, L. J. Daston, & M. Heidelberger (Eds.), *The probabilistic revolution. Vol. 1: Ideas in history* (pp. 157–190). Cambridge, MA: MIT Press.

Jungnickel, C., & McCormmach, R. (1986a). *The intellectual mastery of nature: Theoretical physics from Ohm to Einstein. Vol. 1: The torch of mathematics, 1800–1870*. Chicago, IL: Chicago University Press.

Jungnickel, C., & McCormmach, R. (1986b). *The intellectual mastery of nature: Theoretical physics from Ohm to Einstein. Vol. 2: The now mighty theoretical physics, 1870–1925*. Chicago, IL: Chicago University Press.

Kahneman, D., Slovic, P., & Tversky, A. (Eds.). (1982). *Judgment under uncertainty: Heuristics and biases*. New York, NY: Cambridge University Press.

Kant, I. (1929). *Critique of pure reason* (N. K. Smith, Trans.). London, UK: Palgrave Macmillan. (Original work published 1781; 2nd ed., 1787)

Kant, I. (1974). *Anthropology from a pragmatic point of view* (M. J. Gregor, Trans.). The Hague, Netherlands: Martinus Nijhoff. (Original work published 1798)

Katz, D. (1911). Die Erscheinungsweise der Farben und ihre Beeinflussung durch die individuelle Erfahrung [The appearances of colours and how individual experiences influence them]. *Zeitschrift für Psychologie, Ergänzungsband, 11*.

Katz, D. (1935). *The world of color* (R. B. MacLeod & C. W. Fox, Trans.). London, UK: Kegan Paul, Trench, Trübner & Co. (Original work published 1930)

Kehrbach, K., Flügel, O., & Fritsch, T. (1887–1912). *Joh. Fr. Herbart's sämtliche Werke. In chronologischer Reihenfolge* [Joh. Fr. Herbart's collected works. In chronological order]. Langensalza, Germany: Hermann Beyer und Söhne.

Kendall, M. G. (1947). *The advanced theory of statistics* (2 vols., 3rd ed.). London, UK: Charles Griffin.

Kilpatrick, R. S. (1996). *Amicus medicus*: Medicine and epicurean therapy in *De Rerum Naturae*. *Memoirs of the American Academy in Rome, 41*, 69–100.

Kim, A. (2015). Johann Friedrich Herbart. In E.N. Zalta (Ed.) *The Stanford encyclopedia of philosophy* (Winter 2015 Edition). Retrieved from https://plato.stanford.edu/archives/win 2015/entries/johann-herbart/

Klemm, O. (1914). *A history of psychology* (E. C. Wilm & R. Pintner, Trans.). New York, NY: Charles Scribner's Sons. (Original work published 1911)

Kline, M. (1972). *Mathematical thought from ancient to modern times*. New York, NY: Oxford University Press.

Köhler, A. (1886). Ueber die hauptsächlichen Versuche einer mathematischen Formulirung des psychophysischen Gesetzes von Weber [On the principal attempts to provide a mathematical formulation of Weber's psychophysical law]. *Philosophische Studien, 3*, 572–642.

Koppelman, E. (1970). Plateau, Joseph Antoine Ferdinand. In C. C. Gillespie, et al. (Eds.), *Dictionary of scientific biography* (Vol. 11, pp. 20–22). New York, NY: Scribner.

Körber, C. A. (1746). *Versuch einer Ausmessung menschlicher Seelen und aller einfachen endlichen Dinge überhaupt, Wie solche der inneren Beschaffenheit derselben gemäss ins Werck zu richten ist, Wenn man ihre Kräffte, Vermögen, und Würkungen recht will kennen lernen* [An attempt at a quantification of the human mind in terms of simple finite entities, as well as an attempt to show how the various forces, capabilities, and consequences associated with these entities can determine the internal structure of the mind] (3 parts). Halle, Germany.

Krantz, D. H., Luce, R. D., Suppes, P., & Tversky, A. (2007). *Foundations of measurement* (3 vols.). New York, NY: Dover. (Original work published 1971–1990)

Kries, J. von. (1882). Ueber die Messung intensiver Grössen und über das sogenannte psychophysische Gesetz [On the measurement of intensive magnitudes and on the so-called psychophysical law]. *Vierteljahrsschrift für Wissenschaftliche Philosophie, 6*, 257–294.

Kries, J. von. (1886). *Prinzipien der Wahrscheinlichkeitsrechnung* [Principles of probability theory]. Freiburg in Breisgar, Germany: Mohr.

Kries, J. von. (1895). Über die Funktion der Netzhautstäbchen [On the function of the retinal rods]. *Zeitschrift für die Psychologie und Physiologie der Sinnesorgane, 9*, 81–123.

Krohn, W. O. (1893). The laboratory of the Psychological Institute at the University of Göttingen. *American Journal of Psychology, 5*, 282–284.

Krueger, L. E. (1989). Reconciling Fechner and Stevens: Towards a unified psychophysical law. *Behavioral and Brain Sciences, 12*, 251–320.

Krüger, L., Daston, L. J., & Heidelberger, M. (Eds.). (1987a). *The probabilistic revolution. Vol. 1: Ideas in history*. Cambridge, MA: MIT Press.

Krüger, L., Gigerenzer, G., & Morgan, M. S. (Eds.). (1987b). *The probabilistic revolution. Vol. 2: Ideas in the sciences*. Cambridge, MA: MIT Press.

Kuntze, J. E. (1892). *Gustav Theodor Fechner (Dr. Mises). Ein deutsches Gelehrtenleben* [Gustav Theodor Fechner (Dr. Mises). The life of a German scholar]. Leipzig, Germany: Breitkopf und Härtel.

Laming, D. (1973). *Mathematical psychology*. New York, NY: Academic Press.

Laming, D. (1989). Experimental evidence for Fechner's and Steven's Laws. *Behavioral and Brain Sciences, 12*, 277–287.

Laming, D. (1993). The antecedents of signal detection theory. *Behavioral and Brain Sciences, 16*, 151–152.

Laming, D., & Laming, J. (1992). F. Hegelmaier: On memory for the length of a line. *Psychological Research, 54*, 233–239.

Laming, J., & Laming, D. (1996). J. Plateau: On the measurement of physical sensations and on the law which links the intensity of these sensations to the intensity of the source. J. Plateau: Report on 'Psychophysical study: Theoretical and experimental research on the measurement of sensations, particularly sensations of light and fatigue' by Mr. Delboeuf. *Psychological Research, 59*, 134–144.

Laplace, P. S., Marquis de. (1809). *The system of the world* (J. Pound, Trans.). London, UK: Richard Phillips. (Original work published 1796)

Laplace, P. S., Marquis de. (1812). *Theorie analytique des probabilités* [Analytical theory of probabilities]. Paris, France: Courcier.

Laplace, P. S., Marquis de. (1951). *A philosophical essay on probabilities* (6th ed.) (F. W. Truscott & F. L. Emory, Trans.). New York, NY: Dover. (Original work published 1840)

Laplace, P. S., Marquis de. (1966–1969). *Celestial mechanics* (5 vols.) (N. Bowditch, Trans.). Boston, MA: Chelsea. (Original work published 1799–1825)

Lasswitz, K. (1902). *Gustav Theodor Fechner* (2nd enlarged ed.). Stuttgart, Germany: Frommann. (Original work published 1896)

Leary, D. E. (1982). Immanuel Kant and the development of modern psychology. In W. R. Woodworth & M. G. Ash (Eds.), *The problematic science: Psychology in nineteenth-century thought* (pp. 17–42). New York, NY: Praeger.

Leibniz, G. W. (1987). A new method for maxima and minima as well as tangents, which is neither impeded by fractional nor irrational quantities, and a remarkable type of calculus for them. In J. Fauvel & J. Grey (Eds.), *The history of mathematics: A reader* (pp. 428–434). London, UK: Macmillan Education in association with the Open University.

Leith, S. (2017, January 13). The blind side: How our minds often ignore logic [Review of the book *The undoing project: A friendship that changed our minds*, by M. Lewis]. *The Times Literary Supplement*, p. 32.

Lewes, G. H. (1879). *Problems of life and mind. Third series. Problem the first, the study of psychology, its object, scope, and method*. Boston, MA: Houghton, Osgood & Company.

Lewes, G. H. (1908). *The life and works of Goethe*. London, UK: Everyman's Library #269. (Original work published 1855)

Lewis, M. (2017). *The undoing project: A friendship that changed our minds*. New York, NY: W. W. Norton.

Link, S. W. (1992). *The wave theory of difference and similarity*. Hillsdale, NJ: Lawrence Erlbaum Associates.

Link, S. W. (1994). Rediscovering the past: Gustav Fechner and signal detection theory. *Psychological Science, 5*, 335–340.

Link, S. W. (2001). Fechner, Gustav Theodor (1801–1887). In E. Erwin (Ed.), *The Freud encyclopedia: Theory, therapy, and culture* (pp. 192–195). London, UK: Routledge.

Link, S. W. (2003). C. S. Peirce, confidence and random walk theory. In B. Berglund & E. Borg (Eds.), *Fechner day 2003. Proceedings of the International Society for Psychophysics* (pp. 151–156). Stockholm, Sweden: The International Society for Psychophysics.

Link, S. W. (2015). Psychophysical theory and laws, history of. In J. E. Wright (Ed.), *International encyclopedia of the social and behavioral sciences* (2nd ed., pp. 470–476). New York, NY: Elsevier.

Link, S. W. (2020) The wave theory of difference and similarity. In (Routledge, Psychological Revivals), New York, NY: Routledge. (Original work published in 1992).

Link, S. W., & Tindall, A. B. (1971). Speed and accuracy in comparative judgements of line length. *Perception and Psychophysics, 9*, 284–288.

Lipps, G. F. (1883). *Grundtatsachen des Seelenlebens* [Fundamental facts about mental life]. Bonn, Germany: M. Cohen und Sohn.

Lipps, T. (1926). The laws of psychic relativity and Weber's Law. In T. Lipps, *Psychological studies* (H. E. Sanborn, Trans.) (2nd rev. and enlarged ed., pp. 266–327). Baltimore, MD: The Williams & Wilkins Company. (Original work published 1905)

Lloyd Morgan, C. (1900). On the relation of stimulus to sensation in visual impressions. *Psychological Review, 7*, 217–233.

Locke, J. (1947). *Essay on human understanding* (4th ed.) (R. Wilburn, Ed.). London, UK: J. M. Dent. (Original work published 1700; 1st ed., 1690)

Loomis, E. (1852). *Elements of analytical geometry and of the differential and integral calculus* (2nd ed.). New York, NY: Harper & Bros.

Lowrie, W. (1946). *Religion of a scientist: Selections from Gustav Th. Fechner edited and translated by Walter Lowrie*. New York, NY: Pantheon.

Luce, R. D. (1986). *Response times: Their role in inferring elementary mental organization*. New York, NY: Oxford University Press.

Mach, E. (1873). Physicalische Versuche über den Gleichgewichtsinn des Menschen [Physical experiments on the sense of balance in humans]. *Sitzungsberichte der Akademie der Wissenschaften zu Wien, mathematische-naturwissenschaftliche Classe, 68*, 124–140.

Mach, E. (1959). *The analysis of sensation and the relation of the physical to the psychical* (C. M. Williams, Trans.). New York, NY: Dover. (Original work published 1875)

Maltin, L. (Ed.). (2008). *Leonard Maltin's movie guide, 2009*. New York, NY: Signet Books.

Maor, E. (1994). *e: The story of a number*. Princeton, NJ: Princeton University Press.

Marshall, M. E. (1969). Gustav Fechner, Dr. Mises, and the comparative anatomy of angels. *Journal of the History of the Behavioral Sciences, 5*, 39–58.

Marshall, M. E. (1974). G. T. Fechner: Premises toward a general theory of organisms. *Journal of the History of the Behavioral Sciences, 10*, 438–447.

Martin, L. J. (1906). The electrical supply in the new psychological laboratory at the Leland Stanford, Jr., University. *American Journal of Psychology, 17*, 274–279.

Martin, L. J., & Müller, G. E. (1899). *Zur Analyse der Unterschiedsempfindlichkeit: Experimentelle Beiträge* [Towards the analysis of sensitivity to difference: Experimental contributions]. Leipzig, Germany: J. A. Barth.

Martzloff, J.-C. (2006). *A history of Chinese mathematics*. New York, NY: Springer. (Original work published 1987)

Maxwell, J. C. (1965). A dynamical theory of the electromagnetic field. In W. D. Niven (Ed.), *The scientific papers of James Clerk Maxwell* (pp. 526–597). New York, NY: Dover Press. (Original work published 1864)

McReynolds, P. (1975). Historical antecedents of personality assessment. In P. McReynolds (Ed.), *Advances in psychological assessment* (Vol. 3, pp. 477–532). San Francisco, CA: Jossey-Bass.

Meischner, W., & Eschler, E. (1979). *Wilhelm Wundt*. Leipzig, Germany: Urania-Verlag.

Merkel, J. (1888). Die Abhängigkeit zwischen Reiz und Empfindung [The dependency between stimulus and sensation]. *Philosophische Studien*, *4*, 545–547, 562–565; (1889) *5*, 245–291, 499–557; (1894) *10*, 203–248.

Millett, K. (1990). *The loony-bin trip*. New York, NY: Simon & Schuster.

Müller, F. A. (1882). *Das Axiom der Psychophysik und die psychologische Bedeutung der Weber'schen Versuche: Eine Untersuchung auf Kantischer Grundlage* [The axiom of psychophysics and the psychological significance of Weber's experiments. An investigation based on Kantian foundations]. Marburg, Germany: Elwert.

Müller, G. E. (1873). *Zur Theorie der sinnlichen Aufmerksamkeit* [Toward a theory of sensory attention] (Doctoral dissertation). Göttingen, Germany: University of Göttingen.

Müller, G. E. (1878). *Zur Grundlegung der Psychophysik. Kritische Beiträge* [On the foundations of psychophysics. Critical contributions]. Berlin, Germany: Grieben.

Müller, G. E. (1879). Ueber die Maasbestimmung des Ortsinnes der Haut mittels der Methode der richtigen und falschen Fälle [On the estimations of the accuracy of the place sense on the skin using the method of right and wrong cases]. [Pflüger's] *Archiv der gesamte Physiologie*, *19*, 191–235.

Müller, G. E. (1904). *Die Gesichtspunkte und Tatsachen der psychophysischen Methodik* [The points of view and the facts of the psychophysical methods]. Wiesbaden, Germany: Bergmann.

Müller, G. E., & Pilzecker, A. (1900). Experimentelle Beiträge zur Lehre vom Gedächtniss [Experimental contributions to memory theory]. *Zeitschrift der Psychologie, Ergänzungsband*, *1*, 1–300.

Müller, G. E., & Schumann, F. (1889). Ueber die psychologischen Grundlagen der Vergleichung gehobener Gewichte [On the psychological foundations of comparisons between lifted weights]. *Archiv für die gesammte Physiologie der Menschen und der Tiere*, *45*, 37–112.

Müller, G. E., & Schumann, F. (1893). Experimentelle Beiträge zur Untersuchungen des Gedächtnisses [Experimental contributions to investigations of memory]. *Zeitschrift der Psychologie*, *6*, 81–190, 257–339.

Murray, D. J. (1966). Vocalization at presentation and immediate recall, with varying recall methods. *Quarterly Journal of Experimental Psychology*, *18*, 9–18.

Murray, D. J. (1976). Research on human memory in the 19th century. *Canadian Journal of Psychology*, *30*, 201–220.

Murray, D. J. (1988). *A history of Western psychology* (2nd ed.). Englewood Cliffs, NJ: Prentice Hall.

Murray, D. J. (1990). Fechner's later psychophysics. *Canadian Psychology*, *31*, 54–60.

Murray, D. J. (1993). A perspective for viewing the history of psychophysics. *Behavioral and Brain Sciences*, *16*, 115–186.

Murray, D. J. (1995). *Gestalt psychology and the cognitive revolution*. Hemel Hempstead, UK: Harvester Wheatsheaf.

Murray, D. J. (2012). Theories of memory (history of). In R. W. Rieber (Ed.), *Encyclopedia of the history of psychological theories* (pp. 1105–1128). New York, NY: Springer.

Murray, D. J., & Bandomir, C. A. (2001). Fechner's inner psychophysics viewed from both a Herbartian and a Fechnerian perspective. In E. Sommerfeld, R. Kompass, & T. Lachmenn (Eds.), *Fechner Day 2001. Proceedings of the seventeenth annual meeting of the International Society for Psychophysics* (pp. 49–54). Berlin, Germany: Pabst Science Publishers.

Murray, D. J., & Barnes, M. E. (2014). Putting feelings into psychophysics: Theodor Lipps (1905) on the perception of weight and other modalities. In G. R. Patching, M. Hohnson, E. Borg, & A. Hellström (Eds.), *Fechner Day 2014. Proceedings of the 30th annual meeting of the International Society for Psychophysics* (p. 50). Lund, Sweden: The International Society for Psychophysics.

Murray, D. J., & Farahmand, B. (1995). The historical background of Weber's research on touch. In C.-A. Possomai (Ed.), *Fechner Day 95. Proceedings of the eleventh annual meeting of the International Society for Psychophysics* (pp. 21–27). Cassis, France: The International Society for Psychophysics.

Murray, D. J., & Ross, H. E. (1982). Vives (1538) on memory and recall. *Canadian Psychology*, *23*, 22–31.

Murray, D. J., & Ross, H. E. (1988). E. H. Weber and Fechner's psychophysics. In J. Brožek & H. Gundlach (Eds.), *G. T. Fechner and psychology* (pp. 79–86). Passau, Germany: Passavia Universitätsverlag.

Needham, J. (1959). *Science and civilization in China. Vol. 3: Mathematics and the sciences of the heavens and the earth*. Cambridge, UK: Cambridge University Press.

Netz, R., & Noel, W. (2007). *The Archimedes codex: Revealing the secrets of the world's greatest palimpsest*. London, UK: Weidenfeld & Nicolson.

Newton, I. (1970). *Opticks: Or, A treatise of the reflections, refractions, inflections and colours of light*. New York, NY: Dover Press. (Original work published 1730)

Newton, I. (1999). *The Principia: Mathematical principles of natural philosophy* (I. B. Cohen & A. Whitman, Trans.) (pp. 371–938). Cambridge, MA: Harvard University Press. (Original work published 1687; 3rd ed., 1726)

Nicolas, S. (1995a). On the concept of memory in the works of Joseph Delboeuf (1831–1896). *Psychologica Belgica*, *35*, 45–60.

Nicolas, S. (1995b). Joseph Delboeuf on visual illusions: A historical sketch. *American Journal of Psychology*, *108*, 563–574.

Nicolas, S., & Murray, D. J. (1999). Théodule Ribot (1839–1916), founder of French psychology: A biographical introduction. *History of Psychology*, *2*, 271–301.

Nicolas, S., Murray, D. J., & Farahmand, B. (1997). The psychophysics of J.-R.-L. Delboeuf (1831–1896). *Perception*, *26*, 1297–1315.

Norwich, K. H. (1993). *Information, sensation, and perception*. New York, NY: Academic Press.

O'Connor, J. J., & Robertson, E. F. (2003). *History topics: Nine chapters on the mathematical art*. Available online in the MacTutor History of Mathematics. Retrieved from www-history.mcs.st-and.ac.uk/HistTopics/Nine_chapters.html

Oberlin, K. W. (1936). Variation in intensive sensitivity to lifted weights. *Journal of Experimental Psychology*, *19*, 438–455.

Pantalony, D. (2009). *Altered sensations: Rudolph Koenig's acoustical workshop in nineteenth-century Paris*. New York, NY: Springer.
Pardies, I.-G. (1960–1967). *Élemens de géométrie* [Elements of geometry]. Paris, France: Institut des Hautes Études Scientifiques. (Original work published 1671)
Parzen, E. (1960). *Modern probability theory and its applications*. New York, NY: Wiley.
Peirce, C. S. (1877). Illustrations of the logic of science. *The Popular Science Monthly, 12*, pp. 1–15, 286–302, 604–615, 705–718.
Peirce, C. S., & Jastrow, J. (1884). On small differences in sensation. *Memoirs of the National Academy of Sciences, 3*, 73–83.
Perruchet, P., & Vinter, A. (2002). The self-organizing consciousness. *Behavioral and Brain Sciences, 25*, 297–330.
Pesic, P. (2014). *Music and the making of modern science*. Cambridge, MA: MIT Press.
Peterson, W. W., Birdsall, T. G., & Fox, W. C. (1954). The theory of signal detectability. *Transactions of the Institute of Radio Engineers: 1954 Symposium on Information Theory, 4*, 171–212.
Plateau, J. (1872a). Sur la mesure des sensations physiques, et sur la loi qui lie l'intensité de ces sensations à l'intensité de la cause excitante [On the measurement of physical sensations and on the law which links the intensity of these sensations to the intensity of the source]. *Bulletins de l'Académie Royale des Sciences, des Lettres et des Beaux-Arts de Belgique*, 2nd series, *33*, 376–388.
Plateau, J. (1872b). Un mot au sujet du Mémoire présenté par M. Delboeuf et intitulé: Étude psychophysique: Recherches théoriques et expérimentales sur la mesure des sensations et spécialement des sensations de lumière et de fatigue [A word on the subject of the Mémoire presented by M. Delboeuf titled: Psychophysical study: Theoretical and experimental research on the measurement of sensations, particularly sensations of light and of fatigue]. *Bulletins de l'Académie Royale des Sciences, des Lettres et des Beaux-Arts de Belgique, 34*, 250–262.
Plateau, J. (1878). Bibliographie analytique des principaux phénomènes subjectifs de la vision, depuis les temps anciens jusqu'à la fin du XVIIIe siècle, suivie d'une bibliographie simple pour la partie écoulée du siècle actuel. Cinquième section. Phénomènes ordinaires de contraste [An annotated bibliography on the principal subjective phenomena of vision, from ancient times to the end of the 18th century, followed by a non-annotated bibliography for the present century so far. Fifth section. Ordinary phenomena of contrast]. *Mémoires de l'Académie Royale des Belgique, 42*, 1–35.
Pribram, K. H. (1986). The cognitive revolution and mind/brain issues. *American Psychologist, 41*, 507–520.
Ramul, K. (1960). The problem of measurement in the psychology of the eighteenth century. *American Psychologist, 15*, 256–265.
Ramul, K. (1963). Some early measurements and ratings in psychology. *American Psychologist, 18*, 633–659.
Rausch, W. (1975). Die Musik im Leben und Schaffen Johann Friedrich Herbarts [Music in the life and career of Johann Friedrich Herbart]. *Göttinger Jahrbuch, 1975*, 145–162.
Reid, T. (1853). *Essay on the intellectual powers of man* (4th ed.). Cambridge, MA: Bartlett.
Ribot, T. (1874). La psychologie physiologique en Allemagne. La mesure des sensations [Physiological psychology in Germany. The measurement of sensations]. *La Revue Scientifique*, 2nd series, 4th year, 7(24) (December 12), 553–563.
Ribot, T. (1875). *La psychologie anglaise contemporain (école expérimentale)* [English psychology of today (the empirical school)]. Paris, France: Baillière.
Ribot, T. (1879). *La psychologie allemande contemporain (école expérimentale)* [German psychology of today (the empirical school)]. Paris, France: Baillière.

Ribot, T. (1886). *German psychology of to-day: The empirical school* (J. M. Baldwin, Trans.). New York, NY: Charles Scribner's Sons.

Richards, R. J. (1980). Christian Wolff's prolegomena to empirical and rational psychology: Translation and commentary. *Proceedings of the American Philosophical Society, 124*, 227–239.

Riggs, L. A. (1965). Light as a stimulus for vision. In C. H. Graham (Ed.), *Vision and visual perception* (pp. 1–38). New York, NY: Wiley.

Romanes, G. J. (1888). *Mental evolution in man*. London, UK: Kegan Paul, Trench, Trübner & Co.

Ross, H. E., & Knott, B. I. (2019). Dicuil (9th century) on triangular and square numbers. *British Journal for the History of Mathematics, 34*, 79–94. doi:10.1080/26375451.2019.1598687

Ross, H. E., & Murray, D. J. (1978). *E. H. Weber: The sense of touch* (1st ed.). London, UK: Academic Press for the Experimental Psychology Society.

Ross, H. E., & Murray, D. J. (1996). *E. H. Weber on the tactile senses* (2nd ed.). Hove, UK: Erlbaum (UK) Taylor & Francis on behalf of the Experimental Psychology Society.

Rouse Ball, W. W. (1960). *A short account of the history of mathematics*. New York, NY: Dover Press. (Original work published 1908)

Royal Society Obituary. (1879). Ernst Heinrich Weber. *Proceedings of the Royal Society of London, 89*, xxviii–xxxii.

Rubin, E. (1921). *Visuell wahrgenommene Figuren* [Visually perceived figures]. Copenhagen, Denmark: Gyldendalske Boghandel.

Rydberg, S. (2017). *Inner experience: An analysis of scientific experience in early modern Germany*. Uppsala, Sweden: Uppsala Universitet.

Sanford, E. C. (1898). *A course in experimental psychology: Part I, Sensation and perception*. Boston, MA: Heath.

Scheerer, E. (1987a). The unknown Fechner. *Psychological Research, 49*, 197–202.

Scheerer, E. (1987b). Was wurde aus der inneren Psychophysik? [Whatever happened to inner psychophysics?]. In H.-G. Geissler & K. Reschke (Eds.), *Psychophysische Grundlagen mentaler Prozesse (in memoriam G. T. Fechner)* [Psychophysical foundations of mental processes (in memoriam G. T. Fechner)]. Leipzig, Germany: Karl-Marx-Universität.

Scheerer, E., & Hildebrandt, H. (1988). Was Fechner an eminent psychologist? In J. Brožek & H. Gundlach (Eds.), *G. T. Fechner and psychology* (pp. 269–286). Passau, Germany: Passavia Universitätsverlag.

Schreber, D. P. (1988). *Memoirs of my nervous illness* (I. MacAlpine & R. A. Humber, Eds. & Trans., New introduction by S. M. Weber). London, UK: Harvard University Press. (Original work published 1903)

Schreier, W. (1993). Die Stellung der Gebrüder Weber in der Geschichte der Medizin, Naturwissenschaften, und Technik [The roles played by the Weber brothers in the history of medicine, science, and technology]. In G. Berg, W. Eisenberg, W. Hergert, & W. Schreier (Eds.), *II Weber-symposium in Halle und Leipzig, Oktober 16 und November 18, 1993* [Second Weber symposium at Halle and Leipzig, October 16 and November 18, 1993] (pp. 1–9). Halle and Wittenberg, Germany: Martin-Luther-University Press.

Shannon, C. E., & Weaver, W. (1949). *The mathematical theory of communication*. Urbana, IL: University of Illinois Press.

Shipley, T. (1961). Foundations of the statics of the soul: Sum and ratio of inhibition in complete contrast [English translation of §41–51 of Herbart's *Psychologie als Wissenschaft*]. In T. Shipley (Ed.), *Classics in psychology* (pp. 22–50). New York, NY: Philosophical Library. (Original work published 1824)

Singer, B. R. (1976). Robert Hooke on memory association and time perception. *Notes and Records of the Royal Society of London, 31*, 115–131.

Slater, J. G. (2005). *Minerva's aviary: Philosophy at Toronto, 1843–2003*. Toronto, Canada: University of Toronto Press.

Stadler, A. (1878). Über die Ableitung des psychophysischen Gesetzes [On the derivation of the psychophysical law]. *Philosophische Monatshefte, 4*, 215–223.

Stahl, S. (2006). The evolution of the normal distribution. *Mathematics Magazine, 79*, 96–113.

Stevens, S. S. (1951). Mathematics, measurement, and psychophysics. In S. S. Stevens (Ed.), *Handbook of experimental psychology* (pp. 1–49). New York, NY: Wiley.

Stevens, S. S. (1975). *Psychophysics. Introduction to its perceptual, neural and social prospects*. New York, NY: Wiley.

Stevens, S. S., & Volkmann, J. (1940). The quantum of sensory discrimination. *Science, 92*, 583–585.

Stout, G. F. (1888a). The Herbartian psychology I. *Mind, 13*, 321–338.

Stout, G. F. (1888b). The Herbartian psychology II. *Mind, 13*, 473–498.

Stout, G. F. (1889a). Herbart compared with English psychologists and with Beneke. *Mind, 14*, 1–26.

Stout, G. F. (1889b). The psychological work of Herbart's disciples. *Mind, 14*, 353–368.

Stumpf, C. (1883). *Tonpsychologie* [The psychology of sound] (Vol. 1). Leipzig, Germany: S. Hirzel.

Suppes, P. (2002). *Representation and invariance of scientific structures*. Stanford, CA: CSLI Publications.

Szasz, T. (1959). Introduction to Dover edition. In E. Mach, *The analysis of sensations and the relation of the physical to the psychical* (C. M. Williams, Trans.) (pp. v–xxxi). New York, NY: Dover.

Tanner, W. P., Jr., & Swets, J. A. (1954). A decision-making theory of visual detection. *Psychological Review, 61*, 401–409.

Tannery, J. (1875a). Correspondance: A propos du logarithme des sensations [Correspondence: Concerning the logarithm of sensations]. *La Revue Scientifique*, 2nd series, 4th year, *14*(37) (March 13), 876–877.

Tannery, J. (1875b). La mesure des sensations. Réponses à propos du logarithme des sensations [The measurement of sensations. Replies concerning the logarithm of sensations]. *La Revue Scientifique*, 2nd series, 4th year, *14*(43) (April 24), 1018–1020.

Thomas, N. R. T. (2016). Founders of experimental psychology: Wilhelm Wundt and William James. In E. N. Zalta (Ed.), *The Stanford encyclopedia of philosophy* [Supplement to entry on mental imagery]. Stanford, CA: The Metaphysics Research Lab, Center for the Study of Language and Information.

Thomasius, C. (1692). *Weitere Erleuterung durch unterschiedene Exempel des ohnelangst gethanen Vorschlags wegen der neuen Wissenschaft Anderer Menschen Gemuther erkennenzulernen* [Further elucidation by different examples of the recent proposals for a new science for obtaining a knowledge of other men's minds]. Halle, Germany: Christoph Salfeld.

Thurstone, L. L. (1927). A law of comparative judgment. *Psychological Review, 34*, 273–286.

Tinker, M. A. (1932). Wundt's doctorate students and their theses 1875–1920. *American Journal of Psychology, 44*, 630–637.

Tischer, E. (1883). Über die Unterscheidung von Schallstärken [On the discrimination of sound-intensities]. *Philosophische Studien, 1*, 495–542.

Titchener, E. B. (1892). Uber binoculare Wirkungen monocularer Reize [On the binocular effects of monocular stimuli]. *Philosophische Studien, 8*, 231–310.

Titchener, E. B. (1901a). *Experimental psychology: A manual of laboratory practice. Volume I. Qualitative experiments. Part I. Student's manual.* New York, NY: Macmillan.

Titchener, E. B. (1901b). *Experimental psychology: A manual of laboratory practice. Volume I. Qualitative experiments. Part II. Instructor's manual.* New York, NY: Macmillan.

Titchener, E. B. (1905a). *Experimental psychology: A manual of laboratory practice. Volume II. Quantitative experiments. Part I. Student's manual.* New York, NY: Macmillan.

Titchener, E. B. (1905b). *Experimental psychology: A manual of laboratory practice. Volume II. Quantitative experiments. Part II. Instructor's manual.* New York, NY: Macmillan.

Tögel, C. (1988). Fechner und Freuds Traumtheorie [Fechner and Freud's theory of dreams]. In J. Brožek & H. Gundlach (Eds.), *G. T. Fechner and psychology* (pp. 131–136). Passau, Germany: Passavia Universitätsverlag.

Tolstoy, L. (1968). *War and peace* (A. Dunnigan, Trans.). New York, NY: New American Library. (Original work published 1869)

Turner, J. (2014). *Philology: The forgotten origins of the modern humanities.* Princeton, NJ: Princeton University Press.

Urban, F. M. (1910). The method of contrast stimuli and its generalizations. *Psychological Review, 17,* 229–259.

Urban, F. M. (1912). Hilfstabellen für die Konstanzmethode [Tables to aid the method of constant stimuli]. *Archiv für die gesamte Psychologie, 24,* 236–243.

Viemeister, N. F. (1972). Intensity discrimination of pulsed sinusoids: The effect of filtered noise. *Journal of the Acoustical Society of America, 51,* 1265–1269.

Volkmann, A. W. (1858). Ueber den Einfluss der Uebung auf das Erkennen räumlicher Distanzen [On the influence of practice on the recognition of spatial distances]. *Berichte über die Verhandlungen der Königlich Sächsische Gesellschaft der Wissenschaften zu Leipzig, Mathematisch-physische Klasse, 10,* 38–69.

Walker, H. M. (1967). Abraham De Moivre. In A. De Moivre, *The doctrine of chances: Or, a METHOD for calculating the probabilities of events in PLAY* (pp. 349–368). New York, NY: Chelsea.

Ward, J. (1910–1911). Herbart, Johann Friedrich. In *Encyclopedia Britannica* (Vol. 13, 11th ed., pp. 335–338). New York, NY: Encyclopedia Britannica Company.

Watson, P. (2010). *The German genius: Europe's third renaissance, the second scientific revolution, and the twentieth century.* New York, NY: HarperCollins.

Weber, E. H. (1817). *Anatomia comporata nervi sympathici* [Comparative anatomy of the sympathetic nerves]. Leipzig, Germany: Reclam.

Weber, E. H. (1834). *De pulsu, resorptione, auditu et tactu. Annotationes anatomicae et physiologicae* [On the pulse, breathing, audition and the touch sense. Anatomical and physiological observations]. Leipzig, Germany: C. F. Koehler.

Weber, E. H. (1851). Ueber die Anwendung der Wellenlehre auf die Lehre vom Kreislaufe der Blutes … [On the application of the theory of waves to the theory of the circulation of the blood …]. In E. H. Weber, *Annotationes anatomicae et physiologicae,* Third series, Vol. 2. Leipzig, Germany: C. F. Koehler. (Original work published in 1850)

Weber, E. H. (1996a). De tactu (H. E. Ross, Trans.). In H. E. Ross & D. J. Murray (Eds.), *E. H. Weber on the tactile senses* (pp. 21–136). Hove, UK: Erlbaum (UK) Taylor & Francis on behalf of the Experimental Psychology Society. (Original work published 1834)

Weber, E. H. (1996b). Der Tastsinn (D. J. Murray, Trans.). In H. E. Ross & D. J. Murray (Eds.), *E. H. Weber on the tactile senses* (pp. 137–250). Hove, UK: Erlbaum (UK) Taylor & Francis on behalf of the Experimental Psychology Society. (Original work published 1846)

Weber, E. H., & Weber, W. E. (1825). *Wellenlehre und Experimente gegründet oder über die Wellen tropfbarer Flüssigkeiten mit Anwendung auf die Schall- und Lichtwellen* [The doctrine of waves based on experiments: How the theory of waves in droppable fluids can be applied to sound-waves and light-waves]. Leipzig, Germany: Fleischer.

Weber, W. E. (1867). Theorie der durch Wasser oder andere incompressible Flüssigkeiten in elastischen Röhren fortgepflanzten Wellen [Wave theory applied to the transmission of water or other incompressible fluids through elastic tubes]. *Berichte über die Verhandlungen der Königlich Sächsische Gesellschaft der Wissenschaften zu Leipzig, Mathematisch-physische Klasse, 18*, 354.

Weber, W. E., & Weber, E. F. (1836). *Mechanik der menschlichen Gehwerkzeuge* [The mechanism of human walking]. Göttingen, Germany: Dieterich.

Weinstein, S. (1968). Intensive and extensive aspects of tactile sensitivity. In D. R. Kenshalo (Ed.), *The skin senses* (pp. 195–222). Springfield, IL: C. C. Thomas.

Weiss, G. (1928). *Herbart und seine Schule.* [Herbart and his School]. Munich, Germany: Reinhardt.

Wertheimer, M. (1945). *Productive thinking.* New York, NY: Harper.

Wertheimer, M. (1961). Experimental studies on the seeing of motion. In T. Shipley (Ed., Trans., & Abridged), *Classics in psychology* (pp. 1032–1089). New York, NY: Philosophical Library. (Original work published 1912)

Whewell, W. (1819). *An elementary treatise on mechanics.* Cambridge, UK: Pitt Press.

Whewell, W. (1966). *The history of the inductive sciences from the earliest to the present time* (2 vols., 1st ed.). New York, NY: Johnson Reprint Corporation. (Original work published 1832)

Whewell, W. (1967). *The philosophy of the inductive sciences founded upon their history* (2 vols., 2nd ed.). New York, NY: Johnson Reprint Corporation. (Original work published 1847)

Whittle, P. (1993). A perspective on viewing the present of psychophysics. *Behavioral and Brain Sciences, 16*, 165–166.

Whittle, P. (1994a). The psychophysics of brightness contrast. In A. L. Gilchrist (Ed.), *Lightness, brightness, and transparency* (pp. 35–110). Hillsdale, NJ: Lawrence Erlbaum Associates.

Whittle, P. (1994b). Contrast brightness and ordinary seeing. In A. L. Gilchrist (Ed.), *Lightness, brightness, and transparency* (pp. 111–157). Hillsdale, NJ: Lawrence Erlbaum Associates.

Whittle, P. (1997). *W. H. R. Rivers: A founding father worth remembering* (Talk given at the Zangwill Club of the Department of Experimental Psychology, Cambridge, UK, December 6, 1997). Downloaded March 22, 2002, from http://human-nature.com/science-as-culture/whittle.html

Wiener, N. (1948). *Cybernetics.* New York, NY: Wiley.

Wise, M. N. (1987). How do sums count? On the cultural origins of statistical causality. In L. Krüger, L. J. Daston, & M. Heidelberger (Eds.), *The probabilistic revolution. Vol. 1: Ideas in history* (pp. 395–425). Cambridge, MA: MIT Press.

Wolff, C. (1968). Psychologia empirica. In J. Ecole (Ed.), *Christian Wolff: Gesammelte Werke* (Part II, Vol. 5). Hildesheim, Germany: Georg Olms. (Original work published 1732)

Wolff, C. (1972). Psychologia rationalis. In J. Ecole (Ed.), *Christian Wolff: Gesammelte Werke* (Part II, Vol. 6). Hildesheim, Germany: Georg Olms. (Original work published 1734).

Wolman, B. B. (1968). The historical role of Johann Friedrich Herbart. In B. B. Wolman (Ed.), *Historical roots of contemporary psychology* (pp. 29–46). New York, NY: Harper & Row.

Woodrow, H. (1933). Weight discrimination with a varying standard. *American Journal of Psychology*, *45*, 391–416.

Woodworth, R. S. (1938). *Experimental psychology*. New York, NY: Holt, Rinehart & Winston.

Woodworth, R. S., & Schlosberg, H. (1954). *Experimental psychology* (2nd ed.). New York, NY: Holt, Rinehart & Winston.

Wootton, D. (2015). *The invention of science: A new history of the scientific revolution*. New York, NY: HarperCollins.

Wright, M. J., & Myers, C. R. (1982). *History of academic psychology in Canada*. Toronto, Canada: C. J. Hogrefe, Inc.

Wundt, W. (1863). *Vorlesungen über die Menschen- und Tierseele* [Lectures on human and animal psychology]. Leipzig, Germany: Voss.

Wundt, W. (1887). *Grundzüge der physiologischen Psychologie* [Principles of physiological psychology] (3rd ed.). Leipzig, Germany: Engelmann.

Wundt, W. (1904). *Principles of physiological psychology* (5th ed.) (E. B. Titchener, Trans.). London, UK: Swan Sonnenschein & Co. (Original work published 1902–1903)

Wundt, W. (1920). *Erlebtes und Erkanntes* [My life and thought]. Stuttgart, Germany: Kröner.

Wyss, J. D. (2007). *The Swiss Family Robinson* (J. Seelye, Ed.). London, UK: Penguin Classics. (Original work published 1812)

Young, J. L. (2013). Profile of Margaret Keiver Smith. In A. Rutherford (Ed.), *Psychology's feminist voices multimedia internet archive*. Retrieved from www.feministvoices.com/margaret-keiver-smith/

Index

This INDEX makes it easy to locate information on specific topics. The INDEX has the property that when there are several sub-entries, the earliest subentries are ordered with respect to the earliest pages in the book. A page number in **boldface** includes a Table or Figure relevant to the entry. A lower case n refers to a footnote; eg "65n11" means "page 65, footnote 11"

For Product Safety Concerns and Information please contact our EU representative GPSR@taylorandfrancis.com
Taylor & Francis Verlag GmbH, Kaufingerstraße 24, 80331 München, Germany

www.ingramcontent.com/pod-product-compliance
Ingram Content Group UK Ltd.
Pitfield, Milton Keynes, MK11 3LW, UK
UKHW022351190926
475702UK00015B/2225

* 9 7 8 0 3 6 7 6 4 9 5 6 2 *